**PERGAMON INTERNATIONAL LIBRARY**
of Science, Technology, Engineering and Social Studies

*The 1000-volume original paperback library in aid of education,
industrial training and the enjoyment of leisure*

Publisher: Robert Maxwell, M.C.

# The Impact of Noise Pollution

## A Socio-Technological Introduction

CEMBER, H.
Introduction to Health Physics

GIBBON, D. L.
Aeration of Activated Sludge in Sewage Treatment

Koren, H.
Environmental Health and Safety

MORGAN, R. F.
Environmental Biology
Vols. 1, 2, 3, 4

SCORER, R.
Air Pollution

# The Impact of Noise Pollution
## A Socio-Technological Introduction

**George Bugliarello**

Polytechnic Institute of New York

**Ariel Alexandre**

Environment Directorate, Organization for Economic
Co-operation and Development

**John Barnes**

Consulting Economist

**Charles Wakstein**

Sheffield Polytechnic

**PERGAMON PRESS INC.**

New York · Toronto · Oxford · Sydney · Braunschweig

*Pergamon Press Offices:*

| | |
|---|---|
| U.K. | Pergamon Press Ltd., Headington Hill Hall, Oxford OX3 OBW, England |
| U.S.A. | Pergamon Press Inc., Maxwell House, Fairview Park, Elmsford, New York 10523, U.S.A. |
| CANADA | Pergamon of Canada, Ltd., 207 Queen's Quay West, Toronto 1, Canada |
| AUSTRALIA | Pergamon Press (Aust.) Pty. Ltd., 19a Boundary Street, Rushcutters Bay, N.S.W. 2011, Australia |
| FRANCE | Pergamon Press SARL, 24 rue des Ecoles, 75240 Paris, Cedex 05, France |
| WEST GERMANY | Pergamon Press GMbH, 3300 Braunschweig, Postfach 2923, Burgplatz 1, West Germany |

---

Library of Congress Cataloging in Publication Data
Main entry under title:

The Impact of noise pollution.

Includes bibliographies.
1. Noise pollution. I. Bugliarello, George.
TD892.I48   1975                    363.6                    74-9634
ISBN 0-08-018166-X

---

Printed in the United States of America

"There is no quiet place in the white man's cities. No place to hear the unfurling of leaves in spring or the rustle of insects' wings. But perhaps it is because I am a savage and do not understand. The clatter only seems to insult the ears. And what is there to life if a man cannot hear the lonely cry of the whippoorwill or the arguments of the frogs around a pond at night? I am a red man and do not understand. The Indian prefers the soft sound of the wind darting over the face of a pond, and the smell of the wind itself, cleansed by a midday rain, or scented with the pinon pine.": CHIEF SEATTLE—*Letter by the Susquamish Tribe in the Washington Territory 1854* (Home, 1971).

# Contents

*Part III    Surface Transportation Noise*

*Part IV    Aircraft Noise*

# Foreword

This book is written not for the specialist but for the layman who as decision maker and citizen is called upon every day to form opinions and to make intelligent decisions about the ubiquitous and ever more serious problem of noise.

It is appropriate that, from the outset, we declare our bias. We believe that noise is a major and urgent threat to the quality of our lives. Our hope, through this book, is to generate a more widespread appreciation of the problem, by providing an overview of its major aspects, from health effects to political economy considerations, from the technology of surface transportation noise and its control, to that of airplane and occupational noise.

Although we have endeavored to deal with the subject in a comprehensive way, not all of these aspects have been treated with equal detail. We have given more emphasis to those aspects, such as automobile and airplane noise, which affect practically everybody in an industrial society and those whose effects are most pernicious, such as factory and process noise. Also, inevitably, we have emphasized aspects in which our expertise was the greatest. Each of us has brought to the book a different background (bio-engineering, Bugliarello; aeronautical and mechanical engineering, Wakstein; public policy analysis and sociology, Alexandre; economics, Barnes) and also a different national perspective—that of the United States, France and of the United Kingdom.

The now distant starting point for the present work was a study performed by Bugliarello and Wakstein for Resources for the Future, Inc., on the overall dimensions of the problem of noise in the United States (Bugliarello and Wakstein, 1968). The part on surface transportation noise (Part III) and the chapter on sleep in Part II were drafted by A. Alexandre (but do not necessarily reflect the views of the Organization for Economic Co-operation and Development).

For more detailed accounts of various facets of the noise problem, the reader should peruse the many excellent publications that deal with specific aspects of the problem. Among them, we especially recommend the recent books by Beranek on *Noise and Vibration Control* (1971) and by Burns and Robinson on *Hearing and Noise in Industry* (1970), the U.S. Environmental Protection Agency "Report to the President and Congress on Noise" (EPA, 1971), the book by Kryter, *The Effect of Noise on Man* (1970), the *Report of the Commission for the Third London Airport* (Roskill, 1970), the *Lectures on Transportation Noise* by Lyon (1973), the proceedings of the 1968 conference on noise as a public health hazard (ASHA, 1969), the old but still significant report of the Wilson Committee (1963) and the also old but useful *Handbook of Noise Control* (Harris, 1957).

One of the difficulties in a comprehensive book of this kind is to provide a completely up to date coverage of all the facts of the subject. This is particularly so in our case with regard to legislation and to the indeces that are being continually developed to describe noise and to correlate it with its various impacts. While we have generally endeavored to describe the more recent legislation and indeces, it has not always been feasible to relate them to every aspect covered in the book.

It is impossible to acknowledge here all those who have assisted us in this endeavor throughout its long genesis. For many, we have done so specifically in the text. However, here we should like to express our gratitude to Virginia Bugliarello, who edited with enormous patience and skill several versions of the text and did much library research, to Myra Martin, for her magnificent job in typing the manuscript, to Carolyn Meyer, Nancy Hirsch, Anita Banoff, Vivian Cardwell, and Lorraine Schoenfeld, who in various ways contributed to the emergence of the last manuscript to Ed Daniels who did many of the drawings, to Pat Krevey for the index, and to Sylvia M. Halpern of Pergamon Press for her editing. We also wish to acknowledge the collaborators to the earlier Bugliarello and Wakstein study (Bugliarello and Wakstein, 1968): C. A. Walker, P. S. Bair, D. R. Braverman, Howard Schwartz, H. S. Green, and M. I. Kamien.

Finally, we wish to acknowledge the institutions where the bulk of the work leading to this book was conducted: Carnegie-Mellon University, the University of Illinois at Chicago Circle, the Polytechnic Institute of New York, and the Organization for Economic Co-operation and Development.

GEORGE BUGLIARELLO
ARIEL ALEXANDRE
JOHN BARNES
CHARLES WAKSTEIN

# REFERENCES

ASHA (American Speech and Hearing Association). Conference proceedings. Noise as a public health hazard. Washington, June 1968.

Beranek, L. L. (Ed.). *Noise and vibration control.* New York: McGraw-Hill, 1971.

Bugliarello, G. and Wakstein, C. Noise pollution—a review of its socio-technological and health aspects. Biotechnology Program, Carnegie-Mellon University, Pittsburgh, 1960.

Burns, W. and Robinson, D. W. *Hearing and noise in industry.* London: HMSO, 1970.

EPA (U.S. Environmental Protection Agency). Report to the President and Congress on noise. Washington, D.C., December 31, 1971.

Harris, J. D. (Ed.). *Handbook of noise control.* New York: McGraw-Hill, 1957.

Home. Excerpted from *Home,* a documentary film production of the Southern Baptist Radio and Television Commission. Adaptation and original material by Ted Perry. Copyright © 1971. Used by permission, 1971.

Kryter, K. D. *The effect of noise on man.* New York: Academic Press, 1970.

Lyon, R. H. *Lectures in transportation noise.* Cambridge, Mass.: Grozier, 1973.

Roskill. Commission on The Third London Airport. In *Papers and proceedings.* London: HMSO, 1970.

Wilson. Committee on The Problem of Noise. Noise, final report. Cmnd. 2056. London: HMSO, 1963.

# The Authors

**George Bugliarello** (Dr. Ing., University of Padua; Sc.D. Massachusetts Institute of Technology) is a specialist in bioengineering, social technology and science policy. In 1973 he became the first president of the Polytechnic Institute of New York, formed by the merger of the New York University School of Engineering and Science and the Polytechnic Institute of Brooklyn.

Dr. Bugliarello is a member of the Board of Science and Technology for International Development of the National Academy of Sciences, and Chairman of its Advisory Committee on Technological Innovation. He is the author of a large number of papers and several books in his fields of interest.

He has been a member of the Commission on Education of the National Academy of Engineering, a member of the editorial advisory boards of a number of scientific journals and has taught at Carnegie-Mellon University where he was Chairman of the Biotechnology program and Professor of Biotechnology and Civil Engineering, and at the University of Illinois at Chicago Circle where he was Dean of Engineering.

Dr. Bugliarello has lectured extensively in the United States and in many other countries, was a State Department representative in Venezuela in 1968, a NATO senior post-doctoral fellow at the Technical University of Berlin, and a member of the 1974 U.S. Engineering Delegation to the People's Republic of China.

**Ariel R. Alexandre** (Doctorate in Social Psychology, Sorbonne University, Paris) is a Principal Administrator in the Environment Directorate of the Organization for Economic Cooperation and Development (OECD), an inter-governmental agency whose headquarters is in Paris. In this capacity, he has been responsible for various OECD studies on noise abatement policies at the national and international levels. Dr. Alexandre is a co-author of other books on noise published in France and in the United Kingdom. He is also a member of the Scientific Committee on Noise of the French Ministry of the Quality of Life.


**J. R. W. Barnes** was born in England. He holds a B.Sc. from the University of London, received his M.A. from the University of New Mexico and a diploma from the University of Birmingham. In 1970, Mr. Barnes won a scholarship to the University of Madrid. Before taking his present position as Head of Housing Research in the London Borough of Islington, he lectured at the University of Illinois at Chicago Circle and at various other institutions in Europe and America.


**Charles Wakstein** (Ph.D., London University) is a technologist/designer with ten years' professional experience in American industry and fourteen years' experience in engineering research and teaching in American and British universities and polytechnics. He has published papers in fluid mechanics, design, noise and the social effects of technology. He has contributed to the books *The Hazards of Work and How to Fight Them*, *Environmental Pollution Control*, and the forthcoming book *Engineering Failures*. His main interests are in the demystification of technology and in direct public involvement in design and decision making. He is at present training as a film maker at the Sheffield Polytechnic.

# Part I  The Socio-Technological Problems of Noise

CHAPTER 1

# Noise: Ubiquity, Threats, and Questions

## THE PROBLEM

No one on our planet can escape the unwanted sound that we call noise—a disturbance to our environment escalating so rapidly as to become one of the major threats to the quality of our lives.

The sound of our cities is the jarring staccato of the jackhammer, the angry roar of the automobile, the bus, and the helicopter. The peace of the countryside and the sounds of the jungle have been shattered, perhaps forever, by the internal combustion engine, both on the ground and overhead. In our very homes, more and more power gadgets surround us, each a source of noise. The effect of these multiple causes of noise can, unfortunately, be cumulative. Noise exposure at work adds to exposure while commuting, to exposure at home, and to exposure during leisure activities. Slowly, insensibly, we seem to accept noise—and the physiological and psychological deterioration that accompanies it—as an inevitable part of our lives. Although we endeavor to set standards for some of the most offensive sources of noise—the airplane at takeoff and landing or the truck just off the assembly line—we often fail to effectively monitor and control them. And we accept and at times enjoy countless other sounds, from the clatter of dishes in a restaurant to loud ads on radio and television to rock and roll music.

The problem knows no political or social frontiers. It affects the socialist countries as much as the United States, Western Europe and Japan, being one of the prices paid for modern industrial development. It affects the rich who sleep in a quiet suburb, but travel by plane and cruise by motorboat,

3

just as much as the poor who must live next to a superhighway, an elevated railway or at the end of an airport runway.

The insidiousness of the noise problem lies exactly in this—in its ubiquity and in our unconcern and lack of awareness. Great difficulties both of a social and a technological nature must be overcome if noise is to be controlled, and if we are thus to restore to our lives the quality that our very technical successes and economic progress are, ironically, threatening.

Unfortunately, there is no hope that noise will vanish by a technical breakthrough, if only because there is no such thing as a noiseless machine. Of the energy put in to run a machine, some must come out as noise, even if it is a very small fraction. An automobile may have an energy input of 100 kW. Of that, only one part in a million, or 0.1 W, comes out as noise. A pneumatic drill may have an input of 3 kW; of that, much more, 1 part in 300 or 1 W, comes out as noise! Noise control, furthermore, is technically very difficult and very expensive, because it requires large reductions in the acoustic energy emitted by the noise source. For instance, to reduce noise by 3 dB,* 50 percent of the acoustic energy must be removed; to reduce it by 30 dB, the energy must be reduced by 99.9 percent.

The situation is, in a sense, getting worse as far as noise is concerned. This is so for two reasons. In the first place, machines are more powerful now than they used to be; for instance, a typical commercial jetliner has a noise power of the order of 10 kW, versus a power of the order of 0.1 kW for a commercial propeller liner. Secondly, we are moving more and more in the direction of modes of living and transportation which inevitably generate more noise. The flight to the suburbs would not have been possible without the automobile, a major source of noise. The internal combustion engine is also becoming a tool of leisure. Speedboats, snowmobiles, trailbikes and motorcycles are high sources of noise that affect not only those who enjoy their leisure use, but, unfortunately, also the non-participating bystanders. Finally, the abandonment of the train for the airplane—a trend particularly pronounced in the United States (Fig. 1.1)—also means the replacement of a relatively confined and minor source of noise with a diffused and far more intense one. Only the energy crisis of 1973 has succeeded in slowing down these trends.

---

*See Appendix 1.

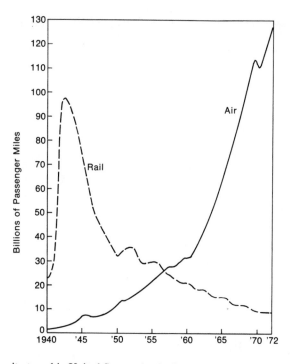

**Fig. 1.1** Inter-city travel in United States: the decline of rail travel and the increase of air travel. (Adapted from *Time*, 1973. Reprinted by permission from *Time*, the weekly news magazine; Copyright © Time Inc.)

It is imperative that techniques and public actions for reducing noise keep pace with the increased power and pervasiveness of machines which the dynamics and style of our society foster. Unless this occurs, the alarming advance of noise levels will not be checked and reversed. Because noise does not pose as obvious and immediate a danger to health as polluted water or polluted air, public awareness of noise and public commitment to noise reduction have been small. Table 1.1 shows indeed how in the United States, where in general the commitment to pollution control has been high, in 1970 the capital investment in noise and sources of pollution other than air and water was insignificant. The projected figures for 1980 become appreciable but still very small in comparison to those for air and water pollution.

**Table 1.1** Investment by Type of Pollution in the United States (Source: Science Policy, 1973).

| Pollutant/ Medium | Capital Investment (Billions of Dollars) | | | | | | | |
| --- | --- | --- | --- | --- | --- | --- | --- | --- |
| | 1970 | | | | (1980) | | | |
| | In Place | % | Annual | % | In Place | % | Annual | % |
| Air pollution | 1.5 | 6.1 | 1.0 | 27.8 | 29.8 | 38.7 | 6.0 | 63.2 |
| Water pollution | 23.3 | 93.9 | 2.5 | 69.4 | 46.1 | 59.7 | 3.0 | 31.5 |
| Solid waste | N.A.* | | 0.1 | 2.8 | N.A. | | 0.3 | 3.2 |
| Other (noise, radiation, land reclamation) | 0 | 0 | 0 | 0 | 1.2 | 1.6 | 0.2 | 2.1 |
| Total | 24.8 | 100 | 3.6 | 100 | 77.1 | 100 | 9.5 | 100 |

*N.A.: not available.

## AN OVERVIEW OF THIS BOOK

In this book, we have undertaken a reconnaissance of the problem of noise that should assist our reader in forming an opinion as to:

- How serious is the noise problem?
- What is known about the effects of noise? What is not known?
- What is the monetary cost of noise to our society? Is there a dollar amount that might be said to represent the damage caused by noise?
- How do we decide how much ought to be spent on noise abatement?
- What are other aspects of the damage that are not well expressed in financial terms?
- What measures are available to solve the problem? What technical measures? What economic measures? What social measures? What political measures? How much will these measures cost to implement?

Although many of these questions are dealt with in the standard references in the field, many others, particularly those of a socio-economic and political nature, generally are not.

And it is precisely these aspects which we shall endeavor to stress. For, as we have seen, noise pollution has reached present levels not only because of the technological imperative of more power, but also because we as a society have allowed it to do so. Just as the causes of noise pollution are partly social and partly technical, so too are the solutions. By the word 'social' we understand all the economic, legal, sociological and political institutions and interrelationships which make up a modern society.

Social questions arise when we consider how a government decides the extent and degree to which people must suffer noise exposure. A distinction must be made between the participating and non-participating environment. Those making the noise may well tolerate it, or even enjoy it, since it is associated with something pleasurable or useful to them. Meanwhile, those who have to endure the noise without benefit from its cause are likely to object strongly to it. The fact that we are all at one time or another noise makers does not alter the basic question: to what extent should the non-participating groups be subjected to noise pollution?

There is a difference between loudness of an unwanted sound and the annoyance it causes. A variety of sociological and psychological parameters determines an individual's or a community's reaction to noise. In general, people tolerate noise more easily if they are causing it, if they feel it is necessary, if they know where it is coming from. As between different groups in society, the more affluent tend to complain more often, although complaints are not necessarily a correlate with annoyance. As living standards improve, and, perhaps more importantly, awareness of the dangers of noise increases, a rise in complaints, legal action and community pressure can be expected.

Noise generates conflicts between the participating and non-participating groups. It is the function of the political process to resolve or reduce these conflicts. If, as seems probable, the present level of complaints represents only the tip of the annoyance iceberg, then community resentment will channel itself into increased political action. The present administrations in most countries are making only limited attempts to solve the problem, and the potential for large scale protests of a violent nature has to be recognized. This is especially true of single event, highly intrusive noise, where the source is readily located—a situation occurring around major airports.

In the pages that follow we deal with: the awareness of noise (Chapter 2), the effects of noise on health (Part II), the ramifications of surface transportation (Part III), aircraft (Part IV), industrial, construction and household noise (Part V), and the political economy of noise (Part VI). In the conclusions (Part VII) we attempt to set noise pollution in the framework of the general class of problems which our society is endeavoring to solve.

## REFERENCES

Science Policy. Counting the cost of pollution. *Science Policy*, March/April 1973.
Time. Light in Amtrak's Tunnel. *Time*, March 26, 1973.

# CHAPTER 2

# The Awareness of Noise as a Risk

## THE LOW AWARENESS

Most of us are now aware that noise can damage hearing. However, short of a threat that disaster would overtake the human race if nothing is done about noise, it is unlikely that many people today would become strongly motivated to do something about the problem.

And yet the evidence about the ill-effects of noise does not allow for complacency or neglect. For instance, researchers working with children with hearing disorders are constantly reminded of the crucial importance of hearing to children. In the early years the child cannot learn to speak without special training if he has enough hearing loss to interfere effectively with the hearing of words in context. In this respect there is a clear need for parents to protect their children's hearing as they try to protect their eyesight. Parents should say, "Don't make that loud noise near Jimmy's ears," in the same way as they say, "Don't poke that stick in Jimmy's face."

If no steps are taken to mitigate the effects of noise, we may expect a significant percentage of future generations to have hearing damage. The consequences would be difficult to predict if the total population were to suffer hearing damage. Conceivably, the loss could even be detrimental to our survival if it were ever necessary for us to be able to hear high frequencies. Colavita (1967) has consistently been unable to find among university students in his classes any who could hear 20 kHz, although the classical results of Fletcher and Munson show 20 kHz as an audible frequency (Fletcher, 1953).

If vision is impaired, each person at least recognizes the value of correcting the loss. Industry has long demanded safety goggles or some form of eye protection for workers on jobs where metal particles, dust or other potential dangers exist to damage their eyes. In some states, such as Illinois, all workers who use wood or metal-cutting machinery must wear safety glasses. This would seem to be a clear precedent for state laws about earmuffs, and warnings of the danger of hearing loss would be desirable by analogy with the warnings which are now required in the United States on all cigarette packages.

Not everybody who needs to wear corrective lenses is happy about wearing glasses, but there is far more general acceptance of this kind of correction than for the wearing of a hearing aid, even when the hearing loss most definitely calls for one. Monocles, spectacles and eye glasses have long been in use, but advances in technology of the hearing aid are relatively recent. Social acceptance has not yet reached the point where a visible hearing aid is considered to enhance esthetics, in the same way as glasses increasingly are.

Thus people live with their hearing loss, even at great psychological cost, as discussed in Part II. In any case, hearing aids are no panacea; they do not work well in noise-induced hearing loss. Amplifying the frequencies where there is hearing damage is not enough to restore hearing to normal. The users still cannot understand speech, because the masking of sounds of one frequency by sounds of nearby frequencies raises thresholds even in people who have normal hearing.

One of the adaptations of living with a hearing loss is the fact that the sufferer is not always aware of his disability. If it is an accumulated loss, a gradual adaptation on the part of the person suffering the damage affects his recognition of it. On account of this insidious effect of adaptation, any educational campaign for hearing preservation ought to be expressed subjectively, for example, "if you have been working at a noise level of so many decibels for so many years, things will sound like this to you."

There is another kind of awareness important to the success of hearing conservation programs, namely awareness in workers or the general population, that long-term exposure to high enough noise levels can cause damage to hearing. Everyday observations of the lack of precautions by operators of pneumatic hammers or chain saws, which reach the 120 dBA level, make it clear that many workers are not aware of the danger. The nature of this problem is illustrated by the fact that workers in noisy industries tend to complain more of the "unpleasantness" of their working environment than of the noise (Noise Control Center, 1972). Awareness is limited to the large and more progressive companies that have hearing conservation programs.

For instance, in Pennsylvania, the total number of manufacturing companies is approximately 18,000. Only one-sixth of the plants, that is, those with more than 100 employees, for which the average number of employees is 250, have the capability of giving this information to their workers because they have well-established industrial hygiene programs. Two-thirds of the factories in Pennsylvania employ less than 50 people and one-third employ less than 9 people. It might be said, therefore, that until the recent OSHA (Occupational Safety and Health Administration) Act, five-sixths of the manufacturing companies in Pennsylvania, as an example, could have been expected to have a low level of awareness of the danger to hearing caused by exposure to noise. This, however, was somewhat mitigated by the assistance given by the insurance companies that carry workmen's compensation insurance for these manufacturers. Even after the OSHA Act, the smaller companies will continue, inevitably, to have less effective industrial hygiene programs. The problem is compounded by the immensity of the task faced by OSHA. In three years, from 1971 to 1974, the agency's 700 inspectors visited 145,000 workplaces in the U.S., but this represented only 2.9% of all workplaces in the country (Time, 1974).

New Jersey has had for some time an active, state-supported program which involves visits to plants, measurements of noise levels and recommendations to management. Where these visits are made, the level of awareness is high. On the other hand, an industrial hygienist stated a few years ago that he had not encountered one case in his long career where noise control was a major issue in collective bargaining (Shimer, 1967).

Some economists believe that in noisy foundries oldtimers are likely to warn the newcomers about noise. If this is so, the noise problem would be "internalized" through higher wages. In Part VI under the heading of "Voluntary Bargains," we show that there is little evidence to support such a notion of an explicit premium being paid to the employee for working under noisy conditions.

## TO INCREASE AWARENESS

### Simulation of Hearing Loss

Awareness of the effects of hearing loss can be increased by appropriate demonstrations. For example, the Department of Audiology at the

Eye and Ear Hospital in Pittsburgh has used magnetic tape recordings in order to show parents of a child with a known hearing loss how speech is likely to sound to their children (Bugliarello and Wakstein, 1968). The tape demonstrates two basic types of hearing loss: loss in sensitivity and loss in intelligibility.

A story that a child might read in the primary grades is recorded first as it would be heard with normal hearing, then at two levels of loss of sensitivity—mild and severe. In the demonstration the listener must focus all his concentration on the voice to hear the words. The degree of concentration might be less if the listener could read the lips of the person talking, or at least see him. A loss of sensitivity may be corrected with hearing aids, but loss of intelligibility cannot. The latter makes the same story sound, at best, as if the speaker were holding his nose. When electronic filters are used to simulate the combined loss of sensitivity and intelligibility, it becomes virtually impossible for the normal listener to understand the story. An adjustment in filters, to simulate the effect a hearing aid would have for a person suffering the combined loss, illustrates why present hearing aids cannot correct completely for intelligibility loss. The normal listener is still unable to understand the words, although the boost in intensity allows him to perceive them at a reasonable level.

Present research in audiology can tell us what the damaged ear cannot hear but as yet cannot ascertain exactly what that ear does hear. Hearing may be measured by having the person listen to pure tones, that is, tones of only one frequency, and measuring the "softest" tone he can hear as a function of frequency. The "louder" a tone must be for the person to hear it, the greater the hearing loss at that frequency. The results are reported in terms of how much "louder" or "softer" the tones must be for him than the mean based on young people with healthy ears. A graph of the function is called a pure-tone air-conduction audiogram—or audiogram. Typical audiograms are shown in Fig. 2.1. The audiogram labeled $D$ is characteristic of the early stages of noise-induced hearing loss;* there is a severe loss of sensitivity (i.e., the tones have to increase in loudness to be heard) between 2000 and 4000 Hz.

In simulating hearing loss for those with normal hearing, electronic filters are used to make the sounds at the "damaged" frequencies "softer" or attenuated. It is possible to set up filters to make the components of various frequencies in sounds as much "softer" for the person with

---

*The loss is also called cochlear hearing loss, sensori-neural hearing loss, or nerve-type hearing loss.

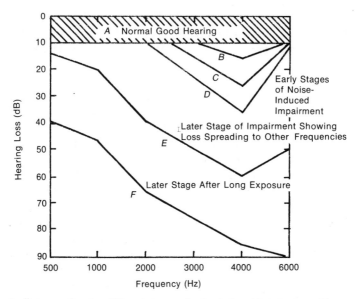

**Fig. 2.1**  Audiograms showing different stages of noise-induced hearing loss. (Source: Bell, 1966. Used by permission.)

normal hearing as they are for the person with damaged hearing. The use of filters in this way helps a person with normal hearing to comprehend the effect of a hearing loss, but it can only approximate the actual sound perception. The damaged ear hears the same sound differently (in general worse) than the normal ear hearing the sound through a filter. The precise workings of the analyzing mechanism of the inner ear, which is the part of the ear most affected by exposure to noise, is still not known.

How are sounds other than speech perceived by a person with marked hearing loss in the frequencies around 4000 Hz? This specific question must be posed for several reasons. In the first place, this particular loss occurs often. Secondly, the loss is usually the first point at which loss occurs across the hearing range. Finally, the 4000 Hz frequency represents the generally recognized "top" of the speech range.*

---

*However, the loss at frequencies beyond 4000 Hz is not trivial. It is interesting for instance to look at the spectra of speech sounds like "sh" and "ss" (as at the end of the work "Hiss"). These quite clearly contain appreciable energy content at frequencies of 5000 and 6000 Hz in the case of "sh" and in the case of "ss" the peak energy content is at 8000 Hz with significant energy extending as far as 9000 Hz. Indeed the entire energy spectrum of the sound "ss" lies above 4000 Hz; this explains why one of the early difficulties with noise induced hearing damage is the loss of the plurals.

There are drawbacks to using a filter to simulate sound perception under these conditions. The filter does not reproduce exactly the accomodations made by a person with an audiogram showing a loss as in a curve $C$ midway between curves $B$ and $D$ in Fig. 2.1. Accepting such limitation, a recording engineer was asked to simulate curve $C$ with a series of sound-effect recordings played through a professional console (Bugliarello and Wakstein, 1968). The objective was to hear the difference between a recording in the flat spectrum curve (representing normal hearing) compared to the same recording played with a filter reproducing a dip at 4000 Hz. It was thought that perhaps the difference would be slight and only a trained ear could distinguish between the two. However, it took no effort to discriminate between a straight and a filtered playback:

• A teletype machine, a printing press, and a treadle-type sewing machine were easily identified, each by its individual and characteristic sound, in the flat spectrum. With the filter cutting off in the 4000 Hz band all three machines sounded alike, or at least similar, and it was difficult to tell which was which.

• Tap water filling a washbasin, filling a kitchen sink, pouring from a shower—all these resembled a more mechanical sound with the filter switched in. The rumbling of the water could just as well have been the rumbling of a machine.

• China or porcelain dishes, rattling as if someone were setting a table or putting them into a cupboard, "became" earthenware or thick pottery.

• The sound of the tappets in a running car engine was no longer discernible, though the rest of the sound remained identifiable.

• Voices in the background of traffic noise at a busy street corner dropped out, as did the screech of tires in a sudden stop.

• Standing by a superhighway, the sound of the approach and retreat of a car being driven by at high speed changed, so that it would be heard only when it is right on top of the listener.

• With rain effects—steady rain, steady rain on a tin roof, rain with thunder—the general change is that instead of being outside in the rain the listener is inside the house. Water rushing in a stream or brook and raindrops splashing in puddles can still be identified but the pleasing musical effect is lost.

• In a general conversation among several women the ability to identify one voice from the others was impaired, if not lost altogether. Phrases and occassional words that came across in the flat spectrum were unintelligible with the filter cut in.

**Public Service Information Campaigns**

Major awareness of noise as a risk can only be generated through large-scale dissemination of information on the subject. But how much would it cost to inform the general public through a multi-media advertising campaign? In the United States this question was asked of the Advertising Council on the assumption that such a campaign could be justified as being in the public interest—similar to such campaigns as "Keep America Beautiful," "Equal Employment Opportunity," or "Continue Your Education" (Bugliarello and Wakstein, 1968). It was estimated that a typical campaign would run around $100,000,* exclusive of personnel costs and of the costs of preparing the material.†

To be effective, a campaign should be repeated at least annually. The value of spending each year between $100,000 and $200,000 to alert the general public to the dangers of noise is clearly modest—but must be weighed against the total cost of other ways of exerting pressure for noise reduction.

As is pointed out in Part VI, the fact that there is little economic incentive to limit noise creates a tendency for more noise to be produced than society—or more specifically the people exposed to it—may consider desirable. An educational program directed towards noise control at several levels then becomes an important and probably indispensable mechanism for encouraging noise reduction.

---

\*In 1973 dollars.
†This range is based upon a general format as follows:

| | |
|---|---:|
| Radio | |
|     Kit mailed to some 450 local stations | $   7,200 |
| Television | |
|     Kit mailed to about 675 local stations and quantities of 35 mm films supplied to networks | 52,000 |
| Newspaper Proof Sheets | |
|     Mailed to about 8500 local and daily newspapers | 6,500 |
| Magazine Proof Sheets | |
|     Mailed to 200–300 consumer magazines | 6,500 |
| Business Press | |
|     Mailed to about 500 business magazines | 3,900 |
| Graphics | 19,000 |
| Miscellanea | 4,900 |
| | $100,000 |

## PRESSURES FOR REDUCTION OF NOISE

If enough people actively work to quiet a source of noise—either acting as individuals or as organized groups complaining to the noise producer—the noise will be quieted.

### Individual Consumers

The individual consumers are a first category of people that can exert pressure. They may be individual homeowners demanding quieter air-conditioners, housewives demanding quieter garbage disposals or mixers, gardeners demanding quieter power mowers. Consumer unions, cooperatives, testing laboratories and their published reports already exist to demonstrate some of the pathways by which the buyer can make his demands, or desires, known to the producer. As competition in a given market increases, more attention is paid to what the buyer says he wants.

Another example of the individual consumer who can influence a noise producer is the buyer of machines or equipment. Several large corporations are writing allowable noise outputs into the specifications for some of their machinery orders. In this way, big business in general is operating, in our present terms, as "individual consumer" and can have a widespread impact on noise reduction by its demand for quieter machinery. Designs by companies competing for bids from large corporations become available to the smaller companies (who may not even be aware that they can profit indirectly by creating a less noisy environment for their employees).

Specifications from the City of New York, which for several years has limited the noise level of official cars, muffler requirements and similar noise ordinances in other states and cities eventually produce quieter vehicles for a more extensive buying public than that covered by the ordinances. In other words, in time more people will unknowingly benefit from an increase in quiet than the few people who knowingly demand it.

### Groups

A second category of people who can exert pressure are groups—persons who are unified in making a single demand or a set of demands of a noise producer. A group may be the members of a union in a single factory, suddenly exposed to excessive noise or recently made aware of the potential damage of noise that has existed for some time. It may be a loosely organized neighborhood group fighting by petition or picket against a noisy shop near their homes, or it may be a citizens' committee or mayor's task force arising from cognizance of a local need. An early example of such groups is the Air Pollution Control League of Greater Cincinnati, which conducted annual noise abatement campaigns from 1958 through 1960. The League used promotional materials from the National Noise Abatement Council (NNAC) and during those years received several awards of recognition from the NNAC. When the NNAC dissolved its organization in 1961, the Cincinnati League also discontinued the promotions for noise abatement and extended efforts into other areas of pollution control.

Another example of an ambitious effort undertaken by a community group is the New York Mayor's Task Force on Noise Control (Task Force, 1970). The task force was constituted by a group of prominent citizens with a broad spectrum of backgrounds and occupations, and enjoyed the co-operation of citizens' groups and of industry. It dealt with five groups of questions:

- Definition of the problem.
- Identification of the chief sources of noise in the city.
- Investigation of the various means and resources by which noise could be reduced in the city.
- Establishment of acoustical criteria, taking into account the needs and requirements of the city for its present and future residents.
- Test of whether principles and methods learned in the course of the investigation could be actually applied in at least one or more limited cases.

The Citizens for a Quieter City, Inc., which participated in the New York Task Force, is yet a further example of an articulated and committed private citizens' group that has spoken informatively on noise (e.g. Baron, 1970, 1972), and has provided "quietude happenings" and dramatic demonstrations of possibilities for noise control.

It would certainly be valuable to understand the motives and forces that underlie the emergence of an effective local group. If a pattern could be found in the evolution of successful citizens' committees for local community action, use of this information in a similar situation might well prove to be the most economical and effective method to bring about desired change.

Sociological studies of the formation of a new institutional agency to achieve collective action on a local issue indicate as a most important factor for success that the agency should act for the public interest, and not to gain private control or personal power [for an example in the case of a watershed district, see Warriner (1961) and Baur (1962)]. Acceptance of a proposal for action comes more readily when it is introduced by authorities or leaders already recognized as such at the local level. Furthermore, when it comes to industry, it is often middle management who needs to be convinced of the value and necessity of parts of the industrial hygiene program conducted by large corporations. Top management can make the decisions and set down outlines for the program, but acceptance and compliance in each separate plant is dependent on the "local leaders."

## AVAILABILITY OF NOISE COST INFORMATION

Particularly useful to an evaluation of the internalized aspects of noise control (Part VI) is a breakdown of costs to those industries which make hearing conservation a distinct part of their industrial hygiene program. Obtaining such costs is difficult. Part of the problem lies in the difficulty of extracting the figures from a plant's total industrial hygiene budget. (Another part may lie in an understandable reluctance to quote costs unless everyone does.) It would be interesting to find out how much Plant B of Corporation A is spending on hearing conservation—how much in audiometric equipment, on earmuffs, on salaries of hygienists, in time or production "lost" by workers while they are being tested or educated, on insulating or masking, etc. Figures of the engineering costs involved in making noisy machines quieter and in designing quieter machines would also be necessary,* as would actual figures of how much it costs a company in settling loss of hearing claims and how much in decreased efficiency of its workers. An estimate of such costs would be useful if no preventive measures were used. As one industrial hygiene manager has pointed out: "the amount of money paid in a single company claim would buy a lot of prevention" (Bonney, 1967). Some of these cost figures exist; they are contained somewhere in Plant B's accounting system, but the problem of how to extract them is far from simple. Other figures simply do not exist, because they are impossible to separate from other costs.

Yet not only economists and government agencies interested in noise control, but also industrial management would profit from having such a breakdown of costs of education and prevention. A useful step in this direction would be the establishment of a clearing house or data center, that could be used by industry for an exchange of such information. Once the desired information is properly identified and programmed, a system

---

*We consider this problem in Part V, Chapter 20.

can be organized by which all the branches or plants of a member corporation provide the necessary budget figures for the corporation's industrial hygiene program. Specific costs for any part of the program could then be computed.

It would be desirable to establish such a center in an urban area containing the key elements required to make its operation successful: headquarters of major industrial corporations (so as to provide direct work relationships with top management), expertise in industrial hygiene, strong computer capabilities, academic skills in audiological and socio-psychological research.

## SOME PROBLEMS IN PUBLIC INFORMATION

An important factor in the enhancement of public awareness of noise and in the development of intelligent public opinion is the availability of public information on the effects of noise. The supersonic transport is an example of a situation in which such information has been very hard to obtain—both in the pre-SST U.S. tests and in the case of the Anglo-French Concorde and the Soviet TU-144. For instance, the economic data needed to support a decision about the Concorde have been deliberately kept secret, and the consortium building Concorde has sent confidential reports to local councillors in what has been criticized as an attempt to influence them, and to bypass the public.

The decision to make information available and to whom and to what extent, is a policy decision that should be made in the open. When, as a result of such a decision, information is made available, it should be clear; when research is described and conclusions drawn, there must be enough detail for the readers to be able to decide whether they agree with the conclusions or not. Authors of papers and reports who fail to adhere to this requirement may be seen in effect as inhibiting the flow of information. Some of the important if difficult questions that an intelligent reader would like and need to know in order to acquire an informed opinion are:

- Is there an unusual rise in complaints?
- Are median or mean values of noise, annoyance or complaints sufficient? What is the spread?
- Are there factors that affect the potential for complaints?
- Were people exposed to a sudden noise—as in a sonic boom— warned before each occurrence of the noise? Similarly, was there adaptation? How defined and ascertained?

• Has a clear distinction been drawn between annoyance and complaints?

• What is the influence of the media on the results (a difficult but important question)? While some authors suggest that the news media have little or no influence, our everyday experience and that of consummate politicians, tell us that the media are indeed very influential, if they give widespread coverage to some event or incident.

• Have the results a predictive value?

Another issue that affects at times our ability in reaching an informed opinion about noise is bias. Although it may be argued that scientific papers are objective by their nature, and that each author writes in good conscience as he honestly sees the problem, subtle biases may be present, often unknown to the authors themselves (this book is no exception). The biases may stem from the psychological attitudes of the authors, their political inclinations, their experiences or from their affiliations. It is important that, as far as humanly possible, when facts are being presented that will be used in making policy decisions, biases and omissions be clearly stated. Since members of the public are going to be using such papers more and more often, the papers ought to be unassailably clear.

## REFERENCES

Baron, R. A. *The tyranny of noise.* New York, St. Martin's Press, 1970.

Baron, R. A. Construction noise. A citizen's viewpoint. International Conference on Transportation and the Environment. Society of Automotive Engineers, New York, August 1972.

Baur, E. J. Opinion change in a public controversy. *Public Opinion Quarterly*, 1962, **26**.

Bell, A. Noise: An occupational hazard and a public nuisance. Public Health Paper No. 30. Geneva: World Health Organization, 1966.

Bonney, T., Director of Industrial Hygiene, Aluminum Corporation of America, Pittsburgh. Personal communication, 1967.

Bugliarello, G. and Wakstein, C. Noise pollution—a view of its techno-sociological and health aspects. Biotechnology Program, Carnegie-Mellon University, Pittsburgh, 1968.

Colavita, F. B., Department of Psychology, University of Pittsburgh. Personal communication, 1967.

Fletcher, H. *Speech and hearing in communication.* Princeton, N.J.: Van Nostrand, 1953.

Noise Control Center, Wymondkam, Leicestershire, U.K. Personal communication, April 1972.

Shimer, P. C., Principal Industrial Hygienist, New Jersey Department of Health. Personal communication, 1967.

Task Force. Toward a quieter city. A Report of the Mayor's Task Force on Noise Control. New York City, 1970.

Time. OSHA under attack. *Time*, July 8, 1974.

Warriner, C. K. Public opinion and collective action: Formation of a watershed district. *Administrative Science Quarterly*, 1961, **6**.

**Part II** The Effects of Noise on Health

# CHAPTER 3

# The Effects of Noise on Hearing

## INTRODUCTION

Almost everyone has had one experience of being temporarily "deafened" by a loud noise. This "deafness" is not total, although it is often accompanied by a ringing in the ears, and one can hear another person if he raises his voice. Moreover, normal hearing comes back within a few hours at most. This sort of partial hearing loss is called Temporary Threshold Shift (TTS). A TTS may be experienced after firing a gun or after a long drive in a car with the windows open.

It may come as a surprise to most people that, if it is continued over a period of years for 8 hours a day and 5 days a week, exposure to noise, even no louder than people shouting, can cause hearing loss. When we say hearing loss, we mean any degree of hearing loss, from partial to "complete." This loss, moreover, is permanent and is not satisfactorily corrected by hearing aids. (The loss is caused by the destruction of the delicate hair cells—and their auditory nerve connections—in the Organ of Corti, which is contained in the cochlea (Fig. 3.1). Every exposure to loud noise destroys some cells, and prolonged or repeated exposure causes the destruction of large numbers of cells, and ultimately the collapse of the Organ of Corti).

There are many jobs that expose workers to enough loud noise to cause hearing loss—some after as little as 1 year (Gallo and Glorig, 1964). Even activities around the home, like mowing the lawn with a power mower, can cause hearing loss if continued long enough and done often enough.

To define hearing loss, we need to ascertain what normal hearing is. This is defined as the hearing of people with healthy ears, who have had very little exposure to noise throughout their lives.

23

HUMAN EAR

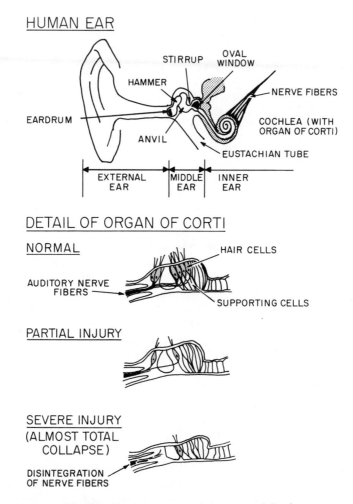

Fig. 3.1   The human ear and the organ of Corti.

### Presbycusis and Sociocusis

Physiologically, the deterioration of hearing is due to the progressive destruction of hair cells in the organ of Corti, and to the reduction in the number of the associated nerve fibers [Fig. 3.1]. This process has two distinct causes: old age and specific noise exposure.

For the average person, normal hearing deteriorates with age; this deterioration is called presbycusis. The main studies of this condition are those of Bunch (1929), Steinberg *et al.* (1940), at the New York World's Fair, and Webster *et al.* (1950), at the San Diego County Fair. These are grouped together and summarized in Fig. 3.2, taken from a Standard of the Acoustical Society of America. It is interesting to note that men have worse hearing than women. Hinchcliffe (1959) attrubuted this difference to the firing of guns, at least in a random sampling taken in Scotland of normally hearing people living in the country (Hinchcliffe, 1959b). As even people living in the country are occasionally exposed to noise, the changes he noted were not exclusively due to age deterioration.

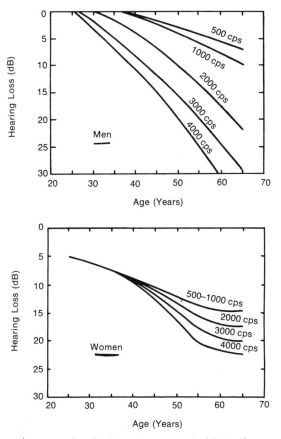

**Fig. 3.2**   Presbycusis: average hearing loss to be expected with age (Source: ASA Standard, 1954).

*The Audiometric Zero*

The zero reference for the presbycusis studies is called an audiometric zero, and is defined as the hearing of young people 18–25 years old who have healthy ears. There are at least three such zero references, called respectively the ASA zero (1951), the more recent ISO zero (1967), and the zero of Hinchcliffe and Littler (1958), which is used in Great Britain. It has been suggested that the ISO zero was a compromise at the request of the American delegation; the Europeans believed that the zero should have been at least 10 dB lower.

Hearing is a statistically distributed quantity. The audiometric zero is a mean value. The variations about the mean have a standard deviation of 7 dB at 125 Hz, 6 dB at 2000 Hz, and 9 dB at 8000 Hz, according to Dadson and King (1952). In the same way, there are presbycusis curves for the various percentiles in the sample population.

When the ISO Committee recommended the new audiometric zero in 1967, a hearing loss of 15 dB re ASA average at 500, 1000, and 2000 Hz (which was compensable) became a hearing loss of 26 dB re ISO. However, the sound-pressure levels of normal speech, that is, the actual physically measured levels remained unchanged by the audiometric zero. Thus, the new low fence, that is, the hearing loss to the beginning of difficulty with speech comprehension becomes 26 dB. The implied assumption must be noted that the only valid criterion for claiming any difficulty is speech comprehension. Yet some other criteria could be considered, such as degradation of the quality of the environment as perceived by the person. We discuss the implication of this point in Chapter 19 of Part V.

*Sociocusis*

Hearing change caused by noise exposure is called sociocusis, which must be separated from presbycusis. For the average person, exposure to loud enough noise will inevitably produce hearing loss. There are extensive data in the literature on the relation of noise exposure to hearing loss. For example, exposure for 8 hours a day, 5 days a week to noise having an overall sound-pressure level of 102 dB produced the median hearing loss at 4000 Hz shown in Fig. 3.3. The subjects were male workers. Similar exposure to noise (Taylor *et al.*, 1964) having an overall sound-pressure level ranging from 87 to 102 dB produced the median hearing loss in female jute weavers shown in Fig. 3.4. It may be seen that the hearing loss progresses most rapidly at a frequency near 4000 Hz. Thus, measure-

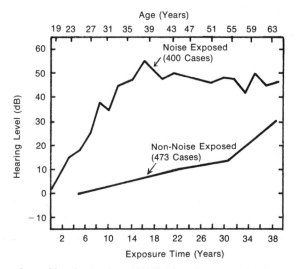

**Fig. 3.3**  Comparison of heating level (at 4000 Hz) in noise exposed and non-noise exposed men (Source: Gallo and Glorig, 1964).

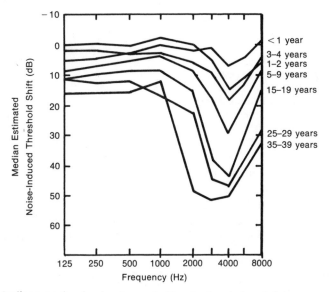

**Fig. 3.4**  Audiograms showing development of hearing loss in female jute weavers (Source: Taylor *et al.*, 1964).

ments at 4000 Hz are crucial for the early detection of hearing loss. (And yet this is the very frequency omitted in the AAOO assessment scheme).

The hearing loss caused by noise can be mild and not apparent even to a person experienced in listening to music, because of the person's gradual adjustment over time. (Indeed, changes in hearing level of less than 5 dB are generally considered not significant, or noticeable.) At the other extreme, the hearing loss can be so severe that the sufferer can only understand someone talking directly to him, even in a raised voice, if he can lip read.

As noise-induced hearing loss progresses in a person, gradually certain sounds—such as bells ringing and clocks ticking—become more and more difficult to hear, and after a time they are lost forever.

Perhaps the most devastating effect of hearing loss is a social one—the inability to take part in meetings and conversations. A recent study by Kell *et al.* (1971) shows dramatically a comparison between a group of weavers working eight hours a day at approximately 100 dBA, and a control group (Table 3.1). Later in this chapter we discuss how speech comprehension can be measured.

**Table 3.1**  Social Consequences of Noise. Comparison of a Control Group with Weavers Working in a 100 dBA, Eight hours a Day Environment. (Adapted from Kell *et al.*, 1971).

|  | Weavers(%) | Control Group(%) |
| --- | --- | --- |
| Difficulty at Public Meeting | 72 | 5 |
| Difficulty in Talking with Strangers | 80 | 16 |
| Difficulty in Understanding Phone Conversations | 64 | 5 |
| Subjective Feeling that Heating is Impaired | 81 | 5 |
| Use of Some Form of Lip Reading | 53 | 0 |

*Military Noise*

Hearing losses induced by exposure to military noise represent a particular but important case of sociocusis. For example, high hearing losses are encountered in audiometric examinations of artillerymen. In a sample of 116 artillerymen, an average loss of 10 dB was found, compared to 0.52 dB for a group of 103 medical students (Reid, 1948). Furthermore:

• Fifty percent had losses (at high frequency) in the worse ear greater than 30 dB, 42 percent had greater than 40 dB, and 23 percent had peak losses greater than 50 dB.

• Twenty percent had average losses (in the range 512–8192 Hz) in the worse ear, greater than 20 dB, and 8 percent had average losses greater than 30 dB.

The artillerymen in the sample who served in proof ranges, and thus experienced a much greater exposure, had a much larger average hearing loss (18 dB) than the group as a whole. In general, although the mean peak hearing loss increased with length of service (reaching 41 dB in subjects with 6 years of service), the greatest portion of the loss (approximately 30 dB) occurred in the first 1 or 2 years. It is interesting to note that in a preliminary sample of 82 artillerymen in an anti-aircraft battery, more than half wore no earplugs, and the remainder wore inefficient, often makeshift, earplugs. The number with adverse hearing symptoms was, of course, much larger among those who wore no earplugs.

## PREVALENCE OF NOISE-INDUCED HEARING LOSS

As there are various stages of hearing loss, and a small variation from normal hearing, say 2 dB, is unlikely to be noise-induced, we must adopt some rule to define what we shall call the hearing loss caused by noise. Let us use the American Academy of Ophthalmology and Otolaryngology definition (AAOO, 1964) of hearing loss, namely one for which the average of the losses at the frequencies 500, 1000, and 2000 Hz is at least 25 dB, with respect to the ISO zero. This hearing loss also is the minimum compensable hearing loss in many states in the United States.

A surprisingly large number of people in the United States have noise-induced hearing loss, thus defined. Glorig (1961) estimated in 1961 the number to be 4.5 million. Independently, we estimated (Bugliarello and Wakstein, 1968) the national loss at about 5 million, by extrapolating Wisconsin State Fair figures (Glorig *et al.*, 1957) for distribution of hearing loss among manufacturing workers. In making such an extrapolation, we assumed implicitly that the Wisconsin manufacturing industry produced the same distribution of hearing loss in its workers as the U.S. manufacturing industry as a whole; that other contributions to hearing loss, such as firing guns, could be neglected; and that the manufacturing workers who came to the Fair were a good sample of all manufacturing workers in Wisconsin.

Although 5 million is only about one-fortieth of the U.S. population, this number must be considered very large. Furthermore, on account of the manner in which noise-induced loss progresses, there will almost always be considerable hearing loss at frequencies above 2000 Hz, before the average loss at 500, 1000, and 2000 Hz reaches 15 dB. This implies that if the method used to evaluate hearing loss is dependent upon these higher frequencies, many more people have hearing loss than if the lower frequencies only are used in assessing the loss. Thus, assessment of the seriousness of hearing damage depends on what method one uses to calculate the percentage.

There are a great many official methods for calculating the monaural percentage of impairment, and there are also a number of ways of calculating biaural impairment from the monaural data. These include those established by: the American Association of Ophthalmology and Otolaryngology (AAOO, 1964); the American Medical Association; the Fletcher 0.8, New York, Wisconsin, California, the Veterans Administration and the Australian methods. The most liberal is the Australian method (Murray, 1962), which uses the four frequencies 500, 1000, 2000, 4000 Hz. Averages are taken of the loss at 500 and 1000 Hz, 1000 and 2000 Hz, and 2000 and 4000 Hz. These three averages are averaged in turn to obtain the hearing loss. The method also makes allowance for cases where the change between the listed frequencies is severe. The use of 4000 Hz is important because it relates to speech comprehension under realistic conditions, and to quality of the environment. The number of people in the United States with noise-induced hearing losses would increase to over 14 million if the losses were defined according to the Australian method versus the 5 million with the AAOO method. Recently Kryter (1973) has stressed again the need to consider frequencies beyond 2000 Hz, by means of an index that would average hearing losses at 1000, 2000 and 3000 or 4000 Hz.

In a previous study, we have also estimated the potential claims in the United States by a criterion of our own (Bugliarello and Wakstein, 1968). This was done by taking, as in the AAOO method, the 500, 1000, and 2000 Hz averages and adding the loss at 4000 Hz, but giving it a weight of only one-tenth, compared to the average of 500, 1000, and 2000 Hz. Roughly speaking, such a method implies that the ability to hear, say music, is one-tenth as important as the ability to hear and understand speech—still a very timid approach to the quality of the environment. The resulting estimate of the number of potential claims turned out to be still higher, by 20 percent, than that given by the Australian method.

## Which Scheme to Measure Hearing Loss?

As the spread of hearing loss estimates can be so great, which method, if any, is most reasonable, in the sense of representing the loss to the person, including the degradation in the quality of the environment as he perceives it?

One opinion argues that speech comprehension is the overriding consideration; to reduce the present incidence of hearing loss at 4000 Hz, we would require reduction of all noise levels to 80 dB. This would be expensive and impractical.

Another view holds that no functional impairment should be tolerated; thus no functional impairment would be permitted, apart from presbycusis. As desirable as this might be, it would mean making factories as quiet as homes; it is doubtful that society would want to assign noise reduction such a high priority, when concerned with many other major social problems, from poverty to energy.

Yet another opinion, which appears to be the most practical under present conditions, seeks to preserve the higher frequencies, as put forward by Hickish (1961) and Verbruggen (1961). Obviously for a person with a hearing loss at a higher frequency, the quality of the environment as he perceives it has been degraded. The preliminary experiments in which we attempted to assess subjectively the change in the quality of the environment caused by hearing loss has been described earlier in the chapter on Awareness (Part I, Chapter 2).

Still another group feels that 3000 Hz is needed in speech (Harris, 1960; Kryter *et al.*, 1962); others set that value at 4000 Hz.

The AAOO scheme is based on a hearing loss just perceptible in terms of occasional difficulty in understanding conversation. This sort of hearing damage has typically taken about 10 years to produce. It is tempting to ask what sounds are like to persons that suffer from it. The question could be answered if one could analyze the impulses of the nerves leading to the inner ear. But to do this would be like trying to troubleshoot one particular wire in a cable containing 30,000 wires, by wrapping a probe around the cable. However, according to Bilger (1967), a person with hearing damage like that shown in the intermediate curve for early stages of noise-induced impairment in Fig. 3.5, hears even less than those described in our simulated hearing loss experiments, (Part I, Chapter 2). Unfortunately, a person who has had 10 years to get used to his hearing loss has also forgotten what his world sounded like before. For instance, in talking to five people who suffered this kind of hearing loss it was found that not one of them considered the loss to be a great disability.

As we have pointed out, hearing conversation with background noise becomes difficult before the loss becomes compensable by the AAOO

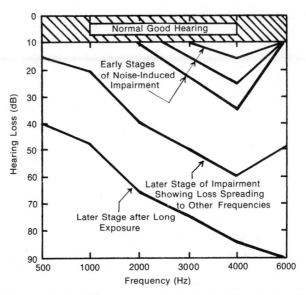

**Fig. 3.5** Audiograms showing different stages of noise-induced hearing loss. (Adapted from Bell, 1966. Used by permission.)

criterion. Furthermore, not enough importance is given to tinnitus (ringing of the ears), and loudness recruitment, a disorder in which loudness increases much more rapidly with intensity than it does in the normal subject. Indeed, tinnitus can in itself be so burdensome as to become disabling.

The common complaint of those suffering from loudness recruitment is that they cannot hear if someone speaks normally, but if someone shouts they *tell* you that you are shouting. The phenomenon is related to the degree of hearing loss: as the hearing loss increases this disorder of the loudness function gets progressively worse and speech discrimination progressively deteriorates. Thus we cannot be concerned only with the ability to hear at different frequencies, but also this extra disability, which is much more serious than a straightforward conductive hearing loss.

**Speech Comprehension**

The area most affected by noise-induced hearing loss is that of speech comprehension. Tests for speech intelligibility generally entail the use of

Phonetically Balanced (PB) words, spoken words, and "cold running speech" (Newby, 1958), but test only what the person *cannot* hear—by measuring the fraction of the words missed. A second shortcoming of this type of test is its failure to measure the subject's ability to comprehend information content: "the cat is on the floor" becomes "the cat is at the door," thus making it difficult to judge how much the previous context has helped him. Miller and Nicely (1955) discuss this problem further.

Speech comprehension, as defined by the AAOO 15 dB criterion, involves about 90 percent comprehension of spoken speech in quiet surroundings. However, most speech is spoken in surroundings that are not quiet: there is almost always background noise, and some people have significant difficulty with comprehension even before the hearing loss has reached a compensable level. In this sense, the question of what hearing loss corresponds to what level of comprehension of speech spoken under realistic conditions is as yet unsolved.

It has been stated that there is no satisfactory way of estimating speech comprehension from the audiogram (Sataloff, 1966). However, it is possible to determine how much speech a person understands by the more time-consuming technique of speech audiometry (Newby, 1958).

Atherley and Noble (1970) have confirmed Sataloff's findings by using assessment schemes like the AAOO one, based on taking the average loss at four, five or even six frequencies. The assessment of the damage based on such schemes was correlated with the assessment based on psychological interviews evaluating people's perceptions of their handicaps. These were classified in terms of speech hearing, non-speech hearing, localization, acuity for non-speech sound, emotional response to hearing loss, speech hearing distortion, tinnitus, and personal opinion of hearing. It was found that the assessment based only on pure-tone audiometry did not correlate with any of the categories, no matter how many frequencies were used in the averaging. The conclusion was reached that an adequate clinical picture cannot be obtained from pure-tone thresholds alone. The use of speech audiometry with background noise appears thus more desirable, for the way speech sounds are presented is important and free-field presentation (where the sound does not come from one source) is preferable to earphones.

Because comprehension of speech is crucial to functioning in society, a method has been worked out to describe how much a person's ability to function in society is impaired by his hearing loss. This is the Social Adequacy Index (SAI), of Davis (1948). A table for determining SAI is given in Fig. 3.6, which shows that the index is a function of the minimum

Table for finding the Social Adequacy Index.

DISCRIMINATION LOSS (% PB WORDS MISSED AT HIGH INTENSITY) vs. HEARING LOSS FOR SPEECH IN DECIBELS

| Disc. Loss \ Hearing Loss (dB) | 0 | 2 | 4 | 6 | 8 | 10 | 12 | 14 | 16 | 18 | 20 | 22 | 24 | 26 | 28 | 30 | 32 | 34 | 36 | 38 | 40 | 42 | 44 | 46 | 48 | 50 | 52 | 54 | 56 | 58 | 60 | 62 | 64 | 66 | 68 | 70 | 72 | 74 |
|---|---|---|---|---|---|---|---|---|---|---|---|---|---|---|---|---|---|---|---|---|---|---|---|---|---|---|---|---|---|---|---|---|---|---|---|---|---|---|
| 0 | 99 | 98 | 97 | 96 | 94 | 93 | 92 | 90 | 88 | 85 | 82 | 79 | 75 | 69 | 64 | 61 | 57 | 52 | 48 | 44 | 41 | 37 | 33 | 28 | 24 | 20 | 17 | 15 | 12 | 10 | 7 | 4 | 2 | 1 | 0 | 0 | 0 | 0 |
| 5 | 94 | 93 | 92 | 91 | 90 | 89 | 88 | 87 | 85 | 82 | 79 | 76 | 72 | 67 | 63 | 59 | 55 | 51 | 47 | 43 | 40 | 37 | 32 | 28 | 24 | 20 | 17 | 15 | 12 | 9 | 7 | 4 | 2 | 1 | 0 | 0 | 0 | 0 |
| 10 | 89 | 89 | 88 | 87 | 86 | 85 | 84 | 83 | 81 | 78 | 76 | 73 | 70 | 65 | 61 | 57 | 53 | 49 | 46 | 42 | 40 | 37 | 31 | 27 | 23 | 19 | 16 | 14 | 11 | 9 | 7 | 4 | 2 | 1 | 0 | 0 | 0 | 0 |
| 15 | 84 | 84 | 83 | 83 | 82 | 81 | 80 | 79 | 77 | 75 | 72 | 70 | 67 | 63 | 59 | 55 | 51 | 47 | 44 | 41 | 39 | 36 | 30 | 27 | 23 | 19 | 16 | 14 | 11 | 9 | 7 | 4 | 2 | 1 | 0 | 0 | 0 | 0 |
| 20 | 79 | 79 | 78 | 78 | 78 | 77 | 76 | 75 | 73 | 71 | 69 | 67 | 64 | 61 | 57 | 53 | 50 | 46 | 43 | 40 | 37 | 34 | 29 | 26 | 22 | 19 | 16 | 13 | 11 | 9 | 7 | 4 | 2 | 1 | 0 | 0 | 0 | 0 |
| 25 | 75 | 75 | 74 | 74 | 74 | 73 | 72 | 71 | 69 | 67 | 65 | 63 | 61 | 58 | 55 | 51 | 47 | 44 | 41 | 38 | 36 | 33 | 28 | 25 | 21 | 18 | 15 | 13 | 10 | 8 | 6 | 4 | 2 | 1 | 0 | 0 | 0 | 0 |
| 30 | 70 | 70 | 69 | 69 | 69 | 68 | 67 | 65 | 65 | 63 | 62 | 60 | 58 | 55 | 52 | 48 | 44 | 41 | 38 | 36 | 34 | 31 | 27 | 24 | 20 | 17 | 15 | 12 | 10 | 8 | 6 | 4 | 2 | 1 | 0 | 0 | 0 | 0 |
| 35 | 65 | 65 | 64 | 64 | 65 | 63 | 62 | 61 | 60 | 59 | 58 | 56 | 54 | 52 | 49 | 45 | 42 | 39 | 36 | 34 | 32 | 29 | 26 | 23 | 19 | 16 | 14 | 12 | 10 | 8 | 6 | 4 | 2 | 1 | 0 | 0 | 0 | 0 |
| 40 | 60 | 60 | 59 | 59 | 60 | 58 | 57 | 57 | 56 | 55 | 54 | 53 | 51 | 48 | 46 | 43 | 40 | 37 | 34 | 32 | 30 | 28 | 25 | 22 | 18 | 16 | 12 | 10 | 10 | 8 | 6 | 4 | 2 | 1 | 0 | 0 | 0 | 0 |
| 45 | 55 | 55 | 54 | 54 | 55 | 53 | 52 | 52 | 51 | 50 | 50 | 49 | 47 | 45 | 43 | 40 | 37 | 34 | 31 | 30 | 28 | 26 | 24 | 21 | 17 | 14 | 11 | 9 | 9 | 7 | 6 | 4 | 2 | 1 | 0 | 0 | 0 | 0 |
| 50 | 50 | 50 | 50 | 49 | 50 | 48 | 47 | 46 | 45 | 45 | 44 | 43 | 41 | 40 | 37 | 34 | 32 | 29 | 26 | 25 | 24 | 22 | 20 | 18 | 15 | 13 | 11 | 8 | 8 | 6 | 5 | 4 | 2 | 1 | 0 | 0 | 0 | 0 |
| 55 | 45 | 45 | 45 | 44 | 44 | 43 | 42 | 41 | 40 | 39 | 39 | 38 | 37 | 34 | 31 | 28 | 26 | 24 | 23 | 22 | 21 | 19 | 16 | 14 | 12 | 11 | 9 | 8 | 7 | 5 | 4 | 2 | 2 | 1 | 0 | 0 | 0 | 0 |
| 60 | 40 | 40 | 40 | 39 | 39 | 39 | 39 | 36 | 34 | 34 | 34 | 33 | 32 | 30 | 28 | 26 | 25 | 23 | 20 | 20 | 19 | 17 | 14 | 13 | 11 | 10 | 8 | 7 | 6 | 5 | 4 | 2 | 2 | 1 | 0 | 0 | 0 | 0 |
| 65 | 35 | 35 | 35 | 35 | 34 | 34 | 35 | 34 | 33 | 33 | 33 | 32 | 31 | 30 | 26 | 22 | 22 | 19 | 18 | 17 | 15 | 14 | 12 | 11 | 10 | 9 | 8 | 6 | 5 | 4 | 4 | 2 | 2 | 1 | 0 | 0 | 0 | 0 |
| 70 | 30 | 30 | 30 | 30 | 30 | 30 | 30 | 30 | 29 | 29 | 29 | 28 | 28 | 26 | 22 | 18 | 18 | 17 | 15 | 13 | 13 | 12 | 11 | 10 | 9 | 8 | 6 | 6 | 5 | 4 | 3 | 2 | 2 | 1 | 0 | 0 | 0 | 0 |
| 75 | 25 | 25 | 25 | 25 | 25 | 25 | 25 | 25 | 24 | 24 | 24 | 24 | 23 | 20 | 17 | 14 | 14 | 13 | 12 | 10 | 11 | 10 | 9 | 8 | 7 | 6 | 6 | 5 | 4 | 3 | 3 | 2 | 2 | 1 | 0 | 0 | 0 | 0 |
| 80 | 20 | 20 | 20 | 20 | 20 | 20 | 20 | 20 | 20 | 19 | 19 | 19 | 19 | 18 | 15 | 12 | 11 | 11 | 10 | 9 | 10 | 9 | 8 | 7 | 6 | 5 | 5 | 4 | 4 | 3 | 3 | 2 | 2 | 1 | 0 | 0 | 0 | 0 |
| 85 | 15 | 15 | 15 | 15 | 15 | 15 | 15 | 15 | 15 | 15 | 15 | 15 | 14 | 14 | 14 | 14 | 15 | 14 | 13 | 12 | 9 | 9 | 8 | 7 | 6 | 5 | 4 | 4 | 3 | 3 | 3 | 2 | 2 | 1 | 0 | 0 | 0 | 0 |
| 90 | 10 | 10 | 10 | 10 | 10 | 10 | 10 | 10 | 10 | 10 | 10 | 10 | 10 | 10 | 10 | 10 | 10 | 10 | 9 | 8 | 9 | 8 | 7 | 6 | 5 | 4 | 4 | 3 | 3 | 2 | 2 | 2 | 1 | 1 | 0 | 0 | 0 | 0 |
| 95 | 0 | 0 | 0 | 0 | 0 | 0 | 0 | 0 | 0 | 0 | 0 | 0 | 0 | 0 | 0 | 0 | 0 | 0 | 0 | 0 | 0 | 0 | 0 | 0 | 0 | 0 | 0 | 0 | 0 | 0 | 0 | 0 | 0 | 0 | 0 | 0 | 0 | 0 |
| 100 | 0 | 0 | 0 | 0 | 0 | 0 | 0 | 0 | 0 | 0 | 0 | 0 | 0 | 0 | 0 | 0 | 0 | 0 | 0 | 0 | 0 | 0 | 0 | 0 | 0 | 0 | 0 | 0 | 0 | 0 | 0 | 0 | 0 | 0 | 0 | 0 | 0 | 0 |

When the discrimination loss is greater than about 90% ordinary speech is not understood at any intensity, and it becomes difficult or impossible to measure the hearing loss for speech.

HEARING LOSS FOR SPEECH IN DECIBELS

**Fig. 3.6** Table for finding the Social Adequacy Index. (Adapted from Davis, 1948. Used by permission of the author and *The Laryngoscope*.

sound-pressure level at which speech can be understood, and of the ability to discriminate between like sounding words (discrimination loss). The discrimination loss is obviously related to the flatness of the audiogram in the speech frequencies; a steeply sloping audiogram, such as that produced by noise exposure, implies a high discrimination loss and accordingly a low SAI.

A SAI of 67 corresponds to the first noticeable difficulty. An index of 33 is the threshold of social adequacy; a person can "get by" in business and social situations only with great difficulty. It is clear from the typical contours shown in Fig. 3.5 that, so long as discrimination is not lost, there can be a large hearing loss for speech without a large loss of social adequacy.

What background noise level is most suitable for the hearing loss tests is an unanswered question. It requires knowledge of the distribution of background noise levels to which a specific person, say a housewife or factory worker, is exposed while conversation is taking place (exemplified in Fig. 3.7), and it requires knowledge of the distribution for a sample

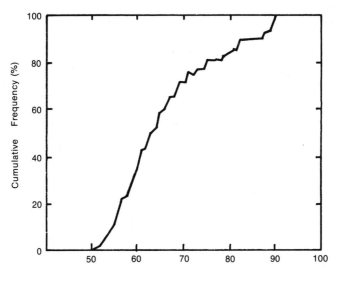

Total Sound Pressure Level (dB)

**Fig. 3.7**  Cumulative daily noise distribution for a student—housewife (Source: Cox, 1967).

population. In the absence of such information, a value-judgment will implicitly be made in the choice of any level.*

### Temporary Threshold Shift

Some susceptible people can suffer larger hearing losses than average when exposed to a particular noise. It would be extremely desirable to be able to identify such people in advance. One approach is to expose them to the noise level in which they are going to work, for long enough to produce a temporary threshold shift. It is hoped that the amount of temporary threshold shift will then be related to the amount of permanent threshold shift, or hearing loss, that would be produced after long exposure to the same noise. Unfortunately, there does not seem to be general agreement about whether this approach is promising (e.g., Nixon et. al., 1965; Sataloff et al., 1965). In any case, it seems clear that the predictive techniques are applicable only in the mean and do not yield a test of individual susceptibility.

How temporary threshold shift is transformed into permanent threshold shift is not properly understood, but the work with soldiers by Kryter and Garinther (1965) suggests that at least for impulsive noise there is a particular Sound Pressure Level (SPL), above which the ear seems to be very severely affected. Above this level, the rate of increase of hearing loss with SPL changes and becomes much larger. This phenomenon has apparently been found in animals as well. It seems that hunters should either wear earmuffs or buy guns that produce lower peak pressures.

## PREVENTION OF NOISE-INDUCED HEARING LOSS

What can be done to prevent noise-induced hearing loss? Clearly the following will help:

- quieting the environment;

---

*In general, a very low background noise level should not be used to determine how well a person can understand speech, because then it would appear that he has a certain amount of difficulty, however great or small, while in fact he would be having more difficulty almost all the time. If a level that is exceeded only, say, 10 percent of the time is chosen, it might be said that his handicap is being exaggerated. Conversely, if a background noise level is chosen that is not exceeded 50 percent of the time, the person will in fact have more difficulty 50 percent of the time. It would be desirable to develop some rational way of deciding on the percentage, whether it be 50, 80, 90, or 95 percent.

- wearing earmuffs and earplugs;
- instituting regular audiometric examinations to confirm whether the protective measures are effective.

These three aspects are part of most hearing conservation programs.

Earmuffs can give as much as 40 dB reduction (Bell, 1966), but it is difficult to insure that they are worn properly all the time. They are moderately uncomfortable and may not fit perfectly for some people; in some cases the frames may be bent so that the earmuffs do not fit tightly—or the earmuffs may be removed. For these reasons, earmuffs or earplugs ought not to be accepted as an adequate protective measure by themselves.

At what noise level should the use of earmuffs be recommended or required? Because hearing loss is statistically distributed, we also need to decide what fraction of the people are to be affected by the noise, and how much they are affected. To answer this question, we must know how much damage a noise or assortment of noises will produce. Until recently, it was thought that a simple answer was not possible. For instance Bell (1966) pointed out that a single decibel figure is an insufficient guide; the spectrum is important, and so are aspects like the length of exposure each day, and the on and off times for interrupted noise. When these are taken into account, and the fraction of the exposed population is decided on for which a certain hearing loss will be tolerated (a loss which, it should be recalled, is a function of frequency), then a Damage Risk Criterion (DRC) can be set up. A typical DRC for one exposure a day is shown in Fig. 3.8.

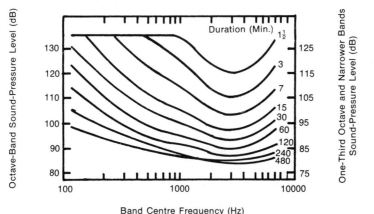

**Fig. 3.8**    Hearing conservation criteria for broad-band noise (Source: Kryter *et al.*, 1962).

Noise having the spectra shown in the figure will produce in the average exposed person a temporary threshold shift measured 2 minutes after exposure of not more than 10 dB at frequencies of 1000 Hz and below, 15 dB at 2000 Hz, and 20 dB at 3000 Hz and above. However, there is no specification of what percentage will suffer what permanent threshold shift when exposed to these noises.

It was thought that it would be simpler and therefore more desirable, especially in industrial situations, to make spectral measurements at only a few frequencies and to derive from these a noise rating. This is the purpose of the ISO-DRC (ISO, 1967). The ISO criterion aims at producing a permanent threshold shift in less than 10 percent of the exposed people of 25 dB or more average at 500, 1000, and 2000 Hz when the noise is on for more that 5 hours a day. In the ISO-DRC, the recommended $A$-scale sound-pressure levels for an 8-hour day are: imperative maximum 90 dBA and recommended maximum 85 dBA. It is interesting to note that the sound-pressure level produced by a chain saw is about 120 dBA at the operator's ear. Certainly the same operators work their saws more than 5 minutes a day. This suggests first that the operators are unaware of the possibility of hearing damage, and, perhaps more important, that damage risk criteria for summer jobs and seasonal work, and for weekend exposure, are needed. If the sound pressures are even higher, of the order of 130 dB, no one ought to be exposed, no matter how short the time or how good the ear protection.

## THE BURNS AND ROBINSON STUDY AND THE 1974 EPA REPORT

All the preceding questions are answered by two recent studies which are a landmark in our ability to assess risk of hearing damage. The first is a study by Burns and Robinson, (1970). The details of the study are perhaps less important than the two major conclusions:

• It is no longer necessary to have detailed information about the spectrum of the noise to which people are exposed. Most fortunately it turns out that for a wide range of industrial spectra the simple $A$-scale weighting is sufficient.

• Integrating the $A$-scale sound-pressure level over the time of exposure (even for exposure levels varying during the day and for impulsive noises) results in a quantity, the immission, that correlates extremely well with the hearing damage observed in a large number of workers. Of course, the damage cannot be uniquely predicted, it is only known statistically; thus, an immission of 121 will produce at 4000 Hz a loss of at least 40 dB in 50 percent of the people exposed. Such a loss would, for example, be found in a lumberjack working for 5 years without ear protection and exposed to 120 dBA from chain saws for 2 hours a day. Further, the odds of loss at 4000 Hz are as follows:

1 in 4 at least 48 dB
1 in 10 at least 57 dB
1 in 50 at least 67 dB

The fact that such tables can now be constructed makes it possible in principle for the first time to suggest to someone contemplating work in a noisy job: "If you take this job, after $x$ years the odds are such and such that *things will sound like this to you.*" Thus he can make a nearly fully informed decision instead of having to rely blindly on experts. The only difficulty is that we are not yet in the position of being able to fill in the italicized part of the previous quote; the relevant research has not been done.

A further important outcome of the Burns and Robinson study is that it makes labeling of noise-producing devices possible in such terms as "This device produces a sound-pressure level of $x$ dBA at the user's ear. This will cause hearing damage of (such and such a severity) in $y$ percent of users, after $z$ years' use. Wear ear protection."

In 1974 a second important study by the EPA (1974) suggests that an equivalent noise level $L_{EQ}$ (see Appendix 1) of no more than 70 dB over a 24 hour day will protect virtually the entire population. The figure is an average daily *energy* (not arithmetic!) level. Thus, the energy contained in an 8 hour (a typical work shift) exposure to 75 dB is equivalent to that contained in a 24 hour exposure to 70 dB. This assumes that the average level in the rest of the day contributes a negligible amount of energy (it should be less than approximately 60 dB).

Hence, the amount of sound energy to which the worker is exposed in the community—in traffic, at home and at play—must be considered in establishing the permissible sound level at work. Conversely, the latter must be taken into account in designing environmental noise guidelines for the community.

## THE EFFECT OF AGING AND PATHOLOGY

It is important to keep in mind that the hearing damage predicted by the Burns and Robinson formulae and nomograms makes no allowance for presbycusis and that this must be added. Moreover, it makes no allowance for the fact that people may contract illnesses that can result in additional hearing damage. The effects of combined noise exposure and pathology have been treated by Baughn (1966); thus corrections for aging and pathology can be added, and should be taken into account when setting acceptable levels of industrial use. At this moment they are not. In the light of this, for instance, the 90 dBA level proposed by the U.K. Department of Employment does not appear to be a safe enough choice. (DE 1971).

## REFERENCES

AAOO (American Academy of Ophthalmology and Otolaryngology). Guide for conservation of hearing in noise. A supplement to the transactions. Revised 1964.

ASA Standard Z24.5. American standard specifications for audiometers for general diagnostic purposes, 1951.

ASA Standard Z24-X-2. The relations of hearing loss to noise exposure, 1954.

Atherley, G. R. C. and Noble, W. G. Clinical picture of Occupational hearing loss obtained with the hearing measurement scale. Occupational Hearing Loss Conference, National Physics Laboratory, Teddington, England, March 1970.

Baughn, W. L. *International Audiology*, 1966, Vol. 5.

Bell, A. Noise: An occupational hazard and a public nuisance. Public Health Paper No. 30. Geneva: World Health Organization, 1966.

Bilger, R. C., Department of Audiology, Eye and Ear Hospital, Pittsburgh, Pa. Personal communication, 1967.

Bugliarello, G. and Wakstein, C. Noise pollution—a review of its techno-sociological and health aspects. Biotechnology Program, Carnegie-Mellon University, Pittsburgh, 1968.

Bunch, C. C. Age variations in auditory activity. *Archives of Otolaryngology*, Chicago, 1929, **9**.

Burns, W. and Robinson, D. W. *Hearing and noise in industry*. London: HMSO, 1970.

Cox, G. V. Unpublished work. Graduate Course in Research Methods, Drexel Institute of Technology, 1967.

Dadson, R. S. and King, J. H. *Journal of Laryngology*, 1952, **64**.

Davis, H. The articulation area and the social adequacy index for hearing. *Laryngoscope*, 1948, **58**.

D.E. 1971 U.K. Department of Employment. *Noise and the Worker*. London HMSO 1971.

EPA (U.S. Environmental Protection Agency). Information on levels of environmental noise requisite to protect public health and welfare with an adequate margin of safety. Washington, March 1974.

Gallo, R. and Glorig, A. Permanent threshold shift changes produced by noise exposure and aging. *American Industrial Hygiene Journal*, May–June 1964, **25**.

Glorig, A. The problem of noise in industry. *American Journal of Public Health*, 1961, **51**.

Glorig, A. *et al*. 1954 Wisconsin State Fair hearing survey, statistical treatment of clinical audiometric data. *American Academy of Ophthalmology and Otolaryngology*, 1957.

Harris, J. D. *et al*. The importance of hearing at 3 kc for understanding speeded speech. *Laryngoscope*, 1960, **70**.

Hickish, D. E. Contribution to the discussion of paper by A. Glorig *et al.*, at NPL Symposium on the Control of Noise, 1961.

Hinchcliffe, R. *Acta Otolaryngolica*, 1959, **50**. (a)

Hinchcliffe, R. The threshold of hearing as a function of age. *Acustica*, 1959, **9**. (b)

Hinchcliffe, R. and Littler, T. S. *Annals of Occupational Hygiene*, 1958, **1**.

ISO. Permissible (low risk) noise exposures for hearing conservation. ISO/TC 43 (Secretariat-275) 405, Draft Proposal, February 1967.

Kell, R. L., Pearson, J. C. G., Acton, W. I. and Taylor W. in D. W. Robinson (editor) *Occupational hearing loss*, Academic, London, 1971.

Kryter, K. D. and Garinther, G. R. Auditory effects from acoustic impulses from firearms. *Acta Otolaryngologica*, 1965, Supplement 211.

Kryter, K. D. *et al*. Auditory activity and the perception of speech. *Journal of the Acoustical Society of America*, 1962, **34**.

Kryter, K. D. Impairment to hearing from exposure to noise. *Journal of the Acoustical Society of America*, 1973, **53**.

Miller, G. A. and Nicely, P. E. An analysis of perceptual confusions among some English consonants. *Journal of the Acoustical Society of America*, 1955, **27**.

Murray, N. E. Hearing impairment and compensation. *Journal of the Otolaryngology Society of Australia*, 1962, **1**.

Newby, H. A. *Audiology*. New York: Appleton-Century-Crofts, 1958.

Nixon, J. C. *et al*. Predicting hearing loss from noise-induced TTS. *Archives of Otolaryngology*, 1965, **81**.

Reid, G. Permanent deafness due to gunfire. *Journal of Laryngology and Otolaryngology*, 1948, **62**.

Sataloff, J. *Hearing loss*. Philadelphia: Lippincott, 1966.

Sataloff, J. *et al*. Temporary and permanent hearing loss. *Archives of Environmental Health*. 1965, **10**.

Steinberg, J. C. *et al*. Results of the World's Fair hearing tests. *Journal of the Acoustical Society of America*, 1940, **12**.

Taylor, W. *et al*. Study of noise and hearing on jute weaving. *Journal of the Acoustical Society of America*, 1964.

Verbruggen, J. Contribution to the discussion of paper by A. Glorig *et al.*, at NPL Symposium on the Control of Noise, 1961.

Webster, J. C. *et al*. San Diego County Fair Hearing Survey. *Journal of the Acoustical Society of America*, 1950, **22**.

# CHAPTER 4

# The Effects of Noise on Sleep

During sleep, the soul drifts away from the sleeper in order to wander. One must never awaken a sleeper suddenly for his soul might not have the time to re-enter the body, and the sleeper would soon die.—MASAI BELIEF

Sleep that knits up the ravell'd sleave of care. . .—SHAKESPEARE

It's only at the price of money that one can sleep in this city.—BOILEAU

## INTRODUCTION

Noise can both awaken people and keep them from going to sleep. For instance, a large jet airplane used for refueling other airplanes in flight, passes over a residential area near a military airbase at 11:45 p.m. during takeoff every three or four nights, but on an irregular schedule. Parents in one family report that their children are awakened every time without exception. These parents decide that it is useless to try to go to sleep before 11:45 any night because the tanker *may* come over that night. They also report that when they first moved there, their children ran into the house crying in fright. At one commercial airport where jet-engine run-ups were carried out between midnight and 6:00 a.m., there was a steady stream of 30 complaints a month, presumably about disturbed sleep (Holland–Wegman, 1967).

Airplane noise can be a much greater disturbance to sleep than other noises. The data shown in Table 4.1 indicate that near a major airport— London (Heathrow) Airport—the number of people awakened by airplanes is about 50 percent greater than the number awakened by other noises (but the number kept from going to sleep is essentially the same).* If we

---

*Unfortunately, these data, which were gathered in annoyance studies, do not show how many people were awakened how many times a night, or how many nights in a specified period of time, or when during the night.

**Table 4.1**   Percentage of People Disturbed by Aircraft Noise and by Other Sources of Noise around London Heathrow Airport. (Adapted from McKennell, 1963. Used by permission. Copyright © Controller of Her Majesty's Stationery Office.)

|  | By Aircraft Noise | By Other Noise |
|---|---|---|
| Kept from going to sleep: | | |
| Very often | 5% | 6% |
| Fairly often | 5 | 5 |
| Occasionally | 11 | 9 |
| Total | 22% | 20% |
| Awakened: | | |
| Very often | 5% | 5% |
| Fairly often | 8 | 5 |
| Occasionally | 27 | 16 |
| Total | 40% | 27% |
| Rest or relaxation disturbed: | | |
| Very often | 5% | 5% |
| Fairly often | 7 | 6 |
| Occasionally | 11 | 12 |
| Total | 27% | 22% |

take the London airport as representative, as many as 40 percent of the people living near major airports may be awakened by noise.

For areas much nearer the airport, where the noise level is above 103 PNdB, the total percentages are approximately twice as large as for other noises. Three percent of the people in a 20-mile diameter around London (Heathrow) Airport live within this band of noise, and are often kept from going to sleep by airplanes. This is likely to be an important factor in their lives. By the definition of the World Health Organization, health is a state of complete physical, mental and social well-being, not merely an absence of disease and infirmity, and loss of sleep is clearly a cause of damage to health. In fact, in the London (Heathrow) Airport Study, about one-fourth of the people kept from going to sleep thought their health was being affected (McKennell, 1963).

Airport and airplane noise is not the only or even the most important source of disturbance to sleep. Automobile traffic noise is particularly significant because of its ubiquitousness. A study by Thiessen and Olson (1968) investigating the effect of truck noise shows that sleeping subjects exposed to a 6-hour tape of a passing truck, with noise in the 40–70 dB range—a comparatively modest intensity—were usually awakened by a 70 dB noise. A 50 dB noise altered the level of sleep, as recorded on an electroencephalogram, in about half of the subjects, whereas between 40 to 50 dB, the chance of awakening the subjects or altering their sleep pattern was between 10 percent and 20 percent. These levels of noise at which sleep is affected are considerably lower than previously suspected.

In brief, it is clear that noise can waken a large number of people, keep them from going to sleep, or disturb their sleep. The question to which we are addressing ourselves in this chapter is: can this be harmful?

## SLEEP—WHAT FOR?

Man, like many plants and animals, follows a daily rhythm of sleeping states (waking and sleeping). "The problem of the alternation of the phases of waking and sleeping, of activity and rest, seems to be a key question in the biology of man and superior animals: it suffices to remember that one survives for a shorter period with lack of sleep than in the privation of food" (Reinberg and Ghata, 1964).

Sleep appears all the more necessary when the individual is young, and thus seems to play a fundamental role in growth, as a Spanish proverb states: "A young person while sleeping becomes cured." Furthermore, the alternation waking–sleeping becomes dependent upon a night–day rhythm only at the end of several years, as shown by Fig. 4.1.

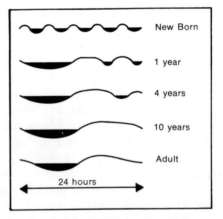

**Fig. 4.1**  Alternation of waking and sleep (dark areas) according to age. (Source: Kleitman, 1963. Used by permission of The University of Chicago Press.)

Therefore, if we wish to assure the well-being of the totality of the population—and not only of adults—protection of sleep ought to be preserved during the day as well as during the night. This is all the more so because a not negligible portion of adults themselves, for instance those on night-work shifts, are obliged to sleep during the day.

But to what necessity does our need for sleep correspond? A functional response would be: we sleep to repair the wearing out of the tissues and to restore their performance. A deterministic reply makes us keep in mind a whole series of chain reactions concerning the influence of darkness on our nervous system, which in its turn exerts various physical and chemical actions favoring sleep. When one considers biological rhythms, the two replies complement each other and cannot be disassociated.

The rhythmic character of sleep depends on cosmic rhythms of all that surrounds us: it thus aids, in a quasi-automatic fashion, to impose upon us the rest without which we could not live.

On this foundation of cosmic rhythm and biological necessity are grafted psychological, sociological, and cultural elements which result in the fact that we do not all sleep in the same manner. The places where one sleeps and the positions one takes in sleep differ according to the country and continent, and durations of sleep vary according to age, habit and daily activity, and according to one's physical and mental health. The physiological rhythm of waking–sleeping is partially taken over by the cultural system which makes it "relative" in terms of existing values and concepts (values accorded to work and to rest, the greater or lesser conjunction of human activities with the seasons, etc.). If it is true that man *is* a body and that the demands of this body are literally imposed upon him, on the other hand, one can say equally that man *has* a body and that he may, to a certain extent, impose upon it the laws of his mind and adapt the behavior of the body to his conscious and unconscious thoughts.

For this reason techniques of rest are not "natural," but "learned" from an early age (Bastide, 1966). According to the characteristics of a society, different exterior stimuli do not assume the same value. Thus, the slight cry of an animal or a cracking of branches will perhaps not awaken a European or an American, but will certainly awaken a primitive for whom these noises could be the sign of danger. As Bastide emphasizes, "There exist differential thresholds of awakening according to cultures." Biologists have neglected until now trans-cultural studies of sleep, which alone would permit us to separate the purely physiological from the cultural. There is a need for a broadened understanding of the unity or of the diversity of the rhythms of sleep according to ethnic groups, according to country and even to regions—urban or rural for example.

Similarly, the relation between sleep and "territory" has never been studied. Everyone knows that when we change beds (while on vacation, staying in a hotel, etc.) we have more difficulty falling asleep because the interruption of habits causes a certain anxiety. There exists then not only a bodily morphology, but equally a social morphology of sleep (places reserved for adults and to children, sleeping alone or with someone, etc.).

In short, sleep depends not only on purely physiological elements, but equally on the spatial and temporal environment, which has a considerable impact on the diversity of individual reactions to noise.

## THE PROGRESS OF A NIGHT OF SLEEP

One generally distinguishes five stages of sleep.* The progress of sleep unfolds approximately through five stages in the following manner:

*Stage I.* In the first part of this stage (stage IA), one is at first sleepy, but awake. The electroencephalogram (EEG) passes from rapid and irregular waves to a regular rhythm of 9–12 Hz—called alpha rhythm. Subsequently, the alpha rhythm diminishes in amplitude by stages.

In stage IB, one floats between a state of being awake and sleep. The alpha rhythm disappears, to be replaced by a low-voltage rhythm, rapid and irregular.

*Stage II.* Rapid wave thrusts of greater amplitude appear—the spindles of sleep. Intermingled with these spindles, waves of peak amplitude and low frequency (1.5–3 Hz) appear (delta waves).

*Stages III and IV.* In these two stages, often called "delta sleep," "slow sleep," or "deep sleep," the spindles disappear and the delta waves become increasingly regular, with a greater amplitude and lower frequency (0.6–1 Hz).

*Stage V.* The fifth stage—"REM" (Rapid Eye Movements) stage or paradoxical sleep—is characterized by rapid waves of weak amplitude (as in stage I) and by numerous eye movements. It is in the course of this REM stage that the majority of dreams take place; the periods of dream activity are repeated four or five times a night.

---

*Given the extreme diversity in the definitions of stages of sleep, we have adopted here a most simple and recent definition as it appears in Morgan (1970), and in EPA (1971a).

The totality of the five stages lasts about 90–120 minutes. A typical night consists of sequences of these stages.

In fact, sleep does not always obey such strict laws, and certain irregularities appear in the succession of the stages of sleep. According to Kryter (1970), each person has a "model" of sleep which is personal for him and which varies, furthermore, from one night to another.

In general, however, one spends the greatest part of sleep in stages II and V (about 20 percent in the latter). After the first 2 hours of sleep, one spends less and less time in stage IV (Fig. 4.2). In the newly born child paradoxical sleep (REM—stage V) constitutes about 50 percent of sleep, and it is only around 18–24 months that the rate of paradoxical sleep becomes identical to that of an adult (Jouvet, 1966). It must be noted that paradoxical sleep exists in all mammals; dream activity constitutes a third functional state of the nervous system, differing from waking and from sleep. Concerning the other stages of sleep, Williams *et al.* (1964) estimates that one spends 2 percent of the time in stage I, 50 percent in stage II, 5 percent in stage III, 15 percent in stage IV, and 8 percent awake.

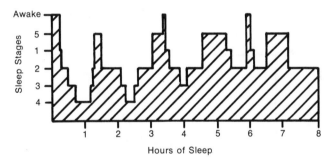

**Fig. 4.2.**  Night sleep of a young adult (alternation of the stages of sleep). (Source: Kales, 1969. Used by permission of Lippincott.)

## THE DISTURBANCE TO SLEEP

### The Intensity of the Stimulus

The disturbance to sleep by noise depends on the stimulus (type of noise, intensity, duration, repetition, etc.), on the stage of sleep at which the disturbance occurs, on the environment, as well as on individual variables, such as age or state of health, etc.

The principal question concerning the stimulus is: what is the intensity of noise that awakens an average individual? There is no precise answer, because of the many factors that we have just outlined. From all the experiments conducted until now, it appears that a sound level oscillating between 35 and 90 dBA is necessary to provoke the awakening of a sleeper! Thiessen and Olson (1968), for example, have noticed that certain subjects are awakened by a noise of a truck at 40 dBA, whereas others are not awakened by a noise of 75 dBA (although changes in the stage of sleep, or modifications of the EEG may be observed). But beyond 40 dBA there are 10 chances out of 100 that sleep will be disturbed (see Fig. 4.3). Rechtschaffen *et al.* (1966), place the threshold of average awakening at 40 dBA for "light sleepers" and at 60 dBA for "heavy sleepers." Steinicke (1957) noticed that if 10–20 percent of the subjects are awakened by a noise of 35 phons, there are still subjects who remain asleep when the noise reaches 70 phons (Fig. 4.4).

These considerable variations make it impossible to define criteria for nightly annoyance that would be applicable in a uniform manner to all noises and to all circumstances. The acceptable nocturnal levels which have been proposed until now depend on pure conjecture, if not upon the simple confusion between acceptable sound levels and existing sound levels.

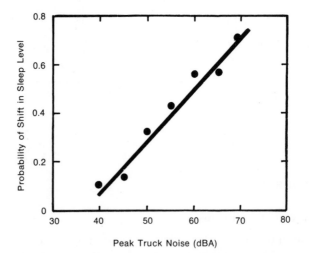

**Fig. 4.3**   Changes in stages of sleep in relation to noise intensity at the time of the passing of a truck (Canada). (Source: Thiessen and Olson, 1968. Reprinted with permission from *Sound and Vibration* magazine.)

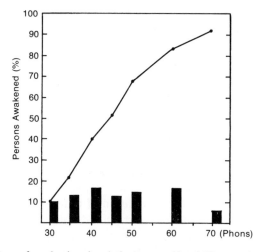

**Fig. 4.4**  Percentage of awakenings in relation to sound level (Germany) (Source: Steinicke, 1957). Bars give percentage incrementally awakened by a given sound level, and curve gives total percentage awakened by sound above a given level.

Each type of noise produces, it seems, a different threshold of awakening, all other things being equal. (We will see in the following section that this threshold of awakening varies, furthermore, in relation to the stage of sleep.) That means that it is not only the intensity of noises which impinges upon the progress of sleep, but also the type of acoustic surroundings (near an airport, near a heavy-traffic street, in a noisy apartment building, near a factory, under the path of a supersonic airplane, etc.). The calculations become still more complicated if, in the course of the same night, one is subjected to different types of noise, a phenomenon which often occurs in reality, but which has been studied very little in the laboratory.

According to present information, it appears that a sound level inside the house, lower than 60 dBA for airplane noise and lower than 40 dBA for road traffic noise, does not disturb the sleep of the majority of the population. These are very approximate figures, in particular for airplane noise, where one must consider the number of flyovers and their distribution in the course of the night. For sonic booms and very brief noises it is still more difficult to fix a limit of acceptability, particularly since certain studies have shown that the disturbance to sleep is often independent of the intensity of impulsive noises, differences of 20 dBA between two stimuli not having produced a significant difference in reaction (Berry and Thiessen, 1970; Lukas and Kryter, 1969).

In any case, it appears that impulsive noises awaken less than traffic noises, for example. On the other hand, the changes in the stage of sleep (lessening the depth of sleep) are as frequent for impulsive noises as for noises of longer duration, such as those due to passing trucks. Furthermore, it appears that if one becomes used to repeated impulsive noises occurring very frequently (say every 10 seconds), this habit diminishes as soon as the interval between noises exceeds 30 seconds. For irregular impulsive noises and infrequent noises, such as sonic booms, it is then scarcely probable that habituation should be produced (Firth, 1971).

In addition to the type of noise and its intensity, the chronology of noise in the course of the night, the alternation of different intensities, and the relation between foreground and background noises play also a considerable role. This has been clearly proven by the experiments of Schieber (1968) on noises of automobile traffic and airplane noises. Reduced automobile traffic was found to disturb sleep more than intense traffic with equivalent foreground and background noise. This leads to conclude that habit to noise is perhaps easier to achieve when noises are regular and frequent than when they are rare and irregular.

Both in the case of automobile noise and airplane noise, sleep was found to be significantly disturbed when the difference between peak value and median level of noise attained 15 dBA.*

These results should be extrapolated only with the greatest caution to other situations, because they were formulated in relation to a determined median sound level, and were based only on observations on young subjects, and also because the maximum difference considered acceptable—15 dBA—between foreground and median noises (or background noise as the case may be) does not take into consideration the various stages of sleep. As will be seen in the next section, certain stages of sleep are more sensitive than others. If one wishes to establish a maximal acceptable difference between foreground noises and median noise, one should then determine it for the most sensitive stages of sleep and not uniformly for the whole night, because most surrounding noises are distributed in the course of the night in a chance manner—rarely in a regular one.

---

*The peak value for automobile noise was determined as the sound level exceeded for 1 percent of the time. The median noise for aircraft noise was taken to be the background noise.

## The Timing of the Stimulus

### Effects at Different Stages of Sleep

In general, it is much easier to awaken someone in the course of light sleep than in the course of deep sleep. This common observation is corroborated by Fig. 4.5, which shows the results of a number of studies (EPA, 1971a). There is, however, far from unanimous agreement as to the influence of noise on the different stages of sleep. Thus Williams *et al.* (1964) points out that it is easier to awaken a subject in the course of stages II and III than during stages IV and V (REM), while Rechtschaffen *et al.* (1966) believes that stages II and REM are the easiest to disturb. The belief that the stage of dreams—REM—is the one that can be most easily disturbed is shared by Lukas and Kryter (1969), as well as by Berry and Thiessen (1970).

As an overall conclusion from studies such as these, one may say that stage IV is the most difficult stage to disturb, and the stage of dreams is often the easiest to disturb. On the other hand, it seems that in the course of the REM stage, certain noises that are not too intense may be incorporated into a dream (Berry and Thiessen, 1970; Lukas and Kryter,

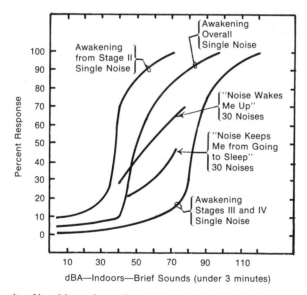

**Fig. 4.5**  Results of inquiries and experimentations showing the relation between stimuli and awakenings according to the stages of sleep (Source: EPA, 1971a).

1969) and for this fact may not produce a behavioral awakening. This is a phenomenon known for a long time to psychoanalysts: dreaming is a protector of sleep, for it includes certain stimuli in its system of symbols.

Such an observation poses the problem of the significance of the stimulus. If on the one hand certain noises are integrated in the dream phase without leading to real awakening, on the other hand it appears that certain stages of sleep [stages II and III in particular (Oswald *et al.*, 1969)] show a remarkable capacity to be interrupted (awakening) by certain very significant noises, eventhough they be low, such as the pronunciation of one's own name or the cries of a baby for its mother. A real evaluation of the signals must occur, and a physiological mechanism must "decide" if the awakening should be produced or not.

At this moment, we know even less about the phenomenon of awakening than about the mechanism of sleep. The real problem is that of the meaning of the noises and consequently of their familiar or strange character. This is particularly important if one tries to differentiate the effects of sudden noises such as a sonic boom, a cry, or the passing of a fast vehicle, from the effects of more continuous noises, such as automobile traffic in general. Unlike a progressive, familiar noise, sudden noise would not permit the releasing of a recognition mechanism.

To return to the effects of noise at different stages of sleep, it is fitting to note that disturbances to sleep can be measured not only in terms of behavioral awakenings, but also in terms of changes in electroencephalographs, of changes in the stages of sleep which may occur without awakening, as well as in terms of the percentage of sleep spent in each of these stages. For instance, a recent study has shown that during nights with airplane noise, the changes of stage were more numerous than during calm nights, and that the stages of light sleep became lengthened to the detriment of those of deep sleep. Thus the depth of sleep diminishes globally during nights spent in noisy surroundings (Metz *et al.*, 1971).

However, modifications of an electroencephalograph are not as easy to interpret as behavioral awakening. It is not known, in fact, if the sole modifications of the EEG are a significant indicator of a disturbance in the health of the individuals.

Finally, changes in the thresholds of awakening depend only in part on the stages of sleep. Differences between individuals (age, sex, etc.) probably play a no less important role in such changes. We shall return later to this problem.

## The Effect of Sleep Accumulation

The depth of sleep gradually diminishes and the probability of being awakened increases (Lukas and Kryter, 1968; Shapiro *et al.*, 1963; Rechtschaffen *et al.*, 1966), as one has accumulated sleep. That holds true for all stages of sleep, but in particular for the stage REM. A recent study concerning the effects of sonic boom on sleep has shown that 75 percent of behavioral awakenings took place during the second half of the night (Morgan and Rice, 1970). The result of these observations is that in order to assure a good sleep to the population, the surrounding noise should be particularly low in the course of the last hours of the night.

## Individual Variables

Researchers concur in pointing out that the reactions to noise during sleep vary notably from one individual to another. Certain variations have found some explanations, but others have very uncertain causes—such as socio-cultural variables—or are completely unknown. In this section, we shall confine ourselves to known individual factors.

## Age

The quality of sleep diminishes with age: sleep becomes subjectively lighter and awakenings are more frequent.

• Gadeke *et al.* (1968) exposed 126 sleeping children, aged 3 weeks to 1 year, to mixed noises (100–7000 Hz), 50–80 dBA. Less than 10 percent were awakened only after having been exposed for 3 minutes to a noise of 72 dBA.

• Steinicke (1957) exposed, in their homes, 350 aged individuals of different sex and professions (a representative sampling) to noises of a duration of 3 minutes. The sound began at a level of 30 phons for a spectrum extended between 50 and 5000 Hz, and increased by degrees from 5 phons until the awakening of the sleeper, who had to stop the apparatus installed near his bed himself. The most easily awakened subjects were young adults and aged people: one-fourth of the men under 30 and more than one-third of the women under 30 were awakened at 35 phons; half of the aged people, more than 60 years old, were awakened at 40 phons.

Lukas and Kryter (1969), in a study of the effects of sonic booms and airplane noises on subjects of different ages, have observed that subjects of more than 70 were awakened by 72 per cent of the noises of 107 PNdB (measured on the outside), while subjects aged 7–8 were awakened by such a noise only in 1 percent of the cases (Fig. 4.6).

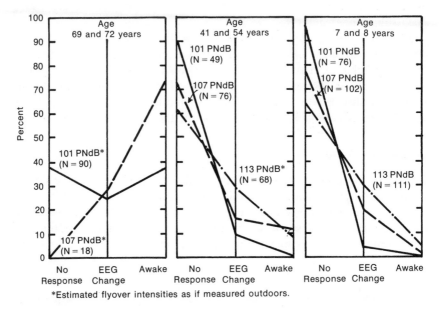

*Estimated flyover intensities as if measured outdoors.

**Fig. 4.6**  Reactions to the noise of airplanes during sleep in relation to the age of subjects (Source: Lukas and Kryter, 1969).

These and other studies show the great influence of age on waking reactions. Adults are more easily awakened by noise than children and the aged are extremely sensitive to noise, even at a very low level.

Thus, if the threshold below which one observes practically no behavioral awakening can be fixed at 50 dBA for children, it should be fixed at 35 dBA for adults and, even more so, for the aged. Since children generally live with their parents, it would be necessary to define the thresholds of acceptability in relation to the sensitivity of the parents—or even of people more than 60 years old, who represent one-fifth of the total population.

In view of the results that we have just presented, one could propose with some cynicism that in dwellings where the predominant noise is that of traffic, it would be suitable to have the children sleep near the streetside and the parents on the interior side (when the latter exists)! Such a conclusion would be hasty, however, for children between 4 and 6 years of age in particular often have their sleep disturbed by enuresis, sleep-walking, nighttime frights, nightmares. A disturbance of sleep by noise could have a disastrous effect on children of this age, who are particularly disturbed if suddenly awakened in the course of the phase of deep sleep (stage IV).

## Sex

Women, in particular housewives who perform no skilled task, are more easily awakened by noise than men. In a study by Steinicke (1957), at 40 phons almost half of the women were awakened, versus only one-third of the men. In reaction to noise, women, much more frequently than men, pass from deep sleep to light sleep (Zung and Wilson, 1966). Finally, airplane noise or sonic boom has been found by Lukas to disturb the sleep of middle-aged women more than of men (EPA, 1971a).

From these studies it is evident that women are more easily disturbed by noise than men in the course of their sleep. This phenomenon seems corroborated by the fact that women take increasingly more sleeping pills as they get older (McGhie and Russell, 1962), but noise is not the only cause for that; menopause and nervousness can play a significant role in this increased sensitivity to noise as one ages.

## Occupation

Certain trying jobs may reduce the total duration of sleep and thus provoke a lack of sleep. This has been observed in personnel working in hospitals as well as in students, school children and certain office workers (Masterson, 1965a, b). Persons in the intellectual professions seem to be less often awakened by noise than manual workers, who in turn seem to be less easily awakened than housewives not performing skilled tasks (Steinicke, 1957). Yet, the studies of the effects of noise in relation to occupation are too few for a definitive conclusion to be drawn from them.

## General State of Health

Persons who suffer from nervous depression have their sleep more easily bothered by noise than those in a good state of health (Zung and Wilson, 1966). At all ages people who have psychosomatic disturbances or neurotic tendencies have their sleep more disturbed and are more often awakened in the course of a night than normal persons (Johns *et al.*, 1970; Morgan and Rice, 1970). Furthermore, persons suffering from cardiac abnormalities or cardiovascular troubles are also more vulnerable to a disturbance of their sleep (Morgan, 1970).

In brief, it seems then that certain mental or physical illnesses render sleep more sensitive to external stimuli,* noise constituting without a doubt only one of these stimuli. Given the greater need for rest of the sick and convalescent, it is obvious that hospitals and convalescent homes should be particularly protected from noise.

### Use of Drugs and Anesthetics

Numerous anesthetics suppress or reduce the stage of paradoxical sleep and produce a sleep whose tracing cannot be compared to normal sleep (Jouvet, 1971). However, most of the information on the subject concerns studies on animals.

Some data concerning the effects on the phase of dreams of drugs utilized in psychiatry for humans are given in Table 4.2. It appears that the majority of psycho-altering drugs have an immediate suppressant action on dream activity but that this action is followed by a "rebound" which is often prolonged. However, definite conclusions cannot be reached in the absence of extended measurements before, during and after therapy.

### Differences in Temperament

Tune (1969) noticed that over 40 years of age, extroverts are awakened later than introverts. Studies of this kind need to be accompanied by studies of emotionality, as was done by Elliott (1971) for noise tolerance among children in the course of the daily period. Elliott has in fact shown that emotionality increases the effects of extroversion and introversion: among the extroverts, emotionality increases the tolerance to noise, while among introverts, emotionality reduces it. The replies to a questionnaire conducted by Monroe in 1967† have permitted the categorization "good" and "bad sleepers," and associated psychometric tests have shown that

---

*But it is uncertain that a relationship exists between psychopathological disturbances and disturbances of dream activity. Certain works (Feinberg *et al.*, 1967) show that the percentage of dream activity is normal among chronic schizophrenics with or without hallucinations. However, the lack of correlation between dream activity and psychopathology may depend on the limitations of the study techniques utilized (particularly the difficulties in performing measures over long periods of time, before, during and after therapy).

†Cited by Morgan (1970).

**Table 4.2**  Effect of Some Drugs on Human Dream Activity.

| | Action on Dream Activity | |
| Drugs | Immediate Effects | "Rebound" after Suppression of the Drug |
| --- | --- | --- |
| Tryptophane | + − | ? |
| 5 − HTP | + or − | ? |
| Reserpine | + or − | ? |
| I.M.A.O. | | |
|   Nialamide | − | ? |
|   Tranylcipromine | − − − | + |
| LSD | + − | ? |
| Amphetamines | − | + |
| Imipramine | − | ? |
| Chlorpromazine (and derivatives) | 0 or − | + |
| Nembutal | − | + |

"Rebound": increase of dream activity when the latter has been suppressed or diminished for one reason or another.

  + = increase of dream activity.

  − = decrease of dream activity.

the "bad sleepers" have more emotional and psychosomatic disturbances than the "good sleepers," and are more anxiety-ridden.

A repeated disturbance of sleep may lead to behavioral modifications: greater aggressiveness, bad humor, etc. (Morgan and Rice, 1970). However, laboratory experiments on the subject have remained thus far too short (we will return to this problem in discussing the effects of prolonged disturbances to sleep). The issue is an important one, for if, as we have seen, persons who suffer from a state of depression have their sleep more easily disturbed, it is not to be excluded that in a normal individual the disturbance of sleep caused by noise may produce in turn such a state of depression or of anxiety. Possibly it is the addition of different disturbing factors—among them noise—which leads or pre-disposes to depression.

How can one determine then the part played by each of the elements which may intervene in the formation of depression? Does noise act as a "multiplier," increasing the depression of the depressed person, the anxiety of the anxious person, etc.?

The present lack of knowledge of the long-term effects of a repeated annoyance day after day, and of the circular effects between causes and consequences is a major gap in our knowledge.

### Sleep Deprivation

The effects of sleep deprivation, whether total or partial, are of a physiological nature. Partial privation of sleep may be either a reduction of the total duration of sleep, or deprivation or systematic disturbance of certain stages of sleep. One may speak, therefore, of a quantitative deprivation of our "ration" of sleep, and of a qualitative deprivation.

#### Deprivation of the REM Stage

In the preceding sections we have stressed the role played in sleep by the REM stage (dream activity) and that played by stages III and IV (deep sleep). Let us now consider what happens when a sleeping subject is deprived of one of these stages.

The reader will recall that a typical night of sleep consists of four or five periods of dreaming and that, in all, one spends about 20 percent of the night in dreaming. The question that has been asked for several years is whether this amount of dreams is absolutely necessary to man.

It has been shown that when one has systematically awakened a sleeper during the REM stage, this sleeper later devotes, when one no longer disturbs his sleep, more time in dreaming than normally (Dement, 1965). Not only does the sleeper attempt to make up later for the period of dreams lost, but he also seeks to prevent his dreams from being disturbed; in the course of nights in which the REM stage is systematically disturbed, the dreamer constantly tries to fall back into the dream phase, and the REM stage becomes much more insensitive to sound stimuli than would normally be the case (Kryter, 1970).

Thus, it would seem that no matter what happens, the quantity of dreams that our body needs cannot be taken from us. This phenomenon is confirmed by the results of a study of the effects of the injections of heroin for one week (Oswald, 1970). Under heroin, the duration of the REM stage sharply decreases, but after the heroin injections are stopped, the duration of the REM stage increases to the detriment of stages III and IV, and it is only 2 months after the injections that sleep becomes normal once again.

From these various studies, one may conclude that:

1. It is simply not possible to completely deprive someone of his dream activity (we have just seen that a "rebound" of dreams takes place in the case of disturbance of REM stage and one knows that waking dreams—hallucinations—are produced if, in spite of everything, the quantity of dreams has been sharply diminished in the course of successive nights). We cannot know then what would happen in the case of total suppression of the period of dreams, since we cannot arrive at completely suppressing them.

2. Laboratory experiments have been too short in duration to affirm that the suppression of dreams is not fundamentally dangerous for health: if it is possible in a strict sense to be partially deprived of dreams in the course of several days or several weeks, can one know what would happen after one or several years of privation of these dreams? Here again no general conclusions can be drawn from laboratory experiments conducted over a short period.

That the dream phase is absolutely necessary to human beings is corroborated by the fact that subjects deprived of the REM stage show symptoms of mental confusion, suspicion and withdrawal, and that the learning of a task in the course of the day is altered by it (Stern, 1969). Various researchers have concluded from this that the REM stage permits the fixating and the maintenance of information in the long-term memory (Fishbein, 1969a, b), that it plays an important role in the "programming" of the brain (Dewan, 1969) and that it aids in assuring the synthesizing and reconstituting functions of the brain (Morgan, 1970 and Oswald, 1970).

## Deprivation of Deep Sleep

The phase of deep sleep appears to be of great importance for the growth of the organism. Subjects deprived of deep sleep (stages III and IV) have depressive and hypochrondriac reactions (measured by psychometric tests after disturbed nights of sleep). The discharge of human growth hormones in the blood appears to diminish if the phase of deep sleep is reduced. Different authors now think that stages III and IV permit assurance of physical growth and the restoration of the tissues of the organisms, while as we have just seen, the phase of dream activity would permit the growth, the maintenance and the restoration of mental and psychic functions.

*Effects on Performance of Moderate Sleep Deprivation*

The tasks that suffer the most from a moderate deprivation of sleep are those of vigilance as well as different tasks performed mentally or with a machine.

A person who has been deprived of a part of his sleep functions more slowly (Wilkinson, 1962). Furthermore, the detection of signals, particularly auditory ones, by a subject deprived of sleep is accompanied by numerous errors (Williams *et al.*, 1959); the times of reaction seem therefore to become longer when one is deprived of sleep. After two nights of 5 hours' sleep the effectiveness for work diminishes (Wilkinson *et al.*, 1966) and a state of somnolence is established which decreases sensitivity. The tasks which are most affected by a moderate privation of sleep are those that are uninteresting, familiar, difficult, and long; some believe that a quantity of normal sleep is necessary in order to maintain a selective attention during the day.

In order to obtain a more complete understanding of these effects, individual and sociological factors should also be considered, such as the average duration of sleep for a given individual, as well as the usual hour of going to bed and awakening. It would be interesting, for example, to compare the effects of the disturbance of sleep among subjects generally needing a long period of sleep (8–9 hours) and among subjects who sleep only 5–6 hours a night.

*Behavioral Effects of Prolonged Sleep Deprivation*

After sleep deprivation for several hours, evoked reflexes (modification of the EEG by stimuli) and behavioral awakenings diminish at all stages of sleep (when again the subject is allowed to sleep), and for all levels of stimulation. The noise needs to be increased by approximately 15 dBA, in order to awaken a sleeper previously deprived of sleep in this manner. At the same time, vasoconstriction reactions diminish only slightly under the effect of new stimuli (Williams *et al.*, 1959).

Prolonged sleep deprivation increases somnolence in a linear manner (Murray *et al.*, 1958), and anomalies in performances follow the progress of somnolence: the frequency and intensity of somnolence is directly related to decrease in performance; subjective and hallucinatory images become superimposed on reality, motor activities diminish and the subject seems to fall asleep; after several seconds of this beginning of sleeping, the subject even sometimes remembers having dreamed (Morris *et al.*, 1960). As previously indicated, it is probable that these hallucinations are due not to the suppression of sleep in general, but rather to that of the REM stage.

## Physiological Effects of Sleep Deprivation

Although in most cases no modifications are observed of pulse, respiratory rhythm, blood pressure and skin reactions with sleep deprivation, no definitive conclusion should yet be drawn concerning these parameters (Morgan, 1970).

Muscular tension, according to some researchers, increases with the loss of sleep, while according to other researchers no significant modifications are revealed.

As far as cerebral activity is concerned, the alpha rhythm decreases with the privation of sleep (e.g., Blake and Gerard, 1937; Tyler *et al.*, 1947). Morgan (1970), in the interpretation of these results, suggests that the changes in the tracing of the EEG ought to be compared to other behavioral modifications.

### Habituation to Noises Perceived during Sleep

Habituation to sonic booms of weak intensity has been found to occur in the course of stage II of sleep, after eight nights of exposure to the noise, but no habituation has been found to appear in the REM stage (dream activity) (Lukas and Kryter, 1968). An experiment by Gastaut and Bert (1961) showed that habituation to repeated visual and auditory stimuli occurring in the course of a cycle of 20 minutes, once a week over a period of 5–7 weeks, was accelerated from week to week. After several weeks, blockage of the alpha rhythm (which occurred at the beginning of the experiment) disappeared at the time of the presentation of the first stimulus. This led to the conclusion that there is a memory of habituation, which grows from week to week.

However, the threshold of awakening in the course of the REM stage decreases as the night progresses, making the sleeper become increasingly sensitive to exterior stimuli (Lukas and Kryter, 1968). Consequently, any adaptation in the course of the first hours of sleep to known stimuli, which have already been encountered in the course of preceding nights, may be annulled by an increased sensitivity to the noise in the course of the last hours of the night. Only the noises interiorized into dreams can give the impression of an adaptation. Furthermore, from all evidence:

- one more easily becomes accustomed to noises of weak intensity than to those of strong intensity (Sharpless and Jasper, 1956; Gastaut and Bert, 1961);
- one becomes more easily accustomed to sounds of low frequency than to sounds of high frequency (Sharpless and Jasper, 1956);
- habituation is facilitated if nocturnal noises are similar to day noises that one has learned to recognize and for which a veritable "neuronic model" has been formed (Berry and Thiessen, 1970).

The habituation, however, is strongly "affected" by personal factors such as one's attitude toward a particular noise and one's anxiety concerning the possible effects of that noise on health. Certain persons will suffer more from a disturbance of sleep by a certain noise simply because they have attached a particular significance to that noise.

In conclusion one must say that the possibility of adaptation to noise during sleep is at best very limited. This is so whether one considers the changes of the state of sleep, the modifications of autonomous reactions and tracings of the EEG, or only behavioral awakening. The apparent adaptation which seems to result from our daily experience is perhaps due to a forgetting of the awakenings and of the disturbances of sleep that one has undergone during the night (EPA, 1971a): it seems that, consciously or unconsciously, one forgets the noise that has bothered our sleep. Many investigators have indeed remarked that the subjects in their studies most often underestimate the number of times they are awakened in the course of a period of exposure to noise (e.g., Morgan, 1970; Mery et al., 1971).

Thus, "the idea that people adapt themselves to noise is a myth" (EPA, 1971b). Several physiologists have shown that in matters of vegetative reactions, there does not exist an adaptation to noise. On the physiological level, other researchers have shown that the cochlear passages—among all higher vertebrates—are the first organs to be awakened and the last to disappear into sleep. Our ears would then be the ultimate guardians of our security.

The biologist René Dubos thinks that if the potential dangers of certain annoyances are at present so unknown it is because damages caused to man appear in a deferred and indirect manner, so that their recognition escapes our habitual analysis of the relations of cause and effect (in EPA, 1971b). Observations of the contemporary world give us *the impression* that man adapts himself to many things. But can one indeed be sure that there do not exist limits to such an adaptation? Can one indeed be sure that an apparent everyday adaptation may not lead in the long run to an acceleration and a facilitation of psychic and organic disturbances, even to a refusal to adapt—conscious or unconscious—which could lead to widespread social troubles?

### Subsequent Subjective Reactions to Sleep Disturbances

We have seen how people tend to underestimate the number of times that they are really awakened by a noise in the course of the night. Yet, psychometric tests show that the disturbance of sleep by noise is felt the next morning. Thus Mery *et al.* (1971), in a study of the effects of airplane noise on sleep, verified through a questionnaire the existence of an impression of poorer quality sleep after nights disturbed by a noise. Morgan (1970), has shown through a series of tests that the fatigue was greater after a night with sonic booms than after a night without booms, and that the *a posteriori* evaluation of the subjective quality of sleep was also affected by the exposure to noise during sleep. Murray *et al.* (1958) has shown that subjects deprived of sleep declare themselves "sleepy" and "indolent." In Part IV we shall discuss the results of sociological inquiries, in which it often appears that one of the major causes of annoyance is the disturbance to sleep.

These tests of subjective valuations of sleep have been generally neglected until now in laboratory experiments. Yet they are particularly important because it is not only the objective disturbance of sleep which affects the population, but equally and perhaps even more the subjective perception of having slept well or poorly. This perception may in effect modify the disposition of people, eventually promote aggressiveness, reduce attention to work and affect social relationships. Taking into account the subjective effects of disturbance to sleep by noise seems particularly necessary if one considers the many new possible sources of noise, such as supersonic planes and non-conventional means of transportation. The subjective impression of having slept badly may modify the attitude of a person concerning his environment. It may polarize his attention and his discontent on what he might consider responsible for his loss of sleep, whether this is the noise itself or the intrusion into his environment of something not habitual or unacceptable.

### Overview

Several major conclusions can be drawn from the considerations presented in this chapter concerning the effects of noise on sleep:

1. The extreme heterogeneity of the methods for defining and measuring disturbance, and of the stimuli utilized, as well as the great variability

of individual reactions to noise, *make an objective definition of a limit of nocturnal noise impossible.* This impossibility is accentuated by the gaps in our knowledge concerning the effects of a prolonged disturbance to sleep.

2. Irregular noise and noise which emerges from the background are particularly disturbing to sleep. Indeed the EPA (1974) considers any impulse noise that exceeds the background noise by more than about 10 dB as being potentially sleep disturbing.

3. Noise not leading to behavioral awakening can however produce physiological modifications, which in certain cases (such as changes in the stages of sleep) can damage the quality of sleep.

4. Noise occurring toward the end of the night, as well as in the course of dream phases and light sleeping phases, is particularly disturbing. Thus, regulatory measures concerning, for example, the circulation of certain vehicles at night, are bound to be ineffective because the dream periods and the periods of light sleep occur several times a night, at unforeseeable moments; in order to protect these fragile stages of sleep it would be necessary to totally suppress the circulation of noisy vehicles during the whole night.

5. Aged people, women beyond the menopause, sick people, people afflicted with psychic disturbances, as well as children between 4 and 6 years old, constitute a portion of the population who are very sensitive to noise or who could be easily disturbed during their sleep by excessive noises. This particularly sensitive group represents more than one-third of the total population. Thus anti-noise measures should take into consideration the reactions of this important portion of the population, and not only those of "adult males in good health."

6. Laboratory studies have the advantage of permitting a controlled and broader study of diverse technical and physiological variables. On the other hand, they place the subjects in an unfamiliar environment, reconstitute specific noises which are less realistic than those perceived in a dwelling, and do not permit a study of long-term effects of a prolonged and repeated disturbance to sleep. In any case, laboratory studies, in order to be complete, should include psychometric tests and thorough interviews, in order to reveal the subjective effects of a disturbance of sleep (effects which, as we have seen, can scarcely be over-emphasized).

## REFERENCES

Bastide, R. Les techniques du repos et de la relaxation. Communication to the Congress on Psychosomatic Medicine, Paris, 1966.

Berry, B. and Thiessen, G. J. The effects of impulsive noise on sleep. National Research Council of Canada, Division of Physics, APS-478, 1970.

Blake, J. and Gerard, R. W. Brain potentials during sleep. *American Journal of Physiology,* 1937, **119**.

Dement, W. C. Recent studies on the biological role of rapid eye movement sleep. *American Journal of Psychiatry,* 1965, **122**.

Dewan, E. M. The P-hypothesis for REMs: Alternate testable versions. *Psychophysiology,* 1969, **6**.

Elliott, C. D. What does "noisy" mean? *New Society,* U.K., May 27, 1971.

EPA (U.S. Environmental Protection Agency). Effects of noise on people. Washington, December 1971. (a)

EPA (U.S. Environmental Protection Agency). The social impact of noise. Washington, December 1971. (b)

EPA (U.S. Environmental Protection Agency). Information on levels of environmental noise requisite to protect public health and welfare with an adequate margin of safety. Washington, March 1974.

Feinberg, I. *et al.* EEG sleep patterns as a function of normal and pathological aging in man. *Psychiatric Research,* 1967, **5**.

Firth, H., University of Edinburgh. Private communication, 1971.

Fishbein, W. The effects of paradoxical sleep deprivation during the retention interval on long term memory. *Psychophysiology,* 1969, **6**. (a)

Fishbein, W. The effects of paradoxical sleep deprivation prior to initial learning on long term memory. *Psychophysiology,* 1969, **6**. (b)

Gadeke, R. *et al.* Der Gerauschpegel in Kinderkrankenhaus und die Wecklarmschwelle von Sanglingen, Mschr. *Kinderheilk,* 1968, **116**.

Gastaut, H. and Bert, J. Electroencephalographic detection of sleep induced by repetitive sensory stimuli. In G. E. W. Wolstenholme and M. O'Connor (Eds.), *The nature of sleep.* London: Churchill, 1961.

Holland–Wegman Productions, Inc. Public Relations for Buffalo Airport. Personal communication, 1967.

Johns, M. W. *et al.* Sleep habits and symptoms in male medical and surgical patients. *British Medical Journal,* 1970, **2**.

Jouvet, M. Activite onirique et neuropharmacologie. *Excerpta Medica International Congress Series,* 1966, **150**.

Jouvet, M. Neuropharmacology of sleep. Article given as personal communication to A. Alexandre, 1971.

Kales, A. (Ed.). *Sleep physiology and pathology, a symposium.* Philadelphia: Lippincott, 1969.

Kleitman, N. *Sleep and wakefulness.* Revised edition. Chicago: University of Chicago Press, 1963.

Kryter, K. D. *The effects of noise on man.* New York and London: Academic Press, 1970.

Lukas, J. S. and Kryter, K. D. A preliminary study of the awakening and startle effects of simulated sonic booms. NASA Report No. CR-1193, 1968.

Lukas, J. S. and Kryter, K. D. Awakening effects of simulated sonic booms and subsonic aircraft noise on six subjects, 7 to 72 years of age. NASA, 1-7892 SRI Project No. 7270, 1969.

Masterson, J. P. Sleep of hospital medical staff. *Lancet,* 1965, **1**. (a)

Masterson, J. P. Patterns of sleep. In G. Edholn and A. L. Bacharach (Eds.), *The physiology of human survival.* London: Academic Press, 1965. (b)

McGhie, A. and Russell, S. M. The subjective assessment of normal sleep patterns. *Journal of Mental Science*, 1962, **108**.

McKennell, A. C. Aircraft noise annoyance around London (Heathrow) Airport. Central Office of Information, SS 337, April 1963.

Mery, J. *et al. Etudes de bruit d'avions sur le sommeil.* Strasbourg: CNRS, 1971.

Metz, B. *et al.* Experience bruit-sommeil. (Scientific Report and results of questionnaires). Strasbourg: CEB-CNRS, 1971.

Morgan, P. A. Effects of noise upon sleep. ISVR Report No. 40, 1970.

Morgan, P. A. and Rice, C. G. Behavioral awakening in response to indoor sonic booms. ISVR Univ. of Southampton Technical Report No. 41, 1970.

Morris, G. *et al.* Misperception and disorientation during sleep deprivation. *A.M.A. Annals of General Psychiatry*, 1960, **2**.

Murray, E. J. *et al.* Body temperature and psychological ratings during sleep deprivation. *Journal of Experimental Psychology*, 1958, **56**.

Oswald, I. Sleep, the great restorer. *New Scientist*, April 23, 1970.

Oswald, I. *et al.* Discriminative responses to simulation during human sleep. *Brain*, 1969, **83**.

Reinberg, A. and Ghata, J. Les rhythmes biologiques. *PUF (Que Sais-je)*, Paris, 1964.

Schieber, J. P. Etude analytique en laboratoire de l'influence du bruit sur le sommeil. Rapport DORST-Centre d'Etudes Bioclimatiques du CNRS, Strasbourg, 1968.

Shapiro, A. *et al.* Dream recall as a function and method of awakening. *Psychosomatic Medicine*, 1963, **25**.

Sharpless, S. and Jasper, H. Habituation of one arousal reaction. *Brain*, 1956, **79**.

Steinicke, G. Die Wirkungen von Laerm auf den Schlaf der Menschen. *Koeln Westdeutschen Verlag*, 1957, **416**.

Stern, W. D. Effects of REM sleep deprivation upon the acquisition of learned behavior in the rat. *Psychophysiology*, 1969, **6**.

Thiessen, G. J. and Olson, N. Community noise-surface transportation. *Sound and Vibration*, 1968, **2**.

Tune, G. S. The influence of age and temperament on the adult human sleep-wakefulness pattern. *British Journal of Psychology*, 1969, **60**.

Tyler, D. B. *et al.* The effects of experimental insomnia on the rate of potential changes in the brain. *American Journal of Physiology*, 1947, **149**.

Wilkinson, R. T. Muscle tension during mental work under sleep deprivation. *Journal of Experimental Psychology*, 1962, **64**.

Wilkinson, R. T. *et al.* Performance following a night of reduced sleep. *Psychonomic Science*, 1966, **5**.

Williams, H. L. *et al.* Impaired performance with acute sleep loss. *Psychology Monographs*, 1959, **73**.

Williams, H. L. *et al.* Responses to auditory stimulation, sleep loss and the EEG stages of sleep. *Electroencephology Clinical Neurophysiology*, 1964, **16**.

Zung, W. K. and Wilson, W. P. Attention, discrimination and arousal during sleep. *Archives of General Psychiatry*, 1966, **15**.

CHAPTER 5

# Other Physiological and Psychological Effects of Noise

The Noise; the Noise; I just couldn't stand the Noise.—SUICIDE NOTE LEFT BY A DESPERATE HOMEOWNER—(Connell, 1972)

## OTHER PHYSIOLOGICAL EFFECTS

Sudden and unexpected noise has been observed to produce marked changes in the body, such as increased blood pressure, increased heart rate, and muscular contractions. Moreover, digestion, stomach contractions, and the flow of saliva and gastric juices all stop. Because the changes are so marked, repeated exposure to unexpected noise should obviously be kept to a minimum. These changes fortunately wear off as a person becomes accustomed to the noise (Broadbent, 1957). However, even when a person is accustomed to an environment where the noise level is high, physiological changes occur. The principal physiological changes are discussed very briefly below.

### Cardiovascular Effects

Well-known studies of physiological effects of noise were carried out by Jansen (1959) with nearly 1400 workers in a large variety of jobs in German industry, who were examined for a number of physiological functions. The workers were assigned to two groups according to the noise exposure. One group was exposed to noise up to 80 phons,* and the other to noise of 100 phons and above. The difference in the incidence of altered cardiac responses between the two groups was statistically significant. However, the differences in the distributions of severity of the symptoms were not reported.

---

*See Appendix 1

Results of measurements of cardiovascular functions in two groups of workers before, after, and at work are also reported by Shatalov *et al.* (1962). The groups were textile workers exposed to 85–95 dB and ballbearing-plant workers exposed to 114–120 dB. The most significant change was a decrease in the maximum blood pressure during work, which was more apparent in the noisy situation. A larger fraction of the workers in the ballbearing plant showed lower heart rates.

Noise, even at relatively lower levels, usually tends to constrict the peripheral blood vessels, in fingers, toes and abdominal organs, and to dilate those in the retina and the brain, possibly leading to headaches. Connell (1972) cites the case of woodsmen in Sweden working with extremely noisy motor saws. After they go home "their fingers first turn blue, then white. This is the symptom of vasaspostic disease caused when small vessels in the hand constrict so as to cut-off the blood supply." On the other hand, measurements on 10 hospital patients of oxygen intake, arterio-venous oxygen difference, cardiac output, cardiac rate, cardiac stroke volume, and pressure of pulmonary arteries before and after a 30-minute exposure to white noise have been reported to show no significant changes (Etholm and Egenberg, 1964). This leaves open the question of whether noise can cause heart disease. The U.S. Environmental Protection Agency suggests that there is some evidence of higher incidence of cardiovascular disease (as well as equilibrium disorders and ear-nose-and throat disorders) among workers exposed to high levels of noise (EPA, 1971b).

Some of the interest in the cardiovascular effects of noise has been spurred from the work of Rosen *et al.* (1964) with the Mabaans, an African tribe, who presumably as a result of their quiet environment have been found to have good hearing and low blood pressure even into old age. Yet these observations are not without experimental difficulties that might affect the results (Ward, 1966).

**Hormonal Effects**

The work of Levi showed that significant changes have been observed in the urinary excretion of adrenaline and noradrenaline of subjects exposed for a short time to noise in a simulated industrial situation and to other stimuli (e.g., Levi, 1966). For some individuals the changes bordered on the pathological; it has been suggested that these people are likely to get excited at the least provocation. When the noise experiments were carried out over a period of time in a work situation, the adrenaline and noradrenaline levels changed very little. This result is consistent with the habituation described by Broadbent (1957).

In rats, exposure to high-frequency sounds of 20,000 Hz has been reported to radically increase adrenaline excretion (The Sciences, 1970). Exposure to low-frequency sounds of 150 Hz released oxytocin, a hormone that stimulates the uterus during labor; noise-induced changes in oxytocin level may adversely affect the fetus and the birth process.

### Gastric Effects

Marked gastric changes occur on exposure to sudden and unexpected noise. Smith and Laird (1930) observed a reduction in strength of stomach contractions during exposure of four subjects for 10 minutes to 80 dB noise, and, after 10 minutes quiet, to 10 minutes of 60 dB noise. The number of contractions per minute decreased by 37 percent during the 80 dB noise, a change that seems unambiguously large. The results for the 10-minute quiet period were variable; the 60 dB exposure following the quiet period produced only slight changes. The 80 dB exposure was not continued for a sufficiently long period of time to determine whether adaptation takes place.

To the layman, these gastric changes spell ulcers; however, there are no indications that noise *per se* is responsible for ulcers.

### Fatigue

A revealing way of measuring the physical effort—fatigue—generated by noise is to measure the activity of muscles, by picking up potentials from the skin above them (Davis, 1932; Ryan *et al.*, 1950). In the investigation by Ryan and his co-workers, 24 subjects carried out 10-minute periods of visual work in noise (N), glare (G), and control conditions (C). Rest periods lasting 3 minutes were used between all work periods. The sequence of the work periods in six series of tests was:

$$CNCG, CNGC, CGCN, CGNC, CCNG, CCGN$$

A test series always included both glare and noise. The sequences were such that the noise was preceded by glare in half the tests. The noise stimulus was recorded laughter, unfortunately of unspecified intensity. A significant difference was observed in the number of electrical pulses produced by noise and control stimuli. In Davis' experiments subjects were exposed for 5 minutes to the noise produced by an electric bell and an electric buzzer together. Adaptation was clearly shown within the 5-minute work period. The noise level, however, was not indicated.

### Effects of High Noise Levels on the Brain

There appear to be some measurable effects on the brain potentials of noise-exposed workers, but the long-term effects are not clear.

Changes in the EEG's of subjects exposed to noise having an SPL of 100 dB with the addition of a tone of 3000–5000 Hz for 2–3 minutes have also been reported (Strakhov, 1962). These symptoms, however, disappeared 5–8 minutes after the noise stopped.

Bell (1966) mentions that in neurological studies of Italian weavers their reflexes were found to be hyperactive; in some cases EEG's showed a diffuse desynchronization similar to that occurring in the psychoneurosis of personality disturbance. Findings such as these are, however, dependent on methods, whether a control group is used, and need to be pursued to assess whether recovery from the epects occur.

Other problems to be considered in tests of this kind are pointed out by Broadbent (1967):

> One study investigated the performance of men who had been working on aircraft engines on certain tests previously found to distinguish people with injured brains from normal persons. The aircraft workers did worse on these tests. But, as the author points out, these men had been subject to emotional stress in their work as well as to noise, since they were anxious about the possible dangers of the task. Any permanent effect on them might be due to this other stress and not to the noise. There is also the danger in such an investigation that people who are by nature somewhat unusual will thrust themselves forward for testing.*

### Effects of Ultrasounds and Infrasounds

Some experiments have shown significant blood sugar changes as a result of exposure to ultrasonic sound—that is, sound at frequencies above 20,000 Hz (Ashbel, 1956), and other experiments have demonstrated extremely severe effects of infrasonic sound—the inaudible sounds at frequencies below 20 Hz (Mohr *et al.*, 1956). Studies such as these suggest that consideration must be given to these components in measurements of wide-band noise.

Infrasounds are the most insidious, because of their unsuspected presence in many activities of our technological society. They can occur in airplanes and other vehicles; they can penetrate the walls of houses exposed to noise from heavy vehicles, and they constitute a dangerous component of the sonic boom. They work on the internal organs, causing a sort of resonance that sets them in vibration. "A person exposed to

---

*Used by permission.

infrasound of 7 cps has a vague impression of sound and a feeling of general discomfort but is totally unable to perform mental work, even simple arithmetic. As the intensity of the unheard sound increases, dizziness sets in, then nervous fatigue and seasickness. At still higher intensity, the internal organs vibrate and the resulting friction produces quick but painful death." (Connell, 1972). However, if the infrasound intensity is less than 130 dB of sound pressure level corresponding to 76 dB(A) for the octave band centered at 16 Hz, the health hazards do not seem to be serious (EPA, 1973).

## PSYCHOLOGICAL EFFECTS

That noise has psychological effects is undoubted. The question is how these effects can be assessed—and whether they lead to damage. No clear case has been made thus far for psychological damage caused by *moderately high levels of noise*—the levels that would cause hearing damage to only a small fraction of the people exposed. Indeed, fears have been expressed that "... over-emphasis on 'damage' may backfire when people come to realize that the truth of the matter seems to be simply that people don't like loud noise and don't like being disturbed," (Davis, 1967). Indeed, people can express violently their dislike about being disturbed by noises. This is recounted vividly by Connell (1972):

> ... A middle aged woman living in Soho became affected by the incessant noise from a newly open discotheque. She complained to the management, the Police, the Local Authority but nothing was done to reduce the noise. Her action took the form of suicide. In Italy a 44-year old man took an overdose of drugs because his eleven children made too much noise while he was watching the Olympic Games on television... In a quiet part of Middlesex with an ambient noise level of 30 to 40 decibels lived Fred, a lusty, healthy builders labourer. The M4 Motorway was built within a few feet of his cottage home. The resultant traffic caused the noise level to rise to 80 and 90 decibels so this poor man suffered an increase of 100,000 times* in the noise level. He took it for some weeks. Discovered there was nothing he could do about it and his action was also directed against the self. He left a note which read "The Noise; the Noise; I just couldn't stand the Noise"...

These are clearly extreme cases of reaction to the intrusion of noise into one's life. But without question the ubiquitousness of the intrusion, even if less severe or less fatally resented, leads to demands for acoustic

---

*This is poetic license. The increase in reality would be a ten-fold one—still a very high one [Authors].

privacy which are psychologically no less important than those for visual privacy (Cohen, 1969; EPA, 1971a).

Exposure to *high levels of noise* does not seem either to result in changes of behavior proceeding from irreversible damage to the central nervous system. However, as one authority has put it: "I would not venture a guess as to the interaction of personality variables with various forms of noise" (Doehring, 1967).

Even without discounting the possibility of psychological damage, the difficulties of attempts to demonstrate its existence cannot be over-emphasized. As Broadbent stated in 1972: ... if one could settle the question of the effects of a long-continued background of noise upon the state of mind or well-being of people who had an opportunity of becoming accustomed to it, this might potentially be very important in its results. However, ... the probability of reaching a definitive conclusion on this is extremely low...."* Although, two years later, Broadbent felt more optimistic about this probability (Broadbent, 1974).

### Irritability

Irritability, tenseness, insomnia are some of the psychological effects of exposure to high levels of noise. It appears, however, that irritability at home (is this an externality?) is more the result of hearing loss than noise, or, to put it in another way, it is not as much noise that makes people irritable as the hearing loss. In an early study, increased irritability and fatigue were observed among men who took part in an experiment to determine possible damaging effects of working near a jet engine (Finkle and Poppen, 1948). The men were also exposed, however, to the mechanical vibrations from the jet engine in the tests, whose effects are not easily separated from those of noise.

A study by the U.S. Navy on the Auditory and Non-Auditory Effects of High Intensity Noise (ANEHIN) on men working on the flight decks of aircraft carriers also observed that: "The most common complaints were increased irritability, tenseness, insomnia, and occasionally fear, because of inability to communicate with other men in the presence of noise. With the exception of the difficulty of communication, however, most of the men stated that they did not believe that their trouble was due to the noise. They felt much more strongly that their trouble was due to the general dangers of the job and to further concern about a delay in their

---

*Used by permission.

return to the United States that had been occasioned by a change in the schedule of operations of the ship"* (Davis, 1958).

According to a "standardized interview," workers in very noisy jobs in German industry reported more disturbances of interpersonal relations than workers in slightly noisy jobs (Jansen, 1959).

In medical studies on about 125 workers in a jet-engine plant exposed to various noise levels (the best defined exposure being for 32 workers in the sheet metal mill, where the noise level was 90–97 phons all day with occasional peaks of 120 phons), increased irritability (Reizbarkeit) was found in 44 percent of these workers, and stomach disturbances like loss of appetite and nausea in 31 percent. Apparently there was no control group. Eighty-four percent of these workers had worked in the plant for more than 3 years. Workers who participated in sports were found to complain less about being irritable.

### Psychological Problems of Adjustment to Hearing Loss

Almost all people with socially inadequate hearing are affected psychologically. In fact, the carefully written and richly detailed descriptions of the psychological problems associated with hearing loss make it clear that the problems are serious ones (e.g., Ramsdell, 1961; Sataloff, 1966).

As suggested earlier in this book (Part I, Chapter 2), ours is a visually-oriented society—suffice it to consider how much people watch television. Thus, inescapably, other people do not recognize and help the person with severe hearing loss anywhere near as much as they do a blind person. Moreover, a blind person can substitute his hearing for his sight, whereas the deaf person has no substitute available except lip reading, and this is a far from adequate substitute. For these reasons, a person with severe hearing loss may be in some ways cut-off from society more than a blind person.

In cases where the hearing loss is not so severe, the psychological problems may be actually more acute. A striking description of the problems of the chipper having noise-induced hearing loss is given by Sataloff *et al.* (1965) [we recall that such a worker is one of the at least 5 million people in the United States with probable noise-induced hearing loss (Part II, Chapter 3, and Part V, Chapter 18)]:

> A hearing impairment may cause no handicap to a chipper or a riveter while he is at work. His deafness may even seem to be to his advantage, since the noise of his work is

*Used by permission of the author and NSAF Directorate for Defense Information.

not as loud to him as it is to his fellow workers with normal hearing. Because there is little or no verbal communication in most jobs that produce intense noise, a hearing loss will not be made apparent by inability to understand complicated verbal directions. However, when such a workman returns to his family at night or goes on his vacation, the situation assumes a completely different perspective. He has trouble understanding what his wife is saying, especially if he is reading the paper, and his wife is talking while she is making noise in the kitchen. This kind of situation frequently leads at first to a mild dispute and later to serious family tension.

The wife accuses the husband of inattention, which he denies, while he complains in rebuttal that she mumbles. Actually, he eventually does become inattentive when he realizes how frustrating and fatiguing it is to strain to hear. When the same individual tries to attend meetings, to visit with friends, or to go to church services and finds he cannot hear what is going on or is laughed at for giving an answer unrelated to the subject under discussion, he soon, but very reluctantly, realizes that something really is wrong with him. He stops going to places where he feels pilloried by his handicap. He stops going to the movies, the theater or concerts, for the voices and the music are not only far away, but frequently distorted. Little by little his whole family life may be undermined, and a cloud overhangs his future and that of his dependents.

The psychological changes that come with hearing loss can be explained by first describing normal hearing as if it occurred on three levels; the language or symbolic level, the signal or warning level, and what can be called the primitive level, which corresponds to the background sounds that we hear without being aware of it. The importance of the loss of this primitive level has been pointed out by Ramsdell (1961):

> It was the constant reiteration, by hard-of-hearing patients at Deshon Army Hospital, of the statement that the world seemed dead which led to the investigation of this third level of hearing and of the psychological effect of its loss upon the deaf. This third level has not generally been recognized, although it is psychologically the most fundamental of the auditory functions. It relates us to the world at a very primitive level, somewhere below the level of clear consciousness and perception. The loss of this feeling of relationship with the world is the major cause of the well-recognized feeling of "deadness" and also of the depression that permeates the suddenly deafened and, to a less degree, those in whom deafness develops gradually. This level of hearing we shall designate as the primitive level.

There are a number of consequences of these well-established patterns. First, since presbycusis produces the same sort of distortion of speech as noise-induced hearing loss, older people are bound to be subject to these psychological difficulties. This is very important to a society such as the American one, in which the average age tends to get older, because the fraction of the population with these problems will increase and the resources needed for their medical and psychological care will also increase. The American society faces the prospect of having a sizeable fraction of its people "sick" and "deaf" old men and women.

However, if presbycusis could be decreased, this trend could be slowed down. To do this, a large scale and obviously very costly program would have to be undertaken to reduce noise levels markedly. To justify such a costly program, one would have to know, among other things, how much the presbycusis could be reduced by a given choice of noise levels and how fast the population is aging biologically. Moreover, such a study would have to be carried out over a period of at least a year with a large population for whom the noise would have to be monitored. Techniques are available for such monitoring and it seems advisable to consider them in detail.

On these grounds alone, quite apart from any considerations of aesthetic experience as described by Ramsdell (1961):

> The sound of the sea, the singing of birds, the patter of rain furnish many people aesthetic experiences as poignant as those received through music.

there is need for a research program aimed at establishing a rational basis for specifying acceptable noise levels. (The program would be promoted indirectly if voters or workers were to demand higher Workmen's Compensation awards for noise-induced hearing loss.) Such a study program might not only reduce noise-induced hearing loss, but might conceivably make some small step towards reducing presbycusis.

Finally, it is important to note that the consequences of hearing loss are changing: ". . . a hearing loss today is far more handicapping than it was before TV, radio, and the telephone began to play such major roles in education, leisure, and the business world. Today, the inability to understand on a telephone is indeed a major handicap for the vast majority of people. The loss of even high tones alone to a professional or an amateur musician or even to a high-fidelity fan also is handicapping. The hearing loss of tomorrow will have a different handicapping effect from the hearing loss of today" (Sataloff *et al.*, 1965).

## A Note on Methodology

One can attempt to asses the psychological effects of noise in a variety of ways:

- through psychiatric interviews;
- through psychological tests;
- through physiological measurements.

Psychological and physiological tests are held by several workers in the field to be preferable, in that order. Many of the different tests of physiological functions used in trying to discover whether there is any psychological damage from exposure to noise levels high enough to cause hearing damage have already been mentioned—for example, the EEG.

Psychological tests are exemplified by those in the ANEHIN (Davis, 1958) and the Jansen (1959) studies. A number of tests are available (such as the Bernreuter Neurotic Index, the Eysenck—2 factors test, the Minnesota Multiphasic and the Cattell-16 factors test). In general, preferable to tests like the Thematic Apperception Test (TAT) that have to be scored by a trained interviewer, are tests that are based on some sort of achievement questionnaire.

## REFERENCES

Ashbel, Z. Z. Effects of ultrasound and high frequency noise in the blood sugar level. Translated into English from *Gigiena Truda i Professional 'nye Zabolevaniya*, Moscow, 1956, **2**, (JPRS-36252).

Bell, A. Noise: An occupational hazard and a public nuisance. Public Health Paper No. 30. Geneva: World Health Organization, 1966.

Broadbent, D. E. In C. M. Harris, Ch. 10. *Handbook of noise control.* New York: McGraw-Hill, 1957.

Broadbent, D. E. Personal communication, 1967.

Broadbent, D. E. Personal communication, 1972.

Broadbent, D. E. Personal communication, 1974.

Cohen, A. Effects of noise on psychological state. In W. Ward and J. Fricke (Eds.), *Noise as a public health hazard.* Washington: American Speech Hearing Association, 1969.

Connell, J. The biological effects of noise. Paper given at the Annual Meeting of the British Association for the Advancement of Science, May 9, 1972.

Davis, H. Effects of high-intensity noise on naval personnel. *U.S. Armed Forces Medical Journal*, 1958, **9**.

Davis, H. Personal communication, 1967.

Davis, R. C. Electrical skin resistance before, during, and after a period of noise stimulation. *Journal of Experimental Psychology*, 1932, **15**.

Doehring, D. G., Royal Victoria Hospital, Montreal. Personal communication, 1967.

EPA (U.S. Environmental Protection Agency). Effects of noise on people. Washington, December 1971. (a).

EPA (U.S. Environmental Protection Agency). Report to the President and Congress on noise. Washington, December 1971. (b).

EPA (U.S. Environmental Protection Agency) Public Health and Welfare Criteria for Noise, Washington, July, 1973.

Etholm, B. and Egenberg, K. E. The influence of noise on some circulatory functions. *Acta Otolaryngology*, 1964, **58**.

Finkle, A. L. and Poppen, J. R. Clinical effects of noise and mechanical vibrations of a turbo-jet engine on man. *Journal of Applied Physiology*, 1948, **1**.

Jansen, G. Zur Entstehung Vegitativer Funktionsstorugen durch Larminwirkug. *Archiv. Gewerbepath. u. Gewerbehyg*, 1959, **17**.

Levi, L. Life stress and urinary excretion of adrenaline and noradrenaline. In W. Raab (Ed.), *Prevention of ischemiac heart disease*, 1966.

Mohr, G. C. *et al.* Effects of low frequency and infrasonic noise on man. *Aerospace Medicine*, 1956, **36**.

Ramsdell, D. A. The psychology of the hard-of-hearing and the deafened adult. In H. Davis and S. R. Silverman (Eds.), *Hearing and deafness*. New York: Holt, Rinehart and Winston, 1961.

Rosen, S. *et al.* Relation of hearing loss to cardiovascular disease. *Transactions of the American Academy of Ophthalmology and Otolaryngology*, 1964, **68**.

Ryan, T. A. *et al.* Muscular tension as an index of an effort: The effect of glare and other disturbances in visual work. *American Journal of Psychology*, 1950, **63**.

Sataloff, J. *Hearing loss*. Philadelphia: Lippincott, 1966.

Sataloff, J. *et al.* Temporary and permanent hearing loss. *Archives of Environmental Health*, 1965, **10**.

Shatalov, N. N. *et al.* On the state of the cardiovascular system under conditions of exposure to continuous noise. Transcript from *Gigiena Truda i Professional 'nye Zabolevaniya*, Moscow, 1962, **6**.

Smith, E. L. and Laird, D. A. The loudness of auditory stimuli which affect stomach contractions in healthy human beings. *Journal of the Acoustical Society of America*, 1930, **94**.

Strakhov, A. B. Electroencephalographic change under prolonged action of noise. Translated from *Byulletin Eksperimental'noy Biologii i Meditsiny*, 1962, **7**, OTS Report 11615.

The Sciences. Shattered sleep. *The Sciences*, May 1970, **10**.

Ward, W. D. Audition. *Psychology Review*, 1966, **65**.

# Part III Surface Transportation Noise

CHAPTER 6

# Introduction

Road traffic is the predominant source of annoyance and no other single source
is of comparable importance.—WILSON COMMITTEE (Wilson, 1963)

## THE PROBLEM

Of all present-day sources of noise, the noise from surface
transportation—above all that from road vehicles—is the most diffused.
In Europe and Japan, it is the source that creates the greatest problems.
Everywhere it is growing in intensity, spreading to areas until now
unaffected, reaching ever further into the night hours and creating as
much concern as air pollution. This is not surprising when it is realized
that road vehicles generate 20 times more power than that developed by
all other sources combined (aircraft, ships, power stations, etc.).

Physical measurements of noise, as well as psychological and sociological measurements of the resulting annoyance, well illustrate the extent of
the problem. They show that in Western Europe the extent of traffic noise
exceeds that of all other sources over the greater part of urban areas. For
example, a survey carried out in London as early as 1961–62, showed that
noise from vehicles predominated at 84 percent of the locations where
measurements were taken (London Noise, 1968).

With regard to subjective reactions, inquiries in several countries show
that road vehicles are a major cause of noise nuisance (Table 6.1) and in
some countries can be *the* major cause of noise nuisance. For instance,
surveys carried out in the United Kingdom, France, Norway, Japan and
Sweden (London Noise, 1968; OECD, 1970; SRI, 1970; IFOP, 1970) show
not only that traffic is considered to generate the most annoying kind of
noise, but that it is often one of the most serious problems that
town-dwellers must face (together with distance from place of work,
leisure, transport, housing, other kinds of pollution, etc.).

**Table 6.1**  Importance of Various Sources of Environmental Noise Annoyance: Percent of People Disturbed By a Given Source of Noise (Source: OECD, 1970).

| Origin of Noise (when at home) | United Kingdom— Disturbances Cited per 1000 People* Central London, 1962 | United States— Percent Citing Principal Source of Bother Los Angeles, Boston, New York Combined, 1967 | Norway 1968 |
|---|---|---|---|
| Road traffic | 36 | 15 | 20 |
| Children/neighbors | 25 | 14 | 6 |
| Aircraft | 9 | 5 | 4 |
| Industry/construction | 7 | 3 | — |
| Trains | 5 | 1 | 5 |
| Pets | 3 | 5 | — |
| Other | 14 | 17 | — |

*Data do not add to 100 because multiple disturbances were recorded for each individual.

**Table 6.2**  Noise Emitted by Different Types of Road Vehicle Traveling at a Constant Speed of 40–50 km/h (25–30 m.p.h.) (Measurements Carried Out at a Distance of 7.5 m) (Source: Stephenson and Vulkan, 1968).

| Vehicle Type | Mean Level (dBA) | Noise Level Range for 80 percent of Vehicles (dBA)* | Relative Sound Intensity |
|---|---|---|---|
| Automobiles | | | |
|   Car under 1100cc | 70 | 67–75 | |
|   Car 1100–1600cc | 72 | 67–75 | |
|   Car over 1600cc | 72 | 68–77 | 1 |
| Light, four-wheeled | | | |
|   commercial | 73 | 69–77 | |
| Heavy commercial | 81 | 76–86 | 10 |
| Buses (London Transport | | | |
|   Buses) | 83 | 80–85 | 16 |
| Motorcycles | 77 | 72–83 | 4 |

*These figures include neither the noisiest 10 percent nor the quietest 10 percent.

Noise from motor vehicles depends partly on the vehicles themselves and partly on traffic conditions, the surroundings and the weather. For instance, the data in Table 6.2 and similar data from other studies (e.g., RRL, 1970) show that under given urban traffic conditions:

- the noise from a heavy truck or bus is equivalent to that from 10 to 15 private cars together;
- a private car in general emits 10 dBA less than a heavy commercial vehicle or a powerful sports car;*
- acceleration can result in 10–20 dBA higher noise levels than at town cruising speed.

Thus, under normal urban traffic conditions noise peaks and sharp variations, which are the basic causes of annoyance, come primarily from two factors: the presence of heavy commercial vehicles (as well as certain motorcycles and sports cars), and the rapid acceleration due to traffic conditions (and sometimes to driver behavior).

Separate consideration of factors such as these is necessary in order to ascertain the most effective noise control strategy. That is, in order to ascertain whether control measures must be applied:

- to the source itself, that is, by reducing the noise emitted by each vehicle or by traffic;†
- to town planning and road design, that is, by modifying the way in which noise is transmitted;
- to buildings, that is, by modifying the way in which the noise is received by the occupants of dwellings.

In this Part, after a brief review in the next sections of the major sources of surface transportation noise, we shall concentrate our discussion on the prevailing source of surface transportation noise—traffic noise from motor vehicles. In doing so, we shall pay somewhat more attention to European conditions, measures and developments, because in Europe the more compact cities and towns make traffic noise a relatively more serious problem than in the United States.

## THE SOURCES OF SURFACE TRANSPORTATION NOISE

Four types of vehicles are primarily responsible for surface transportation noise: automobiles, buses or trucks, rail vehicles (both regular trains and urban subways), and motorcycles. Off-road vehicles, such as trail

---

*It is well to recall that the unit of sound measurement, the decibel, is a logarithmic unit: an increase of 3 dBA is equivalent to an increase of sound intensity by a factor of 2, an increase of 10 dBA by a factor of 10 and an increase of 20 dBA by a factor of 100.

†Although they are both methods of reducing noise at the source, a distinction must be drawn between the noise emitted by each individual vehicle and that caused by traffic—the ensemble of all vehicles on the road.

motorcycles and snowmobiles, are also becoming an important source of noise; in the future, ground effect vehicles are likely to become an additional source.

### Automobiles

Modern automobiles, particularly those of the large American type, are, in general, not very noisy. The Society of Automotive Engineers has established an acceptance standard of 88 dBA for vehicles weighing less than 6000 lb (SAE, 1968). Except for vehicles which have been specially modified to be "noisy" and for some sports cars, the modern automobile easily meets this standard.

The noise heard in a car, while moving fast, is mainly that generated by the contact of the tires with the road, for sub-audio vibration and noise are thus transmitted to the vehicle interior through the body mounts, steering controls and suspension. Most of this noise is eliminated by the use of rubber in body mounts and suspension components. This use of rubber for damping must be kept to a minimum, however, so that there will be no adverse handling effects.

In American cars, not only does tire noise affect the passenger compartment, but it is also the dominant source of roadside noise. Tire noise has a continuous spectrum over the audible range, and rough pavement tends to increase the noise in the middle-frequency ranges (100 Hz–1000 Hz) by about 12 dBA. In the high and low ranges the spectra for rough and smooth pavement overlap (Wiener, 1960).

Other problems, such as exhaust noise and noise generated by engine parts—which are the main problems of European and Japanese cars—are handled by acoustic isolation or damping of the particular part responsible for the noise; a more detailed account of these measures is given in the chapter on the technology of reducing motor vehicle noise.

In general, expensive automobiles have a lower noise level inside than economy or sports cars. This is so, however, only if the windows are kept closed. When the windows are opened, the noise level in the car will approach that of the background traffic for any type of car. Acoustic insulation in this case makes no difference (Apps, 1957a). The manufacturer, however, concentrates on reducing the noise which reaches the passenger compartment and not the noise that the vehicle projects to the outside. In a sense, this is faulty reasoning because, as we have seen, if a person is riding with the windows open, he hears the noise coming from outside the vehicle rather than directly through the vehicle wall.

A 1970 report by the California Highway Patrol gives measurements made at a distance of 15 m (50 ft),* on 9000 vehicles, each weighing less than 6000 lb (CHP, 1970). In urban surroundings, the average noise level recorded was 60 dBA when the speed was below 55 km/h (35 m.p.h.), a level equivalent to about 74 dBA at a distance of 7.5 m. Some vehicles emitted less than 63 dBA and others more than 74 dBA, equivalent to 68–80 dBA at 7.5 m.

According to an investigation of automobiles by the French Institut de Recherche des Transports (IRT, 1971), at 7.5 m with the vehicle traveling at 50 km.p.h.—a typical rate of speed in an urban area—the noise varies, depending on engine capacity and the make of car, between 65 and 75 dBA when the vehicle is cruising in third gear, and between 75 and 85 dBA when it is accelerating in second gear.

## Trucks and Buses

Diesel-powered highway vehicles add another dimension to the highway noise problem. Ignition in a diesel engine occurs at a higher pressure than in a gasoline engine and there is more noticeable airborne vibration emitted by the engine. This is particularly true for vehicles when under heavy load, on upgrades, or accelerating from a stop. Furthermore, with heavy trucks in particular, the engines are operated most of the time at full speed and maximum power—unlike passenger cars and light trucks.

The engine air intake and exhaust add considerably to the noise of a diesel engine. Investigations have shown that the noise from the engine inlet heard inside the cab can be reduced by 5 dBA by fitting the inlet with special silencers (Priede, 1967).

The reduction of diesel vehicle noise proves to be a complex problem, once the relatively simple measure is taken of providing a truck with an effective muffler—a measure that has brought down the noise of trucks emitting more than 100 dBA to about 92 dBA (Ringham, 1973). Further reduction, to the lower limits specified by a number of regulations, such as the 88 dBA limit in some states and cities in the United States, or the standard proposed by the EPA (1974b) for medium and heavy duty trucks (83 dBA at low speed in 1977, 80 dBA in 1981 and 75 dBA in 1983) is a much more difficult problem, involving very careful redesign. Even with mufflers alone, in the case of heavy trucks, there is often a problem of acceptance, and of making fleet owners, purchasing agents and drivers aware of the

---

*This distance is the general practice in the United States, whereas in Europe, measurements are usually made 7.5 m from the path followed by the vehicle.

favorable public relations to be gained from quieting the trucks. To many drivers the roar of a truck is a symbol of the "power" of their vehicle. There have been cases where holes have been punched in "quiet" mufflers in order to increase the noise level. The trucking industry could gain in public acceptance if the reputation of the large trucks for being noisy could be eliminated.

The public transit system in many cities of the world consists primarily of diesel-powered buses. In the United States alone there are approximately 120,000 miles of routes (ATA, 1966). The buses have a comparatively high noise level, particularly when accelerating from a standing start. At the start the noise level is 88 dBA, rising to 94 dBA at about 0.80 seconds after start and then dropping off almost linearly until about 4 seconds at a dBA level of 80, the peak being due to the use of a torque converter.

### Motorcycles

The motorcycle is a particularly disturbing "point source," from which not even the vehicle occupants can be shielded. Noise can be as high as 120 dBA immediately behind the cycle, particularly with racing machines; new machines range usually from 95 to 115 dBA (EPA, 1971a).

Under maximum noise conditions, the sound at 50 ft, that is, in the vicinity of homes, ranges from 77 to 88 dBA for current production models, from 90 to 95 dBA for older machines or machines with poor mufflers, and from 105 to 110 dBA for racing machines (EPA, 1971a). Other factors being equal, the noise of a motorcycle increases with engine displacement. Motor scooters have lower noise levels, but the noise spectrum has relatively more energy at the higher frequencies (1000–3000 Hz) than motorcycles (Apps, 1957b).

### Rail Vehicles

The use of rail systems—which include subway, elevated and surface rapid transit—is extensive in major cities, with more systems being developed to meet present and future urban needs. Most of the subways in operation today are particularly noisy systems which expose millions of passengers to high levels of noise. Often these high noise levels are due to the use of older equipment and outdated maintenance practices. Examination and comparison of various rail systems show that the older subways constructed in the United States tend to have the highest interior noise levels (Table 6.3). Although some noise levels have been reduced by

**Table 6.3**   Ranking of Transit Vehicle Interior Noise Levels for Operation in Subways at 30 m.p.h. (Source: Davis and Zubkoff, 1964).

| Average Sound-Pressure Level in dB | |
| --- | --- |
| Philadelphia | 98 |
| Boston | 95 |
| New York | 94 |
| Chicago | 92 |
| Madrid (Talgo)* | 92 |
| Lisbon | 91 |
| London | 87 |
| Berlin | 86 |
| Paris (rubber tire) | 86 |
| Stockholm | 86 |
| Toronto | 85 |
| Hamburg | 80 |

*Measurements taken on suburban expressway.

the introduction of new vehicles and by extensive noise-reduction treatment, as in the recent Toronto subway system (Paterson, 1956), the levels remain in general exceedingly high. The surprising element is the tolerance of the public who seem to accept the noise, or to accept it without effective protest.

The most critical operational condition in terms of noise for a transit vehicle occurs in tunnels where the noise level in the interior of the cars can increase by as much as 10 dBA (Table 6.4). At the exterior of the vehicle, noise levels are of course higher and have an impact on the large number of people at the stations as well as on a deep area along the right of way when the track is in the open.

Interior noise in a subway car is affected by the opening of doors and windows, the presence of air-conditioning, the degree of occupancy of the car, and the position in the car. According to Huss and McShane, (1973):

- the closing of an end door reduces interior noise levels at the end of a car by an average of 7 dB;
- the closing of all the windows reduces the noise level at mid car by an average of 3 dB;

**Table 6.4**    Existing Car Interior Noise Levels. (Source: Wilson, 1971. Used by Permission of the American Transit Association.)

| Car Type | Interior Noise Levels in dBA Open Track | In Tunnels |
|---|---|---|
| New York Subway | | |
| St. Louis car | 83 | 89 |
| Various cars | — | 85–90 |
| Montreal Metro | — | 83 |
| Toronto Transit Commission | | |
| (H type car) | 77–78 | 83–85 |
| Transit Expressway | | |
| (rubber tire skybus) | 70–72 | — |
| Washington Metro Car Specification | 65–69 | 75–77 |

- in an air-conditioned car the noise level is some 8 dB lower than in the same model car (an R-40 car used in the New York subways) with doors and windows open, but it is the same if the doors and windows are closed and the train is moving;
- the position inside the car makes a difference in noise levels only when doors and windows are open, in which case the noise level at the end of the car is higher by 4 dB on the average;
- an empty car (of the R-40 type) is noisier by an average of 8 dB than a crowded car.

On the other hand, the position of a car in a train seems to make little difference in the interior noise levels.

The data in Table 6.5 show how the noise in subway stations can be unbearably high. Indeed, recent data show even higher levels: as much as 109 dB in New York (Huss and McShane, 1973). A further aggravation is that the noise from the rail vehicles of a subway decreases less rapidly with distance than that of a bus—even in a relatively quiet system like that of Toronto (Fig. 1).

The primary sources of noise in rail vehicles is the interaction between the wheel and the guideway. Noise can be reduced by careful design and maintenance of both. Wheel grinding, rail grinding and rail alignment are important in this connection. Contrary to popular belief, the adoption of rubber tire systems does not necessarily reduce noise (Davis and Zubkoff, 1964; Huss and McShane, 1973). For instance, the Hamburg and the Toronto subways, both relatively very quiet, are "steel on steel" systems. In a system with rubber wheels, if braking action is to be effective when

**Table 6.5** Noise-Measurement Data in Subway Stations (Source: Davis and Zubkoff, 1964).

| Systems | Average Sound-Pressure Level, dB | | | Average Loudness Level, Phons | | |
|---|---|---|---|---|---|---|
| | Arrival | Stop | Departure | Arrival | Stop | Departure |
| Chicago | 100 | 78 | 92 | 106 | 82 | 99 |
| New York | 100 | 75 | 98 | 108 | 78 | 103 |
| Toronto | 87 | 81 | 87 | 96 | 84 | 93 |
| Berlin | 94 | 73 | 88 | 98 | 82 | 92 |
| Hamburg | 97 | 78 | 88 | 105 | 81 | 95 |
| Lisbon | 105 | 88 | 104 | 110 | 94 | 109 |
| Paris (rubber tire) | 88 | 65 | 96 | 101 | 68 | 93 |
| Paris (steel wheel) | 99 | 77 | 96 | 108 | 81 | 106 |
| Stockholm | 96 | 82 | 93 | 103 | 89 | 100 |

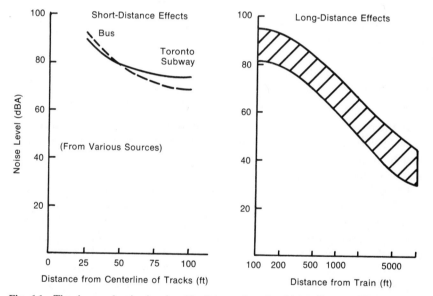

**Fig. 6.1**  The decay of noise levels with distance in rail vehicles (Source: EPA, 1971b).

the rail is wet, the treads, which are a major source of noise in a rubber tire, cannot be eliminated. On rough guideways, furthermore, considerable tire rumble is generated by the vibration of the tire carcass.

Practically no attention to noise was paid in the design of the older subway systems. The newer systems, on the other hand, have established criteria for the noise limit inside the vehicles. The usual criterion is to have noise levels that permit normal conversation at a reasonable distance—for example, 3 ft* for the Toronto subway (Murray, 1967), corresponding to a Noise Criteria Curve, NCA 60,† which is the same figure commonly used as a limit for noise inside the cabin of airliners. Outside the vehicle, at the station, somewhat higher levels may be acceptable, but the tendency in new systems is to keep the noise low. Thus, while the Toronto subway system accepts an NCA of 65, the BART system in San Francisco (BART, 1965) specifies an NCA of 60 when a train passes through a station, or stops and leaves. The criteria as to the noise acceptable away from the track vary from system to system, and according to the nature of the area.

Successful noise-control measures in the design of a subway system include (Huss and McShane, 1973):

- rubber suspensions or air springs;
- special wheels, either damped or resilient;
- damped and isolated car bodies;
- continuous welded rails;
- lubricated rails on curves;
- sound-absorbing ceilings and walls in stations;
- sound-absorbing concrete blocks between rails in stations.

In the New York subway system, a program was initiated in March 1975 to weld 39 feet sections of rail into a continuous rail over 10 miles of routes, and to provide noise arsorbing installations in more than half a dozen stations (New York Times, 1975).

Long-distance railroads are also significant noise generators. The basic components of train noise are locomotive noise, wheel noise, coupler interaction, other miscellaneous structural vibrations and refrigerator car cooling system noise (EPA, 1974a). The dominant source of noise is generally the locomotive, with a normal range of 86 to 98 dBA at 100 feet. The other sources of noise, combined, produce from 70 to 93 dBA, depending on speed. In the U.S., diesel-electric locomotives are by far the most numerous, with 27,000 in service in 1974, divided in two categories:

---

*The Manchester Rapid Transit Study suggests the general criterion that the wayside noise should not exceed the noise generated by existing road traffic—a noise that may in turn be regulated by zoning ordinances (De Leuw, 1967).

†See Appendix 1.

"switcher" locomotives (less than 1500 HP, and used primarily for yard work) and "road" locomotives (more than 1500 HP, and used primarily for long distance hauling. The same technological considerations apply to quieting engine and exhaust noise of diesel-electric locomotives, as to other internal combustion vehicles (Chapter 8). The most important component of the locomotive noise is exhaust noise. The EPA (1974a) estimates that mufflers can reduce such a noise by approximately 10 dBA, at a cost of $250 to 550 for switcher locomotives, and $1900 to 5100 for road locomotives.

Though trains are normally not a continuous source, the noise and annoyance caused by a passing train is usually greater than that caused by trucks. This problem of annoyance may be particularly acute near a railroad track where a passing freight may cause a disruption of several minutes in audio activities. In urban areas, noise levels outside residences caused by trains passing nearby have been found at times to have levels of 90–95 dB, and to reach as high as 103 dB (BBN, 1967). One passing train, measured immediately outside a home at 2:00 a.m. in Los Angeles, California, showed a noise level of 94 dB (BBN, 1967).

## REFERENCES

Apps, D. C. Recent developments in traffic noise control. *Noise Control*, September 1957. (a)

ATA (American Transit Association). Transit fact book. 1966 edition.

BART (San Francisco Bay Area Rapid Transit District). Architectural standards. June 1965.

BBN (Bolt, Beranek and Newman, Inc.). Literature survey for the F.H.A. contract on urban noise. Cambridge, Mass., January 1967.

CHP (California Highway Patrol). Passenger car noise survey. January 1970.

Davis, E. W. and Zubkoff, W. J. Comparison of noise and vibration levels in rapid transit vehicle systems. Technical Report 216, prepared for the National Capitol Transportation Agency by Operations Research, Inc., Silver Springs, Maryland, 1964.

DeLeuw, Cather and Partners. Manchester Rapid Transit Study. Prepared for the City of Manchester, England, 2 Vols, August 1967.

EPA (U.S. Environmental Protection Agency). Report to the President and Congress on noise. Washington, December 1971. (a)

EPA (U.S. Environmental Protection Agency). Transportation noise and noise from equipment powered by internal combustion engines. Washington, December 1971. (b)

EPA (U.S. Environmental Protection Agency). Proposed emission standards for interstate rail carrier noise. The Bureau of National Affairs, Washington, July 1974. (a).

EPA (U.S. Environmental Protection Agency). Transportation equipment noise controls. Proposed standards for medium and heavy duty trucks. Washington, October 1974. (b).

Huss, M. F. and McShane, W. R. Noise in transit systems. *Traffic Quarterly*, April 1973.

IFOP (Institut Francais d'Opinion Publique). Les difficultes quotidiennes des banlieusards. Survey carried out for *France-Soir*, September 21, 1970.

IRT (Institut de Recherche des Transports). Motor vehicle noise in urban traffic. Paris, 1971.

London Noise. *London noise survey.* London: HMSO, 1968.

Murray, R. J. Noise and vibration theories. Report No. 107, Subway Construction Branch, Toronto Transit Commission, Toronto, May 1967.

New York Times. Welding project begins on subway. March 30, 1975.

OECD (Organization for Economic Co-operation and Development). Urban traffic noise, strategy for an improved environment. Paris, 1970.

Paterson, W. H. and Northwood, T. D. Noise control in Toronto's new subway. *Noise Control,* September 1956.

Priede, T. Noise and vibration problems in commercial vehicles. *Journal of Sound and Vibrations,* 1967, **5**.

Ringham, R. F. The truck noise problem and what might be done about it. *Automotive Engineering,* 1973, **81** (4).

RRL (Road Research Laboratory). A review of traffic noise. Report LR 347 (U.K.), 1970.

SAE (Society of Automotive Engineers), Vehicle Noise Committee, Standard J-986, Report. Sound level for passenger cars and light trucks. 1968.

SRI (Stanford Research Institute). Noise pollution control. Report No. 418, California, 1970.

Stephenson, R. J. and Vulkan, G. H. Traffic noise. *Journal of Sound and Vibration,* 1968, **7** (2).

Wiener, F. M. Experimental study of the airborne noise generated by passenger automobile tires. *Noise Control,* July/August 1960.

Wilson. Committee on The Problem of Noise. Noise, final report. Cmnd. 2056. London: HMSO, 1963.

Wilson, P. W. Rapid transit noise and vibration. Presented at the Rail Transit Conference of the American Transit Association, April 1971.

CHAPTER 7

# Trends in Motor Vehicle Noise

## PAST DEVELOPMENTS

The previous chapter has already stressed the importance of motor vehicles as a source of noise in our society. That the problem of automobile noise is growing from year to year is illustrated by the comparisons of the results of two inquiries conducted in London—one in 1948 and one in 1962. Whereas more than half the citizens made no reference to noise in 1948, 90 percent were conscious of it in 1962; during this same period, persons annoyed by noise doubled in number, rising from 23 percent to 50 percent (OECD, 1971).

Growing urbanization, the rising number of automobiles and trucks and the quantity of traffic have had the effect of increasing noise levels generally. A survey conducted in 1967 in Norway showed that while 8 percent of the people living in rural areas were annoyed by noise, the proportion of annoyed persons increased with the size of the city (16 percent annoyed in built-up areas of 200–2000 inhabitants, 20 percent in built-up areas of 2000–20,000 inhabitants, and 27 percent in built-up areas of more than 20,000 inhabitants) (OECD, 1971).

In the United States between 1954 and 1966, noise due to traffic increased appreciably (Fig. 7.1), with an estimated mean annual increase between 0.3 and 0.7 dB (Donley, 1969). Similarly, a study in Osaka (Japan) has shown that between 1955 and 1968, mean noise levels increased by 5 dBA during daytime and by 15 dBA at night in residential areas, while in busy quarters of the city the increase was much smaller (e.g., 3–5 dBA at night) (OPG, 1970). This points to the fact that noise-level estimates must actually be qualified, since sound levels have increased substantially in

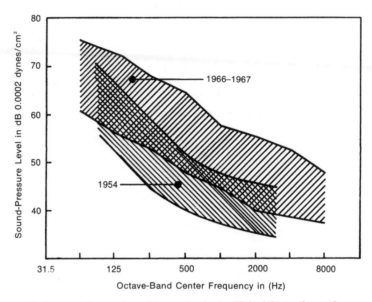

**Fig. 7.1** The increase in sample ambient noise in the United States for a 12-year period. (Source: Donley, 1969. Used by permission of *Sound and Vibration*.)

certain urban areas (particularly in suburbs) over the last ten years, but they have risen only slightly in the central core of cities, where any increase is limited by congestion. The phenomenon with regard to road traffic is therefore more one of noise extension in time and space, rather than one of noise intensification.

Quiet areas have become noisy and the traffic-free period during the night has shortened. The 1962 London enquiry showed that the duration of an average "noise night," that is, the time during which sound level is lower, was surprisingly short: only $5\frac{1}{2}$ hours (from midnight to 5:00 or 6:00 a.m.). This period of quiet began before midnight only in about 25 percent of places where measurements were made and extended beyond 6:30 a.m. only in 11 percent of cases (London Noise, 1968).

Even more disturbing, however, is the fact that measurements made in London since 1962 show that this quiet period is becoming ever shorter (Vulkan, 1968): since night traffic is steadily rising, the period of quiet is steadily diminishing. Such a trend means that ultimately the night noise levels may approach those currently recorded during the day, at least in big cities. Thus, while daytraffic is usually already so congested that there is little likelihood of any further rise in noise levels recorded during daytime traffic peaks, nighttime levels may still rise substantially, since night traffic is still far from being saturated.


## FORESEEABLE TRENDS

To predict what the levels of noise from motor vehicles will be over the next few years is, like all forecasts, a hazardous enterprise, which requires the consideration of a number of factors:

- technical evolution of motor vehicles and progress in reducing their noise;
- population and urbanization trends;
- economic trends and trends in motor vehicle ownership;
- traffic trends, particularly in urban areas;
- changes in legislation;
- changes in public attitudes toward the noise problem.

Several of these factors are very difficult to predict. Others, such as the progress in noise reduction made possible through technical evolution in motor vehicle design, are amenable to reasonable forecasts, as discussed in the next chapter. Here we shall make the assumption that in the near future noise emissions from vehicles will be similar to those of today, and we shall proceed to consider future trends in the development of traffic and of the annoyance caused by noise.

### Urbanization and Increases in Traffic

- The world motor vehicle population (private cars and commercial vehicles) rose from 100 million units in 1960 to 200 million in 1970 and is expected to exceed 300 million units by 1980. In the United States alone, 60 million units were in use in 1960; 130 million units will be in use in 1980 (OECD, 1971).
- Between 1959 and 1965 the number of metropolitan areas in the world with populations of 100,000 or more increased by 40 percent, from an estimated 1046 to an estimated 1409, and between 1951 and 1964 the percentage of world population in metropolitan areas of 1 million or more increased from 8.2 percent to 11.3 percent (from 1.5 percent in 1900) (Forstall and Jones, 1970).
- Between 1960 and 2000, the fraction of the population in urban areas of 100,000 or more is expected to increase from 60 percent to 77

percent in North America, and from 29 percent to 48 percent in Europe. The greatest growth is expected to occur in the larger areas, rather than in the smaller ones of 100,000–300,000 inhabitants (Table 7.1).

• In urban zones, the area is increasing twice as quickly as the population (OECD Observer, 1971).

• In the United States, where, as shown by Table 7.1, the urban fraction in areas over 100,000 in population is expected to reach 77 percent of the total population in 1985 and probably 90 percent by the year 2000, it is believed that urban concentration will take place primarily in 40 metropolitan areas each containing from 1 to 20 million inhabitants. By the year 2000 nearly one-half of the population of the United States will be living in 2 percent of the country's area, in spite of a decline in densities at town centers.

• While the mileage covered each year by private cars or commercial vehicles remains fairly steady, in metropolitan areas it is rising quickly. The pattern for the United States is shown in Fig. 7.2. In France traffic in concentrated residential areas is expected to rise by 55 percent between 1970 and 1985 (OECD, 1971).

From these facts and forecasts it is thus evident that all conditions are fulfilled for a substantial rise in urban motor traffic during the coming years, an increase which should be especially noticeable in metropolitan areas of small density—such as the near and distant suburbs—which are poorly served by public transport. This trend may be checked as a result of

**Table 7.1**  Projected Percentages of Population in Towns of Europe and North America (Adapted from Paix, 1971).

| Year | Over 1 Million Inhabitants | 500,000 to 1,000,000 | 300,000 to 500,000 | 100,000 to 300,000 | Total over 100,000 |
|---|---|---|---|---|---|
| *1960* | | | | | |
| North America | 34 | 9 | 6 | 11 | 60 |
| Europe | 13 | 5 | 3 | 8 | 29 |
| *1975* | | | | | |
| North America | 35 | 9 | 6 | 10 | 60 |
| Europe | 18 | 8 | 5 | 8 | 39 |
| *2000* | | | | | |
| North America | 40 | 12 | 10 | 15 | 77 |
| Europe | 20 | 12 | 7 | 9 | 48 |

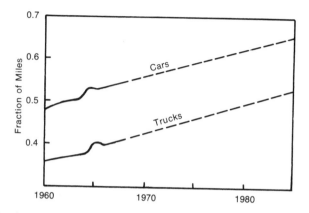

**Fig. 7.2**  Fraction of vehicle miles traveled in metropolitan areas in the United States (Source: NASA, 1970).

the current energy crisis, if motor vehicle traffic is strongly controlled and public transport vigorously supported by governments.

**The Rise in Noise Levels**

The rise in noise levels over those of the present levels can be very roughly predicted from estimates of the growth of the motor vehicle numbers, the annual mileage covered, and the average vehicle speeds in urban areas. In France, for example, such computations indicate an increase of 2–3 dBA between 1970 and 1985 (OECD, 1971).

However, in view of the fact that local conditions play a decisive role where transport and its disagreeable aspects are concerned, it is clear that estimates of this kind are of but limited value. In the saturated centers of big cities, while daytime noise is unlikely to increase much further, it will rise appreciably by night. On the other hand, in suburban areas noise will increase significantly, especially in the neighborhood of fast highways, which are increasing in number.

The more scattered the dwellings in suburban areas, the more marked will be the increase in noise. In fact, contrary to what happens in city centers, where the buildings are contiguous and rooms not opening directly onto the streets are thus protected from noise, in residential suburbs the buildings are separated from one another, thus promoting the transmission of noise to all sides of a building.

Some results of an analytical model recently developed for predicting traffic noise in the United States for different population densities (which

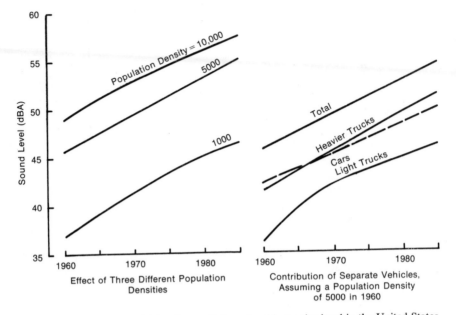

**Fig. 7.3**   Results of a model for the prediction of ambient noise level in the United States (Source: NASA, 1970). (Population density per square mile).

also, in turn, imply a certain traffic level) are shown in Fig. 7.3. While the results are valid only for the United States, they do give some idea of how ambient noise levels are likely to develop as determined by the degree of urbanization.

Two points are particularly noteworthy:

- According to these estimates average noise levels will rise by some 0.4 dBA per year.
- Although large trucks account for only 5 percent of the total number of road vehicles, they will produce a noise level equal to that of all other vehicles combined.

**The Growth in Exposure**

The NASA model also shows that in the United States the urban population exposed to average noise levels above 55 dBA will have increased by a factor of four between 1960 and 1985 (NASA, 1970).

Forecasts for the United Kingdom by the Working Group on Road

Traffic Noise (RRL, 1970) show the trend between 1970 and 1980 of urban population exposed to excessive noise levels (sound level $L_{10}$ (level exceeded 10% of the time) equal to or greater than 65 dBA), for three hypotheses: whether the noise emitted by vehicles remains unchanged, rises, or diminishes (Table 7.2).

**Table 7.2**   United Kingdom: Trends in Population Exposure to Excessive Noise Levels. (Source: RRL, 1970. Used by Permission of Road Research Laboratory.)

| Situation | Urban Population Exposed to an $L_{10}$ Equal to or Greater than 65 dBA | |
|---|---|---|
| | 1970 | 1980 |
| Vehicle noise unchanged | 21 million 46% | 29 million 30–61% |
| Increase of 5 dBA by 1975, then no further change | 21 million 46% | 45 million 93% |
| Reduction of 5 dBA by 1980 | 21 million 46% | 14 million 30% |
| Reduction of 10 dBA by 1980 | 21 million 46% | 4.3 million 9% |

If instead of peak noises ($L_{10}$) trends in mean sound levels ($L_{50}$—i.e. level exceeded 50% of the time) were considered, the increase in numbers exposed to excessive noise would be even higher, since peak noises rise less quickly than mean sound levels.

The predicted increase in vehicle numbers and in traffic is such that a reduction of 5 dBA in 10 years would not be enough to halve the number of persons exposed to excessive noise. On the other hand, a reduction of 10 dBA would have a substantial effect, since in 1980 the number of persons subjected to excessive noise would be no more than one-sixth of what it was in 1970. Forecasts of the same kind could be made for other countries and would probably yield similar results.

## REFERENCES

Donley, B. Figure from the cover. *Sound and Vibration*, 1969, **3** (2).
Forstall, R. L. and Jones, V. Selected demographic, economic, and governmental aspects of

the world's major metropolitan areas. In S. R. Miles (Ed.), *Metropolitan problems.* Toronto: Methuen, 1970.

London Noise. *London noise survey.* London: HMSO, 1968.

NASA (National Aeronautics and Space Administration). Transportation noise pollution, Control and Abatement. Langley Research Center and Old Dominion University, U.S., 1970.

OECD (Organization for Economic Co-operation and Development). Motor vehicle noise. Paris, November 1971.

OECD Observer. Urban growth in O.E.C.D. countries. *OECD Observer*, No. 54, October 1971.

OPG (Osaka Prefectural Government). Environmental pollution in Osaka prefecture. Osaka, 1970.

Paix, C. Urbanization: Statistiques et réalitiés. *Revue du Triers Monde*, No. 46, Paris, 1971.

RRL (Road Research Laboratory). A review of road traffic noise. Report No. LR 347, U.K., 1970.

Vulkan, G. H. Tackling the problems of big-city vehicle noise. *Municipal Engineering*, London, August 1968.

# CHAPTER 8

# The Technology of Reducing Motor Vehicle Noise

The ubiquity of motor vehicles as a source of noise makes it desirable to dwell in some detail on the technology for reducing their noise.*

## SOURCES OF NOISE IN MOTOR VEHICLES

The principal sources of noise in the motor vehicle are shown in Fig. 8.1. The noise depends primarily upon two groups of factors:

- *engine* speed;
- *vehicle* speed and how the vehicle is used.

Noise related to engine speed has a number of components: intake and exhaust noise, cooling-fan noise, noise emitted by the engine proper, and noise from that part of the transmission (gearbox) which rotates at engine speed. The predominant engine noise is, in general, in the frequency range of 300–4000 Hz.

The sources of noise related to road speed are that part of the transmission affected by engagement of the different gears and the rolling of the tires; at higher speeds, aerodynamic noise may be a factor. Certain operational factors, such as the load, age and general condition of the vehicle and the fuel used, also have an influence on the noise emitted.

---

*We are grateful to Professor T. Priede and his collaborators at the Institute of Sound and Vibration Research in Southampton for a review of the technology of motor vehicle noise reduction.

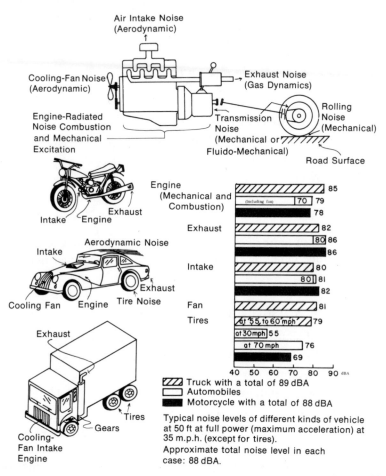

**Fig. 8.1**  Principal sources of noise in a motor vehicle (Adapted from EPA, 1971).

## Engine Speed Effects

### Intake and Exhaust Noise

If they are not silenced, exhaust and intake noises are predominant in an internal combustion engine. Intake noise is produced by the opening and the closing of the intake valves—by the high-speed airflow through the valve seat. The process sets in vibration gas columns at high pressure which communicate directly with the atmosphere.

## Fan Noise

Internal combustion engines are usually cooled by either centrifugal or axial fans. Axial fans, which are the most common, are used exclusively in water-cooled engines to draw air through the radiator, while centrifugal fans are sometimes used for air-cooled engines.

All fans produce broad-band aerodynamic noise, originating primarily from lift fluctuations on the blades due to vortex shedding at the trailing edges. Any large-scale turbulence in the flow ahead of the blades will set up additional lift fluctuations which can significantly increase the broad-band noise radiated. As a broad generalization, the intensity of fan noise increases very rapidly with the speed of the blades—for example, by 55–60 dBA when the blade tips increase in speed tenfold.*

## Engine Noise

Combustion is the primary noise source in the internal combustion engine. In diesel engines, the gas temperature in the combustion chamber after compression is sufficiently high to cause self-ignition of the injected fuel, while in gasoline engines, the gas mixture entering in a combustion chamber is ignited by an electric spark.

Engine noise is primarily determined by three parameters:

- *Engine size.* Engine noise increases faster than engine capacity— for example, by about 17.5 dBA for a tenfold increase in total cylinder capacity.
- *Engine speed.* Noise from diesel engines increases by approximately 30 dBA for a tenfold increase in engine speed, while that from gasoline engines rises by approximately 50 dBA.† The tendency of modern engines to be over square (very short strokes) to save space increases both their bore and speed, and hence their noise.
- *Engine load.* For diesel engines, the effect of load on the gas forces resulting from combustion is, in broad terms, less important than the other two effects—but this effect is substantial for gasoline engines.

The variations of sound intensity with speed and size lead to the general

---

*If $I$ is the intensity, and $N$ the speed of the blade tip, $I \propto N^{5.5 \text{ or } 6}$.

†More generally, the noise intensity $I$ is proportional to the $n$th power of the engine speed $N$ ($I \propto N^n$) with the exponent $n$ ranging from 2.7 to 3.5 for normally aspirated diesels, to 4 for turbocharged and two-stroke diesels, to 4.5 to 5 for gasoline engines and for some diesels with special combustion systems.

observation that for the same horsepower, the larger but slower engines are considerably quieter. For instance, it has been shown that a 30 litre/cylinder engine running at 500 r.p.m. and developing 600 h.p. has the same level of noise as an engine of 0.4 litre/cylinder developing only 40 h.p. at 4000 r.p.m. Yet the ratio of power is 150:1. *Thus, noise is generally independent of horsepower—the amount of work done per unit of time; the main parameter that governs engine noise is rather the operating speed,* or the shortness of the time interval within which the machine performs one cycle.

Investigations into the effect of the number of cylinders show that there are no appreciable differences in noise between four cylinders in line, six cylinders in line and a V8 arrangement for engines of the same bore running at the same speed. However, the choice of the stroke/bore ratio has an important effect: engines with a larger bore have a higher overall noise level.

### Vehicle Speed Effects

*Transmission Noise*

The source of transmission noise is not altogether clear. In most cases, the gearbox is closely coupled to the engine; therefore, it is likely to be excited by vibration forces transmitted from the engine or by vibratory forces caused by gear meshing. Levels of gearbox and rear-axle noise in trucks under ISO test conditions are of the order of 75–85 dBA in the worst cases.

*Tire Noise*

Much of the rolling noise from tires is of an aerodynamic nature—due to the compression and decompression of the air trapped between the treads as the tire rolls over the road surface. Thus, it depends both on the design of the tire—the width of the tire, the dimensions and shape of the treads, the tire pressure—and on the operational factors—the speed of the vehicle, but also the weight and load of the vehicle, and the nature of the road surface (whether smooth or rough, dry or wet). In general, tire noise is greater for trucks than for automobiles, but for a given type of vehicle increases only moderately with load. In particular, for trucks, the noise:

- increases with tire width (almost in direct proportion, other factors being equal);

- increases by about 30 dBA for a tenfold increase in vehicle speed (Waters, 1971);
- increases as the depth of grooves in the treads decreases, that is, as the tire becomes worn out;
- varies with the design of the tread. Treads with unvented or poorly vented cavities are particularly noisy. Longitudinal treads are quieter than transversal treads, which in turn are quieter than recaps (Fig. 8.2). A recap may be noisier by as much as 20 dBA than a longitudinal tread tire, and a tire with a partially worn out transversal tread by as much as 10 dBA with respect to the corresponding tire with a longitudinal tread. Randomization of tread patterns can spread pure tones in the frequency spectrum, with a concomitant reduction in community annoyance (EPA, 1974b);

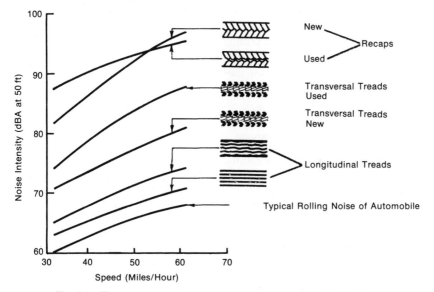

**Fig. 8.2**  The noise from tires in trucks (Adapted from NBS, 1971).

## Operational Factors

*Payload*

Both in commercial vehicles and cars a reduction of payload does not necessarily result in a reduction of noise. In most cases noise levels obtained in constant-speed drive-past tests are lower for fully loaded vehicles than with the driver alone (Waters, 1970). Traffic situations, rather than any inherent characteristic of the vehicle, are usually responsible for increases in noise when the vehicle is fully loaded. On gradients, heavily loaded vehicles tend to be in a lower gear at high engine speed than their unloaded counterparts and spend a longer time at high engine speeds when accelerating.

Vehicles deteriorate with age. Tests in Germany and Austria have shown that 3–4-year-old vehicles emit 2–3 dBA more than new ones (OECD, 1968). The maximum increase in noise due to age is 3–4 dBA both for diesel and gasoline vehicles.

## Fuel Used

The kind of fuel used does not seem to affect the noise from gasoline engines unless the octane rating is insufficient, in which case backfiring and "pinking" can occur. For diesel engines, on the other hand, the cetane rating (which varies from one country to another) has a significant effect: noise increases of 2–3 dBA can be observed if the cetane rating is low. These increases are not uniform, as some engines are more sensitive than others to the cetane rating.

## Engine Speed versus Vehicle Speed

For commercial vehicles, the influence of vehicle and engine speed can be described from measurements of the noise produced at various constant vehicle speeds. The results exemplified by Fig. 8.3 show that:

### For diesel trucks:
Noise level in different gears does not change much, in spite of considerable change in vehicle-road speed.

- If the noise levels are plotted against engine speed, they reduce almost to a single line.
- The same rate of increase of noise (11 dBA for a doubling of speed) is observed with vehicle speed at any chosen gear.
- Rolling noise, whose principal component is tire noise, is appreciably below engine noise.

### For automobiles with a gasoline engine:
- The trends are similar to those for trucks: the noise is again to a large extent controlled by the engine (although other sources such

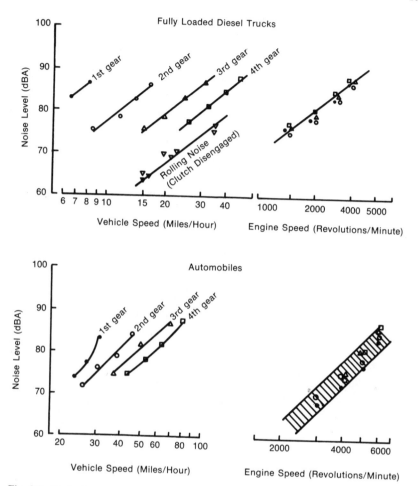

**Fig. 8.3**  Noise levels for trucks and automobiles at 7.5 m (Source: OECD, 1971).

as road and transmission contribute to a much greater extent than in the case of diesel trucks).
- Noise levels plotted against engine speed do not reduce to a single line as distinctly as those of diesel commercial vehicles.
- The rates of increase of noise with engine and road speed is substantially higher than for trucks (an increase of 15 dBA when the speed doubles and of 50 dBA for a tenfold increase in speed— versus 37 dBA for trucks).

## NOISE REDUCTION WITHOUT RADICAL CHANGES IN DESIGN

A motor vehicle is a system; the suppression of a single source of noise, such as exhaust noise, does not necessarily suffice to solve the noise problem. If a particular type of noise predominates, its suppression or reduction could well unmask other significant sources of noise. Thus, all dominant sources of noise in the vehicle must be dealt with if the total noise emitted by the vehicle is to be reduced.

The development of a new vehicle and engine costs both time and money. Some 5–7 years are needed between the design of a new model and the beginning of quantity production. The manufacturer therefore hopes that a vehicle will continue in production over a number of years without changes to the vehicle or engine that would necessitate major changes in the production plant.

Yet, as legislation on pollution and noise becomes more severe, changes in vehicle design will be impossible to avoid. Certain changes are not of a radical kind and are feasible when standards are not yet too severe, or can be adopted as interim measures before basically new models are developed. These changes include more effective control of engine noise by appropriate engine design, total engine enclosures, appropriate design of the entire vehicle, appropriate design of the intake and exhaust system, and of tires. The EPA (1974a) estimated that only 8% of the total 1975 U.S. fleet of 5.2 million motor vehicles over 10,000 lbs in weight would exceed the agency standard for interstate motor carriers, of 90 dBA (at 50 feet) at highway speeds. For the vehicles exceeding the noise standards, a modest set of "retrofitting" measures, costing on the average $135 per vehicle, would suffice to achieve compliance.

### Control of Engine Noise—The Case of the Diesel Engine

As we have seen, at moderate speeds—that is, in urban areas—the noise of both gasoline and diesel vehicles may reasonably be assumed to depend primarily on the engine speed. Since diesel engines are considerably noisier than gasoline ones, this section will concentrate on them as an example of measures that can be taken to reduce engine noise. Most considerations are also quantitatively valid for gasoline engines. To place the control of engine noise in perspective, it is useful to note at this point that the engine cost represents only 10–20 percent of the total vehicle cost. Operational factors are also important. For instance, intake noise decreases markedly with engine load—by 10–15 dBA in diesel engines, and by as much as 20–25 dBA in gasoline engines.

*Choice of Engine Design Parameters*

To reduce noise, a correct initial choice of design parameters becomes very important. For a given horsepower, a quieter engine is obtained by the choice of smaller bore, larger number of cylinders, and lower rated speed (for the same horsepower, the greater the cylinder capacity the less the noise). A design taking into account these parameters can, however, result in an increase of total engine weight for the same horsepower, but this could be offset by turbocharging.

*Control of Noise Due to Combustion*

Considerable changes can be made in a combustion system by modifying the injection arrangements—the number of sprays, the rate of injection and the injection timing.

A critical balance is needed to reduce combustion noise, since any change in injection characteristics will also result in a change in exhaust emissions and fuel consumption. Usually to retard injection in a direct-injection diesel engine effectively reduces noise but adversely affects fuel consumption and smoke emission. Similarly, as we shall discuss again later, in a gasoline engine the use of lean mixtures to reduce emission results in a more rapid cylinder pressure rise and more noise.

*Noise Reduction by Turbocharging*

The initial pressure rise in the cylinder is the determinant factor in engine noise. Thus, engine load should have no effect on noise, and engine power can be increased without corresponding increases in noise by pressure-charging, rather than by increasing cylinder bore and rated speed. Alternatively, to reduce the noise of an existing engine, the speed can be decreased, while the load is increased by turbocharging, to maintain the same power. With its higher combustion chamber temperatures resulting in a shorter ignition delay period, it is even possible that, other factors being equal, a pressure-charged engine will be nominally quieter than a normally aspirated engine.

*Cover Design*

A large area of the external surface of an engine, often as much as 60 percent, consists of casings or covers, such as the oil pump, front timing and valve gear cover. If cover noise could be completely eliminated (it can be done experimentally with lead sheet shielding) the overall engine noise can be reduced by 2–6 dBA, depending on the type of engine.

Thus, there is considerable scope for appreciable noise reduction through improved cover design. Another satisfactory method of reducing cover noise is vibration isolation, in which the main area of the cover is isolated from its fixing flange by a bonded rubber strip. This method offers considerable production difficulties and is not reliable enough at present for oil sump applications. In general, an improved cover should have a natural frequency falling outside the 300–4000 Hz range of predominant engine noise.

The cost of covers represents only a small fraction of the total engine cost (on the order of 1 percent). Therefore, even if the cost of an improved cover should increase by 100 percent or more, the total engine cost would not be affected significantly.

### Engine Shielding and Enclosure

Close-fitting shields can be used to reduce noise emitted by the basic engine casting—the cylinder block and the crankcase structure (Fig. 8.4); the resulting overall engine noise reduction can reach 2–3 dBA.

Engine noise can also be reduced by enclosing the engine—by fitting an

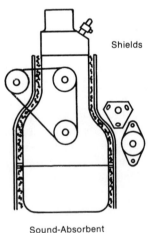

Fig. 8.4  Close-fitting shields to reduce engine noise. (Source: Grover, 1968. Used by permission of Institute of Sound and Vibration Research.)

acoustic box around it. The main difference from the close-fitting engine shields is that the enclosure is some distance from the noise-radiating surface of the engine (usually near the walls of the vehicle forming the engine compartment). Thus the enclosure has to deal with both normal and random incidence noise and is at a disadvantage with respect to the shields, which have to deal only with normal incidence noise, because of their close proximity to the noise-radiating surface of the engine. The attenuation of a panel at random incidence is generally about 10 dB less than at normal incidence. Moreover, because of the large reverberant volume, the enclosure must always be lined with absorbent material. The use of a large quantity of porous material around the engine constitutes a serious fire risk which may be reduced to some extent by the use of fire-retarding foams and perforated metal guards.

A reduction of 6–10 dBA is possible by complete enclosure with absorbent lining, as exemplified by the results in Table 8.1 which underscore the importance of the sound-absorbing material. The achievement of a wholly satisfactory design is impeded, however, by a number of factors. In addition to the fire hazard, the enclosure causes poor cooling of the engine surfaces (particularly the oil sump), difficulties in passing through controls and pipes, increases in weight (about 50 kg), poor accessibility for engine servicing, and, finally, is costly in both material and installation (between $200 and $300 for a commercial vehicle). In reality, an effective enclosure that eliminates overheating and many of the other problems can probably be achieved only through drastic changes in the configuration of the vehicle—for instance, by locating radiator and fan away from the engine.

**Table 8.1**  Noise Reduction Due to Engine Enclosure. Motor Industry Research Association (MIRA) Results for Two Trucks. (Source: Aspinall and West, 1966. Used by Permission of the Motor Industry Research Association.)

| Vehicle condition | Vehicle 1 dBA | Vehicle 2 dBA |
|---|---|---|
| Normal with additional muffler | 90.5 | 88 |
| Plus underpan (engine undertray) | 89.5 | 87 |
| Plus engine enclosure | 88.5 | 85.5 |
| Plus gearbox enclosure | — | 85 |
| Plus absorbent lining of enclosure | 80.5 | 82 |
| Radiator intake blanked off | — | 81.5 |

**Intake and Exhaust Noise**

*Intake Noise*

Intake noise can be lowered by appropriate silencers that reduce the vibrations transmitted to the air by the aspiration of the engine. The whole intake system needs to be considered—the inlet manifold, air filter, and intake silencer. The latter require space, making the problem more severe in automobiles than in trucks, because the limited space in the engine compartment demands very compact air-intake silencers.

*Exhaust Noise*

Making better exhaust systems would be neither difficult nor expensive. However, disagreement persists as to the methods for producing quieter exhaust systems (Serendipity, 1970). The methods generally used depend more on an empirical approach than on theory: every model poses a specific problem calling for a specific solution.

Exhaust noise is affected by a variety of factors and mechanisms, which demand in turn different approaches for reducing it. These approaches fall into the following basic categories: approaches concerning the engine itself, and those covering the design and positioning of the muffler.

In the first type of approach, exhaust noise can be reduced by as much as 10–15 dBA by modifying the exhaust valves (e.g., a fluted exhaust valve to divide the flow of the exhaust gas at the valve seat between a number of separate channels), or by an appropriate design of the exhaust cam (giving a very gradual initial opening so as to release the high-pressure gases through a narrow opening) (Mansfield and Nestorides, 1965).

In the approaches aimed at modifying the manifolds and the exhaust muffler, various investigations have shown that the noise emitted can be reduced by adopting additional expansion chambers or a second exhaust system, and by correct positioning of the exhaust pipe. For instance, on diesel-engined commercial vehicles, when sufficient space is available the addition of a second exhaust chamber appears to reduce noise by 3–4 dBA (Aspinall and West, 1966).

A quieter exhaust system should not lower performance (it is generally assumed that the exhaust system should not absorb more than 5 percent of the maximum effective engine power). These systems should not be allowed to deteriorate with age and use, and need to be compatible with air pollution standards and measures, such as special mufflers for reducing the emission of pollutants.

In cases where exhaust noise predominates over other sources of noise, as in sports cars and motorcycles, the design of quieter exhaust systems has the advantage of allowing fairly rapid correction, since "retrofit" replacements of the exhaust system are possible at acceptable cost for vehicles in use, whereas to replace the engine is a much more difficult task.

## General Vehicle Design

We have seen that there are substantial differences in the characteristics and sound levels of different categories of vehicles (motorcycles, automobiles, trucks, tractors, buses, etc.). However, the overall design of a vehicle is based upon functional considerations and therefore does not lend itself easily to adequate acoustic treatment.

*In automobiles*, there is a large variety of possible engine installations, but by far the most common is the front axial position. In this position, the engine is well shielded by the engine compartment, except at the front where the radiator is a weak point. Ground clearance is low.

*In buses*, the body is low and gives a small ground clearance, thus making a fairly effective screen for the engine. The engine can be installed in a variety of positions, the most common being a horizontal position between the longitudinal chassis members or a transverse position at the rear. Both these positions permit adequate shielding and enclosure. They also allow the radiator and fan to be placed at a certain distance from the engine itself.

*In many heavy trucks*, the engine is behind the cab or under it. In cases where the vehicle is of the tractor type, the rear of the engine and the gearbox protrude behind the cab and are fully exposed. In general, because of operational requirements, trucks have a high ground clearance. The engine surfaces are usually exposed between the chassis and the front wings. The radiator, which is large, is at the front of the vehicle, very close to the front engine surfaces.

In light trucks, the engine is often positioned on the centerline of the vehicle between the driver's and passenger's seats. As most light trucks are designed to operate on good roads, the body of the vehicle extends down to the normal road clearance, about 15–30 cm from the ground. Thus, the body makes a fairly effective screen for the engine. In certain cases, the front of the vehicle is well forward of the radiator and also provides a kind of screen.

In brief, therefore, in common types of heavy trucks, the vehicle walls do not shield the engine. On the other hand, in light trucks, in cars and buses, the engine noise is substantially masked. For instance, if a bus and a heavy truck of the same power are compared, the bus is found to emit 4–5 dBA less than the truck.

### Tires

Just as for exhaust silencers, the tires of vehicles in operation could be replaced by quieter ones, especially since a set of tires has to be changed several times during a vehicle's lifetime.

Since tire noise becomes predominant only at high speed, the effect of its reduction is bound to be felt more on highways than in the cities or other densely built-up areas. In urban centers, the beneficial effects of reducing tire noise will be felt only in the long run, after other sources of vehicle noise have been significantly reduced.

As we have seen, vehicle speed, type of road surface, wheel loading and tread depth, to a varying extent, all influence tire noise. For instance, noise increases as tires wear out, that is as the tread depth diminishes. Thus, frequent replacement of tires, although costly, can reduce somewhat tire noise. Also, changes in tread design can eliminate certain frequencies and harmonics.

Current efforts in tire design are concentrated primarily on designing new tires to improve safety and roadholding quality rather than to reduce noise. Tires should, of course, not be made quieter to the detriment of safety, but research is needed to find tire designs that can be both safe and less noisy.

### Motorcycles

Noise from motorcycles is a particular problem, since the inherent features of these vehicles can vary substantially according to cylinder capacity, whether they employ a two-stroke or four-stroke cycle, etc.— and since they can be variously used and converted (e.g., changes to the exhaust system) by the driver.

The noise emitted by motorcycles comes primarily from the exhaust and, to a lesser extent, from the air intake and from the engine itself, which diffuses noise in all directions. Thus, the simplest and more effective step in quieting motorcycles is to provide them with more effective silencers. Problems of space and weight arise, however, and also have an adverse effect on performance, especially in two-stroke engines. Investigations have shown that noise from a motorcycle could be reduced from an original value of 94–80 dBA by damping the crankcase and cylinder cooling fans and modifying the exhaust and air-intake systems. Acceleration was, however, then reduced, especially at low speeds, and too much space was taken up by the various altered components (Priede and Grover, 1971).

## RADICAL CHANGES IN DESIGN

If significant noise reductions of the order of 10 dBA are desired (primarily in diesel engines), they can be obtained only by radically changing the basic design of the engine. The design objective is to achieve an optimum combination of all possible parameters influencing noise— engine configuration, number of cylinders, bore, bore/stroke ratio, operating cycle, speed, degree of pressure charging, etc. Should compromises become necessary with other requirements, such as emission control or fuel economy, an engine that is designed especially for low noise characteristics has the advantage of offering, from the beginning, scope for overall improvement.

### New Designs for Conventional Engines

When intake and exhaust noise are properly suppressed, the noise from an internal combustion engine is transmitted by its basic components, such as the engine crankcase and cylinder block. Experiments carried out in the United Kingdom show that noise reductions of as much as 10 dBA can be obtained by careful design of the crankcase and the structure of the cylinder block (Priede *et al.*, 1964). Two designs are possible: either a stiff load-carrying framework with separate, highly damped outer walls, or engine walls of enormously increased stiffness, using magnesium or other light metals, so as not to increase engine weight.

Experimental engines have been designed following these criteria, to show their possibilities. They have not, however, reached the production stage because they require costly materials and are quite possibly considered by engine manufacturers to represent too drastic a departure from present designs (a consideration that may lose some of its significance with the advent of new types of engines, which require major plant changes).

More conventional materials and construction methods have been employed by the U.K. Institute of Sound and Vibration Research in a "crankframe" engine—an experimental structure of entirely new design, whose basic principles can be adapted to most engines. The crankcase walls were completely eliminated and the crankshaft was supported by a crankframe enclosed by a non-rigid, highly damped sheet metal cover. The cover also formed the oil sump, which was bolted to the lower deck of the cylinder block where the vibration levels are low. The result was a considerable reduction in noise and vibration with respect to that of a normal engine using the same basic running parts (Fig. 8.5). A British firm has shown that by incorporating the concepts of Priede and his colleagues at the Institute of Sound and Vibration Research, a production-type V8 diesel engine can be designed which would emit 4–9 dBA less than existing diesel engines of the same power (*Automobile Engineer*, 1971).

It is difficult to assess the cost of a production model of a new—but conventional—engine. Ringham (1973), in a discussion of the problem of reducing noise in trucks, states: "At International Harvester we have found it impossible to derive accurate costs on a broad base for possible future improvements in sound levels of our wide variety of products. As engineers, we would have been delighted to be able to derive and present some precise measure of cost–benefit relationship, even as simple as dBA reduction versus cost. But we found our collective judgments to be the only workable means, for now, of coming up with future projections of likely technical attainment within reasonable cost impact."*

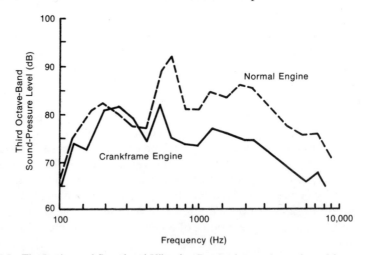

**Fig. 8.5**   The Institute of Sound and Vibration Research experimental crankframe engine. (Source: Priede *et al.*, 1964. Used by permission of the Institution of Mechanical Engineers.)

---

*Reprinted by permission. Copyright © Society of Automotive Engineers, Inc., 1973.

A study by Cummins Engine Company has shown that a 4–5 reduction in present diesel-engine noise levels can be obtained with a reasonable increase in costs (Cummins, 1971). In general, it seems that for standard diesel engines of 300 h.p., a reduction of 5–6 dBa can be achieved at a cost of approximately 5 percent of the engine cost—or of about 1 percent of the total cost of the vehicle. For reductions greater than 5 dBA, costs begin to increase significantly, (e.g., between $1200 and $1800 for a 10 dBA reduction) (Cummins, 1971), but the increase is perhaps only due to our present lack of knowledge concerning reductions of more than 5 dBA on existing engines. Because of its importance, the problem has attracted considerable government attention. For example, the German Ministry of Transport is sponsoring a broad, government-supported research program, carried out by the Association of German Engineers (VDI), for the purpose of reducing air pollution and noise from motor vehicles. This program included cost–benefit analyses and extends to psychophysiological considerations.

Similarly, in the United Kingdom, the government, including the Department of the Environment, is supporting an ambitious research program with the goal of developing a less noisy commercial vehicle—a diesel-engine truck whose total noise, under all traffic conditions, will not exceed 80 dBA (Mills, 1971). Thus, the study covers not only the engine but also the exhaust system, cooling fan, the tires and the body, as well as problems of pollution and safety. Several years are likely to pass before this program can yield any concrete results as to feasibility and cost of quantity production.

The breadth of the British program serves to stress once again that vehicle noise reductions must be considered in a *systems* context. To achieve an overall reduction of motor vehicle noise, all the major sources of noise (intake, exhaust, engine structure, fan, etc.) must be reduced together. This is the reason why the total costs of reducing noise at source may be more substantial than they would appear at first glance.

### New Designs for Unconventional Engines

It is very unlikely that the internal combustion engine will be replaced by another mode of propulsion before 1990. On the other hand, it is certainly possible that before the end of the century other kinds of engines will be developed commercially, if they prove capable of replacing the piston or the internal combustion engine to advantage.

Electric motors and steam engines (or other engines based on the

**Table 8.2**  Methods of Noise Reduction for Different Categories of Vehicle. (Source: Priede, 1971. Used by Permission of Institute of Sound and Vibration Research.)

| Origin of Noise | Principal Noise Reduction Methods | Remarks |
|---|---|---|
| **Motorcycles** | | |
| Air intake | Muffler | Little space is available |
| Exhaust | Improved muffler | Engine efficiency is reduced |
| | | Space is available |
| | | Engine efficiency is reduced |
| Vibrations of covers, valves, gearbox casing, crankcase | Damping vibrations by isolation | Procedure probably ineffective unless intake and exhaust are modified first |
| Cylinder block | Enclosure | Problems: See Table 8.3; also, vibration |
| **Cars** | | |
| Exhaust | Improved muffler | Space not necessarily a problem; muffler can be designed to fit available space |
| Air intake | Improved muffler | Space not necessarily a problem; muffler can be designed to fit available space |
| Fan | Choice of fan position to avoid obstacles; Aerodynamic model of blades, optimization of parameters for limiting blade tip speed | Shape of front of the car can be important. The same applies to grill in front of the radiator and air circulation to radiator |
| | Operation controlled by thermostat (declutchable or electric fan) | |

| | |
|---|---|
| Vibrations of engine cylinder head | If necessary, improved model, e.g., by soundproofing and isolation |
| Tires | Problem only arises at high speeds |
| Engine vibrations | Unlikely that a new engine structure (system of screens or engine enclosure) will be used on cars |
| | Engine is generally well protected by its compartment |
| | To reduce reverberation, the engine compartment can be lined with absorbing material |

Trucks and Buses*

Noise is emitted chiefly by the engine and in a subsidiary way by the exhaust, air intake, cooling fan, tires, and transmission.

| | | |
|---|---|---|
| Engine | See Table 8.3 | See Table 8.3 |
| Air intake | | |
| Exhaust | | |
| Fan | As for cars | As for cars |
| Tires | | |
| Transmission | Screens, | See Table 8.3 |
| | Enclosure, | |
| | Improvement of structure | |

*In the case of buses, the body is a better screen for the engine, and noise can be reduced by enclosure.

Stirling or Rankine principle) would be appreciably quieter than conventional internal combustion engines; on the other hand, gas turbines and rotary piston engines, such as the Wankel engine, do not seem to offer a better noise emission solution than conventional ones.

Noise is particularly minimal in an electric motor, so that the noise from an electric vehicle is virtually equivalent to its rolling noise—the noise from the tires. The use of electric motors in vehicles would thus substantially reduce noise in urban areas. However, with today's battery systems, engine performance (acceleration, speed, payload, distance traveled without refueling, maintenance record) cannot match that of internal combustion engines. Today, electric vehicles could best be used and are used in certain countries as delivery vehicles or as garbage trucks, where distances are short and a return to base is possible for battery recharging.

The Stirling and Rankine engines also produce much less noise than a conventional engine (about 20 dBA less for a Stirling engine) and therefore can offer definite noise-emission advantages.

Neither the gas turbine nor the Wankel engine seem to offer at this moment advantages over conventional engines. This is particularly distressing in the case of the gas turbine, because they are already being used experimentally on some heavy trucks—the vehicles for which engine noise is the most important component of noise.

Noise from a gas turbine engine is less uneven and comprises less pulses than a piston internal combustion engine. Since the gas turbine is designed to operate at high speed, its idling speed is high, thus at traffic lights, for instance, the noise from a stationary vehicle with a gas turbine engine is louder than that with a conventional one. In general, noise from a turbine-driven truck corresponds roughly to the limits currently imposed by some countries; considerable efforts need to be made to reduce inlet and exhaust noise if the gas turbine is to become less noisy.

## NOISE, SAFETY, AND AIR POLLUTION

In certain cases noise abatement requirements will conflict with pollution control or safety requirements. Thus, a less noisy vehicle might turn out to be more air polluting, or less safe, or vice versa. For example, in direct-injection diesel engines, where the combustion chamber is in the piston crown, if the engine timing is advanced to reduce smoke emission, noise increases, typically by some 3 dBA. On the other hand, with an indirect-injection diesel, where the fuel is injected in a pre-combustion

**Table 8.3**  Cost and Technical Problems of Reducing Engine Noise (Source: OECD, 1971).

| Method of Reduction | Reduction in dBA | Cost | Remarks |
| --- | --- | --- | --- |
| Combustion | 2–3 | None | Possible effects on emissions and operating economies |
| Pressure-charging by turbocharger | 2–3 | Cost of turbocompressor assembly | Difficulties at present with emissions. Advantage of increased power. For a given power, the rated speed can be reduced, leading to additional noise reduction |
| More effective covers | 2–5 on poor initial designs | Possible increase in cost of covers by 100% and more (1–2% of the total engine cost) | Research needed on suitable cover designs (development of highly damped sandwich materials and anti-vibration isolation techniques). |
| Screens | 2–3 | About 2% of total cost of engine | Considerable research needed, particularly on suitable materials and mounting methods |
| Enclosure | Up to 10 | Up to 3% of total cost of vehicle | Numerous side problems: fire risk, accessibility, weight, difficulties of maintenance, cooling, etc. Particularly suitable for buses |
| Change in operating parameters (e.g., for long to short stroke) | Depends on parameter (e.g., 6 dBA possible by change in stroke for same engine power) | Not necessarily increased | Characteristics must be brought into the initial design. Allowance must be made for: weight, size, torque, etc. |
| Structure | Up to 10 dBA possible | Impossible to estimate accurately (some present-day assessments indicate cost increases of more than $1000 per engine) | Requires substantial research and development. Same remarks as for screens and enclosures |

chamber, noise can be reduced by retarding the injection timing, with no increase in smoke emission.* Similarly, radial ply tires, which are increasingly in use because of their roadholding qualities, are somewhat noisier than others on stone-paved roads and on roads made of concrete slabs. However, there is no necessary conflict between the safety and tire noise, because tire noise does not seem to increase as adherence increases (even if it varies with tread design); on the contrary, as treads wear out, noise increases and adherence decreases.

In any case, research is necessary to produce engines that are both quieter and less air polluting, and to produce tires that are both quieter and safe. At this moment tire manufacturers are pre-occupied primarily with increasing safety, and car manufacturers do not have enough information concerning the effect of several anti-air pollution measures on noise (even if it is unlikely that such measures will prove incompatible with noise reduction).

## SUMMARY OF APPROACHES FOR REDUCING MOTOR VEHICLE NOISE AT THE SOURCE

By way of an overview, the principal methods which appear feasible for reducing the noise of motor vehicles at the source are summarized in Tables 8.2 and 8.3, both for the various sources of noise and for the various basic processes that can be used to reduce noise.

## REFERENCES

Aspinall, D. T. and West, J. The reduction of the external noise of commercial vehicles by engine enclosure. Motor Industry Research Associated, U.K., Report No. 1966/17, 1966.

Automobile Engineer. October 1971.

Cummins Engine Company. Diesel-powered system noise. Report presented to EPA, Noise Abatement Hearings, November 1971.

EPA (U.S. Environmental Protection Agency). Transportation noise and noise from equipment powered by internal combustion engines. Washington, December 1971.

EPA (U.S. Environmental Protection Agency). Motor carriers engaged in interstate commerce. Noise emission standards. Washington, October 1974. (a).

EPA (U.S. Environmental Protection Agency). Transportation equipment noise controls. Proposed standards for medium and heavy duty trucks. Washington, October 1974. (b).

---

*An indirect-injection diesel is generally more noisy than a direct-injection one, however, and is economically convenient, in general, only for smaller engine displacement (individual cylinder displacement of less than one liter).

Grover, E. C. Control of road noise by engine design. Institute of Sound and Vibration Research, Southampton, U.K., 1968.

Mansfield, W. P. and Nestorides, E. J. Recent development in engine noise reduction. Diesel Engineers Users Association, U.K., 1965.

Mills, C. H. G. The measurement and control of road transport noise. Paper given at the meeting of the Institution of Mechanical Engineers, London, November 1971.

NBS (National Bureau of Standards). Interim progress report of research activity, truck tire investigation. Report No. 10567, Washington, 1971.

OECD (Organization for Economic Co-operation and Development). Urban traffic noise, status of research and legislation in different countries. January 1968.

OECD (Organization for Economic Co-operation and Development). Motor vehicle noise. Paris, November 1971.

Priede, T. Institute of Sound and Vibration Research, Southampton, 1971.

Priede, T. and Grover, E. C. Private communications to A. Alexandre, 1971.

Priede, T. et al. Effect of engine structure on noise of diesel engines. In *Proceedings*, Institution of Mechanical Engineers, 1964, **179** (4), Part 2A.

Ringham, R. F. The truck noise problem and what might be done about it. *Automotive Engineering*, 1973, **81** (4).

Serendipity, Inc., Arlington, Va. *A study of the magnitude of transportation noise generation and potential abatement*, Volume IV, 1970.

Waters, P. E. The control of road noise by vehicle operation. *Journal of Sound and Vibration*, 1970.

Waters, P. E. Some aspects of commercial vehicle noise reduction. Paper given at the Institution of Mechanical Engineers' Symposium, U.K., July 1971.

CHAPTER 9

# Noise Emission Standards

## PRESENT LEGISLATION

Many countries have adopted regulations to control maximum permissible noise levels for the different categories of motor vehicles—Canada, Denmark, France, Italy, Japan, Netherlands, Norway, Sweden, Switzerland, and the United Kingdom all have legislation to this effect.* In the United States the Noise Control Act of 1972 (see Part VI on the Political Economy of Noise), gives the Environmental Protection Agency (EPA) broad authority to establish noise levels for motors and vehicles, among other sources of noise. In October 1974 the EPA (1974b) issued noise emission standards for interstate trucks and buses weighing over 10,000 lb (the sound level to be measured, as usual, at 50 ft from the centerline of the lane of travel). The sound level is not to exceed 90 dBA on highways with speed limits of more than 35 m.p.h., and 86 dBA on highways with speed limits of 35 m.p.h. or less. Compliance with the regulation would affect some 70,000 vehicles† at a cost of $10 million, and require the noisiest diesel to be reduced by 5–10 dBA. (A reduction of 10 dBA would, as we have seen, reduce to half the noise as perceived by our ears.) More efficient

---

*The legislation is described in Annex 1 of the OECD report "Urban Traffic Noise," (OECD, 1970). The Annex shows in particular how the regulations are enforced, whether in connection with new vehicles and their official approval, or with vehicles already in use. Noise is measured in checking stations at the time of the compulsory regular inspections instituted in certain countries, or by means of spot checks designed for detecting excessively noisy vehicles, etc.

†Out of a total fleet of one million vehicles over 10,000 lbs engaged in interstate commerce.

mufflers and the elimination of certain tire treads are the chief means for achieving this reduction.

In 1974 the EPA (1974c) also issued proposed standards for all medium and heavy duty trucks (over 10,000 lbs in weight).* A low speed standard was proposed of 83 dBA for all trucks produced after January 1977, 80 dBA for those after January 1981, and 75 dBA for the trucks produced after January 1983. The corresponding total increases in capital costs for the users (truck purchasing industries) were estimated at $34 million in 1977 for 83 dBA, $117 million in 1981 for 80 dBA and $294 million (but probable less) in 1983 for 75 dBA. These costs are based on the following individual cost projections:

- 83 DBA level: gasoline truck, $0; medium diesel, $105; heavy diesel, $195
- 80 dBA level: $125, $265 and $490 respectively
- 75 dBA level: $300, $1120 and $1130 respectively.

Action has also occurred at the international level. Thus, in 1968 the United Nations Economic Commission for Europe adopted uniform provisions concerning the approval of vehicles with regard to maximum permissible noise limits (Table 9.1).

The Council of the European Communities (Common Market) laid down a directive in 1970, to harmonize the legislation of member states regarding acceptable noise levels (Table 9.2). The member states to which the directive applies (Belgium, Denmark, France, Germany, Ireland, Italy, Luxembourg, the Netherlands and the U.K.) agreed to bring the necessary national provisions into effect within 18 months from the date of notification (September 1971).

## CURRENT TRENDS

Methods of noise measurement need to be suitable for the different driving conditions encountered in urban areas and for different types of vehicles (automatic transmission vehicles, for example). Some countries would prefer a method in which noise is measured on stationary vehicles so as to speed up and simplify periodic checks. Others prefer that current regulations, which take into account only noise emitted during maximum

---

*In 1972 the U.S. medium and heavy truck population (EPA, 1974c) was 3.5 million, of which 67% were medium trucks (98% gasoline, 2% diesel) and 33% heavy duty trucks (44% gasoline, 56% diesel).

**Table 9.1**   United Nations Economic Commission for Europe: Maximum Limits of Sound Level for New Vehicles (1968) (Source: OECD, 1970).

| Category of Vehicle | Maximum Noise Level (dBA)* |
|---|---|
| Two-wheeled motor vehicles | |
| Two-stroke engine: | |
| Between 50 and 125 cm$^3$ | 82 |
| Over 125 cm$^3$ | 84 |
| Four-stroke engine: | |
| Between 50 and 125 cm$^3$ | 82 |
| Between 125 and 500 cm$^3$ | 84 |
| Over 500 cm$^3$ | 86 |
| Three-wheeled motor vehicles (except public works vehicles, etc.) | |
| Over 50 cm$^3$ | 85 |
| Motor vehicles with four or more wheels (except public works vehicles, etc.) | |
| *Private automobiles and their conversions* | 84 |
| Trucks: | |
| Not exceeding 3.5 tons | 85 |
| Between 3.5 and 12 tons | 89 |
| Over 12 tons—with an engine of 200 h.p. DIN or less | 89 |
| —with an engine of more than 200 h.p. | 92 |
| Buses: | |
| Less than 3.5 tons maximum weight | 85 |
| Over 3.5 tons—with an engine of 200 h.p. DIN or less | 89 |
| —with an engine of more than 200 h.p. DIN | 92 |

*Maximum noise possible under normal town driving conditions, that is, during acceleration at full throttle in an intermediate gear, starting from an engine speed corresponding approximately to the speed of maximum torque (the initial speed before acceleration being limited to 50 km.p.h.) along a line at 7.5 m from the microphone (ISO measurement procedure).

acceleration, be supplemented by measurements of the noise emitted at cruising speed, so that annoyance due to the noise of traffic on highways and urban expressways can be better allowed for.

It might prove interesting to develop a standard cycle of noise emission

**Table 9.2**    Council of the European Communities (Common Market): Maximum Permissible Noise Levels for New Vehicles (Source: OECD, 1970).

| Class of Vehicle | Acceptable Noise Levels (dBA)* |
|---|---|
| Passenger vehicles with seating capacity of no more than 9 persons (including the driver) | 82 |
| Passenger vehicles with seating capacity of more than 9 persons (including the driver) and maximum permissible weight less than 3.5 tons | 84 |
| Trucks with maximum permissible weight less than 3.5 tons | 84 |
| Passenger vehicles with seating capacity of more than 9 persons (including the driver) and a maximum permissible weight more than 3.5 tons | 89 |
| Trucks with a maximum permissible weight more than 3.5 tons | 89 |
| Passenger vehicles with seating capacity of more than 9 persons (including the driver) and engine of 200 h.p. DIN or over | 91 |
| Trucks with an engine of 200 h.p. DIN or over and maximum permissible weight of over 12 tons | 91 |

*Measurement procedure as in Table 9.2.
(To allow for uncertainties in the measuring instruments, the result of each measurement made at a distance of 7.5 m is the instrument reading less 1 dBA.)

by motor vehicles in urban areas, similar to that developed for air pollution. The practice of measuring in dBA (which emphasizes the medium and high frequencies) could well permit an increase of noise in the low frequencies, which would lead to very serious problems for town planners and architects since low frequencies are extremely difficult to attenuate. Some suggestions have thus been made that sound-pressure levels throughout the frequency spectrum be covered.

Regarding the future lowering of noise limits, the United Kingdom plans to lower noise standards gradually to 75 dBA for private cars and to 80 dBA for commercial vehicles (RRL, 1970). However, as recognized in the recommendations, it will be particularly difficult to attain such standards for commercial vehicles; several years of research will be necessary before engines and vehicles are designed to meet these standards. Therefore, it is hardly likely that the entire fleet of commercial vehicles will be replaced by less noisy ones before 1985.

In the United States, bills have been introduced in certain states and various cities. For instance, in Chicago an ordinance concerning maximum permissible noise levels was formally adopted on March 10, 1971 by the Municipal Council, and came into force on July 1, 1971 (Chicago, 1971). The ordinance prescribes that by 1980 every new vehicle—whether motorcycle, heavy truck, or private car—should emit no more than 75 dBA when measured at a distance of 50 ft (equivalent to 80 dBA at 7.5 m, the measurement distance adopted in Europe). The details and timetable of these restrictions are given in Table 9.4.

According to both the U.K. proposal and the Chicago ordinance:

• noise from the noisiest vehicles (motorcycles and heavy trucks) would be reduced more quickly and to a greater extent than that from automobiles, in order to eliminate peaks emerging from the background noise;

• in the long term, noise from every vehicle would be reduced by at least 10 dB so as to at least halve the peak noise level and significantly reduce the average noise level from traffic.

Unfortunately, however desirable, reductions of this kind may be very difficult to obtain because of their great economic and social impact. For instance, results from measurements recently carried out in France show

**Table 9.3** United Kingdom: Noise Standards in Force (1970) (Source: OECD, 1970).

| Class of Vehicle | 1970 Limits (dBA) |
|---|---|
| Motorcycles | |
| Not more than 50 cc | 77 |
| More than 50 cc but not more than 125 cc | 82 |
| More than 125 cc but not more than 500 cc | 86 |
| More than 500 cc | 86 |
| Passenger cars | 84 |
| Light goods vehicle not less than 3.5 tons gross weight | 85 |
| Motor tractor not more than 1.5 tons | 89 |
| Heavy vehicles | |
| Of not more than 200 h.p. | 89 |
| Of more than 200 h.p. | 92 |

that if the current standards were reduced by 2 dBA, one-fourth of all private cars and one-third of all heavy trucks would be refused certification. Undoubtedly, this would affect more the poorer owners of vehicles who would find themselves deprived of the possibility of using a means of conveyance that has unfortunately become practically indispensable in our society.

**Table 9.4**  Chicago Ordinance for Noise Emission from Vehicles (Adapted from Chicago, 1971).

| Date of Construction | Maximum Limit in dBA (at 50 ft) |
|---|---|
| Motorcycles | |
| Before January 1, 1970 | 92 |
| After January 1, 1970 | 88 |
| After January 1, 1973 | 86 |
| After January 1, 1975 | 84 |
| After January 1, 1980 | 75 |
| Vehicles heavier than 8000 lb | |
| After January 1, 1968 | 88 |
| After January 1, 1973 | 86 |
| After January 1, 1975 | 84 |
| After January 1, 1980 | 75 |
| Private cars and other motor vehicles | |
| Before January 1, 1973 | 86 |
| After January 1, 1973 | 84 |
| After January 1, 1975 | 80 |
| After January 1, 1980 | 75 |

## RAIL VEHICLES

Noise standards for rail vehicles have received much less attention than standards for road vehicles. However in 1974 the EPA (1974a) proposed a set of standards for such vehicles, expressed in terms of measurements of 100 feet from the centerline of the track.

*For locomotives*, effective 270 days from the issuance of the standards, the noise should not exceed 93 dBA under stationary conditions (and 73 dBA when idling), and 96 dBA under moving conditions, regardless of grade, acceleration or deceleration. Effective 4 years from the date of issuance, the noise should not exceed 87 dBA under stationary conditions (67 dBA when idling) and 90 dBA under moving conditions.

*For railroad cars*, effective 270 days from the date of issuance of the standards, the noise is not to exceed 88 dBA at speeds up to 45 m.p.h. and 93 dBA at higher speeds.

The total net cost to the railroad industry for compliance with the proposed noise emission standards is estimated at 83 to 103 million dollars.

## REFERENCES

Chicago new noise regulation. Department of Environmental Control, Chicago, 1971.

EPA (U.S. Environmental Protection Agency). Proposed emission standards for interstate rail carrier noise. The Bureau of National Affairs. Washington, July 1974. (a).

EPA (U.S. Environmental Protection Agency). Motor carriers engaged in interstate commerce. Noise emission standards. Washington, October 1974. (b).

EPA (U.S. Environmental Protection Agency). Transportation equipment noise controls. Proposed standards for medium and heavy duty trucks. Washington, October 1974. (c).

OECD (Organization for Economic Co-operation and Development). Urban traffic noise. Paris, 1970.

RRL (Road Research Laboratory). A review of road traffic noise. Report No. LR 347, U.K., 1970.

# CHAPTER 10

# The Characteristics and Impact of Surface Transportation Noise

In the previous chapters, we have looked briefly at the nature of the noise in surface transportation vehicles in terms of the characteristics of the vehicle and its interaction with road or rail, as well as the approaches to the design of the vehicle for noise reduction. In this chapter and in the next, we look at surface transportation noise in the aggregate—as it reaches those exposed to it through the operation of a transportation system—that is, through the combined effect of many vehicles of different characteristics—as in traffic—or through the operation of a rail system.

It is useful to note from the outset that a person may be exposed to several types of surface transportation noise, either as a vehicle occupant or outside of a vehicle. As a vehicle occupant, he may not be too annoyed by the noise no matter what type of transportation he is using, because he is "part" of the traffic flow and thus expects and tolerates a higher noise level (however, a driver can become very annoyed when forced to ride immediately behind or alongside a bus or large truck). Outside a vehicle, a person is exposed to surface transportation noise on sidewalks, in residences, in places of business, and here the exposure to noise has no compensating utility.

Nearly all of the urban and suburban population is exposed to surface transportation noise, both as vehicle occupant and as bystander, and increasingly the rural population is becoming similarly exposed—so that in a modern developed country almost no one escapes. An extremely rough estimate of the total U.S. population thus affected indicates that as

131

many as three-fourths of the entire population may be exposed to annoying levels of surface transportation noise (Bugliarello and Wakstein, 1968).*

## CHARACTERISTICS OF TRAFFIC NOISE

Of all the kinds of surface transportation noise, traffic noise, as we have noted, is the most ubiquitous. It is also intrinsically discontinuous: as a vehicle approaches an observation point, the noise level rises, reaches a maximum (peak) level and then decreases as the vehicle moves away. However, a steady flow of traffic (e.g., average or dense traffic conditions) generates an almost constant road noise, from which only the noise emitted by certain vehicles (such as trucks and motorcycles) consequently stands out. Thus, traffic noise is caused by a number of vehicles of different characteristics moving together under variable conditions.

Noise levels recorded in London during a 1961 investigation showed that already at that time traffic noise predominated in 84 percent of the locations examined (Wilson, 1963). The noise levels measured varied

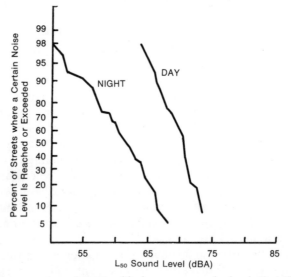

**Fig. 10.1**   Paris: percentage of streets with given average noise levels ($L_{50}$) (Source: CSTB, 1971).

---

*The estimate was developed by extrapolating from figures of a Bolt, Beranek and Newman study of residential areas in Boston (BBN, 1967).

**Table 10.1**  London: Range of Noise Levels at Locations in Which Traffic Noise Predominates. (Source: Wilson, 1963. Used by Permission.)

| Group | Location | Noise Climate (in dBA)* Day (8 a.m.–6 p.m.) | Night (1 a.m.–6 p.m.) |
|-------|----------|------|-------|
| A | Curb of arterial roads with many heavy vehicles and buses | 80–68 | 70–50 |
| B | Major roads with heavy traffic and buses<br>Side roads within 15–20 yd of roads in groups A or B1 above | 75–63 | 61–49 |
| C† | Main residential roads<br>Side roads within 20–50 yd of heavy traffic routes<br>Courtyard of apartment houses screened from direct view of heavy traffic | 70–60 | 55–44 |
| D | Residential roads with local traffic only | 65–56 | 53–45 |
| E | Minor roads<br>Gardens of houses with traffic routes more than 100 yd distant | 60–51 | 49–45 |
| F | Parks, courtyards, gardens in residential areas well away from traffic routes | 55–50 | 46–41 |
| G | Places of few local noises and only very distant traffic noise | 50–47 | 43–40 |

*Range of noise level recorded for 80 percent of the time. For 10 percent of the time the noise was louder than the upper figure of the range and in the case of Group A attained peak levels of about 90 dBA; for 10 percent of the time the noise was less than the lower figure in the range.

†In Groups C–F, noise from other sources, such as trains or children's voices, predominated over road-traffic noise at particular times, but traffic was the most frequent noise source.

enormously according to location, type of street, density of traffic, and time of day (Table 10.1).

A more recent Paris survey indicated that average noise levels (noise levels exceeded 50 percent of the time—$L_{50}$) of 65 dBA or higher were registered during daytime in front of 60 percent of the buildings surveyed (Fig. 10.1). At night the noise was found to be particularly variable from one location to another, with a 15 dBA difference between the 5 percent noisiest and 5 percent quietest streets.

Some noise levels measured in Tokyo are shown in Fig. 10.2, while Fig. 10.3 is a summary of noise exposures in many cities in the United States. Both figures concur with the British survey in indicating the great variation in noise levels depending upon location and traffic conditions.

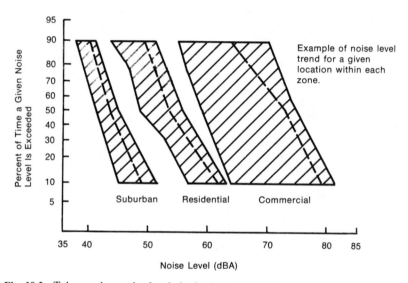

**Fig. 10.2**    Tokyo: urban noise levels in daytime, 1966 (Adapted from Schultz, 1970).

## FACTORS INFLUENCING TRAFFIC NOISE

Unlike the noise emitted by a single vehicle which depends solely upon the vehicle's own characteristics and on the tire-road contact, traffic noise, in addition to the characteristics of the different kinds of vehicle involved, depends also upon a number of parameters independent of the vehicle:

- *Traffic parameters*
  - Speed and density.
  - Composition.
  - Traffic "fluidity" (traffic lights, one-way streets, etc.)
  - Driver behavior.

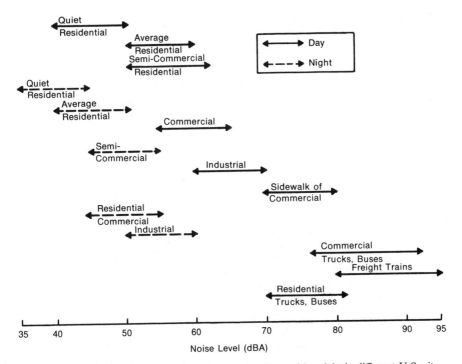

**Fig. 10.3** Summary of existing noise exposures by day and by night in different U.S. city areas (Adapted from Schultz, 1970).

- *Road parameters*
  - Road design (tunnels, cuts, embankments, or on a level).
  - Gradients and degree of curvature.
  - Nature of road surface.
  - Width.

- *Environmental parameters*
  - Distance and height from the road of the recipient of noise.
  - Presence of natural or artificial screens.
  - Condition of ground between the road and point of reception (noise absorption).
  - Reflection of noise from buildings along the road.

- *Weather parameters*
  - Rain, snow, or dry conditions.
  - Wind direction and speed.

- *Dwelling parameters*
  - Orientation of living areas.
  - Attenuation of noise through windows.
  - Size of windows.

These parameters are not all of equal importance: some affect the observed noise significantly and deserve to be reviewed in some detail. Others affect noise only negligibly.

### Traffic

The average noise levels (level exceeded 50 percent of the time—$L_{50}$) emitted by traffic flows of more than 50 vehicles per hour, rise by 3–5 dBA whenever the traffic speed is doubled, and by 4–6 dBA whenever the speed is doubled over 24.6 m.p.h. The peak levels increase at a greater rate with increased traffic flow, but the reduction due to distance becomes more pronounced (see the section below on "Surrounding Areas").

As can be expected, the average sound level also rises with the number of vehicles.* Increases in traffic density are indeed a leading factor contributing to higher noise levels. The combined effects of speed and traffic density are exemplified by Fig. 10.4, which shows the results of a computer model for estimating the traffic noise from a lane† (or single-lane equivalent) of passenger car traffic. (The model has, however, some limitations as it assumes that the traffic flows freely with constant speed, uniform spacing between vehicles and constant power, that is, no hill climbing.)

Under normal urban conditions, that is, excluding high-speed highways, the composition of the traffic assumes special importance, as shown in Fig. 10.5. The noise level is particularly affected by the proportion of heavy trucks, while the effect of buses is less pronounced, as shown by the data in Table 10.2. The increase due to trucks also becomes more marked on a gradient. These facts are hardly surprising when it is remembered that an average heavy truck is 10 dBA noisier than a private car.

On superhighways, on the other hand, the noise difference between

---

*Sound level increases approximately as $10 \log N$ (where $N$ is the number of vehicles) on highways and as $K \log N$ (where $K$ is coefficient between 10 and 20) in ordinary streets.

†In the case of multiple-lane roadway, the total traffic density of all the lanes is assumed to be concentrated in a "pseudolane," whose distance from the actual lane nearest to the observer increases with the number of lanes.

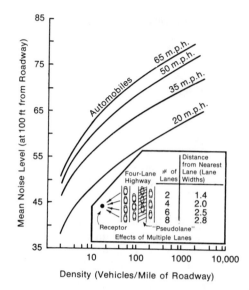

**Fig. 10.4**  Estimated mean noise level at 100-ft distance from a lane (or single-lane equivalent) of automobile traffic. (Adapted from NCHRP, 1969. Used by permission.)

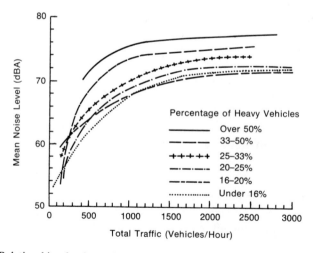

**Fig. 10.5**  Relationship of noise and traffic composition on urban roads (Source: Stephenson, 1967).

**Table 10.2**   The Different Influence of the Addition of Trucks or Buses to Vehicle Mix (Source: IDA, 1972).

| Percentage of Trucks in Traffic | Percentage of Buses in Traffic | Additional Noise (dBA) |
|:---:|:---:|:---:|
| 0 | 0 | 0 |
| 2.5 | 12 | 1 |
| 5 | 25 | 2 |
| 10 | not considered | 4 |
| 20 | not considered | 8 |

heavy trucks and automobiles tends to be less marked. This indicates that speed has a greater effect on noise from private cars than from heavy trucks. In other words, noise generated by intense traffic on high-speed roads is little influenced by the proportion of heavy trucks and is relatively constant, whereas noise generated in a city street fluctuates and comprises sound peaks in proportion to the number of heavy trucks traveling on it.

Discontinuous traffic—traffic involving frequent stops and starts—causes higher peaks, but is apt to lower the average noise level. Traffic that is continuous but very slow gives a low average level with relatively small peaks. Traffic which flows steadily at high speeds gives the highest average levels.

Noise is affected not only by the absolute speed of traffic, but also by variations in this speed, and these are especially noticeable at intersections. When vehicles approach a red light, they slow down and the noise diminishes. When the light changes to green, they accelerate, generating a sharp rise in noise of 15–20 dBA. After the acceleration stage, but while the traffic light system is still in the green phase and the flow resumes, the sound level falls by about 5 dBA (OECD, 1971).

## The Road

The second set of parameters influencing the traffic noise level concerns the road itself. Noise is propagated differently according to whether the road is built at the level of adjacent land, on an embankment, in a cut, or in a tunnel.

A tunnel is obviously the best from the viewpoint of reducing noise propagation, since noise is no longer transmitted to the surrounding area.

Road tunnels are, however, rare, because of construction difficulties and cost.

Roads placed in cuts with vertical walls or sloping banks show strong noise reduction, especially in attenuating frequencies above 500 Hz, provided dwellings are located sufficiently far away. However, in a dense urban area, where buildings are close to the road, a road in either type of cut would yield hardly any reduction of the noise level in dwellings. Thus, cuts are only suitable for urban expressways, with only low buildings built nearby.

Certain road surfaces—especially stone paving (pavé) typical of the streets of some European cities—play a significant role in generating noise. According to certain estimates, stone-paved surfaces can increase noise by 6–8 dBA, at least when the vehicles move at steady high speeds (Burt, 1969).

The gradient and width of the road also influence the noise level. A narrow street lined with high buildings is a veritable "noise canyon" where, if all other factors remain unchanged, the noise can be up to 6 dBA higher than in an open space. Finally, in a street with a steep gradient, the noise can be 6 dBA higher, owing primarily to heavy trucks climbing the hill (RRL, 1970).

## The Surrounding Areas

When considering the area adjacent to the road, the main parameters are the distance between the source of noise and the observation point, the latter's elevation, whether screens are present between it and the road, and finally the various absorption and reflection characteristics of the ground and neighboring buildings.

The closer the observer is to the road, the better he can perceive noise peaks against the background noise; the farther he moves away the less the peaks will stand out from the background. Each time the distance from the road is doubled, the noise peaks are reduced by 7–8 dBA and the average sound level ($L_{50}$) by 5 dBA (Lamure, 1972). Therefore, in an urban area, where the buildings are close to the road and where the discontinuous nature of traffic requires a large number of accelerations, the sound peaks become especially annoying.

The height from which the noise is perceived seems to play but a very minor role in an urban area. This is because, although the observer is higher up and away from the sound source, noise is heard from a larger area. In the case of buildings at some distance from a high-speed road with grass borders, the lower floors may even prove quieter than the upper floors as a result of the absorption effect of the ground. These variations in noise intensity, however, tend to diminish with height.

The other leading parameters concerning the road surroundings are natural or artificial screens. Natural screens along roads usually consist of rows of trees, which reduce noise to a negligible extent. Significant attenuation is provided only by dense and deep plantings which are difficult to achieve in urban areas.

In the case of artificial screens, estimates vary as to how much they reduce noise. Experiments in Germany with 16 different types of shield for attenuating traffic noise have shown sound reductions varying between 15 and 26 dBA, depending on the system used (Rüker and Glück, 1966). In France, simulations of the acoustic effectiveness of various arrangements of screens on a one-twentieth scale model showed that in every case, the attenuation of the average sound level by screens was limited to 15–20 dBA (Josse *et al.*, 1969). Further, the acoustic attenuation provided by a screen depends on the distance and especially the height from which the noise is heard. In any event screens appear to be of real value only along urban roadways or country highways. If they are put up in ordinary streets not only do aesthetic, safety and other problems arise, but the screens must be very high to prevent sound waves from reaching the upper floors of buildings bordering the roads.

**Weather Conditions**

Rain can significantly increase the noise emitted by a single vehicle; increases as high as 10 dBA have been observed (Priede and Grover, 1971). On the other hand, when it rains, traffic speed tends to decrease. For this reason, measurements carried out in Paris show that the sound level exceeded 50 percent of the time ($L_{50}$) does not change significantly even during rain (CSTB, 1971).

It should also be noted that in countries where winters are severe, studded tires are commonly used: when used on dry roads, they cause an appreciable increase in noise, especially at high frequencies.

Finally, in urban areas, wind and temperature profiles only slightly affect the transmission of sound along streets.

**Dwellings**

Noise in an urban area is primarily associated with the annoyance caused in homes. Thus the final group of parameters of concern is the actual design of dwellings, and therefore their insulation rather than the propagation of noise. Because the exterior walls of a building attenuate sound appreciably more than do windows, the noise transmitted into a dwelling thus depends on window characteristics.

Ordinary closed windows attenuate sound by some 15–20 dBA. However, even when open or ajar they reduce noise by some 5–10 dBA. With certain types—double windows or those fitted with heavy glass—reductions from 30 to 45 dBA may be obtained.* Thus traffic noise can be reduced substantially by heavily soundproofing.

Sound levels inside a dwelling also depend upon the arrangement of the rooms. Sound differences of more than 20 dBA may be observed between rooms facing the street and those overlooking a courtyard or garden.

## SUMMARY OF FACTORS CAPABLE OF PRODUCING SIGNIFICANT CHANGES IN TRAFFIC NOISE

From the review in this chapter of the different parameters affecting the propagation, transmission and perception of traffic noise, it is clear that noise, as observed, varies a great deal according to circumstances. Some of the principal factors capable of producing significant change in noise are summarized in Table 10.3. The table lists various factors producing differences of some 10 dBA, corresponding to a change by a factor of 10 in the acoustic energy and of approximately 2 in the subjective impression of annoyance. The values given in the table must, however, be regarded with caution since they are only orientative.

## EXPOSURE TO TRAIN NOISE

Although train noise is more confined and affects a much smaller portion of the population, it can be very strong in areas adjacent to the rails, and it penetrates considerably into developed areas, with sound which is recognizable for several thousand feet from the source. For instance, a U.S. marine officer at training camp for a summer, reported that the officers' group had very little difficulty with the 5:30 a.m. reveille because at 4:45 a.m., 5:00 a.m., and 5:20 a.m., a train passed near their barracks and at 5:30 a.m. everybody was awake. This is one possible way

---

*Estimates vary according to country. In France an ordinary window when closed gives an attenuation of about 15–17 dBA. In the United Kingdom, it is estimated that an ordinary closed window reduces noise by 20 dBA.

**Table 10.3** Some Factors Approximately Doubling the Perceived Noise Level From Automobiles (i.e., Increase of 10 dBA) (Adapted from OECD, 1971).

| | Change of 10 dBA | |
|---|---|---|
| | Quieter ⟶ Noisier | |
| Noise from single vehicles in typical urban conditions | Quietest 10% of automobiles | Noisiest 10% of automobiles |
| | Quietest 10% of heavy trucks | Noisiest 10% of heavy trucks |
| | Noise from automobile (gasoline engine) | Noise from heavy truck (diesel engine) |
| | Noise from automobile at moderate cruising speed | Noise from same automobile while accelerating |
| Noise from traffic. | Median traffic noise on highway at a given flow rate | Median traffic noise on highway at 8 times such a flow rate |
| | Median traffic noise in a street at a given flow rate | Median traffic noise in a street at 4–6 times this flow rate |
| | Red light (traffic stopped) | Green light (traffic flowing) |
| | Nighttime noise | Daytime noise |
| | Noise peaks heard at a given distance | Noise peaks heard at $\frac{2}{3}$ of the same distance |
| | Background noise heard at a given distance | Background noise heard at $\frac{9}{10}$ of same distance |
| | Windows closed | Windows open |
| Noise inside dwelling | Double windows | Ordinary windows |

to derive positive benefit from train noise, but more often the noise has negative value—interrupting conversation or other activities.

As described earlier, trains have been observed to cause noise levels outside nearby residences of 90–95 dBA both during daytime and at night (Chalupnik, 1970). Assuming the average noise attenuation of a house to be some 20 dBA, this gives an interior noise level in a house due to a passing train of 70–75 dBA, both for day and night—a level often sufficient to wake a sleeping person, disturb a baby, or interrupt normal activities.

On the basis of data from a study of 10 cities with widely varying population, the U.S. Environmental Protection Agency (EPA, 1974) estimated that in 1974 one million people in the United States were exposed to peak overall railroad sound levels of 80 dBA or greater. In general, detailed estimates of the number of people who hear various noise levels from trains can be reached by an approach similar to the contour method used in airport noise surveys. Noise contours can be established for rail lines and the number of people and dwellings within each noise contour by using census data and aerial photographs. Problems arise when two or more railroads are within hearing distance of each other.

## EXPOSURE INSIDE VEHICLES

### In Automobiles

As mentioned earlier, acoustic insulation in an automobile is of little value if windows are open. By closing the windows, a driver can attenuate the noise by 15–20 dBA. For example, the noise level inside an auto on a high-speed, interstate-type highway, is about 70 dBA with windows closed and 85–87 dBA with windows open. In compact cars the noise can be appreciably higher. Driving alongside a truck may increase the noise level a further 8 dBA and being in a tunnel near a truck a noise level as high as 104 dBA can be observed.

There has been a great deal of work in automobile insulation measures and many new models are advertised for their quietness. This emphasis, however, has been for the benefit of the vehicle occupant; for until spurred by legislation, very little consideration had been given to the exterior airborne noise which reaches people living and working along roadways. From the point of view of the automaker this is reasonable because he is directing the benefits and quality of his product toward the consumer and does not find economic advantage in reducing noise external to the vehicle.

Long-distance truck drivers are exposed to a continuous high noise level. The cabin of a truck without any special sound insulation may have a sustained noise level of almost 100 dB on an open highway. This suggests that there exists the possibility of hearing loss among truck drivers who regularly operate vehicles not meeting noise-reduction criteria.

### In Public Transit Vehicles

In a modern American bus with rear engine and adequate soundproofing, interior noise of 72–80 dBA is typical (with the bus almost full, and all passengers seated). In older buses with the engine in front, less effective soundproofing, or in poorer condition, the noise can be 85 dBA and higher.

A large number of bus riders are regular commuters, going to jobs or school, and then returning by the end of the working day. It is reasonable to assume that the average time a commuter spends in the transit vehicle is one-half hour for each trip—a total travel time of 1 hour each day. According to the ISO standard for hearing conservation, a person exposed to 85 dBA (interior noise in a noisy bus) for a short time interval, should have a rest period of 3 hours. Thus, if the bus rider is going from a noisy bus to a noisy job or other noisy destination, there is, in fact, no opportunity for achieving the recommended off-time. If the noise level on the job is the same as on the bus, or higher, a worker will, in essence, be adding his commuting time to the exposure time of the noisy job.

Rail transit systems are comparatively less widespread than the urban bus. Particularly in the United States, rail transit systems operate only in a few cities—as subways, elevateds, or surface lines. However, these systems carry a large number of passengers: in the United States alone, close to 2 billion per year, with some 900 miles of track, of which approximately 500 miles are at grade.

This figure will increase significantly in the near future as more such urban systems are constructed. The large number of users of urban rail systems is composed primarily of commuters. With noise in American subway cars reaching levels of 85–90 dBA,* the exposure which a commuter suffers is substantial and needs to be treated in the same way as the exposure to bus noise. Thus, to an increasing degree, noise has been given consideration in the planning and construction of the new rapid-transit systems. The Metro and the Expo Express in Montreal and the BART system in San Francisco are three examples of transit systems where the comfort and the convenience of users have been considered, with emphasis placed on making the system quiet.

## REFERENCES

Bolt, Beranek and Newman, Inc. Literature survey for the FHA contract on urban noise. Report prepared for the FHA, Cambridge, Mass., 1967.

Bugliarello, G. and Wakstein, C. Noise pollution—a review of its techno-sociological and health aspects. Biotechnology Program, Carnegie-Mellon University, Pittsburgh, 1968.

---

*See Table 6.4.

Burt, M. E. Aspects of highway design and traffic management. Paper presented at a seminar on Road and Environmental Planning and the Reduction of Noise. Southampton, U.K., 1969.

Chalupnik, J. D. (Ed.). *Transportation noise—a symposium on acceptability criteria.* Seattle, Washington: University of Washington Press, 1970.

CSTB (Centre Scientifique et Technique du Bâtiment). Etude de la gêne due au trafic automobile urbain. Paris, 1971.

EPA (U.S. Environmental Protection Agency). Proposed emission standards for interstate rail carrier noise. The Bureau of National Affairs, Washington, July 1974.

IDA (Institute of Defense Analyses). Economic characteristics of the urban public transport industry. Prepared by U.S. Department of Transportation. U.S. Government Printing Office, Washington, 1972.

Josse, R., *et al.* Etudes des modes de protection phonique aux abords des voies rapides urbaines. (Investigation of methods of sound protection along high-speed urban highways.) Centre Scientifique et Technique du Bâtiment (CSTB) on behalf of the Institut de Recherche des Transports (I.R.T.), 1969.

Lamure, C. Institut de Recherche des Transports, Lyon, France. Personal communication to A. Alexandre, 1972.

NCHRP. Highway noise: Measurement, simulation, and mixed reactions. National Cooperative Highway Research Program Report 78, Washington, 1969.

OECD (Organization for Economic Co-operation and Development). Motor vehicle noise. Paris, November 1971.

Priede, T. and Grover, E. C. As quoted in OECD, 1971.

RRL (Road Research Laboratory). A review of road traffic noise. Report No. LR 347, U.K., 1970.

Rüker, A. and Glück, K. Bauliche Schutzmassnahmen fur Minderung des Strassenwerkehrslarms. *Strassenbau und Strassenverkehrstechnik*, 1966, **47**.

Schultz, T. J. Technical background for noise abatement in HUD's operating program. Bolt, Beranek and Newman, Report No. 2005, Cambridge, Mass., 1970.

Stephenson, R. J. and Vulkan, G. H. Urban planning against noise. *Official architecture and planning*, London, 1967.

Wilson. Committee on The Problem of Noise. Noise, final report. Cmnd. 2056. London: HMSO, 1963.

# CHAPTER 11

# Reducing Exposure to Traffic Noise

In this chapter we shall consider methods of reducing exposure to noise from *traffic*, as distinct from the methods for reducing noise at the source through improved vehicle design, which were discussed in Chapter 8. These methods, which are applied in different ways from place to place, are essentially of three types:

- noise reduction by urban planning and road design (including the use of sound screens or barriers);
- noise reduction by architectural means, such as soundproofing and arrangement of rooms;
- noise reduction by means of traffic control and police measures.

## URBAN PLANNING AND ROAD DESIGN

We have seen that a large number of parameters influence the noise levels caused by traffic. Substantial reductions in noise can be achieved by changing the design of roads and their surroundings, that is, by appropriate urban planning.

### Tunnels

From the standpoint of suppressing the noise transmitted towards dwellings, tunnels are the most radical solution—yet a solution that creates many difficulties. In traditional cities and towns, considerable topographical and technical problems can arise—because of the state of the subsoil, the space taken up by sewers, underground railways, etc.—factors that make excavation difficult and sometimes even impossible.

Furthermore, when an underground road can be built, it is generally entirely new rather than a substitute for an existing surface road to be closed as soon as the underground road is opened. In addition, building a road underground is by far the most costly solution. According to a British estimate, building a road in a bored tunnel is 13 times more expensive than building it at ground level (RRL, 1970). According to another estimate, the additional cost of building 1 km of roadway using the cut and cover technique would be £3 million (Waller, 1970).

Noise and pollution from ventilation systems are also among the various problems which arise with tunnels (as they do with underground parking lots). The outlets from these systems must be provided with suitable deflectors, and in some way must remove (filter) the exhaust gases, the noxious fumes and pollutants. Tunnels must also be treated acoustically, so that sound levels inside do not exceed the levels which can be tolerated by motorists. Further, the effect on surface buildings of vibrations due to traffic can be serious. In brief, solving a given problem should not go so far as to create a new type of annoyance.

### Roads in Cuts

Noise from a raised road affects a greater area than noise from a road at the level of the adjacent ground. Thus building a raised road is clearly the least desirable solution from one standpoint of noise transmission, unless the road is bordered by a solid parapet.

On the other hand, an effective way of preventing the propagation of noise is, as we have seen, to place a road in a cut (Fig. 11.1). In general, vertical walls give better noise protection than sloping banks (Fig. 11.2), but there is a danger of reflection towards adjacent buildings. A road in a cut with sloping banks is likely to protect only the lower floors from noise, but when the adjacent ground is grassed over, reflection effects are avoided. According to British estimates, if the cost of constructing an urban roadway at ground level is equal to 100, building it in a cut with sloping banks will vary between 130 and 200, and with vertical walls between 400 and 600.

Roads in cuts can prove especially suitable for expressways and main roads in suburban areas, at some distance from dwellings, provided these are not too high. The vertical walls or sloping sides of the cut thus act as barriers, and noise reduction at any point will depend on the distance and height of this point with respect to the barrier. However, from an acoustic standpoint, to build roads in cuts is virtually valueless in congested

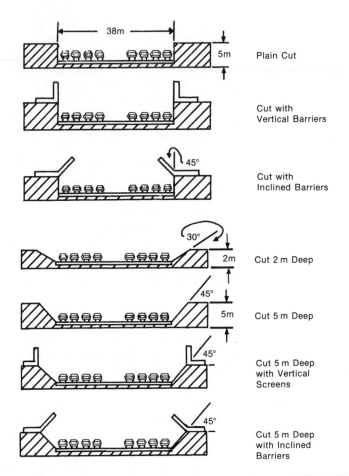

**Fig. 11.1** Roads in cuts with vertical or sloping sides (Source: CSTB, 1969).

districts—as in old towns—with narrow streets and high buildings. It is only in new or renovated districts, where it is possible to alter the width of streets and the height of adjacent buildings, that construction in cuts—particularly in the case of expressways—can prove really worthwhile.

### Road Surface

In order to reduce to a minimum noise due to the road surface, all roads that are still stone-paved should be covered with asphalt: this can result in

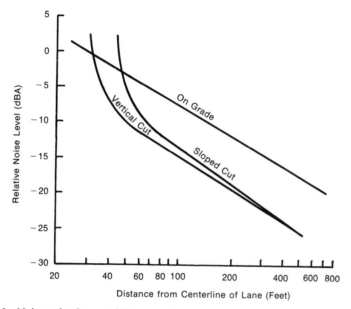

**Fig. 11.2**   Noise reduction provided by vertical and sloping cuts. (Source: NCHRP, 1969. Used by permission.)

noise reductions possibly exceeding 5 dBA. The economics of surfacing is, however, difficult to assess in view of the substantial variations (such as geography) that affect the cost of surfacing.

Yet an asphalt paving needs to be replaced or repaired much more often (about every 3–5 years) than a stone or concrete surface. Thus, the expenditures for road maintenance (and the resulting disturbance to traffic) should not be overlooked in attempting to assess the advantages and costs of different types of road surface.

### Protective Barriers

As was seen earlier, the side walls or banks of roads built in cuts act as acoustic barriers. But it is also possible to erect barriers along roads built on grade, at ground level.

The effectiveness of trees and shrubs as acoustic screens is hard to predict. Foliage density varies, growth patterns are affected by the environment, car exhausts, salt spray, disease etc. Deciduous trees cost less and more adaptable to city conditions than evergreens, but are of limited use during winter. In favor of natural barriers, it must be remembered that the interaction of wind and trees produces a pleasant, soothing sound.

The effectiveness of an artificial barrier depends on its height and type of construction, and also on the distance and the height of the observer with respect to the barrier. A barrier is better at reducing noise peaks than background noise (since part of the sound energy diffracts around it). Thus, the closer the observer is to the barrier, the more effective will be the barrier. Various types of barriers are shown in Fig. 11.3, as well as in Fig. 11.1 (CSTB, 1969).

The maximum noise reductions that can be expected in practice from an acoustic barrier are limited to between 10 and 15 dBA. Figure 11.4 shows the noise reduction obtained at different heights and distances from a barrier 3 m high (Scholes and Sargent, 1971). A specific mass of $15 \, kg/m^2$ is sufficient for a barrier to be effective. However, the requirements a barrier has to meet because of its position in the open air—safety, wind resistance, and durability—are such that this specific weight will in fact need to be exceeded.

The main acoustic requirement for a barrier is that it should be airtight.

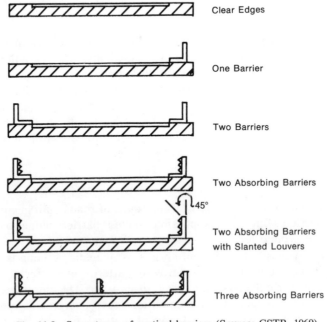

Fig. 11.3 Some types of vertical barriers (Source: CSTB, 1969).

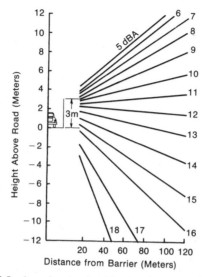

**Fig. 11.4** Reduction of $L_{10}$ by a 3-m barrier (distance between source and barrier: 25 m) (Source: Scholes and Sargent, 1971).

Special attention must be given to any joints. Furthermore, when dwellings are so situated that they can receive reflected sound from the barrier, it may prove necessary to cover it with some absorbent material. The process is very costly, however, and gives rise to problems of maintenance and weather resistance.

Protective barriers have been tested in a number of countries. In England, for example, a barrier 300 m long and 2.6 m high has been erected along the expressway linking London with the Heathrow Airport at a total cost of £30,000 (i.e., £100 or $240 per running meter) (Vulkan, 1970). The barrier consists of plastic panels mounted on a metal frame, which are reported to give a 10 dBA attenuation. A summary of assessments made in Canada, France, and the United Kingdom of the characteristics and costs of various barriers is given in Table 11.1.

Often choices are possible. Dwellings may be built near a main road, and protected from traffic noise by a screen. Or, they may be built farther away from the road. The selection between the two solutions must be guided by an assessment of the respective costs of a barrier and of the amount of land necessary if no barrier is used.

In building a barrier, a number of factors need to be considered in

**Table 11.1** Acoustic Barriers in Some Countries (Source: OECD, 1971).

| Type of Barrier | Country | Characteristics and Maintenance | Price per Meter |
|---|---|---|---|
| Cement blocks (3 m high) | Canada | Construction fairly long; maintenance minimal; appearance unattractive | $60 |
| Laminate of lead (3 m high) | Canada | Construction rapid; thickness of lead to be determined by tests | $60–90 |
| Brick wall (3 m high) | Canada United Kingdom | Maintenance minimal; fairly long in building | $90 $80–90 |
| Pre-stressed concrete wall (3 m high, 15 cm thick) | Canada | Maintenance minimal; construction rapid | $120 |
| Concrete wall, cast in site (3 m high, 22 cm thick) | Canada United Kingdom | Maintenance minimal; slow construction requiring substantial equipment | $150 $150–160 |
| Wooden hoarding, plywood or other (4 m high) | France | Inflammable; requires maintenance | $80–160 |
| Panels of asbestos cement (4 m high) | France | Non-inflammable; requires maintenance | $40 |
| Panels of asbestos cement as base and panels of "altuglas" between 1 m and 4 m (4 m high) | France | Inflammable; transparent; risk of reflection of light | $100 |
| Panels of toughened glass 10 mm thick, resting on wooden posts (4 m high) | France | Non-inflammable; transparent; danger of reflection of light | $160–200 |

addition to cost and acoustic effectiveness:

- wind resistance;
- degree of inflammability;
- degree of sound reflection or non-reflection under different weather conditions;
- ground area required (need for props);
- aesthetic aspects (opacity or transparence).

In general, like roads in cuts, protective barriers are not effective in traditional streets of congested districts, since the buildings are too near the road and the intersections too numerous. On the other hand, the use of barriers along certain sections of highways can be an optimum, short, or medium-range solution to reduce *peak* traffic noise until the noise from engines and exhausts can be substantially reduced; once engines and exhaust are quieter, it can also be a long-range solution to reduce tire noise.

**Urban Planning Schemes**

Separation of noisy areas from residential areas (zoning), whenever feasible, can be an adequate noise control solution in certain cases. Geographical separation according to function can prove to be relatively simple in building new factories away from residential areas, or new residential areas away from industrial zones. But it is a far more difficult process when it comes to the location of roads, since their *raison d'être* is to link together as many points as possible rather than to isolate them.*

In spite of this difficulty, some amount of road planning is possible. Fast roads can skirt congested residential districts, while the residential character of certain areas can be preserved by adopting strict zoning directives, such as limits to the height of buildings or restrictions in building areas.

In new districts, the construction of screening buildings (air-conditioned offices, garages, stores, factories) between roads and dwellings can be promoted. This has been done, for example, at Thamesmead in the United Kingdom and at Bijlmermeer in the Netherlands, where buildings exclusively used for car parking act as screens between residential areas and main roads. The effectiveness of screen buildings of

---

*See section on separate facilities and zoning in Part VI (Chapter 24).

course depends on their height and their arrangement with respect to the dwellings they are intended to protect.

The placing of non-residential buildings to screen buildings from arterial roads is not without problems, however: if land in the area is expensive, the screening buildings may prove impossible or difficult to build economically. Furthermore, the screening buildings themselves can become sources of noise (as in the case of factories) or can be unattractive in appearance.

The best solutions often consist of adopting a set of complementary measures. For instance, if a road is built in a vertically walled cut, it could be bordered by low buildings. High buildings could be erected farther away from the road, thus benefiting from the cumulative protection provided by the cut and by the screen of low buildings.

Urban planning schemes involve considerations that range from road design, to land-use planning, and to the location and architecture of buildings. Thus their configuration and cost are heavily influenced by local conditions. If an area between the road and dwellings must be kept clear, the costs may well turn out to be high, especially if the road is in an urban area. For example, in London the price of land adjacent to a suburban road is 10 times higher than along a road built in a rural area, and 2.5 times higher in Central London than in the suburbs (OECD, 1971).

## SOUNDPROOFING AND ARRANGEMENT OF LIVING SPACE

Methods of attenuating the noise between the road and the front of the dwelling—through appropriate urban planning and road design—need to be coupled with measures for reducing the noise at the dwelling—through soundproofing and appropriate arrangements of the living spaces.

### Soundproofing

In a building, in general, the insulation provided by the external walls is appreciably greater than that attainable with windows. Thus, in almost every case, the determining factor in soundproofing a dwelling is soundproofing of the windows, and, if necessary, air-conditioning the entire dwelling.

The acoustic insulation of a window depends on the spectrum of external noise. Characteristic reductions observed with traffic noise are given in Table 11.2.

If windows must be intensively soundproofed, care must be taken to

**Table 11.2**  Noise Reduction for Various Window Arrangements (Source: OECD, 1971).

| Window Arrangement | Noise Reduction (dBA) |
| --- | --- |
| Ordinary window wide open: | 5 |
| Ordinary window ajar: | 10 |
| Ordinary window closed: | 15–20 |
| Single-sealed window, or with improved airtightness: | 20–25 |
| Double window* with staggered opening: | 20 |
| Double window closed: | 30–35 |
| Double window closed, or with improved airtightness: | 35–45 |

*Two windows each with panes 8–10 mm thick, 15 cm apart.

provide mechanical ventilation. In practice, soundproofing possibilities must match minimum comfortable summer temperature requirements (corresponding to a renewal of the air at least five times per hour).

Soundproofing costs—and the cost of providing air-conditioning where necessary—depend on the amount of insulation required, the size of the openings, the method adopted and on different geographical and economic variables—such as whether the dwellings to be soundproofed are detached houses or flats, whether the windows are of standard size or not, etc. Costs also vary substantially according to whether existing dwellings must be modified or special soundproofing measures are adopted at the design stage. If modifications are made to existing dwellings, the cost will obviously be much higher.

The cost of soundproofing new dwellings to afford protection not only from noise outside but inside the building varies in the United States between 2 percent and 10 percent of the total cost of the dwelling (SRI, 1970). In the United Kingdom, it has been calculated that to protect all houses in the country exposed to a level of traffic noise considered to be unsatisfactory (greater than 65 dBA at the front), the total cost would vary between £440 million and £1320 million ($1.2–3.5 billion) (RRL, 1970). In France, an "acoustic comfort" standard has been instituted that permits the grant of an additional 2–3 percent to low-cost housing financed by the State if their acoustic qualities are deemed to be adequate (French Ministry, 1971).

In the United Kingdom, a recent investigation included a calculation of unit costs as determined by the desired acoustic attenuation (Urban

Motorways, 1971). According to the type of dwelling, the kind of room to be soundproofed (bedroom or living room) and depending on whether a ventilation system was necessary, the cost per room was calculated to vary between £80 and £130 for a noise reduction of 25–29 dBA, between £100 and £150 for one of 30–40 dBA and between £120 and £180 for one of 35–40 dBA. Often only that part of the dwelling which is exposed to the main road was found to require improved sound insulation.

In any event, acoustic insulation of dwellings (and, where appropriate, hospitals, schools and all premises requiring a certain amount of silence) is not a universal remedy. It offers no protection against noise perceived outside the buildings. Furthermore, in order to be really effective, it requires an air-conditioning system, and permanently closed windows.

However, soundproofing becomes essential to provide protection against the most serious cases of noise, primarily those along expressways as well as near airports and other very noisy places. Acoustic insulation, although having the disadvantage of only giving protection against noise at the point of reception, has the advantage of giving protection against all types of external noise.

## REFERENCES

CSTB (Centre Scientifique et Technique du Bâtiment). Investigation of methods of acoustic protection along urban main roads. Paris, 1969.

French Ministry. Communiqué from the French Ministry for Equipment and Housing in Le Moniteur des Travaux Publics et du Bâtiment. Paris, June 9, 1971.

NCHRP. Highway noise measurement, simulation and mixed reactions. National Cooperative Highway Research Program Report 78, Washington, 1969.

OECD (Organization for Economic Co-operation and Development). Motor vehicle noise. Paris, November 1971.

RRL (Road Research Laboratory). A review of road traffic noise. Report No. LR 347, U.K., 1970.

Scholes, W. E. and Sargent, J. W. Designing against noise from road traffic. Building Research Station, Report No. 20/21, U.K., 1971.

SRI (Stanford Research Institute). Noise pollution control. Report No. 418, California, 1970.

Urban motorways project team—remedial costs. Lord Austin-Smith, London, July 1971.

Vulkan, G. H. Personal communication, 1970.

Waller, R. A. Environmental evaluation. Paper given at the seminar on Environmental Standard, London, May 1970.

# Part IV  Aircraft Noise

# CHAPTER 12

# *Introduction*

The advent of the internal combustion engine placed ubiquitous sources of noise not only on the surface of the earth, but also in the sky. Aircraft noise began to be a major problem with the great surge in air transportation which followed World War II. The introduction of jet airplanes, which came into widespread use by the end of the 1950's, led to a second revolution in aviation, as well as to an escalation of the noise level from aircrafts (Fig. 12.1). Since then, annoyance to people living near airports caused by the noise of jet takeoffs and landings has become a psychophysiological and economic problem of enormous magnitude and complexity. Still a third escalation in aircraft noise will occur when supersonic transports come into commercial operation, and if general aviation and, above all, vertical or short take-off and landing aircraft reach their potential.

As a result of the diffusion of air traffic, airports tend to occupy very large land areas* with multiple runways, and large airspaces involved in landing and takeoff procedures. At the same time, under the pressure of population, communities tend to expand toward airports and thus to enter into zones of higher noise. For instance, in the area around London (Heathrow) Airport, the population has increased by 30 percent since the Wilson Report, a well publicized 1963 study of the noise problem around that airport (Wilson, 1963). Also, an increasing number of people are

---

*The shape of things to come is perhaps given by the new Dallas-Fort Worth Airport, which occupies a land area larger than Manhattan Island (Fig. 12.2). The airport is already operational in its first stage and will be completed by the year 2001.

159

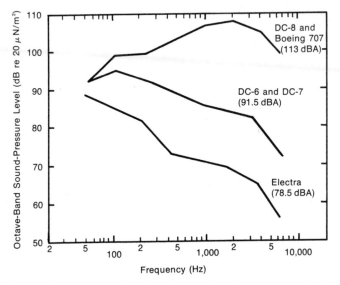

**Fig. 12.1** The escalation in noise introduced by jet aircraft: mean noise level spectra at approximately 1000-ft altitude during takeoff (Adapted from EPA, 1971b).

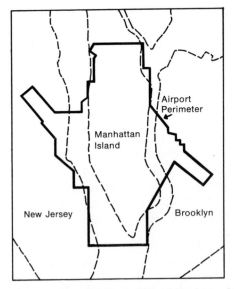

**Fig. 12.2** Comparison of Dallas/Fort Worth Airport and Manhattan Island. (Adapted from *Time*, 1973. Used by permission of Time.)

working in airports and in other areas of the aviation industry. Finally, there are signs that people's tolerance to aircraft noise around airports is decreasing, particularly as socio-economic status improves. Thus, the need for community planning becomes both obvious and urgent.

The aircraft noise problem has been felt sooner and to a greater extent in the United States than in other developed countries, because of a number of factors, including the larger geographical extension of the United States. In 1966, in the United States there were 500 commercial air passengers per 1000 inhabitants, versus 106 for the United Kingdom, 85 for West Germany, and 36 for France (Alexandre, 1970). By the end of 1971, U.S. scheduled airlines carried nearly 80 percent of all U.S. intercity passenger traffic traveling by common carrier (NIPCC, 1972); the major portion of the fleet (in 1969 over 80 percent) of passenger and cargo planes was powered by jet engines, and accounted for the near totality of the capacity flown. General aviation aircraft (personal and corporate aircraft, agricultural aircraft, etc.) have also increased significantly in recent years (from 45,000 in 1950 to 136,000 in 1970 in the United States). Even more rapid has been the rate of growth of helicopters (from 85 in 1950 to 2800 in 1970 in the United States), which at present dominate the vertical or short takeoff and landing (V/STOL) fleet (EPA, 1971a). Considerable numbers of short takeoff vehicles are expected to come into commercial operation in the next few years.

Short range overall world previsions for passengers and freight are chancy. Those shown in Fig. 12.3 indicate that between 1970 and 1980

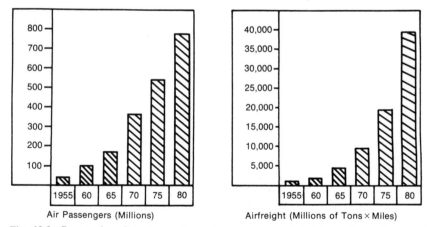

**Fig. 12.3** Past and projected growth of air passenger and freight traffic in the world (Source: Alexandre, 1970).

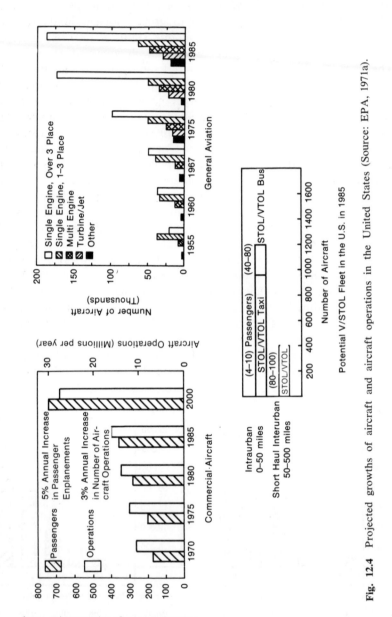

**Fig. 12.4** Projected growths of aircraft and aircraft operations in the United States (Source: EPA, 1971a).

passenger air traffic could be expected to have doubled, and airfreight traffic to have quadrupled. The projected growth in the United States of commercial aircraft traffic to the year 2000, and of general aviation aircraft to the year 1985, as well as the probable composition of the U.S. V/STOL fleet in 1985 are shown in Fig. 12.4. However, the current energy crisis may drastically slow down these rates of growth.

Unlike the case of surface transportation noise, for aircraft noise the participating environment is much smaller than the non-participating environment. At present, aircraft noise affects people near airports, but the development of vertical and short takeoff and landing aircraft and of the SST will affect the entire countryside. The SST alone, if it were to come into operation in the United States, would produce sonic booms felt by approximately one-fourth of the population.

Between 1958 and 1970 the total area impacted by aircraft noise in the United States (in which the Noise Exposure Forecast index (NEF) exceeded the recommended level of 30) increased some fifteenfold, from approximately 100 to 1450 square miles (EPA, 1971a) and the population within that area increased from an estimated 0.5 millions to 7.5 millions. Figure 12.5 shows projections of how such an area can be reduced by

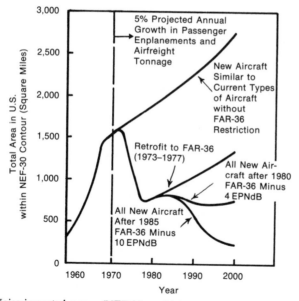

**Fig. 12.5** Noise-impacted areas (NEF-30 or higher) as function of jet-engine noise-reduction goals (Source: Congress Report, 1972).

various jet-engine noise-reduction measures, to reduce by 1990 the noise impacted areas to 1960 levels (but not to reduce the impacted population, as high-density population can be expected to characterize the areas near airports). In the United Kingdom, it was estimated that in 1970 two and a half million people were exposed to aircraft noise corresponding to 35 NNI* or more—a noise level causing extensive annoyance (Mil Research, 1971).

The problem of aircraft noise is complicated by the great economic significance that the aviation industry holds to the economies of developed countries. For instance, at the end of 1971 the U.S. scheduled airlines alone had revenues of close to $10 billion, and employed almost 300,000 employees. Without airlines, a number of economic activities of great importance to national economies—from business and tourism, to the transportation of mail—would be severely affected.

In examining the problem of aircraft noise in the subsequent chapters, we shall proceed, as in the case of surface noise, by considering the sources of aircraft noise, the technical and operational remedies and the impacts of the exposure.

## REFERENCES

Alexandre, A. Prevision de la gene due au bruit autour des aeroports et perspectives sur les moyens d'y remedier. Laboratoire d'Anthropologie Appliquée, Faculté de Medecine, Paris, 1970.

Congress Report. U.S. Congress, Subcommittee on Air and Water Pollution. Hearings on Noise Pollution. Serial No. 92-H35, 1972.

EPA (U.S. Environmental Protection Agency). Report on transportation noise. December 1971. (a)

EPA (U.S. Environmental Protection Agency). Surface transportation noise. December 1971. (b)

Mil Research, Ltd. Second survey of aircraft noise annoyance around London (Heathrow) Airport. London: HMSO, 1971.

NIPCC (National Industrial Pollution Control Council). Airports and the community. Sub-Council Report, Washington, February 1972.

Time. Airport for 2001. *Time*, September 24, 1973.

Wilson. Committee on The Problem of Noise. Noise, final report. Cmnd. 2056. London: HMSO, 1963.

---

*See Appendix 1.

# CHAPTER 13

# *Sources and Propagation of Aircraft Noise*

## SOURCES OF AIRCRAFT NOISE

### Engine and Aerodynamic Noise

The dominant noise from most aircraft is power-plant noise which generally increases with the output of the power plant. However, aerodynamic noise dominates in the case of the helicopter (blade noise) as well as the SST (sonic boom). Aerodynamic noise is also dominant in portions of the interior cabin of certain jet aircrafts.

The noise spectra for selected types of aircraft and power plants are shown in Fig. 13.1. In *propeller aircrafts* the noise is produced primarily by the propellers and contains a harmonic series of discrete frequency tones. For general aviation propeller planes, which are the only kind of propeller planes with a significant future, the dominant fundamental tone is in the range from 40 to 250 Hz. An important group of propeller aircrafts are powered by turboprop engines—basically turbojet engines in which the energy of the exhaust gas is transmitted through a speed reduction gearbox to a conventional propeller.

In *jet aircraft* there are two distinct kinds of engine noise (Fig. 13.2). The first is a low-frequency "roar" caused by the mixing of hot exhaust gases with the relatively stable air around the aircraft, and proportional in noise intensity to approximately the eighth power of the velocity of the exhaust gas relative to the surrounding area. The second is a high-frequency "whine," generated in the compressor section of the engine. The composition and level of the noise due to the relative contribution of these two kinds of noise varies with the type of aircraft and power plant.

165

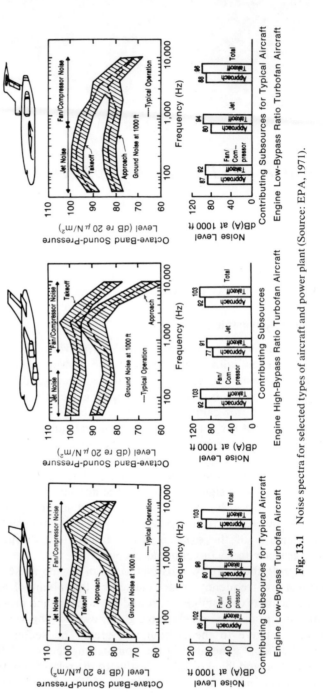

**Fig. 13.1** Noise spectra for selected types of aircraft and power plant (Source: EPA, 1971).

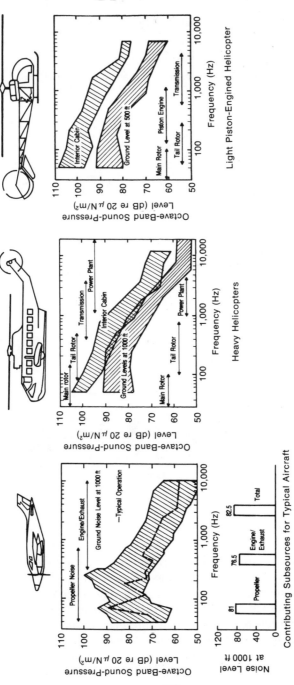

Light Piston-Engined Helicopter

Heavy Helicopters

General Aviation Propeller Aircraft

Contributing Subsources for Typical Aircraft

**Fig. 13.1** *Continued*

167

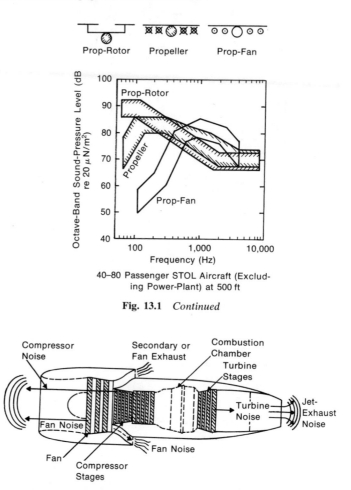

40–80 Passenger STOL Aircraft (Excluding Power-Plant) at 500 ft

**Fig. 13.1**   *Continued*

**Fig. 13.2**   Sources of jet-engine noise (Source: DOT, 1972).

The jet engines currently in operation are basically of two types: turbojets and turbofans. The turbofans differ from the turbojets in that some of the air entering the inlet bypasses the engine combustion system and rejoins the burned gases at the exhaust tailpipe. The bypass ratio— the ratio of the airflow bypassed to that entering the combustion system— varies considerably; it is less than 2 in low-bypass engines and higher than 2 in high-bypass engines. To achieve the bypass, larger diameter stages (fans) are placed in front of the compressor, or a compression stage is added as an extension of turbine blading. While in turbojets exhaust noise usually predominates, in turbofan engines the dominant noise is high-frequency fan noise which is generated internally and propagates both forward and out of the fan-discharge ducts. (Whereas in turbojet engines the high-frequency compressor noise propagates only rearward.) Most of the fan-noise energy is in the mid- and high-frequency ranges; when the blade tips operate at supersonic speed, a multiple-tone noise consisting of a series of tones separated in frequency by the rotational frequency of the engine is also radiated out of the inlet ducts (NIPCC, 1971). In general, for the same power, turbofan engines have lower jet exhaust noise levels than turbojet engines, because the turbofan has higher airflows and thus needs lower exhaust velocities.

Turbojets constituted the first generations of jet engines introduced in commercial service. Because of their higher fuel consumption and higher noise they now represent a rapidly diminishing portion of the commercial fleets: it is expected that by 1980 no turbojet engines will remain in commercial operation in the United States, and that approximately 40 percent of the aircraft will have high-bypass turbofan engines. The wide-bodied jets such as the Boeing 747 are all powered by quieter high-bypass turbofan engines.

On the other hand, the current generation of supersonic transports—the Concorde and the TU-144—unfortunately has had to revert to noisy turbojet engines, with very high jet exhaust velocities (900 m/sec for the Olympus 593 engine of the Concorde at takeoff). The turbojets used in the supersonic transports were the only solution possible in terms of the state of the art of the early sixties, when the Concorde and the TU-144 were initially designed. They are more efficient at supersonic speeds than turbofans, and provide a much higher thrust to weight ratio. But their noise at takeoff equals that of some of the noisiest turbo-jet powered subsonic long-distance transports of the early sixties (NAC, 1974).

In helicopters the principal source of noise is the rotors, which rotate at relatively low speed, generating very high-amplitude pulsating sound pressures in the region of the blade tips. The resulting noise is a low-frequency throb which increases in level and becomes more "slapping" during maneuver, high-speed operation and descent. Under certain conditions, such as engine-idle operation while embarking or disembarking, other sources of noise can become very annoying: they include the piston or gas-turbine engine and the tail stabilizing rotor. Engine and tail-rotor noise are particularly strong in the flight of light utility helicopters.

The problem of helicopter noise is accentuated by two factors. In the first place, low-frequency sounds propagate through the atmosphere more efficiently than those of a higher frequency, and render most sound-insulation methods inefficient. This creates problems in the reduction of both internal cabin noise and the noise in buildings exposed to helicopter noise. Secondly, the throbbing or slapping nature of the rotor noise is not sufficiently taken into account in subjectively weighted noise scales, such as dB(A), which are used to correlate noise with disturbance.

Thus, as we have seen, *short takeoff and landing vehicles* (V/STOL's) at this moment are still largely underdeveloped. Their propulsion may involve propeller rotors, or exclusively propellers, either open or ducted propeller fans, and their noise-frequency characteristics vary with each type.

### The Sonic Boom

The sonic boom is an aerodynamic phenomenon which occurs when a plane flies faster than the speed of sound.* An audible shock wave is generated from the rapid compression of the air. The wave is pushed

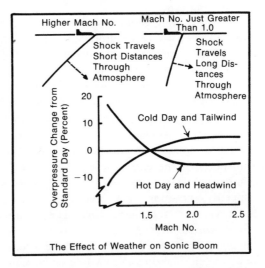

**Fig. 13.3**    The sonic boom (Source: DOT, 1972).

---

*That is, it flies at a Mach number greater than 1, the Mach number being the ratio of the airplane speed to the speed of sound.

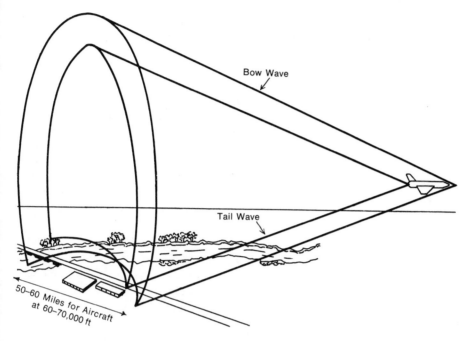

Fig. 13.3  *Continued*

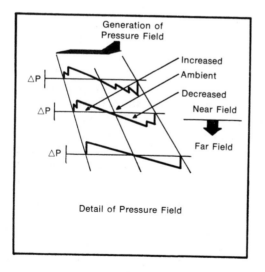

Fig. 13.3  *Continued*

ahead of the plane and forms a cone of increased air pressure, with the airplane at its tip (Fig. 13.3). For a supersonic aircraft operating at 50–70,000 ft, the intersection of the cone with the ground may have a width of 50–60 miles. If the plane flies at low level, the overpressure created by the sonic boom wave is greatly increased, while it is decreased if the plane operates at higher altitudes.

Each component of the aircraft generates its own shock wave so that close to the plane (the "near field") the overall shock wave generated by the supersonic aircraft has a very complex configuration. At a greater distance, the different shock waves interact and coalesce into a bow wave and a shock wave whose signature ("far-field signature") has a characteristic "N"-shape ("N-wave"); an observer on the ground then hears two booms, one for the bow and one for the tail shock, separated by a time interval of 0.1–0.4 seconds.

The intensity of the shock wave decreases with the three-quarter power of the distance from the aircraft. The wave is strongly affected by the speed and weight of the aircraft. The higher the aircraft speed, the smaller is the angle of attack necessary for lift, and the smaller the shock wave; the greater the weight (one of the most difficult factors to reduce in a commercially profitable SST), the greater the intensity of the shock waves. The conditions of the ground also affect strongly the boom felt on the ground, as it may be totally reflected or totally absorbed. If reflected, its intensity becomes twice the magnitude of the incident wave. At Mach number greater than 1.5, if it is a cold day and there is a tailwind, usually the overpressure increases with respect to that on a standard day by not more than 3–4 percent; on a hot day with a headwind, it decreases by not more than 3–4 percent. In general, at Mach number just greater than 1 the shock travels for long distances through the atmosphere, while at higher Mach numbers the shock travels shorter distances. Finally, the shock-wave characteristics are strongly influenced by airplane configurations, the shock being greater, the greater the bluntness of the airplane. The distribution of the lift is also significant, with higher boom intensities occurring if the lift is not evenly distributed over the length of the aircraft.

## Operational Aspects of Aircraft Noise

Noise produced by aircraft and aircraft engines varies during different phases of the operation of an aircraft: ground, takeoff, and landing noise have a major impact; while, with the exception of the SST, of general aviation aircraft flying at a low altitude, and of vertical or short takeoff and landing aircraft, in-flight noise under cruising conditions has a generally small impact.

Ground noise is caused by the ground movements of aircraft as well as by "run-up" tests on engines for power plant and maintenance work. The noise due to ground movements can become particularly severe when certain configurations of the airports concentrate the noise field or fail to shield sufficiently the persons on the ground. Noise from run-up tests is particularly strong when run-up facilities are placed too close to other facilities, or are not properly sheltered.

Takeoff noise is generally the most intense, because during this process the engines are operating at maximum power. Landing noise can also be very intensive. For instance, tests conducted at the Zurich Airport showed that in some portions of the region impacted by the airport, landing noise was actually stronger than takeoff noise (EPA, 1971). In general, certain features of jet engines make their noise particularly intrusive when the engines are cut back for landing (Wilson, 1963).

## PROPAGATION AND MEASUREMENT

### Factors Affecting Propagation

Each of the individual sources that comprise the noise field produced by an aircraft have distinct characteristics of distribution and directivity. Among the factors affecting the propagation of noise from such airborne sources the principal ones are:

- Distance.
- Aircraft altitude.
- Temperature.
- Humidity.
- Wind, temperature, and humidity gradients in the path of propagation.
- Turbulence.
- Ground "Impedance" to the propagation of noise.
- Topography.

For normal conditions the most significant factors are altitude, temperature, and humidity. Beyond a mile from the source all noise spectra from the same category of aircraft (jets, propeller-driven planes, helicopters) become similar, although they may differ in overall noise levels (Large,

1970). In general, high-frequency noise decays rapidly, leaving low-frequency noise as the predominant component.

At present, under "standard" atmospheric conditions the noise generated from *individual* aircraft can be estimated with reasonable accuracy at short distances (less than 3000 ft). At distances greater than 3000 ft, as well as under non-standard atmospheric conditions, such as high winds, humidity beyond the range of 30–70 degrees, and low or high temperatures (less than 30°F or greater than 90°F), the accuracy of a noise estimate becomes greatly reduced (Large, 1970). More accurately predictable are contours of indices such as the NNI,* which describe average levels of aircraft noise.

### The Measurement of Aircraft Noise

Where should aircraft noise be measured so as to establish standards and make it possible to institute comparisons?

For the purpose of establishing standards, in the United States the FAA has instituted a regulation (FAR-36) which applies to all subsonic jet aircraft certified after December 1, 1969. The regulation prescribes noise measurement at 3 points (Fig. 13.4).

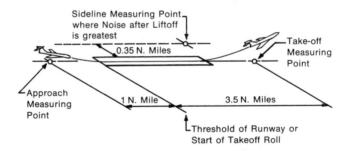

**Fig. 13.4**   Measurement of aircraft noise: noise-measuring points for subsonic commercial jet aircraft, FAA certification (Source: FAA, 1970).

Approach noise is to be measured 1 mile before the threshold of the runway below; takeoff noise is to be measured 3.5 miles beyond the point of brake release on takeoff, and sideline noise at 0.35 miles from the centerline of the runway at the point of greatest noise level (or at 0.25 miles for aircraft with three engines or less).

---

*See Appendix 1.

In general, aircraft noise can be measured in a number of ways, according to the purposes of the measurement. Most large airports possess computerized monitoring equipment with microphones converting the noise into electrical information, which in turn provides the inputs to sound-level meters. For instance, at the Schiphol Airport in the Netherlands, the information from the sound-level meters is transmitted over telephone lines scanned every second and transmitted to a computer that calculates the time, level, and duration of the excess noise; at the Zurich Airport, computerized monitoring equipment is installed at a number of villages around the airport; the Paris airports, both Orly and Charles de Gaulle at Roissy, are equipped with automatic telemetering systems.

## REFERENCES

DOT 1972 (Department of Transportation). Third federal aircraft noise abatement plan. FY 1971–72, January 1972.

EPA (U.S. Environmental Protection Agency). Transportation noise and noise from equipment powered by internal combustion engines. Washington, December 1971.

FAA (Federal Aviation Administration). Noise abatement. Washington, February 24, 1970.

Large, J. B. A note on the propagation of aircraft noise. In *Papers and proceedings*. Commission on The Third London Airport—Vol. VIII, Pt. 2, Section VI. London: HMSO, 1970.

NAC (The Noise Advisory Council). Aircraft engine noise research. London: HMSO, 1974.

NIPCC (National Industrial Pollution Control Council). Noise from gas turbine aircraft engines. Sub-council Report, Washington, February 1971.

Wilson. Committee on The Problem of Noise. Noise, final report. Cmnd. 2056. London: HMSO, 1963.

# CHAPTER 14

# The Technology for Reducing Aircraft Noise

Aircraft noise can be reduced by engineering measures aimed at the power plant and other aircraft components, by operational measures aimed at modifying the operation of the aircraft so as to reduce noise, and by zoning, insulation and other measures aimed at reducing the impact of noise on its recipients. In this chapter we discuss the engineering and operational measures; the other measures, which apply also to other sources of noise, are discussed elsewhere in the book (particularly in Part VI).

## REDUCTION OF NOISE THROUGH ENGINEERING

In discussing the reduction of noise through engineering we shall limit ourselves exclusively to jet engines: in addition to being the loudest noise source, they constitute the overwhelming majority of the commercial fleets and an increasing portion of the general aviation fleet.

### Jet Engines

Turbojet engines powered the first generations of jet aircraft and the current supersonic transports. In these engines, low-frequency exhaust noise predominates, two basic techniques can be employed for reducing the exhaust noise:

• to decrease the exhaust velocity of the jet. Since the engine thrust is directly related to the exhaust velocity, this approach leads to reduction in power and can be resorted to only during climb-outs after takeoff;

• to change the characteristics of the mixing of the hot, high-velocity exhaust gases with the surroundings. This can be achieved by employing exhaust-noise suppressors consisting of nozzles of various shapes. Modest noise reductions are obtained during takeoff and only very small reductions during landing, because the effect of the suppressor decreases as the air velocity decreases.

A very considerable reduction in noise levels has been achieved with the introduction of turbofan engines. In these engines, which have powered the subsequent generations of subsonic commercial jet aircraft, a given thrust is produced with lower exhaust velocities, and hence lower noise. Low-bypass turbofan engines achieve reductions of approximately 25 percent in the exhaust velocity with respect to turbojet engines, and, correspondingly, very pronounced reductions in noise, given the eighth-power relationship between noise and exhaust-jet velocity. With higher-bypass ratios the reduction in exhaust noise is correspondingly higher (NIPCC, 1971).

With the decrease in exhaust noise, the dominant source of noise in turbofan engines becomes the high-frequency "whine" in the fan blade, which propagates both forward and rearward of the engines. A number of measures can be taken to reduce this whine. In the first place, the number and spacing of the vanes and blades can be acoustically optimized. Secondly, the inlet vanes can be eliminated and the fan stages can be reduced (to a single one); exit guide vanes can be placed well aft and sound absorbing linings can be placed in the inlet and discharge ducts. These measures, summarized in Table 14.1, apply not only to commercial aircraft, but also to general aviation aircraft. A recent example of a commercial aviation engine incorporating both a high-bypass ratio, and perforated, honeycombed sound-suppression material on the duct walls is the Q-fan (*Automotive Engineering*, 1973).

In the case of supersonic jets, noise reduction is still very much in an experimental stage (NAC, 1974). Among the possible remedies, it has been found that weak shock waves from small rods placed at the periphery of a supersonic jet can reduce noise (DOT, 1971) and that the use of a shroud in connection with the rods can reduce the noise appreciably. Other measures could include sound-absorbing linings in the tailpipe and in the intake, increased exhaust-nozzle area, as well as modification of engine and airframe so as to allow changes in operational techniques, such as steeper climbs after take-offs (NAC, 1974).

## The FAA Goals for Noise Reduction

In the United States on the basis of the authority assigned to it by the Aircraft Noise Abatement Act of 1968 (Public Law, 90–41), the Federal

**Table 14.1**    Jet Engines: Summary of Noise Sources, Characteristics, and Remedies.

| Engine Type | Noise Sources | Characteristics | Remedies |
|---|---|---|---|
| Turbojet | Exhaust noise | Proportional to eighth power of relative exhaust velocity | Exhaust suppressors |
|  | Compressor noise | Radiates rearward |  |
| Turbofan | Exhaust noise | Lower because exhaust velocity reduced | High-bypass ratios |
|  | Compressor noise | Partially masked by other sources |  |
|  | Fan noise | Radiates forward and rearward | Elimination of inlet vanes |
|  |  | Related to number of blades and vanes | Optimization of vane and blading numbers and spacing Reduction of fan stages (only one) Sound-suppressing linings |

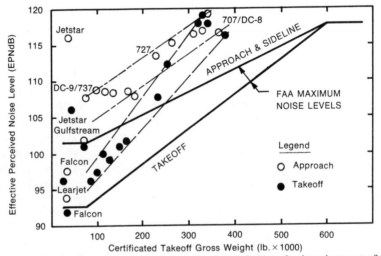

**Fig. 14.1**    FAA maximum noise limits for certification and range of noise prior to retrofitting of commercial aircraft entered into service before December 1, 1969 (Adapted from FAA, 1970).

Aviation Administration established noise limits for subsonic jet aircraft certified after December 1, 1969 (the FAA regulation FAR-36). The limits pertain to the maximum noise on approach and on takeoff, and the maximum sideline noise, measured at the point shown in Fig. 13.4 in the previous chapter, as a function of the aircraft gross weight. Some limited tradeoffs are allowable: noise may be exceeded slightly at one or two of the three measuring points (approach, takeoff, or sideline) if compensated by reductions at the other points.

Figure 14.1, which compares the maximum FAA noise limits for certification with the noise produced by selected types of jet aircraft prior to retrofitting, shows the considerable reductions that must be achieved to bring such aircraft in line with the FAA regulation.

### Retrofitting

The more recent commercial jet planes have achieved very significant reductions in noise levels. For instance, the Boeing 747,* the DC-10 and

---

*The principal types of aircraft mentioned in this and other chapters of this book are:

| | | |
|---|---|---|
| BAC 111 | | 2 jets in rear portion of fuselage |
| Boeing | 707 | 4 jets in wings |
| | 720 | 4 jets in wings |
| | 727 | 1 jet in tail and 2 in rear portion of fuselage |
| | 737 | 2 jets in wings |
| | 747 | Wide-bodied, with 4 jets in wings |
| Concorde | | Supersonic transport, 4 jets in wings |
| Douglas | DC-3 | 2 propeller engines in wings |
| | DC-6 | 4 propeller engines in wings |
| | DC-7 | 4 propeller engines in wings |
| | DC-8 | 4 jets in wings |
| | DC-9 | 2 jets in rear portion of fuselage |
| | DC-10 | Wide-bodied, with 2 jets in wings and one in tail |
| Lockheed Tristar (L-1011) | | Wide-bodied, with 2 jets in wings and one in tail |
| TU-144 | | Supersonic transport, 4 jets in wings |
| VC 10 | | 4 jets in rear portion of fuselage |
| B 58 (Military) | | Supersonic delta-wing bomber, with 4 engines slung from the wings. Mach 1+ |
| XB 70 (Military) | | Experimental supersonic bomber, 6 engines in tail, delta wings, 2000 m.p.h. |
| F 104 (Military) | | Supersonic fighter, one jet in fuselage, Mach 2. |

the L-1011 were all designed to comply with the FAA regulation FAR-36. The noise reductions achieved by the L-1011, the newest of this group, are actually much greater than those demanded by the FAA regulations. But for older, noisier aircraft not originally designed to meet stringent noise regulations, only *a posteriori* corrective measures can be taken, the measures that go under the name of retrofitting. Basically two approaches can be followed in retrofitting. The first leaves the power plant unchanged and modifies or redesigns the exhaust ducts, or completely redesigns the nacelle structures of the engines, to provide, for instance, "daisy"-shaped exhaust nozzles (Fig. 14.2). The second approach makes changes in the power plant, primarily to achieve higher-bypass ratios (Fig. 14.3).

Using the first approach, for two- or three-engine aircraft in U.S. service (Boeing 727 and 737, DC-9 and BAC-111) only slight modifications

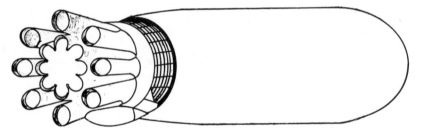

**Fig. 14.2**   A "daisy-shaped" exhaust nozzle (Source: NIPCC, 1971).

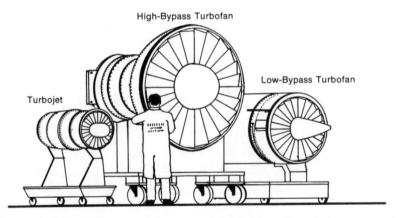

**Fig. 14.3**   Three jet engines. The high-bypass ratio turbofan produces the lowest amount of noise of the three (Adapted from NIPCC, 1971).

are generally necessary to meet the FAA regulation FAR-36, at a cost of approximately $100,000 per aircraft (M. R. Segal, Congress Report, 1972). For four-engine aircraft (Boeing 707 and 720, DC-8) more complete modifications are necessary, at a cost of approximately $1 million per aircraft. The total cost of retrofitting the U.S. fleet in service as of 1975 (about 1200 aircraft) is slightly less than $500 million. A more advanced and more expensive retrofitting program being developed by NASA using the second approach can lead to stronger reductions in noise (5–10 dB better than those achievable for the FAA program), but presents greater technical difficulties, requires a longer time, and would cost approximately $500,000 per engine. In general airport operators are strong proponents of immediate implementation of the first approach, limited to lining the engine nacelles with sound absorbing materials (the "SAM" retrofit). This approach is particularly effective in reducing landing noise, which is a major cause of community annoyance (Congress Report, 1974).

A major political question arises in connection with retrofitting: if the decision is made to retrofit, who should pay: the airlines? the Federal Government? Also, is it not desirable to give incentives to retire earlier the older four-engine jets which, as we have seen, are the noisiest?

### What Limits for Engine Noise Reduction?

There are two limits beyond which little is gained in further quieting aircraft engines (NAC, 1974):

• *The noise "floor"* due to aerodynamic conditions, that is the noise generated by the aircraft's passage through the air. The floor will depend on flying conditions as well as on the aircraft configuration (e.g. landing gear lowered, flaps extended, etc.)

• *The noise "cut-off" point* determined by the general noise level in the community surrounding the airport and by the measures the community is undertaking to quiet other sources of noise.

### OPERATIONAL NOISE REDUCTION

A number of operational procedures can be followed to reduce aircraft noise both in flight and on the ground. In flight, the principal procedures include:

• Rerouting flight paths away from critical areas. This involves making turns away from densely populated areas, both on landing and takeoff, and the use of preferential runways. Rerouting is particularly important in the case of supersonic transports, where the flight paths throughout the supersonic portion of the flight* must be designed so as to minimize the number of people on the ground exposed to the sonic boom. In order to remain within an acceptable noise level even at takeoff, supersonic transports, with their noisy turbojets, may need to resort to hazardous maneuvers. For instance the Concorde can comply with the takeoff noise limits at New York's J.F. Kennedy Airport only by rolling into a 26 degree turn at an altitude of only 100 feet (Witkin, 1975).

- Dispersal of routes, to reduce the frequency of overflights.
- Reduction of the thrusts of the engines following takeoff. This leads to a procedure in which the full thrust necessary to the immediate takeoff is used for a steep initial climb, which is then continued at reduced thrusts over the populated area, and resumed at a normal rate beyond that area (Fig. 14.4).

---

*In the operation of a supersonic transport, the takeoff and landing portions of the flight are subsonic, and so are likely to be additional and at times quite extended portions of the flight after takeoff and before landing, which occur over crowded areas.

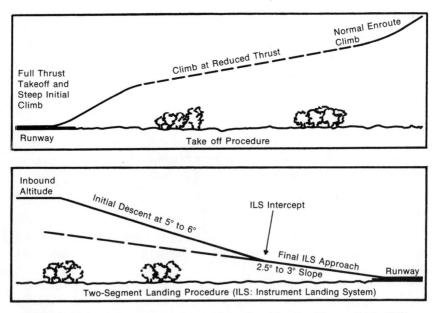

**Fig. 14.4**   Noise abatement procedures at takeoff and landing (Source: FAA, 1970).

• Steeper approach slopes. For instance, a considerable noise reduction can be achieved with a steep initial descent at 5–6 degrees followed by a milder final approach slope of 2.5–3 degrees (Fig. 14.4).

To be effective, in-flight operational noise-reduction procedures require the presence of monitoring systems at and near airports. The modified takeoff and approach procedures to reduce noise must take into account tradeoffs with safety, as well as with the comfort of the passenger. Too steep an initial climb after takeoff may lead to stall and to acute discomfort in some passengers, and too steep an initial approach slope may also lead to major passenger discomfort.

On the ground, noise control operational procedures are also required if the noise level generated by the aircraft on the ground is excessive. These procedures may include the towing of the aircraft to and from the terminal, the placing of the run-up areas for engine testing at a greater distance from the passenger terminal, and the screening of them. Run-up hangars with considerable sound reduction (up to 40 dB) can be achieved at costs not exceeding those of an ordinary hangar (Kurtze, 1968).

## REFERENCES

Automotive Engineering. New engine developments. *Automotive Engineering*, 1973, **81** (4).

Congress Report. Ninety-second U.S. Congress, Sub-Committee on Air and Water Pollution. Hearings on Noise Pollution, 1972.

Congress Report. Ninety-third U.S. Congress, Subcommittee on Aeronautics and Space Technology. Hearings on Aircraft Noise Abatement, 1974.

DOT (Department of Transportation). Second federal noise abatement plan—FY 1970–71. Washington, January 1971.

FAA (Federal Aviation Administration). Noise abatement. Washington, February 24, 1970.

Kurtze, G. Recent advances in silencing ground testing of aircraft. Proceedings, 6th International Congress on Acoustics, August 1968.

NAC (The Noise Advisory Council). Aircraft engine noise research. London: HMSO, 1974.

NIPCC (National Industrial Pollution Control Council). Noise from gas turbine aircraft engines. Sub-Council Report, Washington, February 1971.

Witkin, R. If Concordes are coming, they won't sneak in. *New York Times*, May 11, 1975.

CHAPTER 15

# Exposure and Reactions to Aircraft Noise

Aircraft, like all other sources of noise, expose to noise both those who are involved in their operation (the participating environment) and those who, without being involved in it, are involuntarily exposed to it (the non-participating environment).

But what is most significant about aircraft noise is the much larger size of the non-participating environment in relation to the participating one—those who are involved in flight operations as passengers and as flying and airport personnel. In absolute terms, nevertheless, the very rapid growth of air transportation has made the participating environment a very sizable one. Thus in 1970 in the United States alone 465,000 passengers per day traveled by aircraft, with an average exposure of 1.4 hours at the characteristic cruise noise level of 82 dBA (*Air Transport 1971*, 1972).

## THE PARTICIPATING ENVIRONMENT

### Passengers and Operators

The noise to which passengers and operators of aircraft are exposed depends on the type of vehicle and on the location of the person in the interior of it. In the commercial jet aircraft the interior noise levels usually range from 79 to 88 dBA with a characteristic value of 82 dBA (EPA, 1971). In general aviation aircraft, the noise is of the order of 90 dBA with appreciable variations according to type of aircraft.

In jet aircraft, internal noise is primarily aerodynamic in nature, resulting from pressure fluctuations generated by the turbulent mixing

184

occurring in the "boundary layer" betweeen the fuselage and the surrounding air (Fig. 15.1). At the aft end of the aircraft, however, the dominant noise source may often be low-frequency exhaust-jet noise impinging on the fuselage and transmitted to the interior. In propeller aircraft, on the other hand, the major source of noise in the cabin is engine noise—particularly low-frequency noise from the propeller, against which internal insulation is only limitedly effective.

In modern jet commercial aircraft the operators and passengers are normally exposed to moderately high noise levels throughout an entire flight cycle, from takeoff to landing. The aircrafts are designed so as to maintain at cruising speed interior noise levels which permit passengers to converse at normal voice with good speech intelligibility. A history of typical cabin noise levels during a flight is shown in Fig. 15.2 (EPA, 1971).

In general aviation aircraft, the noise level is usually higher than for commercial aircraft, for a number of reasons. The engine is mounted close to the cabin so that there is little distance attenuation (a situation aggravated in the case of two-engine aircraft); the fuselage noise-insulation techniques are largely ineffective against the dominant low frequency of the propeller noise; the interior wall absorption is limited by the small volume within the cabin; and, in the case of propeller planes, the

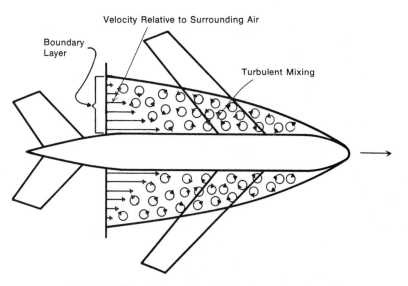

**Fig. 15.1**   The air flow around the fuselage of an aircraft.

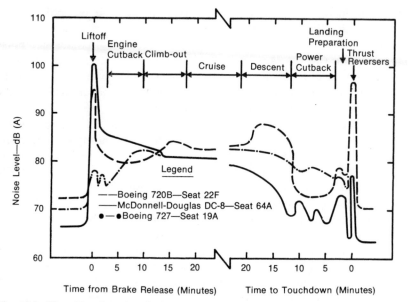

**Fig. 15.2** Time histories of typical cabin noise levels in a commercial aircraft (Source: EPA, 1971).

fuselage noise-insulation technique cannot be very effective against the dominant low-frequency propeller noise.

**Ground Personnel**

Ground personnel range from ramp and maintenance staff to other airport employees. Their numbers vary from airport to airport and so do their exposures. In the United States, about 300,000 airline employees are involved in air traffic operation of about 100 million movements per year—or three airline employees per 1000 movements; the study of the Commission on the Third London Airport (Roskill, 1970) assumes the need of 25,000–57,500 persons in jobs of all kinds for the 400,000 air transport movements predicted for the year 2000 for such an airport (corresponding to 72.5–142 jobs per 1000 movements). The range of exposure can vary from over 150 dB for maintenance personnel involved in the testing of turbojet engines, to levels as high as 120 dB for ramp personnel, to relatively modest noise exposures for personnel at the ticketing counters of an airport, and for personnel working away from the airport to exposure levels which are the same as those of the general population.

## THE NON-PARTICIPATING ENVIRONMENT

The major impact of aircraft noise on a community is due to commercial aviation, primarily in the zones near airports. At this moment general aviation provides no significant impact, since for most of the airports from which it operates an index such as the Noise Exposure Forecast (NEF*) is low—well below 30 even at very close ranges. However, in the future, general aviation is bound to become an increasingly significant and widespread source of noise; already today, at airports with high density of executive jets, the NEF and annoyance levels can be quite high.

Helicopters, with their extended low-altitude operation, generate high-noise impacts; they represent high levels of single-event noise, often more than 25–30 dBA higher than the background, and are therefore bound to annoy many in the community. Hovering, as it occurs in police operation or traffic surveillance, adds to the impact. However, no major reactions to helicopter noise have occurred until now, primarily because of the randomness of most flight patterns. One exception is New York City, where a strong reaction arose against helicopter air taxi services operating from downtown.

### Exposure

How many people are exposed to noise near airports? The answer is a difficult one. It could be obtained in principle from the details of every flight from every airport. Or, if actual noise measurements are available, it could be obtained by superimposing on population density maps noise-level contours such as the one shown in Fig. 15.9. A typical cumulative noise-exposure contour for a single-runway airport is shown in Fig. 15.3.

The first approach entails a huge data collection effort, while the second is made difficult by the belief of some airport authorities that a noise-level map is dynamite—once made public, the people in the high-noise areas will complain and bring suit in droves. On the balance, the noise-exposure contours offer the only practical approach; they provide a predictable measure of noise levels, which must then be related to community reaction.

---

*See Appendix 1.

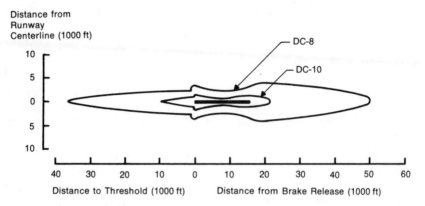

**Fig. 15.3**  Contours of 100 EPNdB during landing and takeoff operations—maximum design weights. (Source: McPike, 1972. Reprinted by permission. Copyright © the Society of Automotive Engineers, Inc.)

## Annoyance

What sort of annoyance is generated by jet aircraft noise near airports? In addition to disturbing rest or relaxation, or to interfering with sleep, jet aircraft noise causes interference with conversation, disturbs reception of television and radio, startles people and makes houses vibrate or shake. However, there is ample evidence that people who are disturbed are not necessarily annoyed by the disturbance and that people who are annoyed do not necessarily complain. This means that complaints are not a sensitive guide to annoyance.

The distinction between community reaction and annoyance is an important one in the context of quality of the environment. Any studies of jet aircraft noise near airports must take into account not just the area near the airport from which complaints come, but the larger area around the airport in which people are annoyed. For instance, in a review of the third stage of the plans of the Commission on the Third London Airport, Mishan makes the point that there is a large population in the zone below the 35 Noise and Number Index (NNI)* contour line, and that there will surely be a portion of this population who will come to resent the extra noise (Mishan, 1970). In the plans of the Commission, the effects of noise below the 35 NNI line were completely neglected (Roskill, 1970).

---

*See Appendix 1.

## European and American Surveys

### British Surveys

Two important surveys on aircraft noise annoyance have been carried out in the United Kingdom around London (Heathrow) Airport. The first was conducted in 1961 (McKennell, 1963), the second in 1967 (Mil Research, 1971). For both surveys a Guttman scale was constructed,* showing annoyance caused by interference with a number of activities.

*The 1961 survey* obtained a high correlation between annoyance score and noise exposure, as expressed in PNdB (Fig. 15.4).† At the same time a

---

*See Appendix 1.

†In the figure each point is the arithmetic mean of the scores on the six-point annoyance scale for informants within the particular noise stratum. The dotted lines indicate the region on either side of the average within which two-thirds of the individuals can be expected to fall. Although the strata are designated in PNdB, the average annoyance caused is actually the joint result of the number as well as the loudness of the aircraft. It is to be noted that, in questions of noise, minority reactions are perhaps even more important than average ones. For an annoyance score of 3.5 as many as one in six people are "annoyed" in the area where the average peak loudness is 92 PNdB, and for an annoyance score of 2.5, at which 50% of people report interference with conversation (Fig. A1.8), the average peak loudness is 85 PNdB. This compares with allowable levels of over 100 PNdB at which airlines are permitted to operate without penalty.

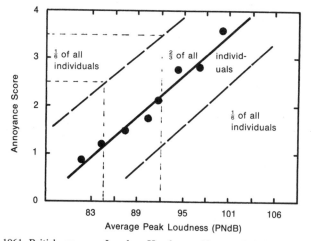

**Fig. 15.4** 1961 British survey—London Heathrow Airport. Relationship between annoyance scores and noise exposure strata. For further explanation see text. (Source: McKennell, 1963. Used by permission. Copyright © Her Majesty's Stationery Office.)

great range of variation was observed in the individual reactions of people exposed to the same noise level—a fact that holds true for other countries, and for traffic noise as well. As we further discuss in the Appendix, the variation reflects personal variables of a psychosocial nature related to factors such as susceptibility to noise or fear of aircraft. To quote McKennell, "Even when all available acoustical knowledge is utilized to the full, by far the greatest proportion of variance in annoyance will remain attributable to the psychosocial factors independent of exposure" (McKennell, 1963).

The total number of adults "annoyed" by aircraft noise was estimated at 378,000, out of a total population of 1,400,000 adults within a 10-mile radius from the airport (Fig. 15.5). The estimate was based on an index of annoyance midway between "moderately annoyed" and "very much annoyed," and corresponds to the amount of annoyance from aircraft noise by which 50 percent of the people were either prevented from going to sleep or had their rest and relaxation disturbed. (If one were to choose to define the annoyance level as that level at which 25 percent of the people would suffer from these disturbances, 700,000 people in a 20-mile area would be annoyed *by this one airport*). As the McKennell report points out: "... the minority in question is a very substantial one. When sensitivity is shown by such large numbers of people, it must be regarded as a normal phenomenon, in the sense that it can be expected to occur among similar large numbers in any ordinary population. It is the feelings of this substantial, largely uncomplaining* yet sensitive minority that the complainants make articulate." A sample of complainants came primarily from that segment of the population which is politically active, and responsive not only to noise but also to other modern disamenities.

The results of the 1961 British survey led to the formulation of the NNI Noise Index,† which takes into account the number of flights as well as the intensity of the noise in order to predict the evolution of future annoyance. The Wilson Committee on Noise concluded from the survey that the limits of acceptability for aircraft noise are 50–60 NNI by day and 30–45 NNI by night (Wilson, 1963).

*The 1967 survey* considered annoyance around London (Heathrow) Airport within a 10-mile radius. In the survey, socio-economic classifica-

---

*(Only 1 percent of the people interviewed said they had complained. It is interesting to note that this turned out to be larger than the actual number of complaints kept on record by the London Airport.)

†See Appendix 1.

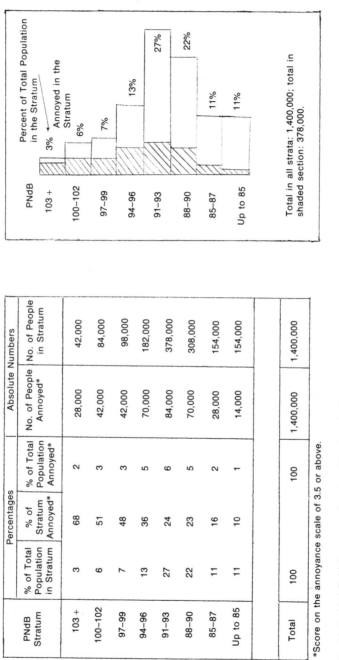

| PNdB Stratum | Percentages | | | Absolute Numbers | |
| --- | --- | --- | --- | --- | --- |
| | % of Total Population in Stratum | % of Stratum Annoyed* | % of Total Population Annoyed* | No. of People Annoyed* | No. of People in Stratum |
| 103+ | 3 | 68 | 2 | 28,000 | 42,000 |
| 100–102 | 6 | 51 | 3 | 42,000 | 84,000 |
| 97–99 | 7 | 48 | 3 | 42,000 | 98,000 |
| 94–96 | 13 | 36 | 5 | 70,000 | 182,000 |
| 91–93 | 27 | 24 | 6 | 84,000 | 378,000 |
| 88–90 | 22 | 23 | 5 | 70,000 | 308,000 |
| 85–87 | 11 | 16 | 2 | 28,000 | 154,000 |
| Up to 85 | 11 | 10 | 1 | 14,000 | 154,000 |
| Total | 100 | | 100 | 1,400,000 | 1,400,000 |

*Score on the annoyance scale of 3.5 or above.

**Fig. 15.5** 1961 British survey—London (Heathrow) Airport. Distribution over noise levels of the total population, and the annoyed* in the population (Source: McKennell, 1963. Used by permission. Copyright © Her Majesty's Stationery Office.)

Total in all strata: 1,400,000; total in shaded section: 378,000.

tion was used as follows:

- *Upper class* (*A*)—A class comprising 3 percent of the total U.K. population and in which the head of the household earns £2000 per year or more.
- *Upper middle class* (*B*)—Comprising 10 percent of the population and in which the head of the household earns between £1000 and £2000 per year.
- *Middle class* (*Cl*)—A class comprising 18 percent of the population and in which the head of the household earns less than £1000 per year, but does some form of minor professional or white collar work.
- *Skilled working class* (*C2*)—A class comprising 37 percent of the population in which the head of the household earns from £14 to £22 per week.
- *Working class* (*D*)—A class comprising 45 percent of the population and in which the head of the household earns between £10 10s. and £14 per week and is employed in semi-skilled work.
- *The lowest economic level group* (*E*)—A class earning less than the last group.

In general, the members of the upper class and upper middle class groups were found to be more vocal and critical than other groups. They are more readily bothered by noise than working class groups and they spontaneously mention aircraft noise, as well as traffic noise, as one of the sources of noise in their area more frequently than did other class groups.

According to the researchers the 1967 survey showed that despite an increase in the number of complaints and in the number of flights between 1961 and 1967, average annoyance scores remained the same. This was taken to imply that other environmental problems and pressures of daily life—suburban transport conditions, housing, air pollution, fear of unemployment, motor vehicle noise, etc.—increased perhaps more rapidly around the London Airport between 1961 and 1967 than exposure to aircraft noise, so that the annoyance caused by aircraft noise seems by comparison more bearable. Also, it was suggested that the formula for the NNI noise index had given too much weight to flight frequency, and that people are more sensitive to noise intensity than to its repetition, at least above a certain number of flights. In reality, a thorough reanalysis of the 1967 survey shows the same relationship between noise and annoyance in 1967 as in 1961. Thus the NNI index appears to be as good as any other index in integrating noise intensity and frequency of occurrence.

*French Surveys*

The first French survey of the annoyance around airports was conducted in 1965–66 by the Laboratory of Applied Anthropology of the University of Paris (Alexandre, 1970). The survey studied four French airports: Paris-Orly, Paris-LeBourget, Marseilles-Marignane and Lyon-Bron. So as to have as wide a range as possible of noise levels and frequencies of occurrence, 20 zones were selected in which the number of noise peaks ranged from 2–200 and the noise intensity from 90 to 112 PNdB. In all, 2000 interviews were conducted—100 in each zone (8 zones around Orly, 5 around LeBourget, 4 around Lyons, and 3 around Marseilles).

The survey showed (Fig. 15.6) a very high correlation (0.93) between the averages of the annoyance scores of the 20 zones considered and the corresponding values of the Noise Index R, which, as shown in the Appendix, is comparable to the American index CNR. Thus, the average annoyance in each zone due to aircraft noise, such as measured by ranking the replies, could be faithfully and precisely quantified. However, as in the British surveys, considerable variations existed between individual reactions to all the noise levels.*

---

*The correlation between the individual annoyance scores of the 2000 respondents and the R noise level index was much smaller, only 0.53.

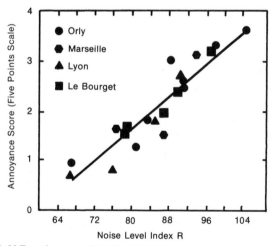

**Fig. 15.6** 1965–66 French survey. Relationship between annoyance scores and noise levels (Source: Alexandre, 1970).

In the course of the survey, two personal factors were identified as possibly influencing the degree of annoyance felt: habituation to noise and sensitivity to noise. The survey also showed that on numerous occasions annoyance increased considerably beyond R = 88 (equivalent to 106 CNR). At this level noise emerged from among the other sources of dissatisfaction with the living conditions of a neighborhood, such as shops, public transport, entertainment, neighbors. An analysis of the replies to specific questions regarding aircraft noise showed that disturbance when listening to the radio or TV was the inconvenience more often cited, and speech interference was the inconvenience which increased the most rapidly with noise level. In other words, a critical annoyance level was reached when noise marred the intelligent comprehension of speech.

## A Dutch Survey

A survey around the Amsterdam Airport conducted in 1964 by the Netherlands Scientific Research Center (TNO), and based on interviews with one thousand persons showed that, as in the British and French surveys, only mean annoyance was highly correlated with exposure (Alexandre, 1970). Observations concerning individual differences were similar to those made in the other countries. The survey led to the conclusion that the limit of acceptability for a 24-hour period was reached at 42 NNI.

## U.S. Surveys

*Earlier surveys.* One of the earliest surveys of community reactions to jet aircraft noise studied communities near two Air Defense Command (ADC) bases and one Strategic Air Command (SAC) base (Borsky, 1961). Because of the special role of military aviation, the results of the survey are atypical for civilian airports. The most significant finding was the small fraction of the population annoyed that complained (from one-eighteenth to one-seventieth). Also, one-fourth of those surveyed believed that no successful response could be obtained to complaints, and another half believed that multiple or organized complaints were necessary for success.

In 1966 the Office of Science and Technology (OST) published a study of its Jet Aircraft Noise Panel (OST, 1966) which reported that "... Communities located in the vicinities of airports serving large cities such as New York, Los Angeles and Seattle, as well as several smaller cities, have displayed increasing annoyance with noise produced by jet aircraft... Evidence of such growing dissatisfaction is the increasing number of complaints and law suits against airport operators and airlines ..." The OST study further indicated that "... if successive belts of PNdB values are drawn around the Los Angeles Airport, then, there is evidence that in belts with perceived noise levels below 90 PNdB there are almost no complaints; in those with values between 90 and 105 PNdB, there are some but not many complaints; and, in those about 105 PNdB the volume of complaints increases rapidly with increasing PNdB level." But, as we have seen, an argument based on complaints can be misleading in many ways.

In 1967 an attempt was made to reach a very rough estimate of the number of people affected in the United States by considering approximately two dozen large air traffic hubs for the fiscal year 1965 (FAA, 1965) and including only those for which the airport was less than 15 miles from the city center (Bugliarello and Wakstein, 1968).* It was concluded that the lowest possible number of people in the United States severely annoyed (annoyance score of 3.5) by jet aircraft noise near airports was 3.1 million.

*The TRACOR study.*    From 1967 to 1970 a study was carried out in the United States by the TRACOR Company (TRACOR, 1970) for the National Aeronautics and Space Administration. The survey was based on a sample of 8000 persons exposed to aircraft noise in the vicinity of several airports: Boston, Chicago, Dallas, Denver, Los Angeles, Miami, and New York. Annoyance was measured by the most sophisticated analytical techniques to date (factor analysis, multivariate analysis, etc.). As in the European surveys, noise annoyance was rated by number on the basis of the kind of activity interfered with. The activities used in establishing the annoyance scale for the airports of Chicago, Los Angeles, Denver, and Dallas are listed in Table 15.1, which for comparison purposes shows also the questions used for the 1961 British survey. The differences between the cumulative percentages are interesting. There are great variations between airports: airports are just not all that similar. For instance, disturbance to sleep varies from 13% at London to 28% at Los

---

*The distance of 15 miles was chosen because London (Heathrow) Airport is 15 miles away from the center of London, and much was known at the time about the London Airport noise problem. Thus, the number of people exposed was underestimated on two accounts: In the first place, only the largest airports have instrument flight rulings. Secondly, the 15 miles criterion led to omitting Kennedy Airport in New York, O'Hare Airport in Chicago, and the Detroit Airport, among others. On the other hand, there were compensating differences in population densities between the United States and the London Airport.

**Table 15.1** Comparative Analysis of Aircraft Annoyance for British and United States Airports (Source: TRACOR, 1970).

| London | | Chicago | | Los Angeles | | Denver | | Dallas | |
|---|---|---|---|---|---|---|---|---|---|
| Disturbance | Cumulative Percent Annoyed | Disturbance | Cumulative Percent Annoyed | Disturbance | Cumulative Percent Annoyed | Disturbance | Cumulative Percent Annoyed | Disturbance | Cumulative Percent Annoyed |
| Various activities | 6 | Various activities | 4 | Various activities | 7 | Various activities | 3 | Various activities | 5 |
| House vibration | 16 | Sleeping | 24 | Sleeping | 35 | Sleeping | 19 | Sleeping | 22 |
| TV/radio reception | 28 | House vibration | 44 | House vibration | 60 | House vibration | 31 | Face-to-face conversation | 40 |
| Face-to-face conversation | 41 | Face-to-face conversation | 51 | Face-to-face conversation | 66 | TV/radio reception | 36 | House vibration | 49 |
| Sleeping | 57 | TV/radio reception | 56 | TV/radio reception | 68 | Face-to-face conversation | 37 | TV/radio reception | 52 |
| General aircraft annoyance | 86 | General aircraft annoyance | 65 | General aircraft annoyance | 80 | General aircraft annoyance | 49 | General aircraft annoyance | 67 |
| Percent not annoyed: | 14 | | 35 | | 20 | | 51 | | 33 |

Angeles; disturbance of face-to-face conversation varies from 1% at Denver to 13% at London and 18% at Dallas; house vibration varies from 9% at Dallas to 25% at Los Angeles; and the percentage **not** annoyed varies from 14% at London to 51% at Denver.

The use of factor analysis and multivariate analysis made it possible to uncover the principal factors which, in addition to purely physical ones, such as distance from airport, permit to predict individual perceived annoyance. The six items in Table 15.2, plus the distance from the airport, account for 61 percent of the "predicted" variance. Hence, we see that certain personal factors, independent of the activities interfered with, play a determining role in predicting annoyance. An improved prediction of individual annoyance can be made by including these variables, but one must be careful not to confuse prediction with causation. When the variables are used in linear models, the correlation between noise exposure and individual annoyance caused by interference with certain activities increased (from 0.37 to 0.67); with a non-linear model the correlation increased further to (0.78). The meaning of these correlations must however be accepted cautiously.

**Table 15.2**    Principal Non-Physical Factors That Affect Individual Annoyance from Airport Noise (Source: TRACOR, 1970).

Fear of aircraft crashing in the neighborhood
Susceptibility to noise
Noise adaptability
City of residence
Belief in misfeasance on the part of those able to do something about the noise problem
Extent to which the airport and air transportation are seen as important

The TRACOR study also concluded that:

- The measurement of noise in dB(A) is sufficient to determine the level of community noise exposure.
- All noise indices are interchangeable, since the correlations between them are always higher than the correlations between any one of them and individual annoyance.
- Above 107 CNR, annoyance steadily increases, while a value of 93 CNR is necessary in order to obtain a significant reduction of annoyance.

*Comparisons between the Surveys*

There is a close correlation* between annoyance and noise for the international airports covered by the European surveys we have described (Fig. 15.7).† This indicates that *attitudes* toward aircraft noise vary little from one country to another. However, the survey also indicates that the critical noise level which represents the level of acceptability of noise does not vary too much from country to country. Thus:

•    in France the maximum noise level should be fixed at 45–50 NNI (R = 88);

•    in Great Britain the daytime level should be between 50 and 60 NNI and the nighttime level should be between 30 and 45 NNI;

•    in the Netherlands, the maximum tolerable limit appears to be at 42 NNI.

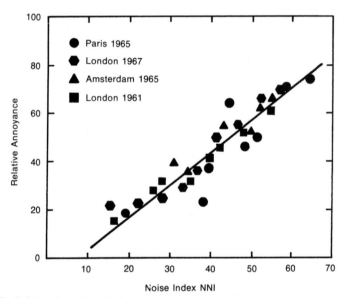

**Fig. 15.7**    Relation between relative average annoyance and noise level (NNI) around the airports of London, Paris, and Amsterdam (Source: Alexandre, 1970).

---

*Given by a coefficient of correlation of 0.92.

†Since the surveys in different countries used different numbers of questions to establish the annoyance scale (five in France, six in Britain, and seven in the Netherlands), valid comparisons can be made only by converting the absolute annoyance scores into "relative annoyance" as a percentage of the maximum score. For the noise levels, the NNI was used because the French and Dutch results were expressed in NNI as well as in R values.

From these findings one may consider that in general in Europe a value of the NNI of 45 is the maximum acceptable level for a 24-hour period, taking into account the fact that the figures given for noise at night are still fragmentary. A 45 NNI level corresponds to noise peaks of about 80 PNdB perceived 100 times in a 24-hour period, *inside a dwelling with closed windows.* Such noise levels interfere with speech, since they mask the intelligibility of a certain number of words and cause the speaker to raise his voice in order to be understood.

Using the results of the three surveys, one finds that *for each 5 NNI increase, there are roughly 10 percent more people annoyed.* The same conclusion can be drawn from American results (Kryter, 1970): beyond 95 CNR, each increase of 5 CNR is accompanied by a 10 percent increase in the number of people annoyed (Fig. 15.8).

The results for the United States where annoyance was found to increase rapidly beyond 107 CNR (that is R = 89) are in close agreement with the European results (R = 88 as the limit). The introduction of the more sophisticated NEF index,* which takes into account any additional

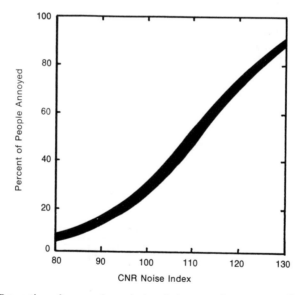

**Fig. 15.8**  Proportion of annoyed people in relation to noise exposure (Source: Kryter, 1970).

---

*See Appendix 1.

factors, shows that residential use should be considered incompatible with an NEF index greater than 40 (Wyle, 1971). The value of 30 for the NEF is the upper recommended value by U.S. Federal guidelines for new residents and constructions; at that value, 30 percent of the population exposed are expected to be strongly annoyed. It must be noted, however, that even at an NEF of 20, 20 percent of the population exposed are expected to be strongly annoyed.

An interesting point emerges from a comparison between noise zone forecasts made at two different times in the past for two airports—the Charles de Gaulle Airport at Roissy in France for 1985 and the O'Hare Airport in Chicago in 1970 (Alexandre, 1970). For both airports the land surface affected by the noise is large, and the noise impact index contours have a rough similarity of shape (Fig. 15.9). However, a much more conservative prognostication of noise contours appears to have been made by the French experts than by the American ones: the two noise patterns have essentially the same extension, although the Chicago traffic used for making the contours for 1970 (as envisaged by the FAA a few years earlier) had twice the intensity (2000 flights) than the traffic forecasts for Roissy in 1985 (1000 flights). Thus, a different group of experts, operating under different conditions, can reach very different forecasts even when using essentially the same noise impact index, and the public more and more must look with a critical eye at reports of experts.

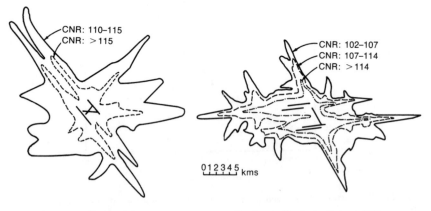

Chicago (O'Hare) 1970            Charles de Gaulle (at Roissy) 1985

**Fig. 15.9** Noise contours for predictions of noise at two different airports (Source: Alexandre, 1970).

**Appeals and Legal Action**

When annoyance reaches a high level, complaints become appeals to authorities and ultimately escalate to legal action. Data by Von Gierke and Nixon (1972) give a quantitative estimate of this progression (Fig. 15.10).

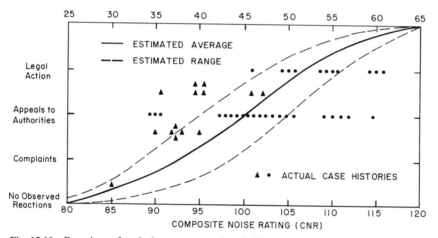

**Fig. 15.10**   Reactions of typical persons to a given habitual environment due to aircraft and industrial noise (adapted from Gierke and Nixon, 1972)

## SOME CONSIDERATIONS ON THE PLANNING OF AIRPORTS

A key problem concerning the exposure to aircraft noise is the planning of airports and of the communities around them. Although the broad question of planning for noise is discussed at length in Part V, it is appropriate here to outline very briefly some of the major questions that face the planner:

 • *The question of subsidy.*   If the inconvenience created by the operation of an airport for the population surrounding the airport is not fully compensated, in effect that population subsidizes the passengers and operators of aircraft and related services.

 • *The question of benefits versus disadvantages.*   Each site selection is a balance between advantages and disadvantages. If the advantages outweigh the disadvantages, the wealth of the nation is increased, and through such an increase there is a greater opportunity to compensate those who will suffer the disadvantages. (The problems of ensuring that such compensation takes place are discussed in Chapter 26.)

•   *The question of land control.*   Problems frequently arise because of a population's tendency to gravitate toward a new airport site— populations who were not present when the airport was initially planned or constructed. The very large area impacted by airport noise makes the control of the land difficult. In the United States the situation is accentuated by the fact that traditionally the power to control the land is in the hands of the individual states and may be delegated to municipalities and counties; there is a need for model protective legislation to be adopted uniformly throughout the country.

•   *The question of individual values.*   One of the most difficult problems for the planner is to assess the real nature of individual values as choices—as they may be indicated by behavior. There is always a great danger of making decisions on the basis of the implicit values of the decision maker or of the pressures exerted by strong pressure groups.

•   *The question of population forecast.*   Another very difficult question is how to forecast the population around the airports. At this moment there are no methods for assessing without substantial margin of error the future population around an airport that would incorporate the population demands arising from the airport.

•   *The question of zoning.*   An airport may create noisy conditions that would tend to drive away residents; but on the other hand it constitutes a hub of transportation that attracts industry and commercial enterprises that can benefit from being in the vicinity of the airport. The question is one of the proper balance between these different uses. In general, land prices around airports have tended to increase when the land is zoned so as to allow both residences and commercial and industrial construction.

•   *The question of space.*   Land-use planning to insure space for new airports is of extreme importance. Land with the characteristics that make possible the siting of new airports is scarce, and is found only at a distance from the cities. Thus the proposed new airport for Milan, Italy will be 85 km from the city. The new airport at Montreal will be at a comparable distance, and will also represent one of the first examples of inclusion—in the land purchased for an airport—of the entire area to be impacted by noise (approximately 300 sq. km).

• *The question of tradeoffs between environmental and other concerns.* The location of a new airport needs also to be governed by a tradeoff between environmental concerns and transportation time. A high-traffic airport with no mass transportation links to the city or cities it serves—a situation that unfortunately prevails in many large airports, from Chicago's O'Hare, to Rome, to La Guardia, to Heathrow, to Washington's Dulles—can be a generator of large amounts of air pollution, as well as of noise due to surface transportation. Where does the optimum lie?

## REFERENCES

*Air transport 1971.* Washington, D.C.: Air Transport Association of America, 1972.

Alexandre, A. Prévision de la gene due au bruit autour des aeroports et perspectives sur les moyens d'y remedier. Laboratoire d'Anthropologie Appliquée, Faculté de Medecine, Paris, 1970.

Borsky, P. N. Community reactions to air force noise, pt. 2, data on community studies and their interpretation. National Opinion Research Center, University of Chicago, WADD Technical Report AD 267057, March 1961.

Bugliarello, G. and Wakstein, C. Noise pollution—a review of its techno-sociological and health aspects. Biotechnology Program, Carnegie-Mellon University, Pittsburgh, 1968.

EPA (U.S. Environmental Protection Agency). Transportation noise and noise from equipment powered by internal combustion engines. Washington, December 1971.

FAA. Enroute I.F.R. air traffic survey, peak day, fiscal year 1965. Federal Aviation Administration, Office of Management Services, Data Systems Division, 1965.

Kryter, K. D. *The effects of noise on man.* New York: Academic Press, 1970.

McKennell, A. C. Aircraft noise annoyance around London (Heathrow) Airport. Central Office of Information SS 337, April 1963.

McPike, A. L. Air transportation system planning: Progress in noise reduction. Proceedings, International Conference on Transportation and the Environment, Washington, 1972.

Mil Research, Ltd. Second survey of aircraft noise annoyance around London (Heathrow) Airport. London: HMSO, 1971.

Mishan, E. J. What is wrong with Roskill. *Journal of Transport Economics and Policy,* September 1970.

OST (U.S. Office of Science and Technology). Alleviation of jet aircraft noise panel. Washington, March 1966.

Roskill. Commission on The Third London Airport. In *Papers and proceedings.* London: HMSO, 1970.

TRACOR. Community reaction to aircraft noise—final report. TRACOR Document T-70-AU-7454-U, Austin, Texas, 1970.

Von Gierke, H. E. and Nixon, C. W. Human response to sonic boom in the laboratory and the community. *Journal of the Acoustical Society of America,* 1975, 51, 2.

Wilson. Committee on The Problem of Noise. Noise, final report. Cmnd. 2056. London: HMSO, 1963.

Wyle Laboratories Research Staff. Community noise. Report Wr 71-17, Office of Noise Abatement and Control, EPA, Washington, November, 1971.

# CHAPTER 16

# The Supersonic Transport and the Sonic Boom

## INTRODUCTION

... it must be considered that introduction of the sonic boom from commercial SST*
operation constitutes a new phenomenon in aircraft noise and environmental pollution
in general; probably never before has a technological development exposed with one
step such a large number and large percentage of the general population to such an
increase in disturbing acoustic stimuli. The new phenomenon will be such that, for
overland flights it would be virtually impossible for people to escape the sonic boom and
avoid boom exposed areas similar to the way some people avoid noise-polluted areas in
our major cities today. The sonic boom from overland SST operation would probably
not make the environment more noisy than the environment many people have to
tolerate today in the vicinity of airports; the main difference would be that instead of a
small minority, a large percentage of the population would be exposed and almost
without the possibility of escape from this new noise... Operation of commercial
supersonic transport aircraft fleets must be consistent with technological progress,
economy, and first of all, human health and happiness (Von Gierke and Nixon, 1972).

The much debated 1971 decision of the U.S. Congress to eliminate
federal support for the development of the Boeing SST highlights the
political impact of the concern with sonic booms. Although other factors
entered into the decision, the environmental concern with the booms was
a preponderant issue. The next test of the weight of environmental
concerns vis-à-vis commercial, economic and prestige concerns will come
with the entrance into regular airline service of the Anglo-French
Concorde and the Soviet TU-144.

---

*Super Sonic Transport.

## PUBLIC REACTION

The big problem as far as the SST is concerned is that it is still not known what peak overpressure the public will find acceptable. This is not just a question of annoying a small fraction of people at airports; a much larger number is involved. As Kryter points out:

> This new noise will be a significant problem, it appears, not because it will have any worse effects upon people than the noise from present-day subsonic aircraft near airports—as a matter of fact, research in Great Britain by Broadbent and Robinson, and also in the U.S., indicates that the effects of sonic booms and noise from subsonic jets near airports may actually be roughly comparable—but because the sonic boom will be heard by so many more people. . . the overall noise problem could become much worse. For example, it is estimated that trans-continental SST operations over the U.S. could expose 50,000,000 or so people to 15 or so booms per day. I think that the "absolute" number of bothered people becomes important (because). . . practically speaking, there probably is a "critical mass" of people required to exert significant political and social action against a nuisance and the number of people near present airports appear in many cases to be fewer than this critical size or number (Kryter, 1970).

Laboratory studies have shown that sonic booms could be compared in annoyance value to recordings of subsonic jets which had previously been well studied (Pearsons and Kryter, 1965; Broadbent and Robinson, 1964). In these studies people were asked to match sonic booms and subsonic jet noise for equal annoyance as expressed by airport noise annoyance indices like NNI.* From the studies, the possibility emerges of assuming that a *sonic boom of 1.9 psf is subjectively equal to a subsonic jet airplane noise of 110 PNdB*. With this equivalence one boom a day will produce a CNR of 98 and the CNR will increase by three for each doubling of the number of booms. Thus two or more sonic booms a day would result in CNR values of 100 or higher; this would lead to vigorous and widespread complaints. In the U.S., where SST schedules could expose 35–65 million people to 10–20 booms a day (e.g., Kryter, 1967), ranging in overpressure from 1.5 to 2.5 psf, there would almost certainly be political and legal actions. A 1974 EPA report suggests that little or no public annoyance can be expected for one sonic boom during daytime of less than 0.75 psf, as measured on the ground. No greater annoyance would be expected with multiple booms if the peak level of each does not exceed $0.75/\sqrt{N}$ psf, where N is the number of booms. Thus for 4 booms a day, the overpressure of each should not exceed 0.37 psf (EPA, 1975).

There are increasing indications that the reactions of a community to

---

*See Appendix 1.

sonic booms cannot be compared to those for subsonic aircraft noise (Rice and Lilley, 1969). The vibration of houses, the startled reactions and the effects on sleep are certainly quite different. More than half of Pearsons and Kryter's subjects said that they could not learn to accept such booms (Pearsons and Kryter, 1965). This was so in spite of the fact that the booms were produced under laboratory conditions at the subjects' will—and thus the subjects had some chance to prepare themselves for the booms.

The sensitivity of people to sonic booms is exemplified by Table 16.1, which shows the nature of some French responses to a survey, and by Table 16.2, which shows the nature of the responses to sonic boom exercise in St. Louis and Oklahoma City.

Another problem in predicting the annoyance caused by sonic booms

**Table 16.1**   Sensitivity to Sonic Boom: Responses to a Survey in France (Source: Rice and Lilley, 1969).

| | |
|---|---|
| 1. Are you disturbed by the boom during your work or daily activities? | |
|     Enormously, very much | 26% |
|     A little, not at all | 74% |
| 2. Do you believe you can tolerate 10 booms per day?* | |
|     Absolutely no | 35% |
|     With much pain | 27% |
|     With some difficulty | 26% |
|     Fairly or very easily | 13% |
| 3. If the booms are produced at night, would you think that they are: | |
|     Absolutely intolerable | 56% |
|     Hard to tolerate, | |
|     Tolerable only if necessary, | |
|     Tolerable without difficulty | 44% |
| 4. Are you used to sonic booms? Can you say whether: | |
|     You are always startled in the | |
|       same way at each boom | 63% |
|     Now you are startled less | |
|       or you are totally used to | |
|       the booms | 37% |
| 5. How much are you disturbed by sonic booms in comparison to the noise generated by all other types of airplanes? | |
|     Much more, a little more | 75% |
|     Not more, rather less | 25% |
| 6. Personally, how much are you disturbed by sonic booms? | |
|     Enormously, much | 83% |
|     Very little, not at all | 17% |

*Total does not equal 100% because of rounding off.

**Table 16.2**  Comparisons between Annoyance Levels and Effects Due to Sonic Booms in the St. Louis (1961–62) Tests (Source: Rice and Lilley, 1969).

| Nature of Effect | Percent of Interviews | | | |
|---|---|---|---|---|
| | Effects Recorded | | Annoyance Recorded | |
| | St. Louis | Oklahoma City | St. Louis | Oklahoma City |
| Shaking or vibration of dwelling | 93 | 94 | 38 | 54 |
| Startling | 74 | 38 | 31 | 31 |
| Interruption of sleep | 42 | 18 | 22 | 14 |
| Interruption of rest | 24 | 17 | 16 | 14 |
| Interruption of conversation | 22 | 14 | 10 | 10 |
| Interruption of Radio or TV reception | 14 | 9 | 6 | 6 |

arises from the fact that, unfortunately, the shape of the N-wave* and its fine structure have a great effect on the annoyance produced; the peak overpressure is not sufficient to characterize the annoyance, and there is some indication that longer duration N-waves might produce more annoyance.

A study of simulated sonic booms in England using specially designed explosive charges (Warren, 1966) suggested that even the group that was "considerably annoyed" adapted somewhat over a period of time; annoyance changed from 20 percent to 10 percent of the group interviewed. In the case of the United States this 10 percent would still represent a considerable number of people, 5 million, if a figure of 50 million in the path of the sonic boom is accepted.

## EFFECTS ON STRUCTURES AND ANIMALS

The sonic boom also affects structures and animals. The effects on structures are relatively minor if the aircraft flies at high altitude and no "super booms" are generated by maneuvers of the supersonic craft. A sonic boom increases dynamically the static load of a building. The dynamic increase factor depends, other factors being equal, on the type of

---

*See Chapter 13.

plane that generates the shock. A large military plane such as the XB-70*
causes the excitation of all structural elements which have a fundamental
frequency of less than 1.5 Hz; on the other hand, for a fighter plane such
as the F-10A, the excitation occurs at about 8 Hz. The dynamic increase
factor is also a function of the damping coefficient of the structure; for
structures with a low damping coefficient, the factor has approximately a
value of two (Lilley, 1969).

Since most building materials, with the exception primarily of large
glass panels, have a natural resonating frequency of 10 Hz, the majority
of the dynamic effects of the sonic boom on buildings are due to the direct
action of the boom waves—direct waves, and the waves reflected by the
ground and other structures. In general, these effects fall well within the
limits of safety for professionally designed buildings. On the other hand,
sonic booms can do damage to buildings in poor state of repair, and
possibly to churches, monuments, and similar structures. As for windows,
it has been reported that during the Oklahoma City tests the boom was
equivalent to a storm of 30 m.p.h. (Wiggins, as reported in Lilley, 1969).

Little is still known about the reactions of animals to sonic booms. It is
possible that animals experience the same reactions of fear as do humans,
but at this moment there is not sufficient information to assert that some
booms affect them appreciably. In particular, in many localities birds are
probably by now accustomed to the sonic booms generated by military
aircraft. Below the sea surface, the overpressure caused by a sonic boom is
less than that generated by surface waves, leading to the conclusion that
the effects on marine life are minimal.

## SOME SIGNIFICANT FIELD TESTS

Given the significance of human reactions to an assessment of the
tolerance to sonic booms, it is appropriate to consider in greater detail the
results of three series of tests performed in the 1960's in the United
States.

### The Oklahoma City and St. Louis Tests

At the end of 1961 and the beginning of 1962 and again in 1964,
airplanes were flown many times at supersonic speeds over two cities in
the United States (the 1961–62 series was conducted over St. Louis and

---

*See footnote at the beginning of Chapter 14 for a brief identification of the types of
aircraft mentioned in this chapter.

the 1964 series over Oklahoma City), and in 1964 extensive interviews were carried out during the flight programs. The object was to observe public reaction, and to obtain information that might be used in predicting the reaction to sonic booms from the SST.

In the Oklahoma City tests (Borsky, 1965), about 1250 daytime booms were produced in the Oklahoma City area with the maximum peak overpressure of 1.5 psf (although 2.0 psf booms had been scheduled). The fraction of people "annoyed" (somewhere between "seriously" and "more than a little") increased to 56 percent by the end of the studies; 5 percent complained to the authorities. Within the fraction of the number of people "annoyed," the number who complained is much greater than found in any other studies of aircraft annoyance. At the end of the study, somewhere between 10 percent and 25 percent of those interviewed said they could not learn to live with eight booms a day for an indefinite period. The ratio of complaint to annoyance was 1 to 11—by coincidence, the same figure as in the London (Heathrow) Airport Study discussed in the previous chapter. However, in the latter study, night operations were taken into account, whereas all the Oklahoma City booms were produced during the day. So it is likely that in practice the 56 percent would increase to perhaps 75 percent. Clearly there is an important question here: can we allow 75 percent of the people in the flight path of an SST and an even larger portion in a more densely populated area, to be "more than a little annoyed"?

In the earlier St. Louis Study (Nixon and Hubbard, 1965), the annoyance was studied by interviews, as well as inferred from the number of complaints per flight. The tests raised several interesting questions that were not satisfactorily answered in the reports:

* The number of complaints rose sharply at the end of the test series when a local newspaper published an editorial against the tests. The same sensitivity to newspaper coverage was shown in the Oklahoma City tests. Since editorial positions are likely to be taken, to what extent do the communication media influence complaints?

* The flight path was chosen to the east of the city, while there is an affluent residential area located to the west: can the information obtained by the tests be used to predict the complaints of these people also?

* There was no information about the complaints from the nighttime booms. Would these not have caused more annoyance?

* Why did the original NASA report (Nixon and Hubbard, 1965) show a larger total of valid incidents than a published summary article (Nixon and Borsky, 1966)?

## The Edwards Air Force Base Tests

Residents of Edwards Air Force Base (EAFB) who were used to hearing sonic booms, were exposed to sonic booms from B-58 and XB-70 airplanes, and also to subsonic jet aircraft noise (NSBEO, 1967). The choice of the XB-70 airplane is important because it is about as large as the supersonic transport and therefore produces a sonic boom very much like the one that may be expected from the SST. Residents of other towns, Redlands and Fontana, California, who had not experienced sonic booms before were also brought to Edwards Air Force Base to listen to the sonic booms. In the tests, the people were warned before each boom. The principal findings (NSBEO, 1967) were that:

> When indoors, subjects from Edwards Air Force Base judged booms from the B-58 at 1.69 psf nominal peak overpressure outdoors to be as acceptable as the noise from a subsonic jet at an intensity of 109 PNdB measured outdoors.
>
> When indoors, subjects from the towns of Fontana and Redlands judged the boom from the B-58 at 1.69 psf nominal peak overpressure outdoors to be as acceptable as the noise from a subsonic jet at an intensity of 118 to 119 PNdB measured outdoors.
>
> When indoors, 27 percent of the subjects from Edwards and 40 percent of the subjects from Fontana and Redlands combined, rated the B-58 booms of nominal peak overpressure of 1.69 psf as being between less than "just acceptable" to "unacceptable". "unacceptable".
>
> When of approximately equal nominal or measured peak overpressure and when heard indoors and judged against the aircraft noise, the boom from the XB-70 was slightly less acceptable than the booms from the F-105 or B-58 aircraft. When heard outdoors and judged against aircraft noise, the boom from the B-58 was slightly less acceptable than the booms from the XB-70 and F-104 aircraft...

The fact that the B-70 booms were "slightly less acceptable" than the F-104 and B-58 booms is significant, because the F-104 and B-58 airplanes were used in the Oklahoma and St. Louis studies. The second conclusion is important because a perceived noise level of 118 dB is unacceptable in any sense and, moreover, the B-70 booms were even less acceptable. Although no adequate criteria are available for predicting public reaction to sonic booms with confidence, it seems unambiguously clear that the annoyance will be considerable, and cannot be ignored.

## TECHNICAL CONSIDERATIONS

As we have seen in Chapter 13 of this Part, the possibility of reducing the sonic boom by altering the design and flight characteristics of the plane is limited. The heavier the plane and the lower and faster it flies, the louder the boom. However, the boom specifications cannot arbitrarily be changed to some lower value. In fact, a supersonic plane becomes impossible to build if the value is too low (Baals and Foss, 1967); the booms can be made less intense by changing certain design features of the airplane, but not by very much (McLean and Shrout, 1966).

Because the atmosphere through which the shock waves are propagated is not uniform, with the temperature profile with height changing from day to day, statistical variations in the peak overpressure of the boom occur. For instance, booms having at least twice the nominal peak overpressure have been observed 10 percent of the time in flights of the XB-70 (Maglieri and Hilton, 1966). These kinds of booms will inevitably be produced in commercial flights.

As it seems clear that sonic booms will annoy some large fraction of the people hearing them, it is reasonable to ask, could the routes be designed to go around the cities? To do this would raise some associated questions concerning variations from the prescribed course and the performance of high-speed turns.

The sonic boom problem could be reduced by having the SST fly more slowly over land, as suggested in numerous newspaper articles following the release of the Edwards Air Force Base Study: this would, however, affect the ability of the SST to pay off as an investment. Recent experience with the Concorde seems to indicate, however, that the sonic boom produced by the aircraft may be tolerable during daytime, as long as the aircraft flies at constant speed without sharp maneuvers.

## A PESSIMISTIC OUTLOOK FOR THE SST

In the report (Nixon and Hubbard, 1965) of the social survey that was carried out during and after the St. Louis test flights, one of the Air Force officers connected with the tests puts forward the hypothesis that a "cumulative saturation point" was reached in people's tolerance. If this is a general feature of exposure to sonic booms, and overland flights are allowed, say in Britain, then a critical mass of people may well demand the stopping of such flights and have their demands met. Clearly this would change the economic picture as far as the airlines are concerned, and the risk of this happening might very well deter the airlines from purchasing supersonic transport airplanes.

The public response to sonic booms becomes even more conjectural when one compares directly the St. Louis, Oklahoma City, and Edwards Air Force Base studies, as well as the results of the Warren study of simulated sonic booms in England [Warren, 1968]. Three different trends in the annoyance with time are shown in Fig. 16.1. Which trend is one to believe? The point here seems to be that even though large amounts of money have been spent in realistic tests and in careful interviewing, the prognosis is still unclear. How different from the conventional scientific experiment after which predictions can be made! In this case experiments have been done and yet we are still no closer to being able to make reliable predictions.

The possibility of political and local action against the boom from the SST appears reinforced by several additional factors. Let us consider the Edwards Air Force Base data. The people who came from Redlands had little experience of sonic booms and, unlike the residents of EAFB, no special connection with the military aircraft that made more acceptable the sonic booms they were used to hearing. If we take the people from Redlands as typical, then their rating of a sonic boom of 1.7 psf is 118 PNdB. For these people one boom a day would produce a CNR of 106, already too high. Things are made even worse if one looks carefully at the relation between CNR and community reaction shown in Figure 15.10. Appeals to authorities could start at CNR values of 95, and legal action is likely to be the most common response at a CNR value of 106 which would arise from just one boom a day! Moreover, in the foregoing we

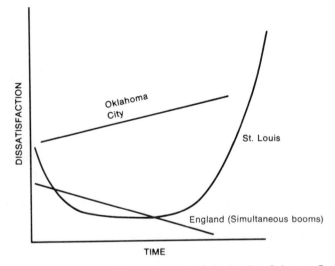

**Fig. 16.1**    Changes in annoyance with time for real and simulated sonic booms. Qualitative trends.

have dealt with averages; a more sensitive minority would still be a very large number of people, because of the width of the carpets.

There is another interesting aspect of the EAFB data. The only airplane that people from Fontana, Redlands, and EAFB heard was the B-58. For the B-58 there are three data points for residents of EAFB listening indoors, so that a simple linear fit would be made, relating the sonic boom overpressure and the equivalent average subsonic jet airplane noise. However, there is only one data point for the residents of Fontana and one for the residents of Redlands. The assumption was made in the study that the slope of the curve for these people must be the same as for the people from EAFB. But this is not all obvious, as the people from EAFB choose to live there and, moreover, are accustomed to hearing sonic booms. Edwards Air Force Base is a well-known establishment that has long been connected with advanced military aircraft; people who were neutral or antagonistic to advanced military aircraft with their well-known sonic booms would hardly choose to live there. So it may be argued that people from Fontana and Redlands may be more sensitive to sonic booms than people from EAFB, and that as such the extrapolation from the one data point at 1.7–2.0 psf, or in the case of Concorde 2.5 psf, may lead to over 125 PNdB, a level so high that there is no previous experience of what public reaction would be.

Finally, in dealing with the SSTs, the question discussed in Chapter 14 of the high noise levels at take-off and landing due to their very noisy turbojet engines cannot be overlooked. Engine quieting programs for supersonic transports are for more expensive and chancy than for the subsonic ones, and are unlikely to achieve substantial reductions in noise level without a drastic redesign of the aircraft.

## REFERENCES

Baals, D. D. and Foss, W. E. Jr. Assessment of sonic boom problem for future air-transport vehicles. *Journal of the Acoustical Society of America*, 1966, **39**, S73.

Borsky, P. N. Community reactions to sonic booms in the Oklahoma City area. National opinion Research Center, University of Chicago, AMRL-TR-65-37, May 1965.

Broadbent, D. E. and Robinson, D. W. Subjective assessment of the relative annoyance of simulated sonic bangs and aircraft noise. *Journal of Sound and Vibration*, 1964, **2**, (2).

EPA (U.S. Environmental Protection Agency). Information on levels of noise requisite to protect public health and welfare with an adequate margin of safety. Washington, March 1974.

Kryter, K. D. Acceptability of aircraft noise. *Journal of Sound and Vibration*, 1967, **5**.

Kryter, K. D. *The effects of noise on man*. New York: Academic Press, 1970.

Lilley, G. M. The Effects of sonic booms on buildings. OCDE Conference on Sonic Booms, August 1969.

Maglieri, D. J. and Hilton, D. A. Experiments on the effects of atmospheric refraction and airplane accelerations on sonic boom ground pressure patterns. NASA TN-D 3520, 1966.

McLean, F. E. and Shrout, B. L. Design methods for minimization of sonic boom pressure field disturbances. *Journal of the Acoustical Society of America*, 1966, **39**, S19.

Nixon, C. W. and Hubbard, H. H. Results of USAF-NASA-FAA program to study community response to sonic booms in Greater St. Louis area. NASA TN D-2705, May 1965.

Nixon, C. W. and Borsky, P. N. Effects of sonic boom on people: St. Louis, Missouri, 1961–1962. *Journal of the Acoustical Society of America*, 1966, **39**, 5.

NSBEO (National Sonic Boom Evaluation Office). Sonic boom experiment at Edwards Air Force Base. Arlington, Va, NSBEO-1-67, July 1967.

Pearsons, K. S. and Kryter, K. D. Laboratory tests of subjective reactions to sonic boom. NASA, CE-187, March 1965.

Rice, C. G. and Lilley, G. M. Effects of sonic boom on man and animals. Report, OCDE Conference on Sonic Booms, August 1969.

Von Gierke, H. E. and Nixon, C. W. Human response to sonic boom in the laboratory and the community. *Journal of the Acoustical Society of America*, 1972, **51**, 2.

Warren, C. H. E. A preliminary analysis of the results of exercise crackerjack and their relevance to supersonic transport aircraft. RAETN No. Aero 2789, ARC 23273, 1966.

**Part V** Occupational, Domestic, and Leisure Noise

# CHAPTER 17

# The Sources of Occupational, Domestic, and Leisure Noise

Industrial processes, construction, and even household and leisure*
activities generate noise that impinges both upon the people engaged in
them and upon outsiders. Lawnmowers affect both those who operate
them and those in the surrounding areas; noise in the industrial plant
affects both the workers in the plant and the neighborhoods around the
plant; the noise of a rock-and-roll band—one of the loudest man-made
noises—affects players and audience alike. It is thus necessary to
consider both the "internal" and "external" aspects of occupational
noise.

From a political economy and legal viewpoint, as we shall discuss in
greater detail in Part VI, the "internal" and "external" aspects are
profoundly different. According to classical economics the internal
aspects—the "internalities"—should, at least in part, be regulated by the
traditional market mechanism that governs manpower supply and compensation, while the external aspects—the "externalities"—require government intervention, or agreements with the surrounding activities that
are affected by the noise. In reality, however, market mechanisms have
been very ineffective in dealing with the internalities. Workmen's insur-

---

*It is difficult to distinguish between some leisure and household activities. For instance,
is gardening (lawnmowing, etc.) a leisure activity or a household chore? For this reason, we
have preferred pragmatically to consider leisure activities together with the sources of
"occupational" noise. We find some rational justification in doing so from the fact that some
people are "working" at their leisure as hard as they are working at their jobs.

ance has not been a sufficient deterrent to noisy environments, and workers, largely unaware of the damage created by exposure to noise, have failed to press for higher wages or, better, for a quieter workplace.

Thus government intervention has become necessary also in the internal aspects of noise. The intervention takes the form of occupational safety regulations which establish limits of exposure for workers and standards of performance for equipment.

Like traffic noise, occupational noise has been growing in intensity and in impact. In modern industrial countries, industry absorbs an increasingly large percentage of the labor force; construction of buildings and other structures is occurring at an accelerated pace; households are acquiring a larger number of mechanized appliances. Agriculture also, in the measure that it must compete with industry in terms of manpower efficiency, is becoming increasingly mechanized, and thus sees the noise level of its activities rise.

The absolute level of noise produced by machinery has increased almost every generation because of new technological developments. For instance, the introduction of the jet engine has raised the maximum level of noise produced in the past 30 years by man-made devices in the same way that the internal combustion engine increased the noise level of the previous generation.

Finally, the numbers of engine-powered leisure vehicles and boats have grown vertiginously during the past 10 years, as have loud rock-and-roll bands.

Regardless of the specific type of device or process, the sources of industrial noise are basically two:

- vibration of a structure or machine, or of their components;
- aerodynamic processes—primarily turbulence, such as the turbulence inside a blower at the contact of a high-speed, high-pressure air jet with the surrounding atmosphere.

## INDUSTRIAL NOISE

From the standpoint of noise, industrial activities can be grouped into four basic categories (EPA, 1971a):

- product fabrication (both molding, such as glass bottle manufacturing, and metal fabrication, such as can manufacturing);
- product assembly;
- power generation;
- processing.

Each one of these activities generates noise, usually with most of its energy in the lower frequencies of the spectrum. As we shall see, although both the workers inside a plant and the persons on the outside are affected, the impact on the workers is generally a much more serious problem.

## External Aspects

Some of the typical sources or avenues of noise transmitted by an industrial plant to the outside are roof ventilators, open windows, steam injectors, compressors, and diesel engines. Before the development of large mass transportation systems, when it was necessary to locate industrial plants close to the houses of the labor force, the noise propagated to the outside from industrial activities had a major impact on the workers' environment. Today, with the growth of both mass and individual means of transportation, the necessity of locating industrial plants in the immediate vicinity of residential areas has greatly diminished.

Thus, the impact of the noise generated by an industrial plant on the environment is generally small. This can be so even at the property line of the plant if the site is properly planned. Furthermore, when a number of plants are grouped together, they tend to elevate the overall noise level in the community to such an extent that the additional noise of an individual plant is limited; only the older plants, located in close proximity to residences, pose a major problem. There are, of course, exceptions. For instance, a glass-manufacturing plant has been found to generate noise that at the property line exceeded the background community noise levels by as much as 29 dBA (EPA, 1971c). Another industrial activity with a strong environmental impact—in this case a single source—are jet-engine testing facilities, which are capable of emitting at the source as much as 150 dB, over a broad spectrum of frequencies.

## Internal Aspects

The principal operations and related noise characteristics in each of the four basic categories of industrial activities are shown in Table 17.1. A more detailed list of noise levels found in specific operations and caused by specific machines in industry is given in Table 17.2. The table is based primarily on measurements by Karplus and Bonvallet (1953) in 40 plants selected from 12 manufacturing industries. A summary of most of the

**Table 17.1**  Some Characteristics of the Most Common Industrial Noise Sources (Source: EPA, 1971a).

| Type of Activity | Examples of Products or Processes | Significant Characteristics |
|---|---|---|
| Product fabrication<br>Metal fabrication | Boilers<br>Cans | Very noisy operations in the metal-stamping process (cutting, shearing, pinching, pressing, etc.); also riveting |
| Product fabrication<br>Molding | Plastics<br>Glass bottles | Major noise source: turbulent mixing with the atmosphere of high-pressure air used in operation, pneumatic control and cooling of molding machines |
| Product assembly | Automobiles<br>Aircraft<br>Dishwashers<br>Radios | Broad-band noise with highest levels at highest frequency, due to operation of electric and pneumatic tools (impact wrenches, riveters, air blow-down devices, grinders, etc.) |
| Power generation | Conventional thermal power plants<br>Nuclear power plants | Some portion of plant indoor (turbine generators and air compressors), other sources outdoors (transformers, forced-draft blowers, induced-draft fans) |
| Process plants | Oil refineries<br>Steel plants | Major noise sources: furnaces (with a broad frequency of noise), heat exchangers, compressors, pumps, air and steam leaks |

data (Fig. 17.1) shows that 80 percent of the noise levels are above 80 dB, and 20 percent above 95 dB. Ranges for noise produced by 11 common tools observed during a more recent study by the U.S. EPA, in a survey of five typical industrial plants, are given in Fig. 17.2, which shows again how machinery and process noise can be extremely high.

The disturbing aspect of data such as these is that many of the types of work processes listed are not unusual; most people know someone in more than half of the occupations involved. Even office work is not without risk of hearing damage, as may be seen from Table 17.3. These again are familiar jobs, some of them with noise levels above 80 dB.

**Table 17.2** Some Specific Sources of Industrial Noise.

130 or more dB*
  Testing a jet engine or turbine
  Riveting a large steel structure

120–129 dB
  Chipping operations on a large steel
    casting
  Testing reciprocating airplane engines
  Riveting on small structures
  Chain saw**

119–120 dB
  Large drop hammer
  Hammer mill
  Rolling mill
  Power house
  Most core manufacturing processes for
    castings
  Metal-forming machines
  Gear-cutting machines
  Testing an internal combustion engine

100–109 dB
  Most mining operations**
  Most operations using pneumatic tools
  Sawing meat and metal
  Sawing, planing, surfacing, and lathe
    operations for large wood pieces
  Textile looms
  Heavy excavation equipment**
  Many paper manufacturing machines
  Many paper products manufacturing
    machines
  Large printing presses
  Boiler room
  Plastic and rubber-molding machinery
  Chemical and food mixers
  Petroleum-refining processes
  Stone crusher
  Tumble cleaners
  All metal furnaces except open hearths
  Forging operations
  Conveyors with steel products
  Punch presses
  Grinders

90–99 dB
  Food canning
  Food preparation
  Most textile, yarn and thread manu-
    facturing operations
  Sawing, planing, etc., of small
    wood pieces
  Small and special purpose printing
    presses
  Many chemical manufacturing processes
  Many leather products manufacturing
    processes
  Welding and cutting, both electric
    and oxy-acetylene
  Polishers
  Drills and borers
  Levelers for steel plates
  Blooming mills
  Strip mills
  Metal shears
  Farm machinery**
  Steel product fabrication
  Machinery assembly lines

80–89 dB
  Textile dyeing
  Carding and combing, textile
  Most apparel manufacturing processes
  Typesetting
  Warehouse operations**
  Fabric-coating processes, chemical
  Raw material processing, chemical
  Finished product handling, steel
    products

*Octave-band sound levels measured at the operator's ear [data from Karplus and Bonvallet (1953) and from the authors (marked**)].

221

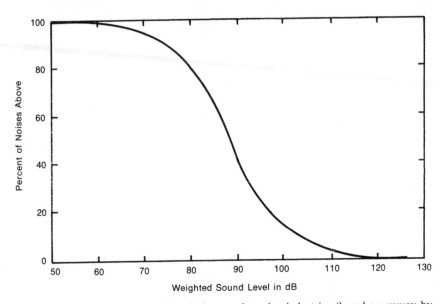

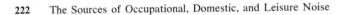

**Fig. 17.1**   Distribution of sound levels in manufacturing industries (based on survey by Karplus and Bonvallet, 1953) (Adapted from Botsford, 1969).

**Table 17.3**   Office Noise—All Measured at the Operator's Level (Source: Stalker, 1955).

| | |
|---|---|
| Private office | 65 dBA |
| Typing office (one typewriter) | 70 dBA |
| Near xerox machine | 75 dBA |
| Accounting office | 79 dBA |
| Business services (copying, printing, etc.) | 80 dBA |
| Keypunch room | 82–84 dBA |
| Computer operations | 85 dBA |

## CONSTRUCTION NOISE

Construction noise is the product of the machines and processes involved in construction. Since much of construction is carried out outdoors, the external noise effects are much more important than for other kinds of industrial noise.

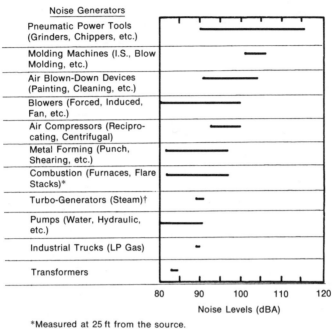

Noise Generators

| | |
|---|---|
| Pneumatic Power Tools (Grinders, Chippers, etc.) | |
| Molding Machines (I.S., Blow Molding, etc.) | |
| Air Blown-Down Devices (Painting, Cleaning, etc.) | |
| Blowers (Forced, Induced, Fan, etc.) | |
| Air Compressors (Reciprocating, Centrifugal) | |
| Metal Forming (Punch, Shearing, etc.) | |
| Combustion (Furnaces, Flare Stacks)* | |
| Turbo-Generators (Steam)† | |
| Pumps (Water, Hydraulic, etc.) | |
| Industrial Trucks (LP Gas) | |
| Transformers | |

80    90    100    110    120

Noise Levels (dBA)

*Measured at 25 ft from the source.
†Measured at 10 ft from the source.

**Fig. 17.2**   Range of industrial machinery, equipment, and process noise levels (measured, except where noted, at operator positions) (Source: EPA, 1971b).

Regardless of the type of structure under construction, be it a high-rise building, a bridge, a highway or a sewer, the equipment employed can be classified into five major categories:

- Earthmoving equipment.
- Materials handling equipment.
- Stationary equipment.
- Impact equipment.
- Other types of equipment.

Figure 17.3 shows noise ranges for typical items of equipment within each of these categories. The noise is clearly quite high, although, with the exception of impact pile drivers, it does not reach the peaks of industrial equipment noise.

Like other kinds of industrial noise, construction noise tends to have more energy in the lower frequency of the spectrum than in the higher

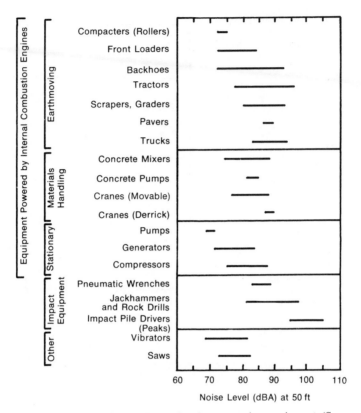

**Fig. 17.3**  Noise ranges of a limited sample of construction equipment (Source: EPA, 1971b).

ones. However, there are differences among the various types of equipment. For instance, among earthmoving machines, the worst offenders are scraper and dozer units, that expose the operator to excessive noise conditions for many hours a day (Benz *et al.*, 1967). The fact that the levels in Fig. 17.3 are reported at 50 feet from the construction machines suggests that the main EPA concern is with the annoyance of people living nearby. However it is easy to extrapolate back to the worker's ear. For every halving of the distance there will be a rise of 6 dB. At 6 feet the levels will be increased by 18 dBA so that the tractors, backhoes and scrapers will produce levels at least as high as 110 dBA.

## HOUSEHOLD NOISE

Although the home is generally a sanctuary from damaging noise, it contains, nevertheless, noise sources with levels above decibels that can damage hearing with sufficient exposure, that is, for many hours a day seven days a week, as well as many other sources that can produce severe annoyance.

There are basically four sources of noise in a household: human-generated noise, appliance noise, building-equipment noise, and background noise impinging upon the household from outside. In each of these categories the noise is either airborne noise, such as voices, or impact noise, due for instance to the fall of an object, which is then transmitted by the structure of the house and converted to airborne noise through vibrations of components of the structure.

*Human-generated noise*—voices, dropping of objects, children jumping, or even just walking—can be a strong irritant, particularly in dwellings designed with insufficient insulation. Indeed in one survey human noise (voices and children playing) was found to be a predominant source of noise even outdoors in a sizable number of cases (Stephenson, 1968).

*Household appliances* generate a broad range of noise, according to the particular type of appliance, as shown in Fig. 17.4. The upper limits of the range can reach very high sound levels. The level of exposure of people in other rooms ("secondary noise") of the household is, of course, less—as much as 10–20 dBA less—but can continue to reach high levels, particularly for certain penetrating sounds, such as those from a noisy home shop tool. An important source of household noise, particularly in those households away from the core of the city, are motor-powered gardening appliances whose noise levels are shown in greater detail in Table 17.4: lawnmowers, hedge clippers and edgers, and trimmers are among the noisiest home appliances. At times gardening involves also the use of chain saws, which are the noisiest of all kinds of gardening equipment, producing some 115 dBA at the user's ear and some 85 dBA at 50 ft.

*Building equipment*, similarly, presents a broad range of noises and can reach high peaks (Fig. 17.5). The portion of the noise that reaches the occupants of the building depends on the location of the equipment—whether the occupants' exposure is direct or indirect, and whether the equipment is segregated in acoustically desirable locations—the acoustic design of the building (walls, ceilings, floors) and the measures taken to insulate the equipment.

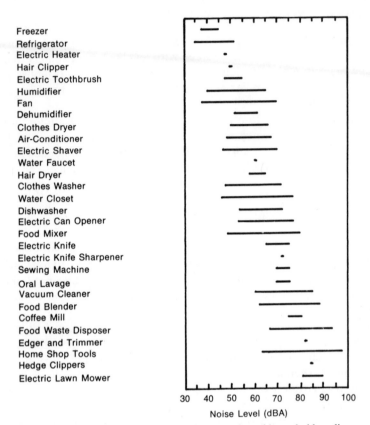

Freezer
Refrigerator
Electric Heater
Hair Clipper
Electric Toothbrush
Humidifier
Fan
Dehumidifier
Clothes Dryer
Air-Conditioner
Electric Shaver
Water Faucet
Hair Dryer
Clothes Washer
Water Closet
Dishwasher
Electric Can Opener
Food Mixer
Electric Knife
Electric Knife Sharpener
Sewing Machine
Oral Lavage
Vacuum Cleaner
Food Blender
Coffee Mill
Food Waste Disposer
Edger and Trimmer
Home Shop Tools
Hedge Clippers
Electric Lawn Mower

Noise Level (dBA)

**Fig. 17.4** Noise ranges at 3 ft from measurements on selected household appliances—both United States and from other countries (Source: EPA, 1971b).

**Table 17.4** Gardening Power Equipment (Source: NIPCC, 1971. Used by Permission.)

| Type | Noise Levels (dBA) | |
| --- | --- | --- |
| | At User's Ear | At 50 ft |
| Chain saws | 115 | 86 |
| Riding mowers | 95 | 78 |
| Rotary and reel mowers | 92 | 68 |
| Snowblowers | 92 | 85 |
| Edgers and tillers | 95 | 78 |

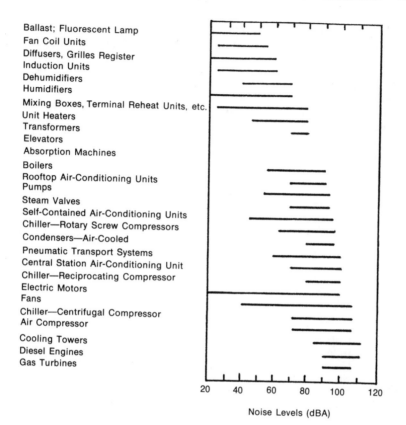

**Fig. 17.5**  Range of noise in dBA typical for building equipment at 3 ft (Source: EPA, 1971b).

*Background noise* is determined by the environment of the dwelling. Street and airplane noises are the most common determinants of the background noise, but construction, industrial, and human noise (e.g., a school yard or a market) can also be important. Clearly the background noise levels vary with the time of the day, and in certain cases, can also be seasonal, thus defying simple categorization. For instance, background sounds due to traffic or air-conditioners tend to mask interior sounds, but when they subside—when traffic noise is reduced at night or the air-conditioner is stopped—obnoxious interior sounds become noticeable. The operation of street-cleaning or garbage-collection equipment whose noise levels, although intrinsically quite high, would be acceptable during daytime, becomes intolerable at night or during the early morning hours.

While accepting these temporal variations in background noise, it is clear that, in general, different areas have on the average different background noise. For instance, the U.S. EPA distinguishes five major types of residential areas, ranging from Quiet Suburban to Very Noisy Residential (Table 17.5). The fact that such classifications can be worked out can be in itself a pointer to social inequalities. The more affluent have an option to move to quiet areas, which may be denied to those in the lower economic layers.

**Table 17.5**  Classification in terms of background Noise of Urban and Suburban Detached Housing Residential Areas (Source: EPA, 1971b).

| | Approximate Daytime Residual Noise Level* | |
|---|---|---|
| Description | Typical Range dBA | Average dBA |
| Quiet suburban residential | 36–40 inclusive | 38 |
| Normal suburban residential | 41–45 inclusive | 43 |
| Urban residential | 46–50 inclusive | 48 |
| Noisy urban residential | 51–55 inclusive | 53 |
| Very noisy urban residential | 56–60 inclusive | 58 |

*$L_{90}$ levels (residual noise levels exceeded 90 percent of the time).

## LEISURE NOISE

Many leisure activities have become a major source of noise and a major hazard. Hi-fi sets are among the worst offenders. Rock groups produce about 100 dB at the performers' ear and more in the front row of listeners. Even children's pop guns can be dangerous to hearing with one exposure. (In dealing with rock and roll music one must be careful, however, about putting it on a par with noise exposure at work. While it is true that levels of 125 dBA are produced by some famous rock groups, e.g. Slade and The Who, and that such levels can give rise to hearing damage in the great majority of people exposed to them, this is only true if the exposure is of the order of 1000 hours total.* This could in fact be

---

*The work of Burns and Robinson reported in Chapter 3 makes it possible to calculate this.

**Table 17.6**  Recreational Vehicles. (Source: NIPCC, 1971. Used by permission.)

| | Noise Levels (dBA) | |
| --- | --- | --- |
| | At User's Ear | At 50 ft |
| Motorcycles | | |
| Less than 240 cc | 105 | 89 |
| More than 240 cc | 112 | 92 |
| Snowmobiles | 118 | 88 |
| All-terrain vehicles | 105 | 85 |
| Pleasure boats | 95* | — |

*For outboard and inboard boats at 8 ft directly forward of engine center line.

accumulated by a devoted fan going to one four-hour concert every week for five years, but it must be understood that even if there is lack of awareness of the risk, this is still exposure by choice. The situation of the worker is very different; even if there is awareness, which is unlikely, there is often very little choice about getting a quieter workplace.)

Recreational vehicles and craft—motorcycles, snowmobiles, all-terrain vehicles, and pleasure boats—which have greatly increased in popularity in recent years, produce noise levels at the user's ear that are so high as to lead to impariment with prolonged exposure. Indeed the 118 dBA reported for snowmobiles (Table 17.6) will produce 50% loss of hearing for weak conversational speech in 10% of the exposed people in as little as 5 years if the exposure is a typical 4 hours a day, two days a week, 13 weeks a year. The noise levels produced are also sufficiently high at 50 ft to severely affect people in the environment of these vehicles. Among recreational vehicles one must include general aviation aircraft which are flown to an increasing degree for pleasure. In their interior their average noise level is around 90 dBA, with peaks as high as 103 dBA.

## OTHER SOURCES

### Sirens

The sirens used by police, firemen, and ambulances serve to communicate an urgent message. Thus, they need to be very intense sources of sound. For example, the sirens of fire trucks in New York City have been observed to emit 124 dBA at 3 ft. Clearly these high levels of sound have distressing and potentially harmful effects both on the occupants of the vehicle and on the people in the street and in the surrounding buildings. The effect on those in the environment of the vehicle is accentuated by the frequency with which sirens belonging to different urban services are heard.

The remedies are not simple. For the operators of the vehicle, the adoption of earmuffs or the soundproofing of the cabin present the obvious disadvantage that other signals and traffic sounds cannot be heard. For the persons in the environment of the vehicle, to attempt to make the sound less irritating by changing some of its characteristics—for instance by giving the signal a musical quality—may remove much of the urgency of the signal.

### Agricultural Noise

An unfortunate and inescapable by-product of the motorization of agriculture is the increase in the noise level in rural environments. A countryside undisturbed by the noise of engines and motor vehicles is increasingly rare.

The principal sources of noise in agricultural applications are primarily tractors, trucks, bulldozers, as well as special purpose machines. These sources are not substantially different in their sound emission characteristics—and hence in their effect on operators and the environment—from those of vehicles and machines used in other occupations.

### Military Noise

It is an unfortunate condition of this earth that a large percent of its inhabitants become involved in military activities—as members of the armed forces or as targets, at best, as bystanders. Military activities can generate some of the loudest man-made noise, because of their intrinsic nature, and because environmental considerations are by necessity secondary to military ones. However, the internal environment of planes, ships, and tanks must be sufficiently quiet so as to reduce fatigue and make voice communication possible.

The sources of military noise are basically four:

- Explosions (from firearms, artillery, bombs, rockets, and construction activities).

- Airplanes and rockets.
- Engines (in combat vehicles, in other vehicles, as well as in ships).
- Other equipment (generators, etc.).

In the case of large explosions and rockets, a single event is often sufficient to permanently impair hearing. Even the explosions from portable firearms can have that effect—and repeated exposure in any case is likely to do so. The other sources of military noise are basically not different from corresponding sources in non-military activities—except that they are often louder, and that less efforts are made to shelter both operators and environment from their long range effects.

## REFERENCES

Bell, A. Noise: An occupational hazard and a public nuisance. Public Health Paper No. 30. Geneva: World Health Organization, 1966.

Benz, L. A. *et al.* A noise and hearing survey of earth-moving equipment operators. *American Industrial Hygiene Association Journal*, 1967, **28**, 117–128.

Botsford, J. H. Control of industrial noise through engineering. In *Noise as a public health hazard.* Washington, D.C.: American Speech and Hearing Association, 1969.

EPA (U.S. Environmental Protection Agency). Noise from industrial plants. Washington, December 1971. (a)

EPA (U.S. Environmental Protection Agency). Report to the President and Congress on noise. Washington, December 1971. (b)

EPA (U.S. Environmental Protection Agency) Noise from construction equipment and operations, building equipment and home appliances. Washington, 1971. (c)

Karplus, B. H. and Bonvallet, G. C. A noise survey of manufacturing industries. *American Industrial Journal*, December 1953, **14**.

NIPCC (National Industrial Pollution Control Council). Leisure time product noise. Sub-Council Report, May 1971.

Stalker, W. W. Evaluation and control of noise in the offices of an industry. *Noise Control*, July 1955, **1**.

Stephenson, R. J. London Noise Survey. HMSO, 1968.

CHAPTER 18

# Exposure to Occupational and Leisure Noise

## THE PROBLEM

In the previous chapter, we surveyed the many and diverse sources of occupational and leisure noise. In this chapter, we ask the question: How many people are exposed to these sources? Since the answer has a bearing on the problem of "internalities" versus "externalities," discussed in Part VI, we find it expedient to separate occupational exposure from leisure exposure. We also find it expedient to separate the internal occupational exposure from the external one (which is primarily construction noise).

The greatest hearing loss from the exposure to industrial noise and to many leisure activities affects the 4000 Hz frequency. Additional losses in the 4000 Hz frequency are due primarily to aging (presbycusis) (Glorig, 1961). The permanent hearing loss at 4000 Hz after 10 years' exposure seems to correlate closely with TTS* after a few days' exposure. Although there is no unanimous agreement among noise experts on this point, this suggests the possibility of screening new employees for probable long-term effects.

The shape of noise spectra is particularly important in the case of industrial noise: industrial processes and devices often produce spectra with sharp peaks, that is, with energy concentrated in a narrow-frequency band (less than an octave in width and/or at a single frequency). These peaks are likely to be more hazardous than noise with a more uniform

---

*See Part II, Chapter 3.

**Table 18.1**   Acceptable Noise Exposures (dBA) for Different Noise Occurrences Per Day. (Source: Guidelines, 1970. Used by permission of Acoustical Publications Inc.)

| Acceptable Cumulative Daily Duration | | Number of Noise Occurrences Per Day | | | | | | |
|---|---|---|---|---|---|---|---|---|
| | | 1 | 3 | 7 | 15 | 35 | 75 | 160 and up |
| 8 hr | | 90 | 90 | 90 | 90 | 90 | 90 | 90 |
| 6 hr | | 91 | 93 | 96 | 98 | 97 | 95 | 94 |
| 4 hr | | 92 | 95 | 99 | 102 | 104 | 102 | 100 |
| 2 hr | Acceptable Exposure (dBA) | 95 | 99 | 102 | 106 | 109 | 114 | |
| 1 hr | | 98 | 103 | 107 | 110 | 115 | | |
| 30 min | | 101 | 106 | 110 | 115 | | | |
| 15 min | | 105 | 110 | 115 | | | | |
| 8 min | | 109 | 115 | | | | | |
| 4 min | | 113 | | | | | | |

spectral distribution (Cohen and Baumann, 1964). Fortunately, the recent Burns and Robinson study discussed in Chapter 3 shows that for a wide range of industrial noise, detailed information about the spectrum is not necessary; the simple A-scale weighting suffices.

Exposure to occupational and leisure noise is usually intermittent and non-uniform rather than continuous and constant. The noise fluctuates in intensity as well as in frequency. Thus, exposure dosimetry—the measuring of the cumulative exposure to noise—becomes important, together with the development of strategies for rotating workers on a particular job.

Until the Burns and Robinson study, and the similar EPA findings also discussed in Chapter 3, few data were available from long-range studies on how the risk of permanent hearing impairment may be reduced by shortening the daily duration of exposure, or by interrupting the exposure from time to time. For instance in the United States an Intersociety Committee had to use guidance from observation of temporary thresholds shifts,* to determine the acceptable exposure levels given in Table 18.1 (Guidelines, 1970). The table shows, for instance, that if a noise of 98 dB occurs 15 times per day, the total acceptable daily exposure is 6 hours, while if the noise is continuous (one occurrence per day), the total acceptable exposure is 1 hour. As a rule of thumb, every halving of the daily exposure would allow an increase of 3 dB in the noise level, without an increase in hearing hazard.

---

*See Part II, Chapter 3.

The EPA study suggests that a 24 hour average exposure level $L_{EQ(24)}$ of 70 dB over a 40-year period is the threshold for hearing conservation that will protect virtually the entire population. Higher average exposure levels are permissible with shorter durations, as long as their average energy does not exceed that given by the preceding criterion. Thus the average threshold level for an 8-hour work exposure with no significant exposure during the remaining 16 hours is $L_{EQ(8)}$ of 75 dB.†

The same study identifies thresholds of annoyance and interference with outdoor or indoor activities (EPA, 1974a):

|  |  |
|---|---|
| Outdoors—Residential areas, farms and places where quiet is a basis for use | $L_{DN}$† less than 55 dB |
| Outdoors—Schools, playgrounds and other areas where people spend limited time | $L_{EQ(24)}$ less than 55 dB |
| Indoors— Residential areas | $L_{DN}$ less than 45 dB |
| —Schools and other areas with human activities | $L_{EQ(24)}$ less than 45 dB |

## OCCUPATIONAL NOISE

### Internal Exposure

A great number of situations expose the worker to high noise levels—levels so high that a person regularly exposed to them risks damage to his hearing (see Part II, and Part III, Chapter 7).

Table 18.2 lists, for 9 major categories of the U.S. labor force, the percentage of workers estimated to be exposed to noise levels equal to or exceeding 80 dB. Unfortunately, most specific noise-level information deals only with specific industrial situations. In the United States, of all the workers employed in over 300,000 industrial plants, specific noise levels can be assigned only to half of the craftsmen, operatives, and other industrial workers.

The significant point brought out by Table 18.2 is that about half of the U.S. work force is employed in areas of high noise level. The portion of the total population exposed to these levels is also high in the advanced economies of Western Europe, Canada, and Japan. In economies where

---

†See Appendix 1.

**Table 18.2**  Estimated Exposure to Noise Levels Above 80 dB in U.S. Civilian Working Population (Source for Population Data: Census, 1970).

| Category | Work Force in Category In Thousands | Work Force in Category Percent of Total Work Force | Population in Category Exposed to over 80 dB In Thousands | Population in Category Exposed to over 80 dB In Percent of Category |
|---|---|---|---|---|
| 1. Professional, technical, etc. | 11,349 | 11 | 1,248 | 12 |
| 2. Farming | 2,380 | 6 | 1,809 | 76 |
| 3. Clerical and kindred | 13,745 | 18 | 6,185 | 45 |
| 4. Sales | 5,443 | 7 | 272 | 5 |
| 5. Managerial and official | 6,371 | 8 | 2,548 | 40 |
| 6. Crafts and skilled labor | 10,608 | 14 | 9,759 | 92 |
| 7. Operative and kindred | 13,454 | 18 | 12,378 | 92 |
| 8. Household and service | 9,777 | 13 | 3,226 | 33 |
| 9. Labor | 3,427 | 4 | 3,296 | 67 |
| | 76,554 | 100 | 40,721 | 53 |

the portion of the population engaged in industry is much lower, a smaller percentage of workers are at risk, but the trend toward mechanization of agriculture makes even these occupations an increasing source of noise hazard.

Figure 18.1 shows an estimated breakdown—by noise level—of the U.S. workers whose job area noise levels have been measured. These workers represent approximately 18 percent of the total working population, and 34 percent of the working population exposed to noise levels greater than 80 dB. The important fact is that approximately 16 percent of them (or some 3 percent of the total working population) work in job areas with noise levels exceeding 95 dB.* Working in such areas for approximately 10 years will cause compensable hearing loss for 50 percent of the workers. Thus a substantial percentage of the U.S. work force risks hearing impairment unless they are somehow protected.

The distribution in Fig. 18.1 cannot be assumed to apply to the remaining people working in areas with noise levels of 80 dB or more, for whom the number of specific measurements are not available; obviously

---

*The number 95 dB was chosen because an ISO damage risk criterion at the time set 87 dBA as a limit for unprotected exposure and because the A-weighted levels are commonly about 8 dBA lower than the unweighted dB or C-scale values.

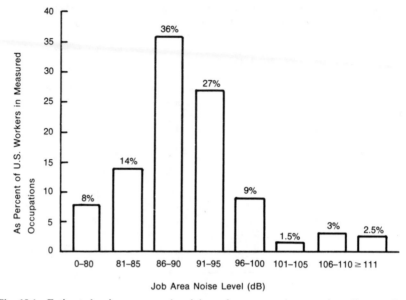

**Fig. 18.1**  Estimated noise exposure breakdown for measured occupations (Source: Bugliarello and Wakstein, 1968).

additional workers are bound to be exposed. Furthermore, the distribution in the figure probably underestimates the fraction exposed to lower noise levels, because the natural tendency is to measure noise levels only in very noisy areas.

These problems in quantitative measurements notwithstanding, the facts are clear. Significant numbers of people are exposed to high noise levels while at work; by the time they have worked for many years in such noise levels, the chances that their hearing is impaired are very high (Fig. 18.2).* In addition, a large number of workers experience noise which is certainly annoying and likely to reduce production efficiency.

---

*The hearing impairment in the figure is the average threshold level in excess of 15 dB ASA (American Standards Association) at 500, 1000, and 2000 Hz. We recall that this is not the only possible definition of impairment; the more compassionate definition of Kryter, for instance (Chapter 3) will give impairments of the order of 25% before the AAOO definition in the Figure acknowledges **any** impairment at all. (Kinnersley, 1973) (See also next chapter.)

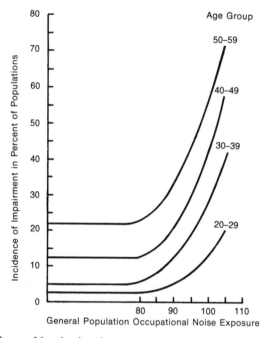

**Fig. 18.2**  Incidence of hearing impairment (average hearing threshold level in excess of 15 dB ASA at 500, 1000, and 2000 cps) in the general population and in selected populations with occupational noise exposure. (Source: Guidelines, 1970. Used by permission of Acoustical Publications, Inc.)

### External aspects

As we have seen, the environmental noise from a modern industrial plant is generally small, and few residents near the plants are affected. Even if a plant is noisy, complaints are likely to be few, as long as the noise from the plant possesses certain acceptable characteristics, such as being continuous, not varying rapidly, not containing fear-producing elements and not interfering with speech communication and sleep; [but unusual exposure conditions or hostility toward plant management may lead to complaints by some individuals or families (EPA, 1971)].

### Construction Noise

On the other hand, an occupational activity that has a major impact on the general population is construction. Large numbers of passersby, as well as the people in dwellings and offices located near construction sites of buildings, subways, sewers, etc., complain about the noise generated by this activity. In a large and dynamic city where construction sites abound, the population affected can be very large indeed, with exposures to a given construction project often prolonged for a number of months.

In the United States some 15 percent of the population (or 30 million people) live and work in the vicinity of construction sites. Passersby are estimated at some 24 billion encounters per year. It has also been estimated that as a result of construction activities, speech communication is severely degraded for about 300 million person-hours per week and the risk of moderate hearing damage is present in about 10 million hours per week, primarily in passersby. Speech interference (due to exposure to more than 60 dB) occurs additionally for as many as 10 million person-hours per week (EPA, 1971).

The level of construction activity in the United States in 1970, given in Table 18.3, shows that building construction is by far the largest activity—and hence the most widespread source of noise. Projections to the year 2000 indicate that building construction will increase more rapidly than the construction of streets and other public works. The pattern of growth in building construction is expected to be distinctly different in the central cities, where growth will occur primarily in non-residential buildings, from outside the central cities, where the growth will be larger on the aggregate and occur primarily in dwellings (Fig. 18.3).

Interference with sleep is usually not a major problem with construction noise as long as construction is carried out during daytime. There is,

Table 18.3 Annual Construction Activity—1970 (Source: EPA, 1971).

| Metropolitan Regions | Residential Buildings (No. of sites) | Non-Residential Buildings (No. of sites) | Municipal, Streets (miles) | Public Works (miles) |
|---|---|---|---|---|
| Large high-density central cities | 8,708 | 1,952 | 273 | 398 |
| Large low-density central cities | 21,578 | 4,903 | 2,150 | 3,140 |
| Other central cities | 102,559 | 12,021 | 6,000 | 8,700 |
| Urban fringe | 262,800 | 30,915 | 11,800 | 16,865 |
| Metropolitan area outside urban fringe | 118,779 | 13,758 | 21,700 | 31,550 |
| Total | 514,424 | 63,549 | 41,923 | 60,653 |

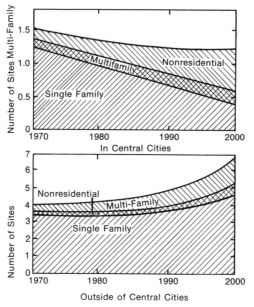

**Fig. 18.3** Number of building construction sites projected to the year 2000—in hundred thousands (Source: EPA, 1971).

however, an appreciable number of people who hold night jobs and sleep during daytime, and are thus affected by construction noise.

Even the sleep of those who hold daytime jobs is affected by construction noise, when it occurs at night—as in the case of street construction or repair, or in the building of a subway. Many city ordinances give discretionary powers to chiefs of police or local administrators concerning permits in emergencies to carry out repairs or construction at night (see Part VI, Chapter 24). This power can be abused if the "emergency" is interpreted with undue broadness.

## Military Exposure

At the end of World War II it was estimated that a significant percentage of all the servicemen would return home with some degree of hearing loss. In the United States, the number of men so affected was conservative: estimated at between a quarter of a million and half a million (Howard, 1943, 1946), or between 2 percent and 4 percent of the peak armed force strength of 12,300,000. The percentage of the forces actually engaged in operation is obviously much larger.

The acoustic trauma in World War II was without doubt severe, and more uniformly distributed than in any previous war when it was confined to the battlefield. In World War II for the first time large amounts of aircraft were used for logistic supply, and for the first time large civilian populations were exposed to aerial bombing and other hostile actions which generated large amounts of noise.

## NON-OCCUPATIONAL EXPOSURE

In modern societies high levels of occupational noise exposure have become the unfortunate corollary of high living standards. Motorized leisure vehicles, radios and highly amplified musical instruments have been the products of both affluence and industrialization.

### Household Exposure

No one in our society escapes household noise. In the United States, for example, from 1960 to 1970 the average number of household gadgets has increased from 1930 to 1970 (Fig. 18.4). Even more dramatic has been the rate of increase in Western Europe and Japan, although the current number of gadgets per household is still below that for the United States. The power and complexity of building equipment is continuously increasing also. An estimate of the current exposure to the noise from home appliances and building equipment in the United States is given in Table 18.4. Although hearing damage risk is not great (certainly a much smaller source of concern than is industrial exposure), speech and sleep interference is at times substantial and should not be tolerated.

### Leisure Exposure

Leisure exposure is not easy to assess in its complete dimensions, as to a large number of persons leisure is to drive an automobile on a holiday, or to fly to a resort with a commercial plane, or to mow a lawn. We have dealt with automobile and airplane noise separately in Parts III and IV, and we must resign ourselves to the ambiguity of whether certain forms of activity are work or relaxation (an important distinction in the political economy of noise).

In any case, there is little doubt that even in our leisure we are exposed in increasing numbers to large amounts of noise. In an action and consumer-oriented society leisure to many is motion and speed, rather

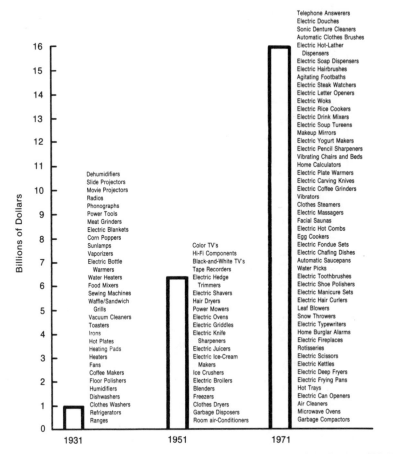

Fig. 18.4   Increase in expenditure on household gadgets in the United States, 1930–70. (Source: McQuade 1972. Tom Cardomone for *Fortune.* Used by permission.)

than contemplation, and the means are available to even those with very modest budgets to acquire some sort of powered leisure vehicle or appliance.

The increase has been as rapid as that of household gadgets. For instance, in the United States in 1960 there were 500,000 motorcycles; by the end of 1970, over two and a half million. In 1962–63 10,000 snowmobiles had been sold; 8 years later, 600,000 (NIPCC, 1971). The data in Table 18.5 show the existence in the United States by 1971 of a large

**Table 18.4** Order-of-Magnitude Estimates of Exposure to Home Appliance and Building Equipment Noise—Millions of Person-Hours Per Week (Adapted from EPA, 1971).

| Noise Source | Average Noise Exposure (dBA) | | Speech Interference* | | Sleep Interference* | | Hearing Damage Risk | |
|---|---|---|---|---|---|---|---|---|
| | Operator Exposure | People in Other Rooms | Moderate | Severe | Slight | Moderate | Slight | Moderate |
| Group 1: Quiet major equipment and appliances (operating levels less than 60 dBA) | | | | | | | | |
| Fans | 51–54 | 44–47 | 1200 | | 0 | | 0 | |
| Air-conditioner | 55 | 48 | 242 | | 121 | | 0 | |
| Clothes dryer | 55 | 48 | 94 | | 10 | | 0 | |
| Humidifier | 50 | 43 | 10 | | 15 | | 0 | |
| Freezer | 41 | 33 | 0 | | 0 | | 0 | |
| Refrigerator | 40 | 32 | 0 | | 0 | | 0 | |
| Group 2: Quiet equipment and small appliances (operating levels between 60 and 70 dBA) | | | | | | | | |
| Plumbing (faucets, toilets) | 62–66 | 51–56 | | 535 | 267 | | 0 | |
| Dishwasher | 64 | 56 | | 461 | 4 | | 0 | |
| Vacuum cleaner | 67 | 60 | | 280 | 0.5 | | 0 | |
| Electric food mixer | 65 | 57 | | 222 | 1 | | 0 | |
| Clothes washer | 60 | 52 | | 215 | 0.5 | | 0 | |
| Electric can opener | 64 | 56 | | 117 | 0.2 | | 0 | |
| Electric knife | 68 | 60 | | 1 | 0.1 | | 0 | |

Group 3: Noisy small appliances
(operating levels between 70 and 80 dBA)

| | | | | |
|---|---|---|---|---|
| Sewing machine | 70 | 62 | 19 | 0.5 | 9 |
| Electric shaver | 75 | 52 | 6 | 1 | 5 |
| Food blender | 73 | 65 | 2 | 0.2 | 0.5 |
| Electric Lawnmower | 75 | 55 | 1 | 1 | 0.3 |
| Food disposer (grinder) | 76 | 68 | 0.5 | 0.5 | 0.5 |

Group 4: Noisy electric tools
(operating levels above 80 dBA)

| | | | | |
|---|---|---|---|---|
| Home shop tools | 85 | 75 | 5 | 2 | 1 |
| Electric yard care tools | 81–84 | 61–64 | 1.5 | 0.1 | 0.4 |

*Figures not directly interpretable in terms of person-hours of lost sleep or speech interference.

**Table 18.5**   Recreational Vehicles, Lawnmowers and Snowblowers. (Adapted from NIPCC, 1971. Used by Permission.)

|  | Numbers in the U.S. |
|---|---|
| Motorcycles | 2,590,000 at end of 1970 of which more than 90% pleasure vehicles |
| Snowmobiles | 600,000 sold in 1970–71 |
| All-terrain vehicles | Reliable data not available; many home-made modifications of standard vehicles |
| Pleasure boats | 4,000,000 outboard motors, 627,000 inboard motorboats, 725,000 inboard motors (diesel and gasoline) |
| Lawnmowers | 89,000,000 sold between 1946 and 1970 (over 5 million sold in 1969–70) |
| Edgers and tillers | Over 300,000 sold in 1969–70 |
| Snowblowers | Over 250,000 sold in 1969–70 |

**Table 18.6**   Approximate Number of Operators or Passengers in Non-Occupational Situations Exposed to Potentially Hazardous Noise from Various Significant Sources in the United States in 1971 (Adapted from EPA, 1971).

| Source | Approximate number of People Exposed* |
|---|---|
| Snowmobiles | 1,600,000 |
| Chain saws | 2,500,000 |
| Motorcycles | 3,000,000 |
| Motorboats (over 45 h.p.) | 8,800,000 |
| Light utility helicopters | 50,000 |
| General aviation aircraft | 300,000 |
| Commercial propeller aircraft | 5,000,000 |
| Internal combustion lawnmowers and other noisy lawn care equipment | 23,000,000 |
| Trucks (personal use) | 5,000,000 |
| Home shop tools | 13,000,000 |
| Highway buses | 2,000,000 |
| Subways | 2,150,000 |

*Single-activity exposures.

number of lawnmowers,* pleasure boats, motorcycles, snowmobiles and related devices.

An estimate by the U.S. EPA of the operators or passengers in the United States exposed to potentially hazardous noise from leisure activities is shown in Table 18.6, which may be over conservative (for instance, the ad hoc panel of the National Pollution Control Council estimated that over 44 million persons participated in recreational boating in 1970) (NIPCC, 1971). The estimate in the table, furthermore, excludes the exposure of persons in the environment, and is also limited to single-event exposures. Most persons are involved, in the course of a week, in more than one of the activities described in the table and thus receive multiple exposures.

## STANDARDS

The task of providing and—and enforcing—noise emission standards for all the sources of occupational, domestic and leisure noise is an immense one. In the U.S. the Environmental Protection Agency is undertaking actions leading to standards for some of the most important sources of noise. For example, a proposed standard for portable air compressors sets a limit of 76 dBA at 7 meters from the compressor (EPA, 1974b).

Approximately 115 thousand people of the one million currently impacted in the U.S. by construction noise would gain relief from the proposed standard. If in addition the proposed noise standards for medium and heavy duty trucks (Chapter 9) are also complied with, construction site noise impact would be reduced according to the EPA by approximately 45%, giving relief to some 470,000 people. The cost of the measures necessary to comply with the proposed air compressor standard would increase the list price of compressor units by about 16%, and lower sales by approximately 4.5%, due to lower demand for the more expensive units.

## REFERENCES

Bugliarello, G. and Wakstein, C. Noise pollution–a review of its techno-sociological and health aspects. Biotechnology program, Carnegie-Mellon University, Pittsburgh, 1968.
Census. (U.S. Bureau of the Census). 1970 census of the population, social and economic characteristics. June 1972.

---

*The total number of lawnmowers in operation is difficult to estimate, but it must involve a considerable fraction—at least 20 million—of the total number of lawnmowers produced between 1946 and 1970.

Cohen, A. and Baumann, K. Temporary hearing losses following exposure to pronounced single frequency components in a broad-band noise. *Journal of the Acoustic Society of America*, 1964, **36**.

EPA (U.S. Environmental Protection Agency). Report to the President and Congress on noise. Washington, December 1971.

EPA (U.S. Environmental Protection Agency). Information on levels of environmental noise requisite to protect public health and welfare with adequate margin of safety. Washington, March 1974. (a).

EPA (U.S. Environmental Protection Agency). Noise emission standards for construction equipment. Proposed portable air compressor standards. Washington, October 1974. (b).

Glorig, A. Age, noise and hearing loss. *Annals of Otology*, 1961, **70**.

Guidelines for noise exposure control. Report of an Intersociety Committee. *Sound and Vibration*, 1970, **4** (11).

Howard, J. C. Jr. Hearing—post war problem. *Annals Otology, Rhinology and Laryngology*, December 1943, **52**.

Howard, J. C. Jr. Auditory impairment in returned service personnel. *Journal Missouri Medical Association*, November 1946, **42**.

McQuade, W. Why nobody's happy about appliances. *Fortune*, May 1972.

NIPCC (National Industrial Pollution Control Council). Leisure time product noise. Sub-Council Report, May 1971.

Kinnersly, P. *The hazards of work.* London: Pluto Press, 1973.

CHAPTER 19

# Workmen's Safety and Compensation Legislation

Nixon's nominee to head the Occupational and Health Administration possesses first-hand knowledge of the problem involved. John Stender, a lifelong
member of the Boilermakers Union, suffers from a hearing impairment caused
by excessive on-the-job noise and has to wear a hearing aid.—
WALL STREET JOURNAL, APRIL 3, 1973

## INTRODUCTION

In this chapter we review the principal provisions society makes for the
prevention of and compensation for occupational deafness. These provisions vary from country to country and are shaped by prevailing legal
doctrines and government practices. In general, legislation follows two
complementary approaches. On the one hand, it prescribes safety and
health practices, which, if enforced, reduce the risk of exposure to noise.
This can be achieved both by limiting the exposure and by technological
solutions, which are discussed in the next chapter. On the other hand,
legislation prescribes compensation to those who have suffered impairment of their hearing through noise exposure at work.

Thus, occupational safety and health acts and workmen's compensation acts are complementary, but, clearly, the more effective the former,
the less need is there for compensation provisions.

## SAFETY LEGISLATION

A number of countries have existing or proposed noise-safety laws.
Discussion here will be limited to the United Kingdom, the Soviet Union
and, in greater detail, to the United States of America—three countries
which present three very different situations.

247

## The United Kingdom

In spite of the very recent passage of a new law, "the Health and Safety at Work Act of 1974" (HSWA, 1974), in the United Kingdom there is still no statutory limitation on exposure to industrial noise.

Prior to passage of the Act the Department of Employment had published a Code of Practice (DE, 1972), which set 90 dBA as the level above which hearing protection should be worn if the exposure were 8 hours a day. The calculations for shorter exposure times and higher noise levels were to be made on the basis of Burns and Robinson's equal energy criterion which is discussed in Chapter 3. On this basis the exposure times recommended are as shown in Table 19.1.

Table 19.1 Recommended Noise-Exposure Levels in the United Kingdom (Source: DE, 1972).

| Exposure Duration Hours Per Day | Maximum Sound Level dBA |
|---|---|
| 8 | 90 |
| 4 | 93 |
| 2 | 96 |
| 1 | 99 |
| $\frac{1}{2}$ | 102 |
| $\frac{1}{4}$ | 105 |

The exposures in the tables are somewhat more conservative than those recommended in either the United States (Table 19.3) or the Soviet Union (Table 19.2)—more conservative in the sense of doing more to conserve hearing. Nevertheless the exposures will still allow one in ten workers to lose a third of their hearing as assessed by the Kryter method. (Kinnersly, 1973).

The Code of Practice also recommends labeling of noise sources and noisy areas. Unfortunately it is not mandatory—a failing in British legislation—but it has been widely circulated and publicized, more so than the booklet "Noise and the Worker" by the Department of Employment in 1971 (DE, 1971). The effect will be that in civil suits an employer will no longer be able to plead ignorance of the risks to hearing, and the way is thus opened to aggressive unions to bring legal actions. We comment further about the role of the unions later in this section.

## History

In general the history of industrial safety legislation in the UK has been one of the piecemeal ad hoc statutes, each one designed to deal with a specific problem. A recent report identified nine groups of statutes and 500 subordinate statutory instruments comprising a haphazard mass of intricate details (Robens Committee, 1972). These instruments are administered by a tangle of jurisdictions: government departments, separate inspectorates and local authorities. As the report puts it:

> "... [there is] an extraordinary variety of provisions which often lay down different standards even when the risk is common to all occupations..."

Provisions, as in the case of the Factories Act (1961), are often weakened by numerous qualifications which allow the employer to comply 'as far as is reasonably practicable.' It is difficult to evaluate from the outside which is reasonably practicable, in a specific situation, both in terms of cost and technology. Furthermore, the onus is often placed on the public to come up with new answers rather than on the noise polluter.

It is to be noted that until the passage of the 1974 act there were probably 6 million workers out of a workforce of thirty million—one in five—not covered by statutory safety standards. Some of the most dangerous jobs such as civil engineering work on tunnels and bridges were not covered. Others not covered included workers in transport and aviation, education, hospitals, pubs, entertainment, postal services, post office engineering, electricity transmission line engineering, parts of the water supply industry, and many others. (Kinnersly, 1973).

## The Health and Safety at Work Act of 1974

The Act (HSWA, 1974) reflects the work of the Committee on Health and Safety at Work, chaired by Lord Robens, which issued a report recommending much of the actual machinery subsequently set up under the Act.

The first result of the new act was to cover about five million more workers: which ones are still not covered is difficult to find out. A Health and Safety Executive is set up to administer the new law, backed by some 900 inspectors (Anderson, 1975). The number is to be increased, according to an answer given by the Minister in the House of Commons, by 50% in the next four or five years (Anderson, 1975) but this increase should be viewed in the light of the fact that in 1971 there were 1,200,000 workplaces covered and only 500,000 visits (not necessarily inspections) by 1000 inspectors—or on average only one visit every two years. A 50% increase will not significantly increase the frequency of visits.

## Penalties

Under the new act the penalties for offences have been increased from a maximum fine of £300 under the old Factories Act of £400. Under the Factories Act there was also a further fine of £75 a day for each day that the offence was continued; this has been reduced under the new act to £50 a day. Osborn (1974) suggests that minimum fines should also be set and that laws should specify that each day of continued violation be treated as a separate offence and subject to a separate fine. These fines compare with the OSHA maximum fines of $10,000. There are however provisions for imprisonment for a maximum of two years under the new act and for unlimited fines as well, in the case of conviction or indictment. The key question is of course whether these penalties will be imposed.

## Controls and Standards

The act provides for Improvement Orders, e.g., to quiet a workplace by x dBA by date y, and Prohibition Orders, e.g., to stop work until the workplace has been quieted by x dBA and /or until hearing protection has been provided. However, there is no legal obligation under the act on Inspectors to abate dangerous practices.

As Osborn (1974) points out, the act in this respect compares unfavorably with the Occupational Safety and Health Act (OSHA) in the United States which allows for prosecution of lax officials (the Administrator of the Environmental Protection Agency) through the avenue of the citizen suit—a civil action in a U.S. District Court for having failed to perform any act or duty under the Act which is not discretionary with him. Osborn further discusses two other important features of OSHA not found in the 1974 act. The act does not require that firms claiming they would go out of business if required to install noise control disclose their costs. Neither does the act expressly forbid advance warnings of visits of Inspectors. These advance warnings were one of the major shortcomings of the old Factories Acts. (Kinnersly, 1973).

The 1974 act provides for making codes of practice *approved* codes; if a code is approved it becomes definitive and can therefore be used by inspectors to issue Improvement Orders or Prohibition Orders. Unfortunately the Department of Employment's Code of Practice has not been approved yet.

In summary, the present situation in the United Kingdom has shown much progress, but is still far from satisfactory, especially in a nation priding itself on its record in public health and industrial hygiene. It is also surprising that the Trade Unions have not pressed for noise-safety legislation earlier and more vigorously.

## The Soviet Union

In the Soviet Union, current standards laid down in the 1969 Sanitary Norm for Industrial Noise are based on the recommendations of the International Standards Organization (TK43 "Acoustic Committee"), (EPA, 1971) and are more rigorous than the U.S. (OSHA) provisions.

Table 19.2 gives the maximum noise levels for an 8-hour shift permitted in various types of workplace. The tradeoffs allowed between noise

**Table 19.2**  Basic Provisions of Soviet Law Concerning Maximum Levels of Noise in Occupational Settings (for an 8-hour exposure). (Source: EPA, 1971).

| Key | ISO Index No. | Approximate Equivalent in dB(A) |
|---|---|---|
| 1. Ordinary work places in factories, etc. | 80 | 85 |
| 2. Laboratories with noise sources | 70 | 75 |
| 3. Remote control and observation stations in factory automated processes | 60 | 65 |
| 4. Offices with office machinery | 55 | 60 |
| 5. Offices where thinking work demanding high levels of concentration occurs | 45 | 50 |

exposure and noise levels are very strict. The duration of the noise has to be less than $1\frac{1}{2}$ hours before the permitted level rises to 90 dBA, and the maximum for a noise lasting less than 15 minutes is 108 dBA.

Enforcement of these regulations is the responsibility of the Sanitary-Epidemiological Service (SES), and violations of the norms can be punished by "disciplinary action, administrative action, or punishment under the criminal code" (EPA, 1971). However, it appears that enforcement is lax. A variety of reasons are put forward for this, including the over-centralized administrative system in the Soviet Union, the lack of priority given to environmental problems, and the economic pressures on factory managers.

## The United States

In the United States, Federal regulation of noise in work places is part of the general Occupational Safety and Health Act (OSHA) of 1970, the aim of which is "to assure so far as possible every working man and woman in the nation safe and healthful working conditions and to preserve our human resources" (U.S. Public Law, 1970).

The Act adopts noise regulations from the Walsh–Healey Act of 1967 (which was limited to industries with government contracts exceeding $10,000 a year), and extends these to cover all employees in businesses affecting interstate commerce. The Act further authorizes the Secretary of Labor to promulgate as occupational safety and health standards any national consensus standards which he finds relevant. The latter term refers to pre-existing rules or standards which have won general (government, industry, and union) acceptance in other contexts.

Although its jurisdiction is nationwide, the Act includes provisions for having the states take over enforcement activities as long as their standards and procedures are at least as effective as the Federal law.

In general the laws provide standards regarding: toxic materials as harmful physical agents; prescription of labels warning of hazards; provision of suitable protective equipment; and monitoring employee exposure to hazards, as well as frequency of medical examinations. Inspectors are allowed to make investigations, which may be on the behalf of an employee or his union, and to issue citations for violations. The Occupational Safety and Health Review Commission, a new quasi-judicial body, has been established to review appeals and set civil and criminal penalties for violations.

The section of the Occupational Safety and Health Standards that deals with noise (Section 1910.95), (U.S. Federal Register, 1972), is divided into two parts. The first deals with the maximum permitted exposure levels (Table 19.3).

In view of the numbers of employees exposed to noise levels in excess of 90 dBA, assessed in the previous chapter, the new OSHA standards mark a definite improvement. And in those plants where the law is effectively implemented, workers who had been exposed to these high levels without protection will gain immediate benefit.

However, the standard is far from ideal. Most medical evidence, and indeed personal experience, argues for a limit of 80 or 85 dB. In the words of the OSHA "The amount of sound energy absorbed during such an exposure (90 dBA for 8 hours) is considered to be the upper limit of a

**Table 19.3** Permissible Noise Exposures Under U.S. Occupational Safety and Health Act of 1970 (Source: U.S. Federal Register, 1972).

| Duration Per Day, Hours | Sound Level dBA Slow† |
|:---:|:---:|
| 8 | 90 |
| 6 | 92 |
| 4 | 95 |
| 3 | 97 |
| 2 | 100 |
| $1\frac{1}{2}$ | 102 |
| 1 | 105 |
| $\frac{1}{2}$ | 110 |
| $\frac{1}{4}$ or less | 115 |

When the daily noise exposure is composed of two or more periods of noise exposure at different levels, their combined effect should be considered, rather than the individual effect of each. If the sum of the fractions: $\quad C_1/T_1 + C_2/T_2 + \cdots C_i/T_i + \cdots C_n/T_n$ (where $C_i$ indicates the total time of exposure at a specified noise level, $T_i$ the total time of exposure permitted at that level, and $n$ is the number of periods considered) exceeds unity, then, the mixed exposure should be considered to exceed the limit value.

†The "slow" response is a setting of the sound level. meter which causes it to average out high level noises of brief duration such as hammering, rather than responding to the individual impact noise.

daily dose which will not produce disabling loss of hearing in more than 20 percent of the exposed population" (OSHA, 1971). Thus under present OSHA standards, one-fifth of the exposed work force will suffer a disabling loss of hearing. The Labor Department under the Johnson Administration recommended the level be 85 dBA.* However, the Nixon

*Perhaps tacit admittance that 90 is too high a level can be gleaned from the following statement from the same bulletin of the Department of Labor, "The Department strongly recommends that any employee who is exposed to high sound levels and requests ear protection, be provided with it, even if the duration of exposure is within the limits prescribed by Table 1" (Table 19.3) (OSHA, 1971). As we have seen, the 1969 Soviet Sanitary Norm for Industrial Noise sets the limit for noise exposure for workers in factories to approximately 85 dBA; in the Netherlands a worker is considered at risk if exposed to more than 80 dBA for 8 hours a day.

Administration kept the level at 90. Further questions can be raised when we consider the meaning of the phrase "disabling loss of hearing," because the definition of "disabling" is clearly arbitrary, as discussed both in Part II and later in this chapter.

Finally it must be noted that, imperfect as the exposures in Table 19.3 are for 8 hours, they become even more dangerous with shorter duration. They fail to take into account the well-established equal energy criterion of Burns and Robinson discussed in Chapter 3. Indeed the level of 115 dBA suggested for exposures of $\frac{1}{4}$ hour a day is 10 dB higher than the 105 dBA that would be recommended by Burns and Robinson on the basis of 90 dBA for 8 hours.

*Remedies*

For those industries where the sound intensity and duration habitually exceed the levels in Table 19.3, the new law is quite explicit. In the first place, "feasible administrative or engineering controls shall be utilized" to reduce the noise; secondly, and upon the failure of the above, "personal protective equipment shall be provided and used to reduce sound levels within the levels of the Table;" and thirdly, "in all cases where the sound levels exceed the values shown herein, a continuing, effective hearing conservation program shall be administered" (OSHA, 1971).

Examples of engineering noise control measures are given in the next chapter. The length of the list in Table 20.1 is indicative of the scope for noise reduction through these measures which are clearly the best solution in that they not only reduce the exposure of the machine operators, but also that of their co-workers, and, indeed, of the community at large. Reservation can be expressed only on the original standards which the engineering controls are designed to meet—a problem we have discussed already—and on the interpretation of the word "feasible."

If a violation of the OSHA standards is ascertained, orders are issued for its abatement by the Occupational Safety and Health Review Commission. While the Occupational Safety and Health Act requires that the employer's first approach to a noise problem be through engineering design and equipment innovations, it is not clear what evidence suffices as proof of "feasibility." If an engineering solution is deemed unfeasible, administrative controls or personal protective equipment must be adopted—decidedly a second best solution.

Administrative controls are designed to limit the duration of individual worker's exposure to the times indicated in Table 19.3. This very straightforward solution is essentially a matter of production planning and allows for a flexible approach to the problem. Its main recommendation is that it is easier to enforce than the requirement to wear personal protective equipment. Its use is limited however to those plants where there is the opportunity to shift employees between jobs, and thus where there are some processes emitting noise levels *below* 90 dBA.

Personal protective equipment (earplugs or earmuffs) has the drawbacks of being uncomfortable to wear and of blocking out auditory signals and warnings. Although the Act specifies that not only the provision but also the use of protective equipment are required and that "in the absence of an observable high proportion of use, the Department would consider the lack of training and promotional program as constituting a violation of the regulation," the enforcement problems are clearly immense.*

On a more philosophic level, protective devices represent another example of man adapting to the machine. The modern workmen, regaled in overalls, face shields, goggles, hard hats, steel-toed shoes, and earmuffs, inhabiting a nether-world of dust, fumes and noise for up to 8 hours a day, can truly begin to wonder whether he has become, in the words of Karl Marx "a mere living appendage".

This is not to deny that in the absence of effective controls, personal protection is essential. However, it is easy to concur with the conclusion of the Department of Labor that "there will be very few cases in which the use of this equipment will be acceptable as a permanent solution to noise problems" (OSHA, 1971).

The final provision of the U.S. Act states that, in the absence of engineering controls, "a continuing, effective hearing conservation program shall be administered." The program must run as long as noise levels exceed those in Table 19.3 and must detect and prevent any incipient loss of hearing. The methods to be used are "audiometry—periodic checks on the hearing ability of individual employees; and noise surveys—periodic checks of the noise level in the areas in which employees are working" (OSHA, 1971).

While the specification of the test facilities, procedures, and audiometrics is exact, the required frequency of the audiometric tests is less clear. It apparently remains up to the plant's "regular or consulting physician," to decide how often the audiograms shall be taken, with the proviso that

---

*It is worth pointing out that at noise levels in excess of 115 dBA muffs or plugs are insufficient and a helmet must be worn as well.

"only under very special conditions shall they be made less than once a year" (OSHA, 1971). The same general observations apply to the noise surveys.

*Assessment*

The 1970 legislation is a marked improvement over the pre-existing situation. Two points emerge, however, as being in need of further attention and clarification. In the first place, the setting of standards for "acceptable" noise exposure is obviously a political, and inevitably an arbitrary decision. To have a completely safe environment would entail noise levels as low as 75–80 dB. Indeed if we accept Kryter's latest conclusions (Kryter, 1973) in this matter, we should aim at 55 dBA. This must be the ideal at which engineering controls measures should aim. However, in view of the fact that a reduction from only 90 to 80 dB entails a tenfold decrease in machine energy escaping as sound, and since only a minute amount of energy can create a considerable noise ($10^{-4}$ W/m$^2$ = 90 dB), the cost of attaining the ideal standard is high and must be carefully considered. It is at this point that the question becomes political. Unless some way is found to calculate a "cost" of hearing disability, with all its economic, physiological and psychosocial ramifications, against which to measure the cost of quieter machinery, a value judgment has to be made on the tradeoffs involved.

Secondly, and in a sense a consequence of the previous argument, it is important to stress the continuing role of the workers (or their union) in securing a decent working environment. The new law does not remove the issue of health and safety from collective bargaining. In contract negotiations, unions have the opportunity to obtain standards of their own; that is, collective bargaining can, and should, be used to reach agreement on working conditions suited to the particular work force in question.

If union members are made aware of the risks involved* in working at 90 dBA for 8 hours, and they determine a lower level than that set by OSHA, such provision can be made in their contract. Negotiations at the plant level are fundamentally more democratic than lobbying sessions in Washington; a "consensus" standard reached over the bargaining table

---

*Recent low-cost workers' handbooks of industrial hazards (e.g., IPPAUNA, 1972) both in the United States and the United Kingdom are a step in this direction. See also Kinnersly (1973).

often can complement an official standard by embodying the perceptions and preferences of the workers.

The crux of the matter, once again, revolves around the awareness of risk. There are highly encouraging signs that in recent years union presidents and negotiators have moved away from an exclusive concern with traditional "bread-and-butter" issues of pay structures, demarcation disputes, and grievance procedures, to a broader concern which encompasses also the less obvious problems of the workplace, such as the effects of air and noise pollution (IPPAUNA, 1972).

### The Military

The concern not only for the health hazard, but also for personnel fatigue and for the impediment of verbal communications caused by noise, make it highly desirable for the armed forces to issue regulations as to the level of noise allowable in and around military equipment. An example of such regulations is given by the recent U.S. Military Standard on Noise Limits for Army Material (Mil-Std, 1973). The standard provides specific noise limits to designers and manufacturers of equipment procured by the U.S. Army. Although it is neither a hearing damage-risk nor a hearing conservation criterion, it evolves "from considerations of hearing damage-risk, speech intelligibility, aural detection, state of the art noise reduction, and federal and state legislation, and [is] intended to cover typical operational conditions."

The standard has the general requirement that when the noise levels from steady-state equipment noise exceed 85 dBA, noise hazard signs must be permanently posted on or in the equipment. Steady-state noise is subdivided in seven categories according to noise levels and the functional requirement of the given military system or piece of equipment (Table 19.4). The first four categories in the table are based primarily on hearing conservation priorities, while the last three are based primarily on communication requirements.

### WORKMEN'S COMPENSATION

Workmen's compensation laws provide cash benefits, medical care, and rehabilitation services for workers who suffer work-related injuries and diseases. The United States has the largest number of workers protected by workmen's compensation laws. In this section we review in detail the U.S. provisions; in the next section, we shall review the situation in the

**Table 19.4** U.S. Standards for Categories of Areas Occupied by Military Personnel (Source: Mil-Std, 1973).

| Octave-Band Limits (Hz) | Center Frequency (Hz) | Steady-State Noise Limit Categories (dB) in Area | | | | | | |
|---|---|---|---|---|---|---|---|---|
| | | A* | B* | C* | D* | E | F | G |
| 37.5–75 | 53 | 133 | 124 | 114 | 109 | 85 | 79 | 76 |
| 75–150 | 106 | 121 | 113 | 103 | 98 | 80 | 73 | 69 |
| 150–300 | 212 | 111 | 104 | 95 | 90 | 76 | 68 | 64 |
| 300–600 | 425 | 107 | 102 | 89 | 84 | 73 | 64 | 59 |
| 600–1200 | 850 | 105 | 100 | 85 | 80 | 71 | 62 | 57 |
| 1200–2400 | 1700 | 112 | 100 | 84 | 79 | 70 | 60 | 55 |
| 2400–4800 | 3400 | 110 | 100 | 84 | 79 | 69 | 58 | 53 |
| 4800–9600 | 6800 | 110 | 100 | 85 | 80 | 68 | 57 | 52 |

| Category | Criteria for Selection |
|---|---|
| A | No direct person-to-person voice communication required. *Maximum design limit.* Hearing protection required. |
| B | System requirement for electronically aided communication via attenuating helmet or headset. |
| C | No frequent direct person-to-person voice communication required. Intermittent shouted communication may be possible at a distance of 1 ft. Hearing protection required. |
| D | No frequent direct person-to-person voice communication required. Intermittent shouted communication may be possible at a distance of 2 ft. *Meets unprotected exposure criteria for 8 hours.* (Levels in excess of Category D require hearing protection.) |
| E | Intermittent electronically aided voice communication required via non-attenuating biaural headset or loudspeaker; occasional direct person-to-person voice communication required; no telephone use required. (Equivalent to NC-70†.) |
| F | Frequent electrically aided voice communication required via non-attenuating biaural headset or loudspeaker; frequent direct person-to-person voice communication required; occasional non-attenuating monaural headset or telephone use required. (Equivalent to NC-60.) |
| G | Frequent non-attenuating monaural headset or telephone use required. (Equivalent to NC-55.) |

*NOTE: Noise hazard caution signs required to be posted in or on equipment when the levels of Category D are exceeded.

†Noise Criteria Curve—See Appendix 1.

United Kingdom which presents a sharply different approach based on civil action in the courts.

## The United States

It is estimated that in 1970, 80 percent of the 71 million U.S. workers were covered by such laws (National Commission, 1972). However, there is a wide variation among states as to coverage, 13 covering more than 85 percent and 15 less than 70 percent. These deficiencies are due to the exclusion of certain types of employment, the fact that in some states the law is elective, not compulsory, and to avoidance by some employers of their legal obligation. If workmen's compensation laws in all states of the United States allowed claims for noise-induced hearing loss in the one-fortieth of the U.S. population that, as we have seen in Chapter 1, Part II, have noise-induced hearing losses, the total amount of such claims could be very large—of the order of $6 billion. Since these workers have been exposed for a mean time of 35 years, potential claims could be building up at a rate of over $160 million a year (Bugliarello and Wakstein, 1968).

Table 19.5 indicates the extent of compulsory coverage in the United States and shows the three types of law, State, Federal Employees, and Longshoremen's and Harbor-Worker's, by which a worker can be covered.

**Table 19.5** Jurisdictions in the United States with Compulsory Workmen Compensation Coverage 1946–72 (Source: National Commission, 1972).

| Year | States* (50) | Other "States" (6)† | Federal (2)‡ |
|---|---|---|---|
| 1946 | 21 | 2 | 2 |
| 1958 | 25 | 4 | 2 |
| 1966 | 27 | 4 | 2 |
| 1972 | 31 | 5 | 2 |

*Alaska and Hawaii are counted among the states in 1946.

†District of Columbia, Puerto Rico, Virgin Islands, American Samoa, Guam, and the Trust Territory of the Pacific Islands.

‡Federal Employees Compensation Act (FECA) and Longshoremen's and Harbor-Worker's Compensation Act (LHWCA).

Discussion here will be limited to State workmen's compensation laws since they are by far the most important. Recently, a National Commission on State Workmen's Compensation Laws came to the conclusion "that State workmen's compensation laws are in general neither adequate nor equitable" (National Commission, 1972). This is confirmed by the fact that out of 16 recommendations published by the Department of Labor in 1971 the average state only met eight. The Appendix includes certain of these especially relevant to noise-induced hearing loss.

Two aspects of the law are of interest here. In the first place the law gives an indication, though not necessarily an accurate one, of how serious society considers hearing loss to be in comparison to the loss of other faculties. Secondly, the law should encourage employers to protect their workers from hearing loss.

### History

Before discussing these points it is useful to review briefly the history of such legislation. As concisely described by the U.S. Department of Labor (BLS, 1960): "The main purpose of workmen's compensation laws was to eliminate the uncertainties of getting damages for injuries at common law or under employers' liability laws. Before workmen's compensation laws were adopted, the employee who was injured on his job got little or nothing in recompense. To recover damages against his employer he had to file suit and to prove that the injury was due to the employer's negligence. The employer, eventhough he had been negligent, could avail himself of three common law defenses: 'assumption of risk,' 'fellow servant rule,' and 'contributory negligence.' That is, the employer could defeat recovery if it was proved that the employee's injury was due to the ordinary risks of his work, if it was caused by the negligence of a fellow worker, or if the employee by his own negligence in any way contributed to the injury.

"The difficulties of obtaining redress under this system led to the enactment of employers' liability acts in many jurisdictions. These acts lessened the severity of the defenses which the employer could use. But in spite of the employer's broadened responsibility, results to the workers were unsatisfactory. The employee still had to bring suit against the employer and prove that the accident was the fault of the employer. There were still the long delays in securing court action, the uncertainty of the results, and the high cost of negligence suits. Often the worker was still denied any compensation or damages.

"With the passage of workmen's compensation laws, workers injured in the course of their employment, if covered by the laws, are assured prompt payment of benefits—regardless of fault, and with a minimum of legal formality."

## The Present

Table 19.6 gives a summary of hearing loss statutes in effect in 1972 in the United States. It can be seen that 40 out of the 50 states award compensation for noise induced hearing loss. But the states that rate the severity of hearing loss by a specific, well defined method, such as that of the AMA are only 23. Furthermore, in at least five states hearing loss must be total in one or both ears for compensation to be given.

This difference between various jurisdictions raises the question of just what injuries and diseases should be compensable. According to the National Commission on State Workmen's Compensation Laws, workmen's compensation benefits will be provided only when

- there is an impairment (either temporary or permanent, and either partial or total) or death;
- the impairment or death is caused by an injury or a disease that is work-related.

If both of these tests are met, the system will provide medical and rehabilitation benefits (National Commission, 1972).

Cash benefits are paid in addition to the above only if the impairment entails disability. The distinction between the two concepts, the former medical, the latter legal, is important in that a total loss of hearing in both ears could conceivably not merit a disability payment if the workman could still do a normal days work and therefore suffers no wage loss.

There is a further complication as to whether hearing loss is a compensable injury. Usually the test for compensation has been "a personal injury" caused by "an accident." A narrow interpretation of the word "accident" clearly excludes hearing damage due to continuous exposure. It could even exclude traumatic hearing loss if the cause of the trauma were a regular part of the job.

Doubt about the etiology of hearing loss can also raise problems. For example, how much of a hearing defect is work related, and how much is due to outside factors? This problem will be dealt with in the future when under the OSHA regulations audiometry is used to assess workers' hearing. As a result of these check-ups the amount of hearing damage suffered from the time a worker joins a firm can be determined.

Non-occupational noise can contribute to hearing loss, but its effects are likely to be much less severe than the effects produced by work exposure. Presbycusis and pathogenic hearing loss also have to be taken into account in any award of damage.

### Hearing Loss versus Other Disabilities

Hearing loss, in one or both ears, is considered to be a permanent partial disability. The seriousness with which states view various disabling injuries can be ascertained from how much and for how long compensation is paid.

The number of weeks for which compensation is payable for hearing loss in both ears varies from 100 to 400, with a median value of 175. For other injuries of the same order of seriousness, the median values for 48 states are:*

| | |
|---|---|
| Loss of an arm at the shoulder† | 228 weeks of compensation |
| Loss of a leg at the hip | 215 weeks of compensation |
| Loss of a hand* | 175 weeks of compensation |
| Loss of hearing in two ears | 175 weeks of compensation |
| Loss of a foot | 150 weeks of compensation |
| Loss of sight in one eye | 139 weeks of compensation |

There is no obvious way of evaluating the handicap caused by the loss of an arm, say, compared with the loss of hearing in both ears. One can imagine ranking these disabilities by the percentage of sufferers who adapt well to them. However, since hearing is a most important sense, the loss of this faculty diminishes every other function. Indeed, unless a deaf person can lip read, he is totally cut-off from social intercourse. Put in this light, the loss of a leg may prove less of a handicap, particularly in a society in which man is becoming less important for his muscular ability than for his ability to communicate and to process the information he receives through his senses.

### The Encouragement of Safety

An important objective of workmen's compensation is the management of safety. This is achieved by the safety engineering and preventive services provided under the program, and by the monetary incentive of

---

*Based on 1969 data—U.S. Department of Labor—Bureau of Labor Standards.
†Major member, that is, right arm for a right-handed person.

lower premiums for better safety records. In some states the agency with the responsibility for workman safety is combined with the workmen's compensation agency, and there is clearly ample scope for co-operation between the two types of organization. Within the workmen's compensation program some $35 million are spent annually by private insurance carriers on safety services. It is not clear how much of this is concerned with hearing loss prevention.

Some industries are inherently more dangerous than others; the injury frequency rate in coal mining in the United States for example is nearly three times that of manufacturing.* Insurance premiums reflect this risk differential; in fact there are some 500 different classes. Each of these has a basic "manual" rate which can be modified up or down according to the safety records of individual firms. Unfortunately, firms with less than 10 employees are too small to be experience-rated in this manner. In fact, according to the National Commission on State Workmen's Compensation Laws, "A firm must have almost 300 employees before an accident rate percent of the average warrants a 25 percent reduction in its insurance premiums" (National Commission, 1972). Retrospective rating can further reduce premiums for larger firms by basing them on the firms' own experience after the policy period is over.

The theory is that firms and industries with poor safety records will face higher premiums, and thus additional costs of production, leading to higher prices. In a competitive market this will cause consumers to transfer their expenditure to safer firms or industries. The power of this argument is almost entirely destroyed, however, when two factors are recognized. In the first place, the market is not competitive, that is, there may not be substitutes for goods made in dangerous industries or firms. Secondly, in no state in 1972 did the average fraction of payroll devoted to premiums exceed 1.5 percent. Even if all the recommendations (for 1975) of the Commission were adopted, the figure would nowhere exceed 2 percent, indicating little financial stimulus to improve safety (by quieter machines). It seems probable that other factors such as the loss of production due to accidents, the new OSHA standards, union pressure, and the growing general awareness of environmental issues, constitute a greater incentive for employers to improve safety than differential insurance premiums.

---

*The 1970 figures for the United States, per million employee hours, were 42 in mining versus 15 in manufacturing (National Commission, 1972).

## Waiting Periods

As can be seen from Table 19.6, several states specify a waiting period before the employee can file a claim. In seven states, 6 months are required. The waiting period applies only to indemnity and not to medical or hospital care: the shorter the period, the less the financial burden on the worker; most States specify a maximum of 7 days.

The purpose of a waiting period in workmen's compensation claims, and the provisions for retroactive payment that usually accompanies it is, in general, to discourage trivial claims. In the case of industrial deafness, furthermore, there is some recovery after exposure to the noise has ceased: the argument is that compensation should be based on the final disability. Unfortunately, claimants may not wish or be able to leave their jobs in order to be eligible for compensation. The case is also put that insurance companies could not remain solvent if there were a flood of claims; neither could the employers if damage claims were awarded by the courts. In general, it seems unreasonable to expect workers to avoid a noisy environment for 6 months before filing a claim, especially since the relationship between temporary and permanent threshold shift seems well enough defined at this moment for provisional compensation to be paid.

## The Assessment of Disability

Finally, the choice of the scheme by which hearing disability is legally assessed is a crucial factor in claims. For instance as we have seen in Chapter 3, the American Academy of Ophthalmology and Otolaryngology (AAOO, 1964; Davis, 1965) and the American Medical Association (AMA, 1961) take into account only the average hearing loss at 500, 1000, and 2000 Hz on the basis that these are the most important from the point of view of speech comprehension. Further, they specify a "low fence" of 25 dB; in other words no impairment is held to have occurred until a person has suffered a permanent threshold shift of this amount.* This is shown graphically in Fig. 19.1, from which it can be seen that 100 percent impairment corresponds to a loss of 82 dB.

---

*The "low fence" was originally 15 dB. A new audiometric zero established by the International Organization for Standards effectively reduced this fence to about 5 dB. This would have had the same effect as eliminating the measurement at 500 cycles and adding a measurement at 3000 cycles—a situation that would approximately double the cost of compensation (Sharrah, 1966). To avoid such an increased cost, the fence was raised to 25 dB.

This approach has several major drawbacks. First, the measurements contain the assumption that the only valid criterion for claiming any difficulty is speech comprehension. There can be other criteria, such as degradation of the quality of the environment as perceived by the person, which are also important elements of impairment. As we have seen in Part II, it seems absurd to define "hearing loss" merely as a loss of speech comprehension. Secondly, the measurements are carried out without any background noise, which means that under realistic conditions the 100 percent impairment would correspond to less than 82 dB; the "high fence" should be lower. Thirdly, a hearing loss at higher frequencies, although not compensable by the scheme, still causes difficulty in understanding conversation under realistic conditions. Finally, noise induced hearing damage is often accompanied by loudness recruitment which makes extra amplification useless for improving intelligibility (Kryter, 1970); again the high fence should be lower.

Figure 19.2 depicts an alternative which could obviate these drawbacks. This alternative is based on the Australian method (Murray, 1962) which includes in the computation of the average hearing loss, the loss at

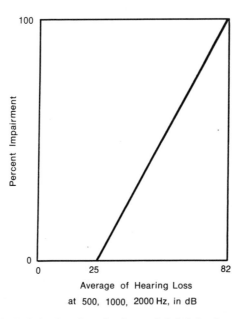

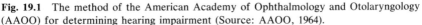

**Fig. 19.1** The method of the American Academy of Ophthalmology and Otolaryngology (AAOO) for determining hearing impairment (Source: AAOO, 1964).

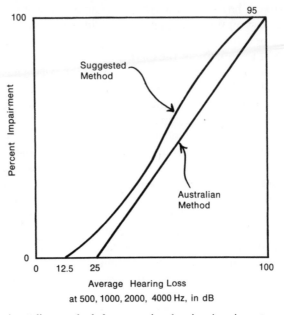

**Fig. 19.2** The Australian method for assessing hearing impairment—and a possible improvement (Source: Murray, 1962).

4000 Hz to provide a much broader measure of the impairment, since hearing loss is always more acute at this frequency. The alternative furthermore could specify that the tests be carried out with background noise at a level exceeded only 10 percent of the time, and with a low fence corresponding to hearing two standard deviations worse than mean normal hearing. Finally, if the relation between average hearing loss and percentage impairment is expressed by an $S$-shaped curve, penalties are increased for hearing loss in the early stages, with the greatest penalty at moderate hearing loss and decreasing penalties for severe loss.

A quite different and attractive approach would be that proposed by Atherley and Noble (see Chapter 3), who suggest that pure-tone audiometry by itself is inadequate to represent the degree of handicap regardless of how many or which frequencies are used in the averaging. Thus the assessment should be based on a battery of tests including speech audiometry and a questionnaire about the degree of handicap experienced by the worker.

Kryter (1970) also strongly disagrees with the AAOO and American Medical Association suggestions that speech comprehension in a quiet environment is a sufficient indicator of the ability to hear everyday speech, and proposes a more compassionate formula to assess the percentage loss for *weak* conversational speech (and why indeed consider only loud or normal levels?)

Every scheme, however, contains within it implicit value-judgments which should be clearly understood and either accepted, rejected or modified by the people affected. What must be said again and again is that it is not only a question of *which* assessment scheme, but also and perhaps more important *who* decides. All these schemes assume that impairment only arises from interference with speech; if instead, for example, we propose a criterion based on using up, say, half of the 25 dB margin between normal hearing and beginning difficulty with speech comprehension then we would add 12.5 dB onto every hearing loss in our calculation, the level of potential workmen's compensation payments would then be increased from $6000 million to at least $15,000 million, or more than double!

The AMA-AAOO formulas have been derived by a subcommittee of experts, in response not only to health considerations, but also to economic and political ones. There is no reason why a workman should not be compensated for the loss of ability to hear sounds such as the kicking up of leaves in autumn, the chirping of birds in the spring, and the fizz of the soda pop bottle his child has opened. The auditory environment is not confined to three or even four frequencies. In the future one should consider the use of adaptations of Davis' (Davis, 1948) Social Adequacy Index described in Part II (Chapter 3), or of a much more complicated "Quality of Life Index" based on what people actually listen to and value.

It seems fair to conclude this section with the observation that both the 6-month waiting period and the AAOO standards have led to a serious underestimation of the size of the problem. Several million workers are being denied compensation at present and are bearing the full social cost of industrial noise pollution alone. Adequate and prompt indemnification of this burden would not only render justice to them, but, by raising insurance premiums, would reinforce the preventive measures of OSHA. While prevention must be the long-term solution to occupational deafness, society should pay its debt to those who have for so long subsidized it at the expense of their hearing.

## The United Kingdom

It is interesting to note that in the United Kingdom for about 50 years prior to 1945 there was a Workmen's Compensation Act which functioned roughly on the lines described above for the U.S. system. The Labor Government of 1945 abolished this system and introduced a national insurance industrial injuries scheme, toward which both the employee and the employer contribute. Unfortunately, under this scheme industrial deafness is not a scheduled injury.

In the autumn of 1973 the UK Department of Health and Social Security published a report (DHSS, 1973) which led to prescribing occupational deafness as an industrial disease under the National Insurance (Industrial Injuries) Act of 1965. As a result since October 1974 it has been possible for workers (not all but some) to claim and receive disablement benefit for occupational deafness.

The amount of the benefit for complete loss of hearing in both ears is £19 a week (DHSS, 1974); this compares with about £35 a week for the average factory worker's gross wage. As it stands the benefit is payable only to workers who have been working at the particular job for 20 years. Thus may leave as many as 25 years in a working life-time for the benefit to be paid, for a total of £25,000.

The benefit is considerably in excess of the amount paid by the state of Hawaii and is probably the most generous in existence today (even if not enough to live on; one would still have to work). It has, however, three serious limitations: Firstly, it is available only to people in a very small number of jobs and thus to very few people. Secondly, a worker must have been working at that job for twenty years. Thirdly, a worker must have *very* serious hearing damage to qualify.

The jobs and processes covered are (DHSS, 1973):

"Any occupation involving (a) The use of pneumatic percussive tools or high speed grinding tools in the clearing dressing or finishing of cast metal or of ingots, billets or blooms; or (b) the use of pneumatic percussive tools on metal in the shipbuilding and/or ship repairing industries; or (c) Work wholly or mainly in the immediate vicinity of drop-forging plant or forging press plant engaged in the shaping of hot metal."

Note that (a) excludes the use of such tools in boiler making and in the manufacture of process plant or of pressure vessels; chippers on welded tanks are excluded. Yet the report itself lists other jobs that are risky to hearing: "metal production work and fabrication; large diesel engines; gas-fired, oil-fired and certain electric furnaces of large size; textile spinning and twisting; and weaving." The further requirement that workers must have been working at the particular job for twenty years can exclude a large number of workers that have been injured from holding noisy jobs for shorter periods of time. In the jobs and processes for which compensation is allowed, the noise levels are so high that serious damage is quite likely to occur in a year, not in twenty years or in ten years or even in five years. This is clear from the Burns and Robinson study. Indeed in a case in which levels of 125 dBA were encountered in the use of pneumatic percussive tools in the shipbuilding and ship repairing industries, an immission that would give one in ten workers a 74% loss of hearing for weak conversational speech as defined by the Kryter method (Kryter, 1970) could be acquired in three months of 8 hour a day, 5 day a week exposure (Kinnersly, 1973).

Undoubtedly it was properly realized that there might be a flood of claims that would in fact overwhelm the National Health Service Ear, Nose and Throat clinics, and that this should be staved off by limiting the jobs and processes, the time of exposure, and the degree of hearing loss. But the result poses an important question. Where to draw the line on those three variables is clearly a value judgment; as such should it not be a proper and important issue for a political decision by elected representatives? Should the House of Commons have an opportunity, for instance, to allow claims for people who had worked in a particular job or process for five years instead of twenty, or to lower the "low fence" to a 27–37 dB average at 1000, 2000 and 3000 Hz?* Should fundamentally political decisions be made by a body which is not elected—such as an Industrial Diseases Sub-Committee—and converted into a regulation by the Secretary of State for Health and Social Security without any direct involvement of the Parliament?

## A Disturbing Thought

In a recent paper based on extrapolation of his own data, as well as data from other sources, Kryter reaches the conclusion that *presbycusis and sociocusis* (these can't really be separated unless one is a hermit) *are equivalent to exposure to a steady level of 40–55 dBA for 45 years* (Kryter, 1973). When we compare this to the 90, 85, and even the 80 dBA steady 8-hour levels recommended in the United States and the United Kingdom, the Soviet Union, and the Netherlands, it is clear that this is setting the cat among the pigeons (see Ward, 1973). What this means in effect is that it is no use pretending that steady levels below 80 dBA are harmless; it might as well be acknowledged that even in choosing such levels as 80 dBA as

---

*This figure was suggested by an expert witness to the Committee on the grounds that people attended hearing aid clinics for the first time with such losses because they considered themselves in need of help (DHSS, 1973).

"safe," society is giving weight to economic considerations and imposing risk on people exposed to levels 10 or even 20 dBA lower.

## APPENDIX: EXCERPTS FROM U.S. DEPARTMENT OF LABOR RECOMMENDED STANDARDS FOR WORKMEN'S COMPENSATION LAWS (ESA, 1971)

### Compulsory and Elective Laws

In general, workmen's compensation laws as they apply to private employers are either compulsory or elective. A compulsory law requires every covered employer to comply with its provisions for the compensation of work injuries. An elective act permits an employer either to accept or reject its provisions. In case the employer elects not to be subject to the law, however, he loses the common law defenses—assumed risk of the employment, negligence of fellow servants, and contributory negligence. Under most types of elective laws, acceptance of the act is presumed unless specific notice of rejection is filed.

Although in practice most employers elect to come under the act, some do not, in which case the employees may be unable to obtain compensation unless they sue for damages.

Recommended Standard: The workmen's compensation law should be compulsory.

### Numerical Exemptions

The effectiveness of workmen's compensation laws is limited in many states by numerical exemptions under which small employers are not covered by the law.

Workers employed by employers who have only a few employees are usually in need of the protection offered by the workmen's compensation laws. The small establishment is likely to lack a formal safety program and the financial resources to protect the injured workers in case of serious injury. At the same time, the employer in a small business establishment needs the protection of workmen's compensation to safeguard himself against law suits for injuries to employees.

Recommended Standard: No exemption of employers based on number of employees.

## Coverage of Agricultural Workers

Available data rank farmwork as one of the most hazardous types of employment. The misgivings of the early farmers of these laws about difficulties of administration which encouraged the exemption of farmers, small firms, and other specified employments no longer hold true. State workmen's compensation laws that provide for broad coverage of their workers have proved that these occupations may be covered without adverse results.

Recommended Standard: Coverage of agricultural workers in the same manner as other employees.

## Occupational Disease Coverage

Complete coverage of occupational diseases has been the trend in workmen's compensation laws that provide for broad coverage of their cover only enumerated diseases, usually termed "schedule" coverage.

Full coverage of occupational diseases can be provided for in the law by various methods. One is by a simple definition of the term "injury" such as is used in the Wisconsin law: "... 'injury' is mental or physical harm to an employee caused by accident or disease . . .." In several State laws, full coverage has been obtained by adding another paragraph to their scheduled listing of diseases. Rhode Island, for instance, accomplished this by adding to its schedule: "Disability arising from any cause connected with or arising from the peculiar characteristics of the employment."

A person disabled by an occupational disease should be entitled to workmen's compensation benefits as much as a person disabled from an accidental work injury.

Recommended Standard: Full coverage of occupational diseases.

## Rehabilitation Division within the Workmen's Compensation Agency

A workmen's compensation agency has a special responsibility with respect to the rehabilitation of the worker shortly after he is injured. Although only a small percentage of the workers who are injured require rehabilitative services, when these services are required it is important that there be an early referral to a rehabilitation program. This can best be accomplished through a division in the workmen's compensation agency that specializes in this type of case. Unless rehabilitation begins soon after the injury, the maximum physical restoration may be prevented.

Recommended Standard: A rehabilitation division within the workmen's compensation agency.

### Maintenance Benefits during Rehabilitation

In order to encourage the co-operation of the injured worker to accept rehabilitation, it is necessary to give him some compensation to help cover his additional expenses and financial loss during the rehabilitation period. This is especially true when the worker must spend a considerable time away from home.

Recommended Standard: Provision for special maintenance benefits during the period of rehabilitation, in addition to such other benefits to which the injured worker may be entitled.

### Medical Benifits for Occupational Diseases

Workers suffering from disability due to occupational diseases are not protected to the same extent as those suffering from accidental injuries. Approximately one-third of the states limit medical benefits in occupational disease cases. These limitations are on either duration or cost, or both.

Recommended Standard: Full medical benefits for occupational diseases.

### Selection of Physician

Most of the early workmen's compensation laws placed responsibility for selecting the doctor upon the employer or the insurance carrier. The trend in workmen's compensation legislation is toward selection of the physician by the injured worker as reflected in statutory amendments and in administrative rules and regulations.

Recommended Standard: Initial selection of physician by the injured worker.

### Time Limit for Filing Occupational Disease Claims

A workmen's compensation law may provide coverage for occupational diseases but its effectiveness may be seriously curtailed if the law provides for an inadequate period of time in which a worker must file for benefits. A worker may not know that he has contracted an occupational disease until: (1) a substantial period of time has passed after the date of last exposure; (2) a substantial period of time has passed before the condition is diagnosed as a disease that occurred as a result of employment. For example, in cases involving overexposure to ionizing radiation, it may be 10, 20, or more years after exposure before a worker becomes disabled and has knowledge that the condition requiring treatment is directly related to his radiation exposure while on the job.

About one-half of the states have a flexible provision relating to the time that a claim must be filed in order that the case may be given favorable consideration. The remainder of the laws require that a claim be filed within a specified period.

Recommended Standard: The time limitation for the filing of claims should be at least 1 year after the date when employee has knowledge of the nature of his disability and its relation to his job and until after disablement.

## Ratio of Maximum Weekly Benefit for Temporary Total Disability to Average Weekly Wages

Most of the laws base cash benefits on varying percentages of average weekly wages received by the worker, usually $66\frac{2}{3}$ percent. However, workers do not as a rule actually receive the amount indicated by the percentages because most laws also set a dollar limitation on the payments. This means that the worker may receive less than the statutory percentage.

It is suggested that a formula based on the state's average weekly wage be provided for determining the maximum weekly benefit in order to eliminate the necessity for constantly adjusting the benefit rate at each session of the legislature.

Recommended Standard: Maximum weekly benefit should be equal to at least $66\frac{2}{3}$ percent of the state's average weekly wage.

## Types of Administration

Two general methods of administration of the workmen's compensation laws exist in the United States. One is by a state agency, such as the State labor department or a board or commission. The other is by the courts. At present most of the laws are administered by state labor departments, or through separate workmen's compensation agencies, but there are five states that have court administration.

No law is better than its administration. If not administered properly, even a good law is ineffective. The administration of a workmen's compensation law includes not only claims administration but also supervision of immediate and continued medical care, supervision of benefit payments, co-operative arrangements for rehabilitation, promotion of safety, and other specialized functions. It is generally agreed that administration by an agency is better adapted for these purposes than administration by the courts.

Recommended Standard: A state agency should be designated to administer the workmen's compensation law.

## Judicial Review

The purpose of workmen's compensation legislation is to take the settlement of claims, so far as possible, out of the courts. Satisfactory claim settlement can be obtained only through a good statutory operating plan and a properly staffed agency.

Recommended Standard: Judicial review should be limited to question of law.

## REFERENCES

AAOO. Guide for conservation of hearing in noise. A Supplement to the Transactions of the American Academy of Opthalmologists and Otolaryngologists. Revised 1964.

AMA. Committee on Medical Rating of Physical Impairment. Guides to the evaluation of permanent impairment, ear, nose, throat, and related structures. *Journal of the American Medical Association*, 1961, **7**, 177.

Anderson, D. A. S., Chief Press Officer, Health and Safety Commission, Private Communication, April 1975.

BLS (Bureau of Labor Standards). State Workmen's Compensation Laws. Bulletin 161. Revised May 1960.

Bugliarello, G., and Wakstein, C. W. Noise pollution—a review of its techno-sociological and health aspects. Biotechnology Program, Carnegie-Mellon University, Pittsburgh, 1968.

Davis, H. The articulation area and the social adequacy index for hearing. *Laryngoscope*, 1948, **58**.

Davis, H. Guide for the classification and evaluation of hearing handicap in relation to the international audiometric zero. *Transactions of the American academy of ophthalmologists and otolaryngologists*, 1965, **69**.

DE (U.K. Department of Employment). Code of Practice for reducing the exposure of employed persons to noise. London: HMSO, 1972.

DHSS (U.K. Department of Health and Social Security), Occupational Deafness, London, HMSO, 1973, Cmnd. 5461.

DHSS (U.K. Department of Health and Social Security), Benefits paid for Occupational Deafness, Leaflet NI 207, October 1974.

EPA (U.S. Environmental Protection Agency). An assessment of noise concern in other nations. Vol. 1, December 1971.

ESA (U.S. Employment Standards Administration). State Workmen's Compensation Laws: A comparison of major provisions with recommended standards. Bulletin No. 212. Revised 1971.

Fox, M. S., M.D. In the U.S. and Canada—hearing loss statutes. *National Safety News*, Chicago: National Safety Council, Vol. 105, No. 2, February 1972.

HSWA (U.K. Health and Safety at Work etc., Act) 1974, Chapter 37. London, HMSO, Reprinted 1975.

IPPAUNA (International Printing Pressmen and Assistant's' Union of North America). Fighting noise . . . A manual for worker action. Washington, 1972.

Kinnersly P., *The Hazards of Work*. London, Pluto Press, 1973.

Kryter, K. D., The Effects of Noise on Man, London, Academic Press, 1970.

Kryter, K. D. "Impairment to hearing from exposure to noise. *Journal of the Acoustical Society of America*, 1973, **53**.

Mil-Std. U.S. Department of Defense. Military standard—Noise limits for army material. Military Standard 1474 (MI), March 1, 1973.

Murray, N. E. Hearing impairment and compensation. *Journal of Otolaryngological Science of Australia*, 1962, **1**.

National Commission. The report of the national commission on workmen's compensation laws. Washington, Superintendent of Documents, September 15, 1972.

Osborn, W. C., "The Law Relating to Noise", in Sinclair, T. C., *et al.*, (eds.), Environmental Pollution Control, London, Allen & Unwin, 1974.

OSHA (Occupational Safety and Health Administration). Guidelines to the Department of Labor's occupational noise standards. Bulletin 334, Washington. Revised 1971.

Robens Committee (Committee on Safety and Health at Work), Safety and Health at Work, London, HMSO, 1972, Cmnd. 5034.

Sharrah, J. S. Compensation for hearing loss. *Industrial Medicine and Surgery*, April 1966.

U.S. Federal Register, Vol. 37, Number 202, Pt. II, Department of Labor Occupational Safety and Health Administration, Occupational Safety and Health Standards, October 18, 1972.

U.S. Public Law. 1970 Occupational Safety and Health Act, 1970, U.S. Public Law 91-596, 84 STAT 1590, December 29, 1970.

Ward, W. D. Comments on impairment to hearing from exposure to noise, by K. D. Kryter, *Journal of the Acoustical Society of America*, 1973, **53**.

CHAPTER 20

# The Technology of Noise Reduction from Machines

## INTRODUCTION

Occupational and leisure noise may be reduced through engineering solutions in many different ways. However, the most economical solution is not always obvious; a great deal of attention must be paid to detail. Problem analysis for noise control breaks down into four basic steps:

- the people affected by the noise must be located;
- the source of the disturbance must be found and a detailed survey made of exactly what causes the noise;
- amount of noise reduction satisfactory to those affected by it must be decided upon (legal action, health studies, or negotiations may influence this decision);
- the method of noise reduction to achieve the desired results most inexpensively must be determined.

In the case of a cost–benefit study, the last two steps are slightly altered. Instead of a particular target for noise reduction (a single point on a noise reduction versus cost graph), a benefit curve listing the dollar benefits for a range of noise-reduction values would be obtained. Assigning dollar values to the benefits involves economic and social considerations, as discussed in Part VI. Finding the cost curve is, instead, basically an engineering problem.

276

## The Mechanics of Noise Generation

Noise has two sources, mechanical vibration and air turbulence. Vibrational energy may be transformed into sound energy if the vibrations are transmitted to a sufficiently large surface. Maximum efficiency occurs when the critical dimension of this surface or sounding board is at least as large as the wave length of the sound being generated. A mechanical source of noise may generate vibrations of many different frequencies. The frequency spectrum of the noise the unit generates will be dependent upon the driving frequencies of the mechanical vibrations present.

Air turbulence creates noise directly in the air. If the shear forces between two air masses moving at different velocities are great enough, a turbulent region forms at the interface of the two masses, to dissipate the resulting frictional energy. Part of this energy leaves in the form of sound-pressure waves. Air turbulence noise tends to be very broad band, with no particular frequency dominating the spectrum.

## Noise Transmission and Attenuation

Several natural phenomena are important in determining the extent to which noise is transmitted or abated. If there are no echoes and only a single source, noise will decrease as a function of distance. For a single-point source in a region having no surfaces which could reflect sound waves, the sound level will decay 6 dB for each doubling of distance from the source. If the noise is produced by a line source (e.g., a crowded highway), the sound will decrease 3 dB for each doubling of distance (BBN, 1967).

Atmospheric and weather conditions are also factors. Sound level will decrease when traveling through air simply because of the frictional forces between gas particles. Higher-frequency noise is more affected. A pure-tone sound with frequency between 75 and 150 cycles per second (cps) will have its level decreased by 0.016 dB every 100 ft, simply due to friction. A sound with frequency between 4800 and 9600 cps will decrease by intensity by 1.2 dB for every 100 ft (Wiener, 1958). Unless the noise has a great many high-frequency components, such as the whine of a jet turbine, atmospheric attenuation has no real effect on its level until the receiver is at least 2000 ft away from the source (BBN, 1967).

If the receiver is downwind from a noise source, he will hear the sound much better than if he were upwind. If the source and receiver are in an area experiencing a temperature inversion condition, the sound close to the ground will carry better than if a normal temperature profile exists with the temperature decreasing as the distance from the ground increases (Parkinson, 1958). Wind and temperature gradient effects are neither exactly known nor easily measured.

The characteristics of the earth surface affect noise to some extent. Thus, some of the high-frequency components of sound traveling across snow-covered or grassy surfaces will be absorbed (Pietrasanta, 1955). Rock cliffs or other hard surfaces will reflect noise; this means that the noise may carry further, into regions where it would not normally be heard.

Sound produced in closed spaces or regions with reflecting surfaces may reach the receiver in two ways. The sound may either travel directly from the source to the receiver, or the wave may be reflected off some surface before it reaches the receiver. Reflected or reverberant sound is often more annoying to the receiver than is direct sound. A reverberant condition prevents the receiver from locating the noise source, and distance laws cease to be applicable (Parkinson, 1955). The sound level in a room does not change as a simple function of distance from a noisy machine. The receiver feels surrounded by noise.


## HOW TO REDUCE NOISE

### Noise Reduction at the Source

Noise-reduction methods are usually classified on the basis of where the sound or vibration is treated. It is convenient to distinguish four main regions:

- the source;
- the sound radiator;
- the region between source and receiver;
- the receiver.

Source solutions attack the noise before it can be generated. When feasible, such solutions are generally quite effective. At times noise reduction is inadvertently achieved as the result of actions taken for other reasons. Thus, a change from jolt squeeze molding to diaphragm molding for economic reasons caused an overall reduction of 3 dB in one foundry (Weber, 1959). Noise reduction in this case costs nothing. Replacement of a worn part in a machine or oiling a dry bearing may also bring a considerable reduction in noise. The cost is no more than that of regular maintenance.

Noise may also be "designed out" of a system. If anti-noise measures are taken during the initial design phase, considerable reductions of potential noise may be obtained for little additional cost. Noiseless plumbing systems with controlled water velocity and special valves are not much more expensive than regular systems. Hence, proper initial planning is effective and cheap, because it attacks the problem before the costs of modification become excessive. If the system must be redesigned or modified after installation, the costs and results are less certain to be satisfactory. U.S. Steel and Alcoa both include noise level specifications when they purchase certain new machinery. Both companies feel it more advantageous to absorb the cost of noise reduction in the initial purchase cost, than to try later to modify the machines. Their actions suggest that machine quietness is a marketable quantity. Encouraging consumers to consider quietness as an important facet of performance may be an effective way of assuring that noise considerations are deemed important in the design of new products.

Ingenuity also plays an important role in achieving noise reduction. There is an example of reduction of the noise of hissing air nozzles achieved by increasing the air velocity in jets (Carter, 1965). At the new velocity, most of the sound is at frequencies too high to be heard by humans. Recently, noise-suppressing metal alloys* have been developed which help stop sounds before they start, by inhibiting vibration. Potential applications are in power tools, propellers, brake disks and subway wheels.

If it is not technically feasible to design the noise out of a system, other methods must be used. For example, the source may be operated in such a manner as to reduce noise. Thus, the air velocity of an air ejector may be lowered so as to just barely knock out the stamped part (Cudworth, 1959). The operation may also be moved to an area where it will disturb fewer people. In either case, the change in operation or location usually costs money because of less efficient production.

Still another solution is the substitution of a less noisy type of machine or process for the old one. Ultrasonic pile drivers, for example, are much less noisy than older types. Usually the methods which employ the fewest moving parts are the quietest. Switching from riveting to welding in a foundry lowered the noise level of the joining operation from 110 to 90 dB

---

*Typically, a compound of copper, manganese, and aluminum.

(Hardy and Porter, 1955). Electric motors are much quieter power sources than internal combustion engines. Direct energy conversion methods of the future will provide the quietest power source.

An interesting but limited method of reducing noise is to destroy it with another noise—a superimposed sound wave, identical to the initial wave, but 180 degrees out of phase. The two waves cancel each other out; such a solution has been attempted with electric transformer noise, with only partial success (Conover, 1956). The initial noise was being generated from a complicated source, and trying to duplicate the wave patterns of the initial wave proved extremely difficult: where the patterns matched, the noise was stopped; where the patterns did not match, the resulting noise was frequently worse than the initial sound.

Sound may also be used to mask noise. A technique used by many stores and offices is to play music at a slightly higher level than the noise.

Assessment of the costs of reducing noise at the source is very difficult. First, few cost figures for reduction programs carried on inside a company are available. Second, substantial portions of many noise-reduction costs involve more than materials or labor; for example, lost production due to downtime for modifications and reduced efficiency of the quieter machine. Lastly, noise reduction is usually just one of a number of reasons for making changes or modifications, making it difficult to determine what portion of the total costs is caused by noise-reduction considerations.

### Noise Reduction at the Sounding Board

Noise may also be attacked at the sounding board. One solution is to isolate the vibrations from any possible radiating surfaces by using flexible connectors and mountings (Vance, 1956). Such connectors can usually be bought commercially and are easily installed. For example, rubber hoses can reduce the compressor vibration being transmitted through an air-conditioning pipe system (Yeng, 1967). Most floor mounts for heavy machinery require careful design, however, making engineering costs a sizable component of the noise-reduction expenditure. The problem here is that the resilient mountings must be massive enough to take the weight of the machine, and the machine itself will ordinarily vibrate with a greater amplitude under these circumstances. Again, the isolators must not have a natural frequency anywhere near that of the mass of the actual machine nor of the driving force itself. A general rule is that the forcing frequency must be $\sqrt{2}$ times the natural frequency of the mounting (the frequency at which the mounting resonates) before any improvement takes place; the higher the ratio, the better the isolation.

The natural frequency of a mounting is related to the amount of deflection under the applied load. Thus, given a forcing frequency, it is fairly straightforward to calculate the required static deflection property of the isolators.

If the vibration cannot be isolated from the sounding board, the board itself may be modified to become a less efficient radiator. One method is to cut the board into several pieces, each smaller in dimensions than the wave length of the most undesirable spectral component of the noise. The vibrations of the board may also be reduced by increasing its mass or its stiffness. Finally, the board may be coated with some mastic material which absorbs the energy of the vibrations and transforms it into frictional heat (Chapman, 1956). As with source treatments, sounding board treatments take many forms, and cost per decibel figures are difficult to establish.

## Noise Reduction between Source and Receiver

A further method of noise reduction is the treatment of the waves before they reach the receiver. Three types of measures are possible between the source and receiver: sound-absorption, sound-isolation, and use of resonators.

### Sound Absorption

Sound-absorption methods are, theoretically, the ideal way to reduce noise. Sound energy is transformed into heat energy by passing the waves through soft fibrous materials. Energy is lost through the frictional interactions of the fibers (Carter, 1965; Mariner, 1957; Purcell, 1957). The problem with absorption treatments is that the sound must pass through a great deal of such materials before a significant amount of energy is removed. Contrary to popular belief, materials like fiberglass have only limited acoustical applications. They are not the answer to every noise problem and their indiscriminate use is ill-advised. Absorption treatments are more effective against high-frequency than against low-frequency noise.

If an absorption material is applied to the walls of an untreated room, the overall noise reduction in the room would be between 8 and 10 dB.*

---

*At a cost of some $0.50–1.00/ft² of wall.

Doubling the thickness of the absorbent material would only yield additional noise reductions of 3 dB (Parkinson, 1958). Since sound-absorbent material is also good for thermal insulation, benefits other than noise reduction may be gained from such a wall treatment program.

Sound baffles are strips of absorbent material hung from the ceiling. This has the same effect as wall treatments with similar costs and results.

Absorbent curtains and spot treatments are limited applications of sound-absorbent materials used to provide localized effects. An example (common but ineffective) of an absorbent curtain is a blanket of fiberglass hung between a machine and a worker. This method does not provide much noise reduction because the sound does not pass through very much material. An example of spot treatment would be a panel of acoustic tile hung behind a machine to stop reverberant noise from bouncing back into the operator's face.

A relatively new use of absorbent material has been in functional sound absorbers. These geometrically shaped units hang directly over the sound source and absorb a large quantity of the sound directed at the ceiling. Since such noise is usually reflected back towards the floor, the absorbers are treating reverberant noise. The effect is felt by all in the room except those very close to the noise source (Gould and Yeng, 1956). Proper installation of such units can result in overall noise reductions of between 8 and 10 dB (Mariner, 1957).

In summary, sound-absorption treatments, by themselves, benefit only receivers in the same ambient as the source. The costs and effects of sound-absorption treatments can be calculated.

### Sound Isolation

Sound-isolation treatments prevent sound from reaching the receiver by some sort of barrier. Two types of barrier are commonly used, each based on different physical principles.

One type completely encloses either the source or the receiver. The walls prevent sound incident on one side from being transmitted to the other side. The wall's effectiveness, measured in terms of sound transmission loss, is dependent on the physical properties of its material, namely density and stiffness. The sound Transmission Loss, or TL, of a wall constitutes the difference between the noise level in decibels on the source side and the level on the receiver's side. Theoretical calculations show that TL is a function of the sound frequency and the surface weight of the wall. A graph of this function appears in Fig. 20.1.

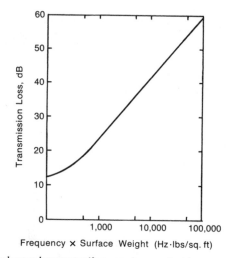

**Fig. 20.1**  Theoretical mass law curve (for sound waves incident to surface from all angles) (Source: Purcell, 1957).

It should be noted that, as with sound-absorbent treatments, sound isolation by total enclosure works best against high-frequency noise; for the same surface weight the TL is greater for high frequencies. The actual TL curves of various materials deviate from the theoretical curve due to resonances, and at higher frequencies due to a so-called coincidence effect.

The TL of a non-homogeneous wall is largely dependent on the smallest TL of a component. If a large brick wall, whose masonry components have a TL of 45 dB, has 20 percent of its space taken up by single glazed windows whose TL equals 20 dB, the TL of the composite wall will be 22 dB. In a regular house, the TL of the walls is usually controlled by the area occupied by doors and windows.

The sound-isolation capacity of a total barrier can be critically weakened by failure to completely enclose either the source or the receiver. Modern office buildings frequently have noise problems because sound may flank the wall partition by going through the false ceilings, as shown in Fig. 20.2. Many industrial machines cannot be sound treated with total enclosures because openings must be provided to pass material into and out of the units.

The other type of sound-isolation enclosure is a partial barrier. Instead of completely stopping noise, this type of barrier deflects it away from the receiver. One prerequisite for a partial barrier is that it must be made of a

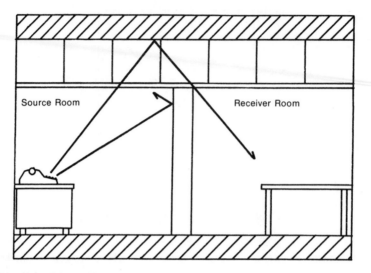

**Fig. 20.2** False ceiling noise problems in an office (Source: Parkinson, 1955).

material solid enough to prevent any sound from being transmitted through it. Any sound that reaches the receiver must have gone around the barrier (the higher-frequency components, in fact, are bent around it). Again, a great deal of information is available for designing a partial barrier for a particular job (Purcell, 1957, Rettinger, 1957). Obviously, the higher the partial barrier between the source and receiver, the greater the noise-level reduction at the receiver.

The noise reduction afforded by sound-isolation techniques is dependent on the physical properties and dimensions of the materials used. Costs can thus be directly calculated.

### Resonators

Resonators are devices specifically designed to treat low-frequency noise. A reflective surface is placed in the path of sound waves. Waves reflected off the surface cancel out incident waves.

The principle is frequently used in automobile mufflers. A well-designed resonation muffler can effectively reduce exhaust noise without increasing back pressure (Nelson, 1956). The only drawback of such a muffler over an absorption type is its greater size and weight. Despite a widely held belief, a well-designed muffler system can quiet an engine while increasing performance at the same time (Rowley, 1967).

*Combinations of Absorption, Isolation, and Resonator Treatments*

Combinations of these three approaches are frequently used to take advantage of the best qualities of each. Resonator plenums in air-conditioner ducts are usually lined with absorption material to eliminate the high-frequency noise the resonator cannot stop (Lemmerman, 1957). Absorption material is used to line the interior of a source-isolation enclosure in order to lower the sound level inside the enclosure (Purcell, 1957). Exact figures for noise reduction achieved by such combinations are difficult to calculate and must be based on specific situations.

## Noise Reduction at the Receiver

The final method of reducing noise is at the receiver, by means of ear plugs (permanent or disposable), semi-insert protectors or ear muffs. In general a pair of acoustical earmuffs costing less than $10 provide the best solution, since they may reduce noise as much as 40 dB if properly worn (Bell, 1966). The actual protection given depends on the frequency of the sound (Table 20.1). However, such devices are often annoying and uncomfortable to wear. In addition, they impede the reception of important acoustical signals and they may produce a sense of isolation from the environment, although this may be overcome by the use of amplitude-sensitive or frequency-selective ear protectors.

**Table 20.1**   Typical Performance of Fluid Seal Ear Muffs. The Assumed Protection is the Sound Reduction Given to the Majority of Users (DE 1972).

| Frequency | Hz | 125 | 250 | 500 | 1000 | 2000 | 4000 | 8000 |
|---|---|---|---|---|---|---|---|---|
| Mean attenuation | dB | 13 | 20 | 33 | 35 | 38 | 47 | 41 |
| Standard Deviation | dB | 6 | 6 | 6 | 6 | 7 | 8 | 8 |
| Assumed Protection | dB | 7 | 14 | 27 | 29 | 31 | 39 | 33 |

A more subtle way of dealing with some kinds of noise at the receiver is to make the sound more acceptable. For instance, people are less annoyed by highway noise if they cannot see the road (Winterbottom, 1965). Air-conditioning noise rarely disturbs people in the area being air-conditioned, because the receiver associates the noise with a beneficial result.

## A Checklist of Measures

In general, no single measure will suffice to reduce the noise from a machine. Desirable as it would be to eliminate the noise at the source, this is seldom totally possible, technically or economically. Thus, mixed strategies become necessary, governed by the characteristics of the specific noise source and its environment. A list of possible measures to quiet machines is given in Table 20.2. Many of the measures in the table are general and apply to all sources of noise.

## Noise Reduction in the Household

Noise can be reduced to a considerable extent in a house which is well designed from an acoustical standpoint, and where the occupants pay attention to the problem. Measures to achieve this end can be classified into three groups:

Architectural measures.
Interior decor measures.
Appliance design and operation measures.

Some of the most effective architectural measures include:

- placing the bedrooms as far away as possible in the layout of the house from traffic noises and other major sources of outdoor noise;
- placing closet, storage walls, and fireplaces between rooms;
- staggering inside doors so as to avoid presenting a straight line path to noise;
- insulating utility rooms from the rest of the house;
- applying acoustic material to walls and ceilings—and even to floors.

Interior decor measures include:

- carpeting (which can be most effective against impact noise);
- heavy curtains;
- upholstered furniture;
- padded doors;
- fabrics on walls;
- plants.

Heavy-duty appliances can be cushioned and insulated by following the same principles outlined in the previous section. For instance, noisy dishwashers can be made some 50 percent quieter with fiberglass insulation, as can air-conditioners. The noise of a fan can be reduced from

**Table 20.2**   Some Noise Reduction Measures for Machines (Source: EPA, 1971b; OSHA, 1971).

Plant Planning

Selection or substitution of processes
   Specify noise level when selecting process
   Compression for impact riveting
   Welding for riveting
   Hot for cold working
   Pressing for rolling or forging
Selection or substitution of machines
   Specify noise level when ordering new equipment
   Larger, slower machines for smaller, faster ones
   Step dies for single-operation dies
   Presses for hammers
   Rotating shears for square shears
   Hydraulic for mechanical presses
   Belt drives for gears
   Large, low-speed fans for smaller, high-speed ones
Location of equipment within plant
   Confine noisy machines to insulated rooms
   Shelter equipment with baffles
Location of plant with respect to community
Maintenance of machines
   Replace or adjust worn and loose or unbalanced parts
   Lubricate machine parts and use of cutting oils
   Properly shaped and sharpened cutting tools
Other controls at source
   Maintain dynamic balance in machine
   Minimize rotational speed
   Decouple driving force
   Reduce velocity of fluid flow
   Reduce turbulence
   Take advantage of directionality of source
Control of transmitted noise
   Vibration—isolate the source
   Use flexible shaft coupling and flexible sections in pipe runs
   Enclose the source
   Absorb sound within room
   Use reactive or dissipative mufflers
   Place fabric sections in ducts
Control of radiated noise
   Increase mass
   Increase stiffness
   Shift resonant frequencies
   Add damping
   Reduce surface area
   Perforate the surface
Control of noise at receiver
   Earmuffs for machine operators and attendants
   Soundproof booth for operators and attendants of one or more machines
   Remote control of machine

100 dBA at 3 ft to 35 dBA received by an occupant of the building, by interposing a wall and insulating the mounting from vibration. Similarly the noise of steam valves can be reduced from 80 to 40 dBA.

Noise levels that are attainable in a household through a normal combination of architectural and mechanical measures are shown in Fig. 20.3. There is no justification for exposing the occupants of a building to higher levels of noise.

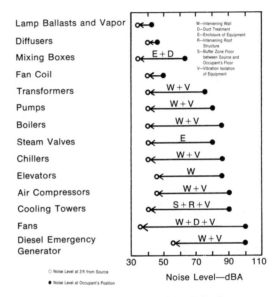

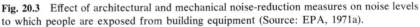

**Fig. 20.3** Effect of architectural and mechanical noise-reduction measures on noise levels to which people are exposed from building equipment (Source: EPA, 1971a).

## THE COST OF QUIETING MACHINES: A VERY ROUGH ESTIMATE FOR THE UNITED STATES

Basically, noise control is very expensive because it requires large reductions in the acoustic energy emitted by the noise source (Table 20.3). The actual costs industry pays to quiet its machines are extremely difficult to estimate, both because of lack of data and because, as we have discussed, noise-reduction measures may be combined with other measures. Table 20.4 gives an extremely rough estimate of what it would cost to reduce noise in those occupations in the U.S. industry whose noise

**Table 20.3**  Reductions in Acoustic Energy Necessary to Achieve Given Noise Reductions.

| Reduction in Noise (dB) | Reduction in Energy (Percent) |
|---|---|
| 3 | 50 |
| 10 | 90 |
| 30 | 99.9 |

levels have been measured, for three hypothetical costs per decibel per worker, ranging from $25 (probably a very low estimate) to $125* (possibly a high estimate for occupations in the lower-decibel range).

The table shows that the cost is high, particularly considering the fact that it is computed only on the base of the workers *known* to be exposed to high levels, rather than in terms of the total number of workers exposed to over 80 dB (Table 18.2). It also shows that the bulk of the cost in reducing occupational noise would be encountered in quieting environments between 85 and 100 dB, rather than the extremely noisy environment, where the number of workers is relatively low.

However, consideration of the large sums of money involved should be placed in perspective. If the assumption is made that machines get replaced every 10 years, one-tenth of the costs given in the table need to be incurred per year. Even with the highest estimates given in Table 20.4, this amounts to less than one fifth of one percent of the U.S. gross national product. It is also instructive to compare such costs with the corresponding ones for earmuffs (at $10 per year and capable of reducing noise by as much as 40 dB). For the 10 million workers considered in the table, the cost of earmuffs would be approximately $100 million, a much lower figure than the annual costs of noise reduction in machines. Clearly, the sensible approach is that being taken by many industries: give every machine operator and attendant earmuffs, and, in addition, attempt to quiet the machines as much as possible, because the workers will not always be willing or able to wear their earmuffs or to wear them properly, and because the quieting of machines has a beneficial effect also on those not in the immediate environment of the machine.

*Data for a particular company indicate an average cost of $90 (in 1973 dollars) per decibel per worker (Bugliarello and Wakstein, 1968). The cost can be expected to vary with type of process and machine, and with noise level.

**Table 20.4** Three Very Rough Estimates of the Cost of Occupational Noise Reduction in the United States. For the Occupations Whose Noise Level Has Been Measured (Fig. 18.1) and for Three Hypothetical Noise Reduction Costs Per Decibel Per Worker.

| Job Area Noise Level | Work Force in Measured Occupations | | Noise Reduction | Noise-Reduction Cost (in Millions of Dollars) | | |
|---|---|---|---|---|---|---|
| | Percent | Numbers (in Thousands) | (dB) | At $25/dB, Person | At $75/dB, Person | At $125/dB, Person |
| 86–90 | 36 | 4.998 | 5 | 624.7 | 1,874.1 | 3,123.5 |
| 91–95 | 27 | 3.748 | 10 | 937.0 | 2,811.0 | 4,685.0 |
| 96–100 | 9 | 1.249 | 15 | 468.0 | 1,404.0 | 2,340.0 |
| 101–105 | 1.5 | 0.208 | 20 | 104.0 | 312.0 | 520.0 |
| 106–110 | 3 | 0.416 | 25 | 260.0 | 780.0 | 1,300.0 |
| 111 and above | 2.5 | 0.347 | 30 | 260.2 | 780.6 | 1,301.0 |
| | | 10.966 | | 2,653.9 | 7,961.7 | 13,269.5 |

# REFERENCES

Bolt, Beranek and Newman, Inc. Noise in urban areas and suburban areas: Results of field studies. Federal Housing Administration Report 1395, Job 11257, January 27, 1967.

Bell, A. Noise. An occupational hazard and public nuisance. Public Health Paper No. 30. Geneva. World Health Organization, 1966.

Bugliarello, G. and Wakstein, C. W. Noise pollution—a review of its techno-sociological and health aspects. Biotechnology Program, Carnegie-Mellon University, Pittsburgh, 1968.

Carter, H. C. Noise and vibration control. *Domestic Engineering*, May 1965, **205**.

Chapman, R. A. Use of coatings in noise control. *Noise Control*, March 1956, **2**.

Conover, W. B. Fighting noise with noise. *Noise Control*, March 1956, **2**.

Cudworth, A. L. Field and laboratory examples of industrial noise control. *Noise Control*, January 1959, **5**.

DE (Department of Employment). Code of practise for reducing the exposure of employed persons to Noise. London, HMSO, 1972.

EPA (U.S. Environmental Protection Agency). Report to the President and Congress on noise. Washington, December 31, 1971. (a)

EPA (U.S. Environmental Protection Agency). Noise from industrial plants. Washington, December 31, 1971. (b)

Gould, H. A. and Yeng L. F. Results of functional sound absorber installations in two industrial plants. *Noise Control*, March 1956, **2**.

Hardy, H. C. and Porter, S. M. General principles of reducing noise in machinery. *Noise Control*, September 1955, **1**.

Lemmerman, R. D. Air conditioning and ventilation noise reduction. *Noise Control*, January 1957, **3**.

Mariner, T. Control of sound by sound absorbent materials. *Noise Control*, July 1957, **3**.

Nelson, C. E. Truck muffler design. *Noise Control*, May 1956, **2**.

OSHA (Occupational Safety and Health Administration). Guidelines to the Department of Labor's occupational noise standards. Bulletin 334, Washington. Revised 1971.

Parkinson, J. S. Control of interior noise. *Noise Control*, January 1955, **1**.

Parkinson, P. H. *Acoustics, noise and buildings*. London: Faber and Faber, Ltd., 1958.

Pietrasanta, A. C. Fundamentals of noise control. *Noise Control*, January 1955, **1**.

Purcell, J. B. Control of airborne sound by barriers. *Noise Control*, July 1957, **3**.

Rettinger, M. Noise level reductions of barriers. *Noise Control*, September 1957, **3**.

Rowley, D. W. Control of farm tractor intake and exhaust noise. *Sound and Vibration*, March 1967, **1**.

Vance, D. H. Use of vibration and shock control in reducing noise sources. *Noise Control*, March 1956, **2**.

Weber, H. J. Foundary noise. *Noise Control*, July 1959, **5**.

Wiener, F. M. Sound propagation outdoors. *Noise Control*, July 1958, **4**.

Winterbottom, D. W. The nuisance of traffic in residential areas. *Traffic Quarterly*, July 1965, **19**.

Yeng, L. F. Keeping systems quiet. *Domestic Engineering*, March 1967, **209**.

**Part VI** The Political Economy of Noise

# CHAPTER 21

# *Introduction*

Noise is an economic problem in the same sense that air and water pollution are economic problems—that is, they are all by-products of producing or consuming activities. However, noise differs in certain important ways.

For instance, noise has a once and for all effect; it does not accumulate over time, like other forms of environmental pollution. This means that it is, in principle at least, easier to apply economic analysis, since future effects are absent:* we are dealing with an essentially current problem. Partly because of this, noise is also a local problem; as was pointed out in previous chapters the intensity of a sound decreases proportionately to the square of the distance from the source. Thus the problem is not global, at least not in the same way as air pollution (see Chapter 24).

Noise levels differ in range, frequency, and intensity, depending on the physical location of the source and the receiver, and, in the case of airborne noise, on wind and atmospheric conditions. Reaction to noise levels varies according to the person affected, the source, and the time. It is difficult to measure annoyance in an objective way, although physiological effects are easier to judge. Thus we are not dealing with a homogeneous function, and the multiplicity of methods devised to measure noise annoyance on a single scale reflects this.

These characteristics of noise account for the relative inattention paid to it as a pollutant. Perhaps the very invisibility and insidiousness of noise

---

*There are of course ill-effects from continuous exposure to high noise levels (see Part II), but noise is not cumulative, although the damage it causes is.

have led to this, but today its toxicity is not in doubt. To add to everyday noise levels, we have the exotic dangers of ultrasonic and infrasonic frequencies, sonic boom signatures, and projected or actual military use of sound (the ability of noise to psychologically disturb people has been well illustrated by the recent use of noise machines by the British Army in Ulster to interrogate suspected members of the IRA) (Parker, 1972). But for the purposes of this chapter, discussion must be limited to the more prosaic confines of noise as an economic problem, although the emphasis will be on economics as a social science rather than as a branch of applied mathematics.

Most environmental noise problems share a common ancestry: the Industrial Revolution, which effectively put an end to the era when man-made noise was a limited if at times severe phenomenon. The clatter of horses' hooves on medieval cobblestones and the rattle of the iron-rimmed wheels were early causes of noise from transport. The din of battle surely left some audiometric casualties. For example, it has been reported in 1782 that after the British flagship *HMS Formidable* had fired 80 broadsides Admiral Lord Rodney became almost stone-deaf for two weeks; what the seaman on the gun deck felt was not recorded. In *Ecclesiasticus* one reads of "the smith .... sitting by the anvil .... the noise of the hammer and the anvil ever in his ear;" and as early as 1670 Swedish scientists stated that deafness was prevalent among coppers-miths and blacksmiths (Groom, 1972). There was even a law passed by Queen Elizabeth I of England forbidding her subjects to beat their wives after ten o'clock at night lest their neighbour's sleep be disturbed! However, these problems, real though they were, do not bear comparison in either degree of noise, or numbers of people affected by it, with those which have presented themselves in the last 150 years. The urbanization of the majority of the population and the concentration of production in factories, coupled with the increasing use of machines in every facet of life, has led to the present intolerable situation, where a large proportion of people in urban areas experience high noise levels for most of their lives.

For the purposes of this part, attention will be focused on noise arising from transport and industry, the two main sources. Other noise sources include demolition, construction, and road works; ventilation and air-conditioning plant in buildings; sports, entertainment, etc.; and human noise arising partly from lack of consideration for others. Following the lines of the Noise Advisory Council Report in the United Kingdom, we have defined this latter category as Neighborhood Noise (NAC, 1971).

Clearly much of this generalized noise also comes from industry and transport and any solution to the latter problems will automatically reduce the former. For this reason the emphasis is here placed on noise in factories and noise from motor vehicles and aircraft.

If noise is unwanted sound, at what point does this become a cost? Could it instead be a benefit?* That is, how does it fit into the economic scheme of things? Noise is a cost if it interferes with production or consumption activities, including (in the latter) leisure and rest. If the existence of a man-made sound lowers the efficiency of a productive input, or the satisfaction derived from a consumptive output (broadly defined), then we can directly or indirectly evaluate the cost.

A person—an agent—producing or causing the production of this unwanted sound is causing a loss to other people if the sound adversely affects their activities. This loss is external to the agent since it is not borne by him. He may either positively enjoy the noise,† or tolerate it in view of the (greater) direct benefits this activity brings him. In the latter case we assume that the noise producer is aware of the noise cost and has in fact internalized it. The economist analyzes these side effects as externalities.‡ These are costs (and benefits) imposed on society by an economic agent, which are not borne by or recouped by that agent. Thus the generator of an externality has no economic motive for altering his behavior. Noise pollution, like any other form of pollution arising from the production or consumption of economic goods, is an example of such an external cost.

The aim of part VI is to show the extent—and the limits—to which economic analysis can contribute to an understanding of the problem of noise pollution. Chapter 22 contains a broad examination of how noise relates to economics, and of how they both relate to social welfare. Chapters 23 and 24 review alternative means of dealing with noise externality, and a comparative evaluation is given in Chapter 25. The

---

*For example, while ultrasound can be highly dangerous if improperly used, it has a valuable diagnostic use in medicine.

†The definition of noise is subjective; while few people relish dead rivers and foul air, some, perhaps many, do enjoy blaring transistor radios, the roar of motorized traffic, or even the crash of machinery. To them the sound is not unwanted, and their enjoyment is an external economy.

‡Other general terms employed are: "intangibles," "neighborhood effects," and "third party effects," all of which can be beneficial or harmful. Also used are the terms "external economies" and "external diseconomies."

entire issue of putting a price on noise is discussed in Chapter 26, while some deeper reflections on this, and the role of economics in general, are reserved for the conclusion of the book.

## REFERENCES

Groom, C. E. Din and deafness. *Medical News Tribune*, February 1972.
NAC (U.K. Noise Advisory Council). Neighborhood noise. London: HMSO, 1972.
Parker. The Parker report. Cmnd. 4901. London: HMSO, 1972.

# CHAPTER 22

# Economics, Welfare, and Noise

## THE AIMS OF ECONOMICS

This chapter sets the scene for an examination in the subsequent chapters of the ways in which a "modern mixed economy" can deal with an externality such as noise.*

To do this we must first discuss what is the aim of economics. The consensus would probably be that there are three goals of economic life: the best allocation of our resources, or *economic efficiency*; an increased volume of our national product, or *economic growth*; and a "fair" distribution of our national product, or *economic equity*. There would also probably be agreement that these goals are themselves subservient to that end of all economic activity—economic welfare.†

Economic welfare is a new concept in the history of economic ideas, and was first coherently formulated by A. C. Pigou of Cambridge in 1920. As he pointed out, economic welfare is subsumed under social welfare

---

*The phrase is Samuelson's and indicates that the analysis will be restricted to those industrialized, western nations, where the government spends roughly 40 percent of national output (Samuelson, 1970).

†All ends-means classifications are especially precarious in economics. There is nothing immutable about Efficiency, Equity, and Growth, nor even sacrosanct (see below); but it seems reasonable to identify them as currently accepted goals of economic policy. Others, such as full employment, price stability, and the balance of payments, are undeniably important, but are essentially short-run. In the jargon of econometrics, they are "target variables" (which can be attained through the manipulation of an economic target and "instrument variables" such as tax rates, credit restrictions, etc.). The distinction between an economic end, is a valid one, and reflects their relative importance.

and cannot be separated "in any rigid way from the broader concept" (Pigou, 1962). It consists of that part of social welfare which has an economic value, that is to say, which can be measured in terms of some unit of account (normally money). Economics deals with those things which give us material satisfaction, and the best single measure of this is the gross national product (or the value of goods and services produced by a nation's economy in a year). Which leads us to the conclusion that the higher the National Income,* the higher the economic welfare, and hence, the social welfare.

During the last two centuries this has certainly been the case. When the Industrial Revolution got under way during the nineteenth century, the living standards of the bulk of the population slowly improved as the western nations got over the "hump" of capital accumulation, and some of the expanded national product percolated downwards. It is incontrovertible that this process has benefited those nations fortunate enough to undergo the transformation. The material standard of living of the industrialized nations transcends the wildest dreams of a century ago, and is astronomically above that of the developing countries. Clearly, in the turbulent years of an economy's drive to maturity, with rapidly increasing material prospects, and a religious, social, and political milieu favorable to continued expansion, there was little time to reflect on the more injurious consequences of untrammeled industrial growth.† When the material condition of life for the majority of people is low, and when poverty and disease handicap spiritual and personal aspirations, a society can perhaps find an excuse for ignoring for a long time the side effects of such progress.

In the years since the second world war this implicit assumption has become an overriding policy objective. The transformation is a recent one, because national accounting concepts such as G.N.P. have only been defined clearly for some 35 years, and the statistics adequate for their quantification only a little longer.

The designation of national targets for economic policy and the discovery of means to influence them, led however to an overemphasis on growth of output. Nations were ranked according to their position on a

---

*The terms National Product and National Income are interchangeable since the value of goods produced must equal the incomes paid out in their production.

†This is not to deny that the horror of child labor, terrible working conditions in factories, and vast pollution of rivers and air constituted far worse externalities than those we have under discussion. Nor is it to recommend that developing nations countenance similar policies during their push for higher standards of living.

league table of percentage increments to G.N.P In those where the rate of growth was inadequate,* plans, commissions, committees of inquiry, etc., were set up to probe the causes of what seemed to be a national dishonor. Indeed the main consideration prompting the politicians in Britain to apply for that country's membership of the Common Market† was that her output could expand that much faster inside than out.

Although graphologists, politicians, and others imbued with a "feel" for progress, still divine and debate the latest 0.5 percent swing in the pace of economic growth, a reaction has set in. From a recent OECD survey of the United States:

> In earlier periods, with lower levels of economic activity, waste could be assimilated with considerable ease. This is no longer the case, and the absorptive capacity of the environment is now becoming severely taxed. Parallel to this development is a change of relative values on the part of the public, which is beginning to place a higher priority on the quality of natural surroundings. This change in preferences springs basically from a concern for health, and from a growing desire to live, work, and plan in a more pleasant environment (OECD, 1972).

The presumption has never been that economic welfare represented the total of social welfare—merely that it is an important part. Society's welfare is clearly a function of more than things economic; people's happiness depends upon a myriad of causes and is an elusive, metaphysical concept. Unfortunately we can no longer conclude that an increased standard of living (in material terms) improves total welfare, if it conflicts with other values such as the desire to live and work in tolerable surroundings. The linkage, higher G.N.P., higher economic welfare, higher social welfare, is not now an automatic one for industrialized countries.

More aircraft movements, increased automobile output, and higher production from noisy factories all represent a rise in the index of economic welfare; but when they are accompanied by noise and other adverse externalities, the total effect on social welfare is equivocal. The failure of the second linkage, that is, between economic and social welfare, is essentially an allocative and distributive problem which will be discussed further under Economic Efficiency. However, the causal mechanism is weakened still further by failures in the statistic of economic welfare, G.N.P.; a matter dealt with below.

---

*Chiefly Britain and the United States.

†Obviously something which entails profound consequences for other aspects of British life than the mere economic one.

## ECONOMIC GROWTH

Economic growth is described by the real* increase in G.N.P. per capita. It is a measure of the total flow of goods (consumer and capital), and services produced by the economic activity of a nation in a given time period. The drawbacks of G.N.P. as an index of economic welfare (and thus as a guide to social welfare) are those of non-inclusion and misrepresentation.†

### The G.N.P. Statistics

*Non-Inclusion*

The exact definition of G.N.P. varies from country to country and, except when imputation is feasible, excludes the results of any activity which is not traded. Thus, the value of housewives' services, of voluntary, unpaid work for charity, and of home decoration and maintenance (e.g., the fitting of double glazing for noise reduction), is entirely omitted from our calculation.

The index of the physical volume of goods and services produced may increase without any reference to quality changes. When these are taken into account, a further element of doubt is cast on the official figures of national well-being.

The relationship between G.N.P. and economic welfare is weakened more when we recall that it is current levels, and current or at best recent, changes in the level of G.N.P., which are under consideration. Scant reference is normally given to the accumulation of wealth in the past. The amount of social overhead capital (docks, railroads, freeways, hospitals, schools, houses, etc.) that the mature industrial nations have inherited far outweighs the effects of current flows on economic welfare. Any comparison between countries which ignores their history in this regard is a false one; even given the wonders of compound interest it will be 12 years at current rates of growth before Japan equals the U.S. per capita G.N.P. figures,‡ and much longer before the effect of centuries of higher

---

*That is, corrected for changes in the value of money.

†Lack of space forbids a full discussion of these points (which can be found in any modern macro-economic textbook, such as that by McDougall and Dernburg (1963).

‡This assumes a continuation of the 1965–70 annual average rates of growth of 12.1 percent for Japan and 3.3 percent for the United States. It is slightly inaccurate since it ignores the 0.17 percent difference in the two countries population growth rates (OECD, 1972).

American standards are outweighed.* Of course, the time scale is lengthened further, if the currently very high Japanese growth rates do not continue.

## Misrepresentation

Misrepresentation is a less obvious source of bias in the national accounts. For example the amount of leisure time we have is clearly a vital part of our standard of living, and as incomes rise the average number of hours worked tends to diminish. Yet the price of leisure is the output foregone, and so never enters our statistics at all. The more leisure taken, the greater the loss in potential G.N.P. and the lower our index of economic welfare. Undoubtedly the G.N.P. of Spain would increase if the siesta were abolished—it is not clear that the welfare of the Spanish would.

For goods and services supplied through the market the value is the market price. This can be broken down into contributions towards: cost of raw materials, labor, depreciation, interest, and indirect taxes plus profit. However, public goods and services, schools, police protection, national defense, etc., are not provided through the market; they are financed through taxation or borrowing, and supplied "free." Thus an important part of national output—government activity—is under-valued.†

Government output is valued at labor cost, that is, wages and salaries to government employees. The current goods and services purchased by the government from business ends up in the accounts as final output of the business sector. There is no allowance made for the value added by the government in its various activities and programs. Further, no allowance is made for the use of government capital equipment (schools, court houses, etc.) in terms of interest, nor is a return imputed to public sector "entrepreneurship" in the form of profits.‡

Therefore, the value of G.N.P. is underestimated the more it is

---

*In 1958 the total assets (tangible and intangible) of the United States were estimated at $3,735,310,000,000. In that year the G.N.P. was $447,300,000,000. If the same wealth/income ratio has merely been maintained, with a current G.N.P. figure of $1,046,800,000,000, the wealth of the United States stands at $8,793,120,000,000 (OECD, 1972).

†This does not apply, for example, to public utilities: their services are charged for at a price which at least attempts to cover costs.

‡Absence of a depreciation allowance makes no difference when comparing public output with *net* private output.

composed of things we consume as a society. Yet there is no presumption that a public health service is less beneficial than one based on private insurance; nor that public transport is less useful than private; nor even that money spent on regulating the by-products of economic activity is, in any but the narrowest sense, unproductive. In fact it is becoming increasingly recognized that the opposite is the case.

In contrast to the above situation, where government services to control noise pollution are undervalued, there arises the irony of anti-pollution measures actually inflating G.N.P.

When a public authority subsidizes the provision of double glazing to house owners near airports (as the British Airport Authority does near Heathrow), to the extent that this is financed by general taxation, G.N.P. is increased by the difference between the cost involved and the reduced after tax consumption expenditures.

The American Medical Association has estimated the total cost of pollution-caused damage to human health to be as high as $38 billion a year (OECD, 1972). This figure is presumably based on loss of production due to pollution. But only if the loss of output due to days off sick, or reduced efficiency, is greater than the medical expenses incurred in treating the silicosis, deafness, etc., is the G.N.P. reduced. Recent evidence shows that industry's output is not greatly curtailed by noisy working conditions, which makes it more likely that the ensuing treatment for ear damage, expenditure on hearing aids, etc., is a net addition to G.N.P. (Kryter, 1970). Furthermore, in the degree to which health expenditures come directly out of savings—from insurance policies—it actually pays (in terms of economic growth) to deafen people. The extra expenditure on medical care supposedly restores the status quo, and in no sense does the higher GNP thus generated represent an increase in welfare, economic or otherwise.

In order to make the G.N.P. figures truly representative of economic welfare, it has been suggested that a measure of the pollution damage be subtracted, and the index presented as net of environmental costs. This might remedy the failure of national output statistics, at least in regard to externalities. There is no market in unwanted goods, but if there were, the value of noise would be negative (McDougall and Dernburg, 1963). However, to conceal the environmental costs in a single index of economic welfare fails to do justice to the problem.

**Social Indicators**

An alternative is presented by recent attempts by social statisticians to devise social or environmental indicators that would supplement the economic ones (Winch, 1971). The exact distinction between economic and social indicators is difficult to define. In fact, the elements of social indicators are already published separately, in figures on housing, health, education, etc. Any consolidation of these figures into one social index is made difficult by the problem of giving an appropriate weight to each figure—a task that would involve complex value-judgments.

Any environmental indicator must reflect the current situation in physical terms, together with the monetary costs and benefits involved in improving it. N. Terleckyj of the National Planning Association (Cazes, 1972), suggests the production of tables showing numbers of workers in the principal noisy industries who are exposed to noise levels in excess of 110 dBA, 100 dBA, etc., with the average length of time of exposure. The cost of reducing the numbers of workers exposed to typical situations could then be compared with the expected benefits. In this connection, increased output is a poor guide to the benefits. Other guides, such as reduction in medical expenses and more subjective measures produced by sample/opinion surveys, or simulation experiments would have to be used. Similar indices could be compiled for numbers of people affected by aircraft and traffic noise, although valuation of costs and benefits would present added problems here (see Chapter 26).

The advantages of these indicators are, as Cazes (1972) has noted, that they express results rather than trends of expenditure, and give more definitive results than G.N.P. or consumption per head. Publication of social and environmental indicators, together with the more usual economic ones, would provide a constant reminder of the real costs of economic growth.

**ECONOMIC EFFICIENCY**

In the previous section we have examined the lack of congruence between official measures for economic welfare and the real satisfactions experienced by society. We now turn to a more detailed appraisal of why, no matter how inclusive and accurate the statistics, an $x$ percent increase in economic welfare may still entail a less than $x$ percent increase in total welfare. Here we take up the discussion of noise as an external cost from where it was left in Chapter 21 and show how its existence implies a distortion in the workings of the economy. Possible remedies are put forward in the subsequent chapters, in the light of the following analysis of what constitutes optimal output.

## Optimal* Output

To discuss "optimal output" implies that a choice can and must be made in the level and composition of the output. Choice is necessary due to the problem of scarcity posed by the clash between unlimited material wants and the limited means of supplying them.† What is actually produced in a market economy depends, apart from public goods provided through the government process, upon what consumers are willing and able to pay for, and on what business is capable of producing. Demand for output depends on peoples' preferences, and on the income and wealth which enable people to express such preferences with differing degrees of intensity. The supply of output is primarily a technological consideration, being a function of the ease with which resources can be combined to produce goods.

Technical efficiency in production is obviously desirable because it enables more output to be produced with the same input, or the same output with less input. Under a price system the spur of losses and the prospect of profits induce firms to cut costs and increase efficiency.

Subjective efficiency in exchange is also desirable, since differing relative valuations of goods fosters trade. Further, the individual himself is not acting rationally if he fails to allocate his budget efficiently, so as to maximize the utility derived from different purchases.‡

The key concept underlying the explanation of efficient behavior by both producer and consumer is that of "marginalism."

The principle involved is a simple one, and entirely general. Any activity should be carried out up to the point where the extra (or marginal) benefit so derived is equal to the extra (or marginal) cost so incurred. In this way the net gain from that activity is maximized. If we accept that the

---

*"Optimal" only with a given distribution of income and wealth, and on the assumption that people are the best judge of their own welfare.

†There is room for scepticism on how fundamental this "clash" is in western societies, a view that has been explicit in the whole of this chapter. For while resources are undeniably scarce, material wants are clearly not infinite, except in a trivial sense.

‡In other words, if Individual $X$ obtains more satisfaction (per dollar spent on it) from good $A$ as he does from good $B$, then it is to his advantage to buy more of $A$ and less of $B$. This is efficient behavior in that with the same income, or budget, Individual $X$ is extracting more satisfaction from a (small) rearrangement of his expenditure pattern.

costs of any activity will increase at an increasing rate while the benefits from it will decrease at a decreasing rate, and that this abstract "activity" can be measured in money, then the principle can be expressed diagrammatically, as shown in Fig. 22.1.

In the figure, the optimal level of the activity, where the marginal costs equal the marginal benefits, is *OA*. At this point total benefit is given by the area *OPQA*, while total cost is equal to the area *ONQA*. Net benefit (benefit–cost) is thus equal to the shaded area *NPQ*, and is a maximum at the level of activity *OA*, any movement away from *OA* causing net benefit to decrease.

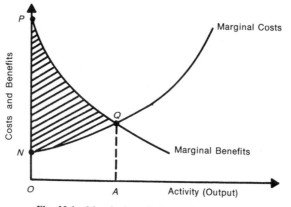

**Fig. 22.1**   Marginal analysis: optimal output.

The precise conditions for achieving maximum economic efficiency can be described by a set of marginal conditions (equiproportional ratios) governing the rates of transformation of economic variables. The rules are universal in the sense of being applicable to a market or a planned system; adherence to them ensures that no reorganization of the economy can increase one person's welfare without diminishing that of another. One of the first neo-classical economists to formulate these conditions was Vilfredo Pareto, and the "Pareto optimum" has become the symbol for efficiency in allocation (Pareto, 1971).

## The Market System

The rigorous formulation of these conditions lent powerful justification to the ideology of laissez-faire, since it can be shown that under a perfectly competitive capitalist system the Pareto optimum is achieved automatically. In theory, individuals and firms maximize utility and profits in response to the blind, uncontrollable, forces of the market. The role of the government was seen as providing the framework in which the price system could best function, and in removing any imperfections, monopoly, barriers to trade etc., which might threaten the workings of "les forces automatiques"—the automatic forces.

The pre-conditions for perfect competition are considerable: many buyers and sellers in every industry—whether in the product or factor markets; perfect mobility of productive resources; profit maximization by producers and utility maximization by consumers; no uncertainty about the present or future; complete divisibility of all economic goods; and the absence of any externalities in production or consumption. Given the above, since all markets are interdependent, the whole system settles down into a general equilibrium held together by the various prices which no buyer or seller can, by himself alone, influence.

Few if any markets, and certainly no economy as a whole, have ever been perfectly competitive, one pertinent reason being the presence of uncorrected externalities such as noise. Thus the importance of the theory lies in its role as a benchmark against which to judge actuality: its relevance depends on the extent to which an imperfect price system approaches the Pareto conditions, that is, allocates resources efficiently. We can use the theory to see how the price system works, and to determine the distortions which noise externality creates.

Prices are set by the interaction of supply and demand, which in turn depend upon marginal cost and marginal benefit (or utility). To individuals, the higher the price of a good the lower the marginal utility per dollar spent on it, and the smaller the quantity they will purchase. To the firm, price is the marginal revenue from the sale of a unit of product. The firm will always expand output as long as the price (marginal revenue) is greater than the additional cost of production (marginal cost); the profit maximizing level of output is where marginal cost equals price.

The quantity demanded and the quantity supplied are equal at the equilibrium price. This is the optimal output level because the value placed on the last unit by consumers is exactly the same as cost of production; and both are equal to the price.

### Social Costs

However, the allocative efficiency of the market is upset whenever social costs exceed private costs, as they do in the case of noise pollution. Parties to market contracts, buyers and sellers, can impose noise costs on society, as can individuals in their consumption activities. In either case little, if any of the effects of noise may fall on those whose activity generates it, and who therefore have no motive to take these effects into account. Unfortunately, on the other hand, the costs, whether objective (such as soundproofing) or subjective (such as annoyance or stress) are real enough to those who bear them. When these social costs* of activity are positive and considerable, it is an *a priori* indication that the activity is over-expanded. In other words, there is a misallocation of resources because the marginal social cost of the last unit exceeds the marginal social benefit from it.†

Application of our efficiency rule to a noise-generating activity requires that such an activity be reduced until the marginal condition is satisfied, and the resources so released transferred to some other activity where price exceeds marginal social cost. This situation is portrayed in Fig. 22.2.‡

In the figure we are assuming that noise costs increase as output rises, which would not seem unreasonable for most noise-generating activities. In the absence of noise costs, optimal output would be *OB* and net benefit maximized as the area *DZC*. Once noise is taken into account the relevant cost curve is the social one, and the optimal output is *OA*. If no

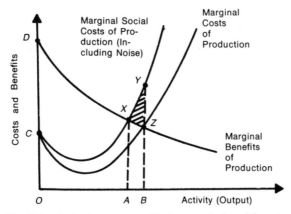

**Fig. 22.2**   Optimal output considering marginal social costs.

---

*“Social” because they fall mainly on society at large.

†This is taken to be the price, unless there is some external benefit from the activity.

‡A more detailed and exact example of this kind of analysis is given in the Appendix to Chapter 23, Part VI.

adjustment is made, and we remain at *OB*, there is a social loss of the shaded area *XYZ*. The excess of social benefits over total social costs can never be greater than at output *OA*, and price *XA*.

The problems involved in estimating the magnitude of the social costs of noise will be discussed in Chapter 26. But, however large the costs of noise are, and in some cases they are clearly very large, their inclusion in the optimization process does not necessarily mean that no noise will be produced at all. As can be seen from Fig. 22.2, up to output *OA* people value the good produced more than they dislike its joint product, noise. (Of course this does not rule out the possibility of closing down an individual source of noise, e.g. a drop-forge plant in a residential area because of its high social cost.)

In the absence of exact information on the social costs of noise it is difficult to estimate the optimal level of any activity with accuracy. Of course the risk of inaccuracy matters less the greater the externality. Furthermore, any corrective measure will involve costs of its own, including those of information gathering. Whether these costs are of devising and administering a tax system, the enforcement of legal standards, or the creation of separate facilities, they must be taken into account in the attempt to achieve optimum output.

**Optimal Noise Output**

But what actually constitutes the optimal level of noise pollution? It is useful to look at this question from both the noise-production and the noise-reduction points of view.

In Fig. 22.3 the marginal social cost of noise pollution is related to the marginal social cost of noise abatement. The latter is made up of the cost of remedial measures, soundproofing, introducing quieter machines, etc., and their administration and enforcement by the government. It also includes any loss of output due to the noise abatement procedures.

The optimal level of noise output *A*, where the marginal cost noise imposes on society is just equal to the marginal cost to society of abating it, is *OA*. If no noise is to be produced, the social cost of abatement will be very high, in most cases approaching infinity, as the noise output shrinks to zero. On the other hand, if no attempt was made to restrict noise, abatement costs would be zero, but the losses to the community would be very large—again, in our diagram, approaching infinity. (As will be seen in Chapter 26, some people already put an infinite figure on the disruption noise can cause to their lives. One only has to imagine unmuffled car

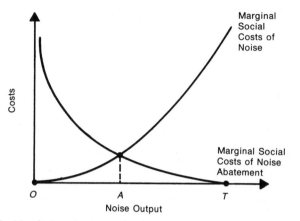

**Fig. 22.3**  Marginal social costs of noise pollution and of noise abatement.

exhausts, nil restrictions on factory location, no noise prevention within work places, and unrestricted jet takeoffs at night, under full power, to conclude that such a view would become a majority one if *no* noise abatement were practiced.)

Perhaps a more familiar treatment of the problem would be to relate the marginal social cost of noise abatement to its marginal social benefit,* as shown in Fig. 22.4. This time, the amount of noise abatement is measured along the horizontal axis. Starting from a position of no abatement, the

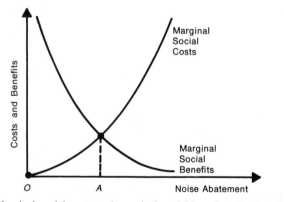

**Fig. 22.4**  Marginal social costs and marginal social benefits of noise abatement.

*The marginal social benefit of noise *abatement* is equal to the marginal social cost of noise *pollution.*

extra benefits from introducing some abatement are very large; as the level of abatement increases, the extra benefits diminish, and the extra costs rise. The optimal amount of abatement is $A$, where the marginal social benefit of reducing noise is equal to the marginal social cost of doing so, is $OA$. The thrust of the whole of this book is, of course, that our society is at present somewhere between $O$ and $A$ in Fig. 22.4.

### An Overview of Economic Efficiency

We have shown that where there are non-marketed costs such as noise pollution, there is a likelihood that an economic activity has been carried out beyond its optimal level. This implies that the value to society of the good or service produced is less than that recorded on market performance alone. Noise clearly diminishes people's welfare, and if this is not taken into account, we cannot maintain that an increase in economic welfare—that is, an increase in the market value of goods and services produced—is an unalloyed increase in social welfare.

Further, we have pointed out that in order to justify correction, it is not enough that noise costs be positive; rather, the criterion should be that the marginal social cost of noise pollution be greater than the marginal social cost of abating it. Once we have *fully* valued the social cost of noise, there is no intrinsic reason why the pursuit of the "good" of noise reduction should not be subject to the same optimization rules as the pursuit of any other good.

Both of these conclusions follow from application of the general efficiency rule governing resource allocation. Unfortunately, however conceptually clear these conclusions may be, the practical problems involved in their implementation are many, and difficult. But, before tackling them, we must turn to the third goal of economics, that of equity.

## ECONOMIC EQUITY

It is important to understand the meaning of economic equity when judging the inequity of noise. Equity is no less germane than efficiency to any discussion of economic welfare, although it is a more difficult concept—dealing as it does with subjective rather than objective problems. In this section we define and illustrate some of these problems.

In Anglo-Saxon jurisprudence equity has long been the division which remedies the inflexibility of Common Law and supplements it with the principles of natural justice while, in economics, the term is used in a narrower sense, to discuss the fairness of the distribution of national output. It can be said that distribution is a part—perhaps a major one—of the broader legal concept of justice. This could be the reason for the preoccupation with distribution shown by economists. There is obviously substance in this; noise is an unfair imposition on pauper and millionaire alike, but it is doubly unfair when those who suffer from it are without recourse. Further, it would seem that low income and high exposure to noise too often coincide. Thus we are justified in devoting the bulk of this section to questions of income distribution.

### The Ideology of Equity

Even the restricted sense of equity holds definitional problems: what is "economic justice?" There are basically two schools of thought: one describes distributive justice—people are in some sense "equal," and thus receive equal shares; the other, commutative justice—people are rewarded in return for their services to society, and to the degree that society values their service. At one end of the spectrum "pure communism" demands not merely an equal distribution but one geared according to need. At the other extreme, "pure capitalism" rewards each factor according to its productivity; to paraphrase Marx: "from each according to his ability and to each according to his ability."

These two ideals are depicted in Fig. 22.5—the utility possibility curve for a two-individual community. (Restriction to two individuals makes it possible to portray the analysis on a plane surface.) The utility possibility curve represents the maximum possible utility that can be extracted from the economy under any conceivable combination of different product

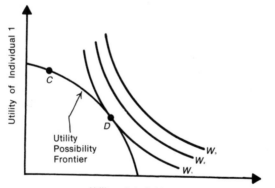

**Fig. 22.5**  Utility possibility curve for a community of two individuals.

mix, different distribution of that product, and different factor input by the individuals. [A formal derivation is given by Winch (1971).]

The Pareto optimum has been defined as the goal of economic efficiency, whether in a planned or a price system. Compliance with the efficiency rules of production and exchange is sufficient to bring us to some point on the utility frontier, where it is impossible to increase one man's well-being without diminishing that of another. It is here that the question of equity arises, for while the Pareto frontier is the goal of efficiency, it is at the same time the constraint of welfare.

A free enterprise system under conditions of perfect competition might bring us to point $C$ on the frontier. However, social welfare is only maximized at $C$ if we accept the existing pattern of ownership, the resulting distribution of income (and the composition of output this calls forth), as being a reflection of the values of the society.

An ideal communist society would put a different emphasis on individuals' utilities: one based on need (however defined) rather than on factor ownership. Superimposed on the utility possibility curve in Fig. 22.5 is a social welfare function of the form $W = W(U_1, U_2 \dots U_n)$ where $n$ is the number of individuals in the society. Each point on a given contour $(W_1, W_2 \dots W_n)$ of the function represents a different combination of individuals' utility which yields the same social welfare. In other words, as far as society is concerned very different distributions of utility between individuals can still yield the same total social welfare. However, it is obvious that to stay on a given contour line one individual will have to be given increasingly large increments of utility to offset the small reduction in that of the second.

As we move higher in the direction of the upper right hand corner of the diagram, welfare increases (we cross higher contour lines), a process constrained by the utility frontier. Thus the optimal position for society must be one where the social welfare function is tangent to the utility possibility frontier; in Fig. 22.5, at $D$.* It is important to note that although the distributional value-judgments are different in the communist example, we are still on the Pareto frontier: a theoretical planned system is just as efficient as a theoretical price system.

In Fig. 22.6, the situation is reproduced for a modern mixed economy, where the social welfare function is weighted by the pattern of ownership and by some egalitarian notions.

---

*In the capitalist case one can imagine the welfare function as shifting to whatever point on the utility frontier the forces of the market arrived at.

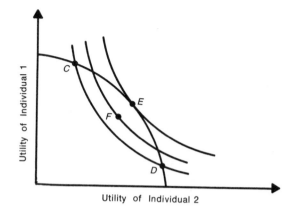

**Fig. 22.6**  Utility possibility curve for a two-individual community in a mixed economy.

The most desirable outcome is clearly at point $E$; however, under a mixed system this may not be possible. In contrast to the extreme points like $C$ where the welfare function reflects the status quo, or $D$ where it reflects the "planners" preferences, point $E$ may be unobtainable because of the very methods necessary to reach it. This type of society may have to rest content with a point such as $F$, a point sub-optimal from the efficiency standpoint. The reason for this is that measures to promote income equality, either by altering ownership returns through subsidies on the things produced (farm-price support programs), or through progressive incomes taxes, violate the marginal conditions of optimality, and thus reduce efficiency. What is noteworthy from Fig. 22.6 is that given the society's values as evinced in the social welfare function, it prefers to be at $F$ than at $C$ or $D$, because at $F$, although below the utility frontier, it has attained a higher welfare contour than at the points on the frontier that a "pure" capitalist or communist system produces.

## Noise and Equity

We now turn to some observations on the effects of noise in a modern mixed economy like the United States. The way in which society views equity—the shape of the welfare function— is reflected, but imperfectly, through the political process. (One reason for the imperfection being that equity considerations may be outweighed by other political issues when the electoral choice is made.)

Programs to reduce noise nuisance have costs and benefits flowing from them. If one considers the types of property aligning railroad tracks, the areas bordering freeways, the high-density living of slum households, and the working conditions of millions of men in factories, the likelihood is that lower income groups are exposed to an above average degree of noise pollution and will therefore receive an above average benefit from its abatement. This thesis does not, of course, always apply; for the very poor in rural areas may not suffer at all from noise, and the worker in a drop-forge plant may be able to live in a quiet suburb. Noise pollution control would be an improvement in the economic sense, because noise can be viewed as a negative good which enters the individual's utility function and requires either stoic acceptance (a psychic and physical loss) or an attempt to reduce or escape it; the latter involves a diversion of spending power from "positive goods" or an actual reduction in income (quitting a noisy job).

Where the cost-burden of improving the sound environment falls will depend on the solution adopted, but in general it will be borne by either industry of the government.

Manufacturers of noise-producing goods can deal with the cost of silence in three ways: they can accept a reduction in profits, pass the cost on by a price increase, or shift the burden backwards through lowering the price they pay for factor inputs. The method or methods adopted will depend upon the degree of competition and the market form which the firms face in the product and factor markets. The most commonly expected result of a tax on pollution, for example, is that it will be passed on by a price increase. Whether or not this is regressive depends largely on whether the good in question is a necessity or a luxury. Backward shifting of the cost through reduction of wage rates (or more likely, a slowdown in the rate of increase) is usually considered regressive, while reduced output of the polluting industry and laying off of workers will result in the unskilled and disadvantaged carrying the real cost of noise reduction.

The government share of the cost will stem from possible subsidies to noise-reducing activities, the provision of separate facilities for this purpose, and the administration and enforcement costs of legislation.

These programs can be financed in several ways, one of the easiest being out of the annual revenue gain, or fiscal dividend, that a growing economy generates. Apart from this, there either has to be a reallocation within the budget, or an increase in taxation or borrowing. Without following through the full ramifications of an increase in the supply of government bonds, to the extent that it raises interest rates, and thus restricts housing starts, we would be improving one part of the environ-ment at the expense of another. As regards taxation, the problems posed by fiscal federalism are considerable and are analogous with those mentioned in Chapter 24 in connection with the legislative solution. In any discussion of public finance, equity considerations loom large;* all that can be said here is that the least regressive of all the taxes which governments rely upon for the main part of their revenue is the personal income tax, and therefore governmental action to reduce noise pollution should probably be financed in this way. (Abstracting from the situation of the previous paragraph where the tax itself is the means of securing noise abatement.)

In sum, allocation of resources by reducing the output of activities whose marginal net benefit becomes negative through the addition of noise costs, can also be approved of on equity grounds, in that it benefits the poor. Nevertheless, such noise-reduction programs do entail costs and the final incidence in real, as well as in financial terms, should be borne in mind. In the words of Baumol (1972): ". . . redistribution measures should be built right into environmental protection policies, to make certain that they do not simply serve, however unintentionally, as another instrument to make the rich richer and the poor poorer."

## REFERENCES

Baumol, W. J. Environmental protection and the distribution of incomes. In *Problems of environmental economics*. Paris: OECD, 1972.

Cazes, B. Environmental quality indicators and social indicators. In *Problems of environmental economics*. Paris: OECD, 1972.

Kryter, K. D. *The effects of noise on man*. New York: Academic Press, 1972.

McDougall, D. M. and Dernburg, T. E. *Macro-economics*. New York: McGraw-Hill, 1963.

Musgrave, R. A. *The theory of public finance*. New York: McGraw-Hill, 1959.

OECD (Organization for Economic Co-operation and Development). U.S. economic survey. April 1972.

Pareto, V. *Manual of political economy*. Translated and edited by A. Schweir, New York: A. M. Kelly, 1971.

Pigou, A. C. *The economics of welfare*, 4th Edition. London: MacMillan, 1962.

Samuelson, P. A. *Economics*, 8th Edition. New York: McGraw-Hill, 1970.

Winch, D. M. *Analytical welfare economics*. Baltimore: Penguin Books, 1971.

---

*For a good treatment of tax equity see Musgrave (1959).

# CHAPTER 23

# Externalities: Voluntary Bargains, Taxes, and Subsidies

## DEFINITION

The economic concept of external costs and benefits has been briefly described in our introduction (Chapter 21). The purpose of this chapter is to enlarge on the theory and examine two possible solutions to the problem.

There are four types of externalities:

• The effect of production on production: the activity of one producing unit affecting the output of others with no change in their factor inputs. That is, with the same combination of land, labor, and capital, output varies due to some outside cause. Thus the noise from one factory in an industrial park may reduce the efficiency of the workers in a neighboring plant.*

• The effect of production on consumption: broadly defined to include leisure time, sleep, daydreaming, even our visual perception of the environment. Traffic noise, with its effect on sleep and relaxation, is a prime example of this, as is air and water pollution. Clearly the loss in this kind of "consumption" from productive activities can be enormous. Yet it is rarely recognized as an external cost, still less is compensation dreamed of. [For an honorable exception see Mishan (1967).]

---

*In the pages to come we are primarily concerned with the social aspects of spill-over effects emphasized first by Pigou, rather than with technological externalities dealing with cost curves.

- The effect of consumption on consumption: an example is the noise from a neighbor's power mower.
- The effect of consumption on production. This externality is exemplified by the power boats of vacationers obstructing fishing activity.

These categories are not always clear cut. Thus traffic noise can be generated both by a truck delivering goods (a production on consumption externality) and a jet full of tourists (a consumption on consumption externality). Yet identification of these four types of externality is useful because of the differing kinds of solutions which they demand. In general there are four alternatives:

- voluntary bargains between the parties involved;
- taxes or subsidies (depending on whether the activity is to be discouraged or encouraged);
- government control of the generating activity;
- the creation of separate facilities.

## VOLUNTARY BARGAINS

Adherents to the voluntary bargains approach (Buchanan and Stubblebine, 1962) place their faith in the ability of the market system to anticipate and avoid divergences between private and social costs. Some risks can be insured against, and where they cannot, the answer may be to revise the law of property rights to include the possession of peace and quiet as an inalienable right, along with justice, or liberty. This group stresses the cost involved in government action to correct externalities, and suggest that some divergence between social and private costs is the price we pay for economic freedom and its attendant advantages. In other words, the aim of government economic policy should be to provide pure public goods (e.g. defense, public sanitation, justice) and perhaps some quasi-public goods (education, postal services), while creating the climate in which free markets can best function. Any gross distortions can be corrected by ad hoc measures and government fiat, but the onus of proof must always be on those wishing to delimit the role of the free-enterprise system in maximizing economic welfare.

In what sense is this solution applicable to the problem of noise as an external cost? Since most economic transactions take place through private contracts (exchanges) between firms and consumers (goods market) and firms and employees (factor market), if noise enters the bargain we can say it is internalized.* Thus, in the case of the goods market a housewife would rationally only buy a noisier food blender at a lower price than another one which was equal in all other respects. The danger here is that, in spite of the high noise levels created by some household appliances, the housewife may be unaware of the dangers involved, or not be given the choice of buying a quieter machine.

In the case of the factor market, to induce men to work in noisy occupations, a premium must in theory be paid to overcome the higher disutility involved. It seems, however, that most workers are unaware of the hearing hazard, complaining more of the "unpleasantness" of their working environment! (See Part I, Chapter 2.) Although some noisier jobs attract better pay, there is no clear-cut method of determining just how noisy a job has to become before it warrants a pay rise, nor is there a consistent link between noise and wage levels (ICI, 1972). Furthermore, it is doubtful whether the worker has a real choice of quitting a noisy job and finding another even at a lower wage. But this discussion begs the broader issue of whether or not we should pay people to suffer ear damage.

One could imagine internalization taking place in a linkage between two production activities, where the recipients of the noise (Firms $A$) are able to come to terms with the creator of the noise, if $A$ is a small number. For instance they could pay the polluter to cut down his noise output as long as the amount was less than their loss of output due to the noise. However, this solution becomes unfeasible whenever the number of injured parties becomes large, as is clearly the case in transportation noise.

Another alternative is a merger between interested parties, wherein external effects would immediately be internalized. Apart from objectives to merger on monopoly grounds, this alternative does not offer in general a practical solution, again because of the sheer numbers involved in noise pollution.

If externalities are seen as uncovenanted risks of other people's activities, it is sometimes held that the market can take cognizance of them through insurance. If movie stars can insure their legs, surely factory workers can insure their ears? Indeed this does happen; most countries see to it that there is some form of compulsory insurance against industrial injury (see Part V, Chapter 19). But as we have pointed

---

*Whether implicitly or explicitly is unimportant theoretically but it raises practical problems.

out in Part II, noise-induced deafness is hard to distinguish from presbycusis. Furthermore, it is far less dramatic than other forms of industrial accident, and its progress is so gradual that it is often not even recognized by the worker until it becomes serious enough to interfere with conversation.

The ordinary citizen, however, cannot insure against the ill-effects of something as ubiquitous as unwanted sound even if he could place a price tag on it. Also, the "pooling-of-risks" principle on which insurance is based, would break down if most people were exposed to the risk most of the time, as they are with noise. Thus, insurance companies specifically exclude sonic boom damage from their policies.

In general the laissez-faire approach to the problem of external costs breaks down because of the high cost of information and organization involved in most voluntary bargains. If these costs are assumed to be zero, it can be shown that the Pareto optimum is reachable (Coase, 1960). But of course the costs are not zero, and increase with the size of the group affected.* Clearly if these costs could be reduced by putting the burden of action, not on those afflicted by noise, but on the relatively smaller number of producers, there would be more scope for private agreement (Mishan, 1967). This is most obvious in factories, where the noise source is readily identifiable, the levels are measurable and the people most affected—the workers—are easily recognized. In this closed situation the management is the decision maker, and information and organization costs are likely to be small.

Thus the possibilities for a free market solution are bounded by the prevailing legislation, a topic discussed in Chapter 24. In most situations it is irrelevant, from the viewpoint of optimal allocation, whether the sufferers bribe the noise producers or are compensated by them. Thus a change in the legal framework giving explicit recognition to peace and quiet rights would also be an improvement in terms of equity; the polluter would pay. Indeed the absence of such recognition opens up the possibility—at least in theory—of blackmail. $A$'s activity which harms others can be stopped if annoyance moves the victims to bribe $A$ sufficiently.

Questions of distribution also figure in any economic arrangement, providing an added deterrant to the voluntary approach. Lower income

---

*It should be noted that if monopoly exists the bargaining solution is undesirable even with zero costs. Wellisz suggests that a Pigovian solution is called for in these situations (Wellisz, 1964).

groups, through choice of occupation or place of residence, are generally those suffering most from noise. If the polluter is richer than those he pollutes, and is bribed for restricting his activity, the situation is clearly unacceptable. If he is poorer, the result may be distributionally and allocatively an improvement, though hardly equitable.

There remains the idea that externalities are something to be put up with in order to have the benefits of a free market economy. That is, people accept noise levels as a concomitant of material progress. Since we are sometimes the offenders, and sometimes the sufferers, there is thus some existential equalizing of the burden. This is an idea that would have some validity only if we were offered an explicit choice between more material wealth and less external costs—a choice non-existent at the moment. One further argument favoring a "do-nothing" stance is the charge of paternalism often leveled at those advocating radical changes. If people are indifferent to, accept, or even enjoy noise; if tolerance of it in factories is a sign of manhood, and production of it on a motorbike is an integral part of the excitement, can politicians or planners impose their preferences on others? (This point will be taken up again in the conclusion of this book.)

In brief, it would thus appear that the free market solution to noise externalities is unusable from the allocative standpoint, except for a limited range of consumer–producer and producer–producer linkages (mainly when reciprocal effects are present, which can encourage mergers). However, while keeping in mind the strictures of this school of thought regarding the real cost of government action it is to this alternative that we must turn.

## TAXES AND SUBSIDIES

In 1920, A. C. Pigou formulated what has become the traditional solution for externalities. When there is a divergence between marginal social and marginal private net* products "self-interest will not, ... tend to make the national dividend† a maximum; and, consequently, certain specific acts of interference with normal economic processes may be expected not to diminish, but to increase the dividend" (Pigou, 1962).

---

*That is, benefits minus costs.
†That is, income.

Hence, activities where social benefits* exceed private benefits should be encouraged by subsidies, while activities in which social costs exceed the private ones should be taxed.

This solution lies mid-way between laissez-faire and controlled approaches, and is conceptually simple even if difficult to administer. A tax on the noise polluter should be designed to equate private costs with social costs, and thus have the result of reducing the noise-generating output to its social optimum. The attraction of this method is that it so modifies the cost function of a firm (or the utility function of an individual) that in pursuing profit (utility) maximization the activity is carried to its socially optimal level.

Practical examples of Pigovian taxes and subsidies are harder to find than the space devoted to them in learned journals would lead one to believe. In Britain the regional employment premium, a subsidy designed to encourage industry to locate in areas of high unemployment, is a practical application of a Pigovian principle. The costs of unemployment in redundancy pay, national insurance benefits, welfare payments, and the loss of potential output, coupled with the social distress and personal degeneration so caused, have led governments to a commitment to high and stable levels of employment. When unemployment is structural, that is, concentrated in a region because demand has shifted from local industry, or a new technology has undercut it, then it costs less for society to pay firms to move there than to adopt a laissez-faire policy.

As regards noise, government expenditure on research into quieter engines is an externality-reducing subsidy. Other subsidies can take the form of night flight concessions to encourage operators to use quieter jets like the Lockheed Tristar (L-1011) or the DC 10.† The British Airports Authority is considering using differential charges (i.e., taxes) to achieve the same end.

Another action that would affect noise is to curb the use of motor vehicles on congested urban roads through extra charges placed on drivers to reflect the social costs of traffic congestion. As Peters has pointed out, this is also an example of Pigovian market modification (Peters, 1968).

Clearly the social costs which motor vehicles impose on society include

---

*Social benefits include private benefits (usually taken as represented by the price paid for the good in question), and social costs include private costs (wages, rent, interest, and profits).

†See footnote, Part IV, Chapter 14.

much more than congestion. They embrace noise and air pollution, the value of lives and injuries in motor accidents (over and above the valuation in insurance premiums), and the general disruption and stress which the present unrestrained levels of traffic cause. The reason that these factors are not usually taken into account in proposals for road pricing is the difficulty in quantifying them.*

Congestion costs are simple to calculate, as the sum of the various extra expenses (in fuel, time, etc.) incurred through traffic delays.† In the case of the other social costs, a relationship between increased traffic, more noise and air pollution, and a dollar amount representing these costs is not nearly so easy to formulate. Any evaluation of the pollution thus caused must be made indirectly, but in theory at least there is no reason why one element of the tax on vehicles in cities should not be an estimate of the social cost of noise. The aim of such a levy must be to bring the private cost of each trip up to its social cost. This would reduce the number of trips to the optimal level where the price paid by the road users is equal to the additional true cost of another trip (see Appendix). It is interesting to note that the Dutch have introduced a tax on all fuels in proportion to the amount of air pollution they cause. The tax ranges from 0.30 guilders on 100 liters of gasoline to 0.00015 guilders on a cubic metre of gas (Times, 1972).

Unlike air pollution, noise does not accumulate in the atmosphere. Therefore the same noisy machine in different localities would incur a different tax. Transport noise is more offensive at night than during the day, and affects more people in towns than in rural areas, which again calls for differential treatment. In the case of factory noise, at first sight there would seem to be more hope for a Pigovian solution: machines could be noise rated and a tax introduced at a zero rate below the 80 dB level, for example (which is regarded by many as the maximum for

---

*Attempts are made to quantify the economic loss of accidents, but those of necessity preclude those sections of the community with no present or future economic worth, that is, those people who are retired. It is also difficult to evaluate the potential earnings of a child. Even if those two problems were absent the personal loss and grief so caused are incalculable and therefore not included.

†A classical example of calculation of congestion costs is given by the Smeed Committee Study of Central London: "Estimates for Central London for example show that the congestion costs imposed by a typical car on other vehicles rose from 4d a mile at traffic speeds of 20 mile/h to 2/- a mile at 12 mile/h and 6/- a mile at 9 mile/h. The costs imposed by heavy vehicles are often two or three times higher" (Smeed, 1964). These calculations are 10 years old; present day figures would be considerably higher.

continuous exposure) and increasing progressively as the decibels rose. However, various factors complicate the issue. The tax will have to be high enough to make the cost of noise reduction preferable to it. Moreover, since it is much easier to design quiet machines than to quieten existing noisy ones, the tax would be more burdensome on firms buying machines before the law was passed; it would thus have to be fairly mild for the first few years of operation. Finally, administration of the tax would pose problems in terms of collection and enforcement.

Some of these drawbacks to a noise tax also apply to the legislative solution; a comparative analysis is undertaken in the next chapter. In general, however, the imposition by the state of "extraordinary restraints," as Pigou called them, is fraught with practical difficulties. Noise is a variable function of time, locality, level, and receiver. When this is added to the multiplicity of noise sources, it clearly brings out the need to examine a less exact but more simple administrative action.

## APPENDIX:  THE PRICING OF HIGHWAY TRANSPORTATION

Before seeking to devise a levy to equate the private and social costs of highway transportation—which include noise—we must examine the total cost situation in more detail.

Among the fixed costs of highway transportation are the long-term capital outlays on land purchase, road construction and what have been called "invariate maintenance" costs (Walters, 1968). These costs are distinguished from variable maintenance costs in that they are due to weather and time and not to vehicle use. Other variable costs are those specific to a given road user (private costs) and those which accrue to all road users and the community at large (social costs). The latter comprise congestion costs and the costs of noise and air pollution, etc., which must be taken into account in the proposed levy.

Thus:

Total cost     = Fixed + variable costs
Fixed cost     = Track + invariate maintenance costs
Variable cost = Variable maintenance cost +
                            private operating cost and social costs

Assuming the government decides to maintain the road, we can regard track and invariable maintenance costs as fixed, and thus ignore them. The only relevant costs in the decision to use the road once it is built are variable ones.* The price which road users pay for a journey should be equal to the extra (or marginal) cost of the journey. In this way the value of the resources used up by the vehicle owners are equal at the margin to the value placed on their journey. This value is the price they are willing to pay in order to make the journey.

We can illustrate this optimum position graphically (after Walters, 1968), for two cases: a rural road and an urban road. In each case we must assume a road of given proportions, and identical vehicles and drivers so that all vehicle trips cost the same for a given traffic level. A further assumption is that variable maintenance costs are covered by vehicle owners, say by a fuel tax.†

## The Rural Road

In the case of the rural road (Fig. 23.1), we assume no congestion, minimal noise, air pollution, accidents, etc. In this situation, social costs are effectively zero. Since the variable maintenance costs are paid for by the fuel tax, the only costs to be covered are the operating ones. As the

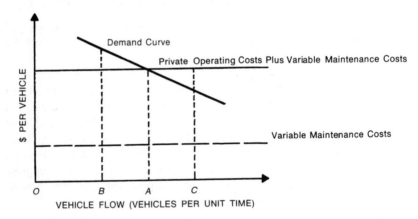

**Fig. 23.1**  Pricing of transportation on a rural highway.

---

*Of course total costs must be covered, but whether this is done through general taxation or through a road fund based on license fees or fuel taxes is an entirely separate question from the one of obtaining maximum efficiency from a road once built. Any revenue raised by the tax *could* be used to cover fixed costs, but perhaps a better use would be to compensate those suffering the (reduced) social costs.

†The variable maintenance costs (VMC) are constant for each vehicle since traffic is assumed homogeneous. They are therefore shown as a straight line on a graph.

latter are entirely private costs they are paid for by the vehicle owner, and no further levy is required.

In the graph the intersection between the demand curve and the cost curve (the line which is the sum of the private operating cost plus the variable maintenance cost for vehicle trips) gives us the optimal flow of traffic, A. The demand curve represents the price people are willing to pay for each level of flow (and hence the benefit to the people), while the cost curve represents the value of resources used up in providing for that level of traffic flow. (The average and marginal costs of a vehicle journey are in this case equal and constant.)

If the flow is restricted to B, the road users are prevented from enjoying a service which they value more than it costs. On the other hand, when the flow is at C, the excess journeys (C–A) are being made at a cost higher to society than the benefits received from making those journeys.

## The Urban Road

In the more relevant case of an urban road, the social costs are considerable. This gap between private and social costs is apparent even at low traffic flows.

If unrestrained, the traffic flow will reach B (Fig. 23.2), where private operating costs plus variable maintenance costs are equal to the demand. But a traffic flow, B, generates external costs, CD, which are borne by society at large. In order to reach the optimal flow A, the government must raise a tax, EF. The marginal valuation of an extra journey, as

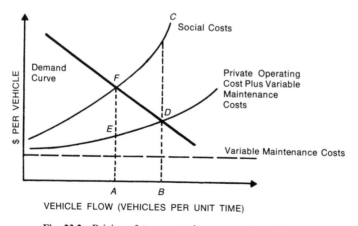

**Fig. 23.2**   Pricing of transportation on an urban highway.

shown by the demand curve, is then equal to the marginal social cost of that journey. Clearly the greater the external costs of vehicle traffic, the greater the pollution (and congestion) tax and the lower the optimal flow.

In this appendix we have discussed a Pigovian solution in terms of an extra fuel tax. Other solutions such as differential licensing, or some form of meter or toll charge, may be more advisable for administrative reasons. The logic of the argument remains the same.

## REFERENCES

Buchanan, J. M. and Stubblebine, W. Externality. *Economica*, 1962, **XXIX**.

Coase, R. H. The problem of social cost. *Journal of Law and Economics*, 1960, **III**.

ICI (Imperial Chemical Industries). Private communication, U.K., 1972.

Mishan, E. *The costs of economic growth*. London: Staples Press, 1967.

Peters, G. H. Cost–benefit analysis and public expenditure. Eaton Paper 8. London: Institute of Economic Affairs, 1968.

Pigou, A. C. *The economics of welfare*, 4th Edition. London: MacMillan, 1962.

Smeed Report. Road pricing: The economic and technical possibilities. London: HMSO, 1964.

Times. *The Times* (London), July 4, 1972.

Walters, A. A. The economics of road user charges. World Bank Staff Paper 5. Baltimore: Johns Hopkins Press, 1968.

Wellisz, S. On external diseconomies and the government assisted invisible hand. *Economica*, 1964, **XXI**.

CHAPTER 24

# Externalities: Legislation and Separate Facilities

## BASIC CONSIDERATIONS

The essential problem in a legislative approach to the control of noise is that of weighing the rights of the individual versus the needs of the community. Each individual in a society is expected to suffer a certain amount of annoyance or interference. The amount to be borne depends on the society's weighing of the harm to the individual against the utility to other segments of society—in this case, the producers of noise. The type of legislation of a particular political jurisdication determines the balance between these two considerations. The decision as to where the balance lies is not easily made, because it involves the answer to the questions: Should we force anyone to protect himself from noise? Should we have legislation that prohibits someone from exposing himself to a high noise level, such as that of a rock band? If so, does this mean that we could, by analogy, prevent him from smoking, or force him to air-condition his house? Who should pay for noise-reduction measures—a question of major implication for urban planning? For instance, in the case of airport or traffic noise, should the noise producer pay or the landowner? In the latter case, the result may be urban sprawl, as housing developments would move away from airports and other areas of major noise.

The situation is further complicated by a number of factors:

• The recognition of noise as a hazard or as a legitimate nuisance has occurred only recently, and many dimensions of the hazard and the nuisance, as we have indicated throughout the book, are still unknown.

• For a variety of reasons, legislation aimed at dealing with general nuisances has proven inadequate where applied to noise, for noise is much more elusive than other nuisances. Some high-level noises, such as that of a rock band, give positive pleasure to a number of people. Therefore, if nuisance legislation is to be successful, it must be cast in a much more specific form than it is at present.

• Jurisdictional conflicts almost inevitably occur among the different governmental agencies involved in noise legislation and enforcement. For instance, more than 20 Federal agencies are involved at Kennedy International Airport in New York. In the case of airport noise, as in the case of industry or of rock-and-roll bands, there is a need for co-operation among many government units.

• The regulatory effectiveness of government units has also been limited by jurisdictional limitations arising from the pre-empting of certain aspects of legislation by a superior authority. Thus, in the United States the power of the states and local governments to regulate traffic—and hence noise generated by it—is completely pre-empted by the Federal government. In the case of aircraft noise, state and local regulations for minimum altitude, noise levels and curfews (limitations of hours of flights) have been held by the courts to be unenforceable. Therefore, cities or states in the United States have no jurisdiction over aircraft flying over their territory, and airport owners and operators can control only the noise emitted by the aircraft on the ground.

• The technical competency of many smaller governmental jurisdictions, such as small municipalities (and at times even that of the large ones), in drafting noise ordinances and enforcing them is limited. This has prevented effective and rational approaches to noise control.

• The ability to enforce noise legislation is frequently hampered by poorly formulated legislation and by the lack of due process in its enforcement. Hence, the courts have failed to uphold many actions by the enforcers of noise ordinances, either because of vagueness of these ordinances or because of the absence of correct legal procedures, such as prior notification of the offender. The lack of due process includes also excessive use of discretionary power by the chiefs of police.

The remedies to some of these problems are obvious. Vagueness, unreasonableness, lack of technical justification and of procedural due processes can be remedied by more attention to technical detail, more precision in the drafting of the ordinances, and by their even-handed enforcement. Jurisdictional conflicts and limitations can be overcome by closer co-operation between governmental units involved, and by the delegation of authority to state and local units.

It is evident, therefore, that a major obstacle to widespread noise abatement lies in the imperfection of the legal instruments rather than in that of the readily available technological means for reducing noise. Legislation has also been hindered by excessively zealous environmentalist approaches, which have led in some cases to the incorporation of unenforceable provisions in noise ordinances and codes. For instance, the 1972 New York City Noise Control Code defines noise as "any sound that annoys the person" (New York Code, 1972), and provides as penalties fines and imprisonment. Clearly, the definition is so vague that the test of its enforceability will have to be determined by the courts.

## COMMON LAW ACTION

Noise annoyance can be tackled either by individual action under common law or through ad hoc legislation. It will be seen that, of the various types of noise pollution, only neighborhood noise is amenable to action under common law. The main advantages of common law are that an individual or group of individuals can file a private nuisance suit without waiting for official action. In the United Kingdom it is no defense for the plaintiff to show that he has taken all reasonable steps to prevent the noise (NAS, 1969)—a provision so powerful that recent statutes have left it out (NAA, 1960).

However, a private nuisance action is only effective against a single stationary noise source: proceedings against a heavy-traffic flow are obviously not viable, nor are they against the rising tide of general noise from all sources. In fact, in the United Kingdom, it has been established that temporary and transient noise will not generally be accepted as a nuisance (NAS, 1969). It would of course be possible to seek relief from aircraft noise by a private action against either the individual airlines, or the airport authority, but in the further interests of the air travel industry, civil action against aircraft noise has been prohibited both in the United Kingdom and in the United States.

Thus common law action would be most effective against neighborhood noise such as that engendered by factories, places of entertainment, etc. However, in addition to the effort and expense of proceedings, the plaintiff must face one hard fact, that the noise creating activity is of economic benefit to a certain segment of the population. If a reduction in noise cannot be achieved without affecting the activity adversely, this will be borne in mind by the courts when making the decision—and they will not readily grant an injunction. This is especially so in long established industrial areas where higher ambient noise levels apparently have to be tolerated (Smith and Keenan, 1969). A factory can even acquire the right to make a noise by prescription if it has been doing so for long enough, and an action for private nuisance cannot then be made.

To summarize, an undesirable feature of common law action based on general nuisance statutes is that it places excessive discretion, particularly in the absence of formal procedures and standards, in the hands of those who administer the ordinance—the police, who are usually subject to many practical pressures against enforcing the laws, and to whom environmental protection may have a lower priority than protection against crime. In general, because common law remedies require that each case be decided on its own merit and by judicial action, it proves too cumbersome a procedure for a nuisance on the scale of noise.

## NOISE LEGISLATION

Thus, we must turn to other legal instruments in order to seek redress from the main sources of noise: traffic, aircraft, industry, and neighborhood noise. Ad hoc legislation to prevent noise pollution is the most common means of handling this externality; mufflers are required on automobiles, permitted noise levels are laid down for jets near airports, and belated attempts are being made to reduce the din from factory machines.

To be effective, a government ordinance must set a noise standard which represents a real improvement over the pre-existing situation, and which is clearly defined in terms of an accepted measure. Laws based on concepts of "unreasonable" or "unnecessary" noise, or even on the common law "nuisance" approach are too vague, and introduce a subjective element of interpretation into what should be an imperative. Limits set in decibels should be introduced with provision for a progressive lowering with time.

The legislation must also be comprehensive, in that no major source of noise is neglected. For example, the Noise Abatement Act in Britain excludes statutory enterprises, a definition that covers the British Rail and National Road Freight organizations, as well as the British Airports Authority and the Iron and Steel industry (NAA, 1960). These organizations—some of the biggest noise sources—are regulated by other enactments, but would be more amenable to action by individuals and public health officials if included in specific noise laws. Similarly, in the

United States, the acts that regulate industrial noise—the Walsh–Healey Act and the Occupational Safety and Health Act of 1970, do not cover Federal, State or Local Government employees [although they may be covered by other equally effective requirements (see OSHA, 1970— Sections 18(c) (b) and 19, Public Law 91-596)].

## Emission Standards

The most efficient way of reducing noise is to set source emission standards for the main offenders—industrial machinery, aircraft, and vehicles. This is particularly crucial in the case of industrial noise, since any reduction benefits both the workers and the general public.

### Industrial Noise

The Noise Advisory Council in Britain has recommended that all machinery offered for sale be noise rated, and that eventually a law regulating noise output of specified classes of machines should be passed (NAC, 1971). However, declaratory aims like this must be backed up by government action, and certainly in a shorter time period than envisaged in the NAC report (10–15 years).* Preventive measures such as earmuffs are not sufficient (and offer no relief outside the factory); still less are expedients such as limiting the duration of noise exposure by working in shifts. Better design and layout procedures do not get to the root of the problem,† and even the Annual Report of the Chief Inspector of Factories which favored this solution concluded: "The total reduction of noise from all these measures may not be very great in terms of decibels, but may be enough to keep the level of overall noise below a point where workers are likely to suffer ear damage" (HM Inspector, 1970). This "point" is taken as 90 dBA for 8 hours exposure in the United States and United Kingdom (compared to the Dutch 85 dBA limit). However, even when we reduce factory noise levels below 90 dBA, there is no cause for complacency since this is the bare minimum for a tolerable working environment. The U.S. Federal regulations for in-plant industrial noise—the Walsh–Healey Act and the Occupational Safety and Health Act of 1970—leave major gaps in the regulation of industrial noise. For they exempt not only

---

*A step in the right direction has been taken under the U.K. Health and Safety at Work Act of 1974 (see Chapter 19), in that producers of machines now have to insure their safety ("so far as is reasonably practicable").

†Of course when individual machine noise outputs are reduced, there will still be the need for isolation, spacing and shielding of some noisy processes.

Federal government employees, but also the myriad industries not engaged in interstate commerce. These inefficiencies of Federal legislation concerning industrial noise point to the need for supplementary state and local legislation.

## Traffic Noise

As we have seen in Part III, traffic noise poses a special problem in terms of measurement, and thus of setting desired standards, since it varies with speed and driving conditions. The difficulty is to decide whether limits should apply to noise emitted by stationary vehicles, vehicles under normal driving conditions, or on the maximum noise a vehicle is capable of emitting—accelerating fast in low gear. There is also the question of how the vehicle is driven: large powerful cars can emit a great amount of noise when accelerating but are usually quieter in city traffic.

The task of devising a single measure to reflect these diverse influences is obviously a very complex one. A procedure has been suggested, similar to that used for aircraft certification, whereby separate measures are made of noise from the vehicle when stationary, during maximum acceleration, and at cruising speed (OECD, 1971). For each class of vehicle the three measures would be entered in the registration papers. The enforcement of such a law would depend upon the practicality of checking noise emissions and upon the penalties for exceeding the limits. Although there is ample scope for increasing the present level of fines, the restraining factor is society's judgment of the seriousness of this offence in relation to others.

Curbside checks on stationary vehicles are the easiest to administer, but since most annoyance from road traffic occurs at night and most disturbance stems from peak level noise, the best single measure would be of noise output at maximum acceleration. The problem is solved if there is a fixed relationship between the noise emission from a vehicle when stationary and when accelerating. This seems to be the case for diesel-engined vehicles but not, under present testing procedures, for gasoline-powered ones.

In the United Kingdom the Motor Vehicles (Construction and Use) Regulations of 1969 (U.K. Regulations, 1969) laid down maximum sound levels for various classes of vehicles, but made the measurement so complex and detailed that 63 out of the 64 Chief Constables refused to operate the system and less than 20 people have been prosecuted in 3 years. The failure of this act has prompted the Noise Abatement Society (NAS) to suggest that noise should be part of the annual vehicle test (NAS, 1971). For enforcement of the law, the Society has produced a small easily portable noise "torch" which lights up when a vehicle exceeds the appropriate level. The police officer or other official conducting the test takes the vehicle registration number and forwards it to a central registry. The onus is then upon the owner of the vehicle to have it tested by more accurate equipment and to carry out any necessary repairs. If the central registry fails to receive a clearance certificate from an authorized mechanic the vehicle road license is suspended. Such a system, in which a roadside check is followed by a more accurate one at the owner's expense,* would certainly simplify enforcement and control procedures.

## Aircraft Noise

In the early years of civil aviation, governments strove to create conditions favorable to its growth, and as early as 1920, the United Kingdom instituted the Air Navigation Act which included a prohibition of private actions against overflying aircraft (ANA, 1920). This provision was continued in the 1949 Civil Aviation Act which is the basis for current regulations (CAA, 1949). These laws, framed at the time of the propeller aircraft, are still very lenient to the aerospace industry. In the United Kingdom takeoff noise limits are 110 PNdB† by day and 102 PNdB by night, although the NAS recommends a maximum tolerable limit of 90 PNdB (NAS, 1969, 1971).

Mild as these limits are, still more lukewarm are the enforcement procedures. The Aviation section of the Board of Trade, which monitors airport noise, admits that about 9000 jets exceeded 100 PNdB in 1971, and that roughly 5000 takeoffs were missed altogether. The 9000 delinquents received letters of complaint, but the ultimate sanction—being barred from the airport—has never been used (BBC, 1972).

In the United States, under a 1968 amendment to the Federal Aviation Act (U.S. 88, 1968), the Federal Aviation Administration (FAA) was given

---

*Unfortunately, the British Standards Institution and the Department of the Environment tested the NAS's noise torch and found it lacking in several respects (NAC, 1972). Even given an accurate, portable meter, there are many problems in obtaining reliable readings under operational conditions. It would seem that improvement in enforcement techniques must wait on the invention of an adequate static test for gasoline-engined vehicles.

†See Appendix 1.

power to license aircraft, subject, among other things, to standards which the agency has set for takeoff, sideline, and approach noise levels, for post-January 1967 subsonic aircraft. These standards vary for planes of different weights, but the maximum is 108 EPNdB in the daytime. These standards, and the corrective actions to meet them, are discussed in detail in Part IV.

In the way of overview, suffice it here to say that only three aircraft currently meet these regulations for takeoff and landing noise: the post 1972 Boeing 747, the Douglas DC 10, and the Lockheed L 1011. For the older, two- or three-engined jets, such as the DC 9 and Boeing 727, the FAA requires noise suppression devices to be fitted. No provision has been made to muffle the bigger and much noisier planes like the DC 8 and Boeing 707, since it is held to be too costly due to their shorter operational life. As these planes were being produced until very recently, there will be an appreciable number of noisy jets in service for 10–15 years; this includes the Concorde, at present excluded from FAA regulations.*

In the short to medium term the situation is still crucial, witness the EPA:

> Projections by the Air Transport Association estimate that by 1975 only 18.6 per cent of the fleet will have been certificated under Part 36, and even this is probably optimistic, given present economic conditions that will retard aircraft replacements. Thus, to the extent that it depends upon type certification as presently structured, the noise problem will have been only slightly relieved by 1975 and indeed, could still be significant as late as 1990 (EPA, 1971a).

Further, an international conference on Aircraft Noise concluded that little could be done in the way of operational procedures (better takeoff profiles, different angles of approach, power reductions while over residential areas, etc.) to reduce noise "since these had in many cases, reached the limits possible without degradation of safety" (Aircraft Noise, 1967). This means that further improvements must come from regulations for muffling existing jet engines.

Several estimates have been made of the cost to quiet the U.S. commercial jets (see Part IV). If one takes the estimate of the Rohr Corporation—$800 million—to quiet a U.S. fleet of 2000 jets (Observer, 1972), this would amount to roughly 1 percent on fares—not much when

---

*The Concorde's manufacturers claim that the in service plane will be no noisier than the Boeing 707 or Douglas DC 8 (FI, 1971). This means that the second most advanced piece of aerospace technology in the world (after the space program) will produce as much noise as subsonic jets designed 15 years ago.

the estimated cost of aircraft noise in the United States alone may range between \$4 billion and \$18.5 billion (EPA, 1971b).

Pressure must be maintained on airlines to retrofit existing aircraft, and on manufacturers to produce still quieter engines. In spite of the present weak financial state of most airlines, pleas of "uneconomic" and "too costly" are a little specious in view of the figures quoted above and the speed at which technical advances in this field are being made.

For example, the technical director of Rolls Royce has stated that one reason for his company's bankruptcy in 1972 was the expensive technology built into the high bypass R.B.211 engine to reduce noise* (Guardian, 1972). [But an official inquiry recorded that the principal reason for the collapse of Rolls Royce was poor management and reliance on fixed-price contracts (RR, 1972).] Other authorities maintain that the main motive behind the development of high bypass turbofan engines was not noise reduction but the lower fuel consumption.

### Building Codes

Building codes, usually in conjunction with land-use prescriptions, offer one avenue for protecting dwellers from excessive noise. The codes are indeed the only avenue left to a municipality to control noise wherever superior government, as in the United States and the United Kingdom, has pre-empted jurisdiction over aircraft and other kinds of noise. Yet, a building code is far from being a panacea, since protection of the receiver is much more costly than control of the source, and furthermore, the code cannot protect a person who is outside the dwelling.

The codes that include provisions for the regulation of noise are of two principal types: performance codes and material codes. *Performance codes* prescribe a certain performance in the reduction of noise for the particular structure or machine being regulated. They can prescribe performance, either on the basis of results of *laboratory tests* of the transmission loss of a particular material or component employed in the construction, or on the basis of *field test* of the performance of the structure or machine. Laboratory test performance presents less of an

---

*Arguments that a pollution control technology is too expensive are often used to delay improvements in pollution control. Where anti-noise laws pose a real threat of economic disruption, unemployment, etc., they cannot be considered in isolation. However, if social costs are to be internalized, a corporation which cannot cover them should go out of business, since its existence represents a misallocation of resources.

unknown to a builder than field test performance, because the latter may lead to expensive modifications if, after construction, the final performance is not satisfactory. *Material codes* specify in detail the material to be used in particular kinds of construction, on the assumption that the compliance with the code will lead to the desired performance.

Each type of code has advantages and disadvantages. Performance codes are more difficult to enforce, but if enforced give a better guarantee of noise reduction. They are usually feasible only if there is an adequate staff to enforce them—for example, in the larger cities. Material codes reduce the burden on the enforcement officials who may not be able to monitor performance; yet they tend to discourage innovation in the use of materials and therefore need periodic updating. In addition, they are usually difficult to write.

### Building Codes for Aircraft Noise

Development of building codes against aircraft noise have been very slow. Thus in the United States, only two codes of this type had been written by the end of 1972: one in Inglewood, California—a town located in the path of the Los Angeles Airport; and the other in Irving, Texas—a town bordering the Dallas-Fort Worth Airport.

The Inglewood code is primarily a performance code with some material specifications. It distinguishes two zones: a high-noise zone (NEF > 40) in which a noise reduction of 35 dBA by a dwelling is prescribed, and a lesser noise zone (NEF 30–40) in which the prescribed noise reduction is 28 dBA noise. The Irving code is primarily a materially oriented code but with optional performance features. No residential dwellings are permitted in a high-noise area, the only exception being that dwellings can be built in a portion of the high-noise area that does not exceed by more than 10 dB the noise boundary of the area (provided noise reductions of 45 PNdB in the sleeping areas and of 35 PNdB elsewhere are achieved, so as to equalize annoyance during daytime and at night).

### Multi-Family Dwelling Codes

In addition to external noise, of which aircraft noise is one of the most extreme examples, noise internal to a dwelling is also of concern, if a desirable internal environment is to be created. This is the noise generated by people, mechanical devices, etc. The development of these codes has also been surprisingly slow: in the United States in 1972 there were only two codes for multi-family dwellings dealing with internal noise—the San

Francisco code and the New York code. Both are performance codes, since material codes would be exceedingly complicated, given the large spectrum of materials and structural arrangements potentially involved in multi-dwelling construction, particularly in high-rise buildings. In the San Francisco code, performance is assessed primarily on the basis of field tests, while in the New York code it is assessed primarily through laboratory tests.

## Jurisdictional Areas

The appropriate authority of control is a further factor in any consideration of noise laws. For aircraft, international agreement is required. In the case of neighborhood noise, which is a highly localized phenomenon the city or county is the relevant government level, but in the case of noise from vehicles and machines, national standards may not always be sufficient.* This is so chiefly for two reasons. Where exports are at stake, few countries will set for their own manufacturers higher noise control standards if this impairs competitiveness. Similarly, few countries will be willing to accept the "polluting imports" of others, even if cheaper. That this problem exists is illustrated by the varying noise limits for new vehicles obtaining under the U.N. Economic Commission for Europe regulations, the latest European Economic Community directive, and the proposed U.K. limits (NAC, 1972). In fact, in the United Kingdom the date of introduction of the new regulations has been postponed until consultation has established a uniform European vehicle code.

Regarding machinery, although noise considerations will only become relevant to trade when domestic regulations are imposed to the same extent as they are now on vehicles, some sort of international noise standard would seem advisable for another reason: multi-national corporations may locate where noise laws are lax, just as they do where labor is cheap, and taxes low. This amounts to exporting the externality to those countries where environmental factors loom less large. Whether this is desirable if it creates jobs in, and attracts investment to, economically less advanced nations, is a question that cannot be pursued here. It is significant to note parenthetically that in the United States, the EPA can apply its general requirements to imported goods.

---

*However, while a noisy export is trans-national, the noise itself is not, which delimits the need for international control as compared with air or water pollution.

## Local Noise Ordinances

A number of noise ordinances have been enacted by local governments, either to control specific noises, such as construction noise or lawnmower noise (by limiting, for example, the hours of the noisy activity), or to provide comprehensive regulation for noise in the community. These ordinances, like the comprehensive noise ordinances, are all subject to pre-emption by a higher level government: if a superior government body has regulated the subject matter of the ordinances, the local government cannot regulate in conflict. Pre-emption may be necessary to remove the uncertainty and confusion of a multitude of different standards, for instance, on autos or die-casting machines, and to ensure that states do not compete with each other as "noise havens" for industry. But there is still scope for state and local action on other noise sources. The ordinances, in general, provide discretionary powers regarding noise generated by utilities, the noise generated in non-residential areas, the noise generated in emergency conditions (e.g., utility repairs), etc. But if the discretionary powers are to be upheld by the courts, guidelines are needed in each case—for instance, as to what constitutes an emergency.

Incorporation of noise restrictions in existing codes and ordinances— such as the building code, the construction code, or the motor vehicle code—is often favored by many municipalities over comprehensive noise controls. If a noise provision is incorporated into an existing code, its enforcement lies with existing mechanisms—with experts on the subject matter of the ordinances (automobiles, buildings, etc.)—and the setting up of a more expensive ad hoc agency is avoided.

On the other hand, comprehensive noise ordinances with power of enforcement vested in special agencies offer a more co-ordinated approach to noise control, and are enforced by personnel with expertise in acoustical matters, and a direct commitment to environmental protection. In the United States, the first state to introduce a comprehensive noise control law was New Jersey, where the State Department became empowered in 1972 to regulate all noise harmful to "physical health and mental serenity."

There is clearly a universal need for comprehensive local codes and zoning ordinances to protect the public from all types of noise, not only aircraft or indoor noise in multi-family dwellings. It may take well into the 1980's before comprehensive codes and ordinances come into existence throughout the United States and Europe, because of the massive effort necessary to have the building industry, the planners, the municipalities, the manufacturing and building industries, and the citizens' groups find a workable and enforceable common ground. Building and zoning ordinances will not be replaced by comprehensive noise ordinances, but will complement them. In general, there is today enough information regarding the noise produced by major sources, such as road traffic or aircraft, to lessen the need for extensive noise surveys in a community. Much money and efforts are spent needlessly in such surveys, frequently for the sole purpose of enhancing acceptance of a draft of a noise ordinance by a city council that is not inclined to believe standard projections for traffic or airplane noise. (But, of course, there will always be the need for localized surveys for unusual types of noise.)

## Federal and Common Market Legislation

In the United States, Federal legislation represents the only feasible approach for the regulation of noise generated by vehicles involved in interstate commerce, such as aircraft, trucks and buses—and by certain industries, such as the automobile industry, whose products are distributed throughout the nation. The same principle is obviously desirable in the case of European countries, where the Common Market has greatly encouraged international traffic and international diffusion of the product of national industries. Yet, both in the case of the United States and of the European Common Market, Federal or international regulations cannot be relied upon exclusively for the control of noise, but must be complemented by local legislation.

In the United States the Federal picture is complex because of the large number of governmental agencies (15 or more) which, until recently, have had jurisdiction over different aspects of the noise problem. As a consequence, Federal action has been slow. Thus, until 1971, the United States had no Federal guidelines for exposure to traffic and railroad noise. The situation was compounded by the slow action of standardizing organizations, such as the American National Standards Institute, in standardizing acceptable practices in building components. Only the Federal Housing Administration had established a criterion for rating of walls and floors of multi-family dwellings. In 1971 the Department of Housing and Urban Development (HUD) (HUD, 1971), proposed limiting noise exposures (in decibels) for a site to be acceptable. Primarily used by HUD in granting loans, the standard gives minimum acceptable rather than desirable noise levels. In a companion standard, HUD also gives noise assessment guidelines—again, minimum acceptable levels—for evaluating external site exposures for given physical conditions and surroundings of the site.

## The Federal Noise Control Bill

The 1972 Federal Noise Control Bill takes a comprehensive view of the noise problem in the United States and is exerting a sweeping influence on noise control. The bill assigns to the EPA co-ordination of all the Federal noise programs in the 15 or more Federal agencies involved. The EPA is also mandated to establish noise source emission standards for new products in construction equipment, transportation and recreation vehicles (other than aircraft), energy powered equipment, and electronics and electric equipment. The EPA is given some authority in the area of aircraft noise, and the authority to label certain products involved in interstate commerce. Finally, the EPA is empowered to do research on facts, measurements, and control of noise.

An important feature of this legislation is the mandate to the EPA to assist the Secretary of the Treasury in issuing import regulations concerning possible products that are potential sources of noise. The legislation, furthermore, envisions the use of the purchasing powers of government in acquiring less noisy equipment, thus exerting a pressure on the market for the development of such equipment. The enforcement provisions involve prosecution in U.S. District Courts with fines up to $25,000 for each violation, or prosecution, by special agreement, in state courts. Military aircraft and some other specialized products qualify for exemption. Particularly noteworthy is the rigid schedule for implementation, which is required within $1\frac{1}{2}$–2 years from the date of approval of a code.

The Federal legislation also has a major influence on the states and local communities, which can be provided with technical assistance and financial support. However, the rights of the states and communities to regulate their own noise are not pre-empted, except for emission standards on new products, which cannot differ from Federal standards, where the exist. The communities and states retain the right to legislate on new products not subject to Federal regulation, and to set limits equal to those set by Federal regulations in the case of new products subject to the latter (a provision aimed at involving local and state authorities in the enforcement of Federal regulations). The noise controls restored to state and local authorities also include those on:

- the manner of operation of products

- the time and the places in which products may be operated
- the number of products which may be operated together
- noise emissions from the property on which products are used
- the licensing of products
- environmental noise levels.

Without doubt, this comprehensive Federal legislation will eventually reduce noise, as a result of the source standards for newly manufactured products set and enforced by the EPA. But these standards are not a panacea, since in the long-run, vehicles and engines, as they age, will again become noisy. Neither can this legislation remove the burden for noise controls from the states and the communities, which will continue to shoulder the major responsability for dealing with community noise.

## *Federal Environmental Impact Statements*

Another major step has been taken in the United States, by requiring Environmental Impact Statements for all major Federal actions significantly affecting the quality of the human environment. This Federal action stems from the National Environmental Policy Act of 1969 (NEPA, 1970) and from the guidelines of the Council on Environmental Quality (CEQ, 1973), which has been established by the Act. Impact statements are required for all projects—private or public—characterized by the presence of sufficient Federal control and responsibility. In addition to the Federal government, environmental impact statements are now being required by a number of states and local governments. A description of the nature of the statements, and of the process leading to their formation, is given in Appendix 3. The ultimate result of the process is to lead to a "go or no go" decision concerning a given project falling under the jurisdiction of the National Environmental Policy Act.

## Separate Facilities and Zoning

As a supplement to passing general laws on permitted noise levels, the government can separate the noise producer from the noise sufferer. The idea of separating the producer of a nuisance from the rest of the public is not new: non-smoking compartments in railroad cars have been in existence for a long time and so has been the designation, in cities, of zones intended for industrial or commercial purposes. Specific attention to noise is, however, more recent.

Separate facilities are advantageous in that there is no need to devise a tax to achieve the optimal level of a noise-creating activity, or to pass laws enforcing national standards, or, in making an investment decision, to subtract from expected benefits a measure of the compensation due to those bearing the cost. Once areas have been designated with differing levels of noise permitted in or over them, factories, airports, vehicles and the use of noisy consumer goods will be allowed only if they comply with the various requirements. Those who like or profit from the sounds so produced may create them in certain zones while others can enjoy the relative quiet elsewhere. Thus zoning or separate facilities are clearly a strong, and sometimes very effective solution to the problem of unwanted side effects—in the extreme case externalities would vanish.

In the United States, urban zoning for noise has tended in recent years to move from what can be called partly specific zoning—"cumulative zoning"—to totally specific zoning—"non-cumulative zoning." (Cumulative zoning bars a particular kind of industry from a given zone, but implicitly permits residential dwellings everywhere. Under non-cumulative zoning, not only is industry barred from a given zone, but also residential dwellings are confined to a specific zone.)

One of the common pitfalls in zoning for noise is the establishment of too many zones, because this makes the problem of monitoring noise and enforcing the code exceedingly complex. It is generally far better to confine, through zoning, specific and identifiable noise sources, such as an airport, or an industrial zone, than to provide a theoretically more rational, but in practice unenforceable general zoning (that would establish, for example, zones of 40, 60, 90 dB throughout a city). General zoning leads to subdivision into a large number of zones, in that even over a small area local conditions determine the noise level, and hence different zones must be established. Thus, an arterial road passing through a quiet residential district would require two or three zones. The recent comprehensive noise ordinance for New York City, which provides for this type of zoning, has been criticized as being indeed too complex for enforcement; it is feared that the cost of enforcement will run into millions of dollars, without a commensurate return.

*Motor Vehicles*

Separate facilities have long been proposed for traffic, although noise has been only one of the factors involved. Traffic-free residential and shopping precincts are now a common feature of many cities, and are almost mandatory in new towns.* In the United Kingdom the Minister for Transport Industries has, for some time, been considering proposals for designating special routes for heavy trucks, especially to and from the ports (FT, 1972). The Greater London Council (the strategic highway authority for London) recently suggested some 425 miles of such routes, to which trucks of over 16 tons in weight or 36 feet in length would be restricted. Residents of the streets affected are naturally opposed to the plan. They will undoubtedly obtain grants for soundproofing, but whether they receive compensation (and how much) under the Land Compensation Act 1973 (LCA 1973), is still to be determined. In general the principle of concentrating the noise is a valid one, because overall annoyance is minimized when the noise peaks suffered by many are transferred to a few, already noisy, routes. However, proposals such as these should be seen in the context of an overall transport strategy. When noise costs as well as other pollution costs are taken into consideration, increased use of alternative transportation systems, rail or canal, becomes more feasible.

Much of the destruction and misery caused by urban highways would be avoided if they could be built in tunnels. Under the combined effect of soaring land prices and rapid advances in tunneling technology this now appears to be a real possibility (O'Reilly and Munton, 1972). For the growing number of city dwellers to whom the idea of an urban highway is a contradiction in terms, this possibility is one actively to be sought after. As the cost of shielding the remaining residential areas from noise, air pollution, and visual blight rises, and the legitimate demands of people in this respect are met, the idea of burying all the externalities underground becomes ever more attractive. The cities can thus be returned to the people.

### Aircraft

A major reason for the annoyance caused by aircraft is the fact that older established airports were sited for use by planes with piston engines, and placed as close as feasible to cities. Since these airports represent huge capital investments, and are often of great importance to

---

*Unfortunately such schemes often end up with pedestrians isolated in covered plazas and subterranean walkways, while the traffic roars above and around them on the urban expressway. Noise and air pollution are not diminished, and although safety is improved, the increased traffic flow caused by the faster speeds possible on expressways, eventually debouches onto secondary roads with no separate facilities and causes accidents to increase there.

the local economy, their closure is not a real possibility (but their eventual running down may be, if alternative facilities are provided). The problem is exacerbated when long established airports themselves expand, by the addition of new runways, and thus increase the area of conflict over land use.

For the present, the only realistic course of action is to control the land use of the area surrounding these airports. Based on a noise contour map, the permitted pattern of activities within the different contours can be scheduled—industrial and agricultural land use being allowed where residential use could not.

Obviously economic, social, and legal complications make it difficult to alter established land uses in this fashion, but the enforcement of compatible development in the future is promising. At London's Gatwick Airport, for example, the Surrey County Council has adopted specific planning policies to limit the growth of residential accommodation within areas badly affected by aircraft noise nuisance (Roskill, 1971).

To a certain extent the need for a separate facilities solution to aircraft noise depends on the success of the legal measures discussed earlier. Mainly because of noise certification, the long-term future regarding aircraft emissions is hopeful, but the increase in aircraft movements—currently of some 7 percent a year—will counteract in part effects of emission reduction. Thus while measurements such as PNdB will show gradual improvement as noisier planes are phased out, measurements like the Noise and Number Index, which reflect both the noise and the frequency of its occurrence, may reveal a deterioration of the situation. Only when accurate predictions of future aircraft noise characteristics can be combined with projections of traffic volumes, will planners be able to decide on the degree and extent of noise nuisance to be expected in the future.

This inevitable spread of the noise "footprint" of airports* can be minimized in effect by operating procedures and by restrictions on night flying. The latter is itself a form of separate facility: by day the sound environment is dominated by the requirements of air travelers, at night the sleeping multitudes hold sway. Heathrow, Paris-Orly, Sydney, and Hong Kong all restrict night flights. Opposition to these restrictions comes mainly from the short-haul operators who are involved in flying people on package holidays. In the United States, the problem of changing night flight schedules is less affected by short-haul operators,

---

*See for example, Fig. 15.9 in Part IV.

but is complicated by the fact that any major flight carrying mail (under contract with the Post Office) cannot change schedule without Post Office permission.

Flight routing policies for departure are operated by most airport authorities, with the intention of concentrating aircraft on narrowly defined paths from take-off to the airway. Other factors such as airport usage, safety, and traffic control techniques, are taken into consideration when deciding upon the number and type of the routes. Subject to the overriding requirement of safety, there should be a minimum of such routes, and they should be aligned so as to concentrate traffic over areas of low population density. These Minimum Noise Routes (NAC Aircraft, 1971) should be permanent, to allow development for residential purposes to avoid the area. As with the truck routes discussed earlier, a minority will suffer disproportionately and must be protected and compensated fully. However the advantages in terms of minimizing total disturbance are greater here, in that, except for general aviation, aircraft noise is eliminated rather than reduced over those areas not on the flight route.

The final answer in terms of reducing aircraft noise nuisance must come from investment in new airports in areas of minimal population density. In Britain the advantage of dissipating a large proportion of the noise over the sea was a factor in the siting of the proposed Third London Airport on reclaimed land near the island of Foulness. In choosing this site the Government overrode the recommendation of the commission set up to study the alternatives, the Roskill Commission, which had opted for an inland airport. The Roskill report had concluded that the additional traffic at regional airports which would result from the Foulness choice would inflict a noise penalty on as many people as if an inland site were chosen (Roskill, 1971). It is probable that the Government was swayed in its original decision by the large and vociferous publicity campaign mounted by opponents of the inland site—an effort which the less affluent and disorganized residents of the Foulness area could not match.

To the degree to which noise was the overriding factor, the Third London Airport decision was an example of the creation of separate facilities. If the Government had ensured by restrictions on the use of other airports that their noise problems decreased or at least did not increase, then the choice of Foulness would have been an unqualified gain in terms of noise reduction.*

---

*For further discussion of the Roskill Report see Chapter 26. For a combination of reasons—bigger capacity jets, the oil crisis and revised (downwards) forecasts of passenger movements—plans for a Third London Airport have been scrapped.

## Noise Abatement Zones

The British Association of Public Health Inspectors (APHI) has suggested in a memorandom to the NAC that noise control areas be set up "to improve living conditions in mixed areas including factories and commercial premises, a substantial proportion of dwellings and roads (other than main through roads) carrying a substantial volume of traffic" (NAC, 1971). The proposals were made with the success of smoke control areas in mind, which were set up under the Clean Air Act in 1956 to deal with air pollution from domestic sources. The NAC followed the suggestion and, in their 1971 Report on Neighbourhood Noise, recommended that local authorities be given the power to create Noise Abatement Zones. The Council agreed with the APHI that there is scope for local authorities to close roads and divert traffic to reduce vehicle noise in the areas, but rejected the ideal of requiring firms to give notice in advance of installation of noisy machinery. The Council preferred instead the setting of target levels for noise emissions from premises, which could vary for different types of machines, and also for daytime and nighttime operation (NAC, 1971).

This excellent concept was designed to counteract the continuous increases in background or ambient noise levels, against which any individual noise-maker could blend with impunity. The legislation would enable local authorities "to deal with all premises which are (individually or collectively) creating an excessively high level of noise in the neighborhood of houses and other noise sensitive establishments" (NAC, 1971). If this approach has a weakness, it is once more in how it will be administered. In reaching the target emission levels firms are only obliged to use the "best practicable means." Although the NAC spells out this requirement in some detail, if a legal decision becomes necessary, there is too much latitude in the interpretation of the regulations.*

Undoubtedly, however, the introduction of this type of scheme, if forcefully administered, can provide a powerful weapon with which to deal with neighborhood and traffic noise. While under the current laws it could not affect aircraft noise, through the pressures brought to bear on

---

*The Noise Abatement Zone concept was adopted and incorporated in the Control of Pollution Act of 1974, which additionally allows the Secretary of State for the Environment to make regulations requiring noise abatement to be carried out by firms on their plant and equipment. Also under the act much tighter control of noise from construction sites is made possible by local authorities (CPA 1974).

firms within Noise Abatement Zones it would increase the demand for quieter machines, and thus also benefit workers subject to factory noise.

As we have seen, isolating the effects of noise producing activities is a question of land-use planning. It seems likely that the many opportunities inherent in this approach can best be explored at the local level. In the United States local governments have the power to restrict certain activities in their areas, but noise control has not until now been a major consideration. A report by the EPA concluded:

> Inclusion of noise standards in zoning codes is generally recent, and most are not well enforced. Many cities with quantitative noise limits in zoning codes have no measuring equipment for enforcement purposes and there is again a need for guidelines in formulating workable standards. Standards are useful for planning and zoning commissions in screening applicants for industrial locations (EPA, 1971a).

The physical separation of externality-generating activities from the people affected by them is clearly the most authoritarian of the proposals discussed.* It involves planning of areas and activities and is an obvious interference with the liberty of firms and individuals. Nor is it a universal panacea; not all airports can be located near the sea, not all roads can be put in tunnels, and industrial noise is not dealt with by noise abatement zones *per se*. But it does provide a solution to general noise from different sources in urban areas, and on these grounds alone it justifies a further extension of government control into the economic life of the country.

## REFERENCES

Aircraft Noise. *U.K. Aircraft noise.* London: HMSO, 1967.

ANA. (*U.K. Air Navigation Act 1920*), Section 9 (1). London: HMSO, 1920.

BBC (British Broadcasting Corporation). Transcript of Programme on Aircraft Noise. Personal communication, 1972.

CAA (*U.K. Civil Aviation Act 1949*), Section 40 (1). London: HMSO, 1949.

CPA (*U.K. Control of Pollution Act 1974*). Part III. London: HMSO, 1974.

---

*Although as Mishan has pointed out, if the right of people to a decent environment were explicitly recognized in the form of legal rights to clean air, privacy, and quiet, then the market might be relied upon to create separate facilities itself. Noisy activities would tend to concentrate in areas where they least infringed amenity rights. "If, for example, the majority of people dwelling within one area preferred motoring to the extent of being quite willing themselves to put up with the accompanying noise, motoring would be far cheaper in, and therefore, would be attracted to, the latter area. On the same principle, airlines would avoid areas where quiet was most appreciated and concentrate on routes over which compensatory payments were smallest" (Mishan, 1967).

EPA (U.S. Environmental Protection Agency). Report to the President and Congress on noise. December 31, 1971. (a)

EPA (U.S. Environmental Protection Agency). The economic impact of noise. Washington, 1971. (b)

FI (*Flight International*). London, April 8, 1971.

FT (*The Financial Times*) London, August 14, 1972.

Guardian. (*The Guardian*), Manchester June 29, 1972.

HM Inspector. Annual Report of HM Chief Inspector of Factories. Cmnd. 4461. London: HMSO, 1970.

HSWA (*U.K. Health and Safety at Work, etc, Act*). London: HMSO, 1974.

HUD (U.S. Department of Housing and Urban Development). Departmental Circular 1390.2, Washington, 1971.

LCA (*U.K. Land Compensation Act*). Part II. London, HMSO, 1973.

Mishan, E. J. *The costs of economic growth*. London: Staples Press, 1967.

NAA (*U.K. Noise Abatement Act 1960*), Section (3). London: HMSO, 1960.

NAC Aircraft (Noise Advisory Council). Aircraft Noise: Flight Routing Near Airports. London: HMSO, 1974.

NAC (The Noise Advisory Council). Neighbourhood noise. London: HMSO, 1971.

NAC (The Noise Advisory Council). Traffic noise: The vehicle regulations and their enforcement. London: HMSO, 1972.

NAS (The Noise Abatement Society). The law on noise. London, 1969.

NAS (The Noise Abatement Society). Chairman's Report. London, 1971.

New York Code (*New York City Administrative Code*). Chapter 57, part III, 1972.

Observer (*The Observer*), London, March 3, 1972.

OECD (Organization for Economic Co-operation and Development. Motor vehicle noise. Working Document U/ENV/71.9, Paris, November 15, 1971.

O'Reilly, M. P. and Munton, A. P. Prospects of urban highways in tunnels. Transport and Road Research Laboratory Research Paper presented at Transport Engineering Conference, London, 1972.

Roskill. Commission on The Third London Airport. The Roskill Report. London: HMSO, 1972.

RR. Rolls Royce, Ltd. and the RB211 Aero Engine. Cmnd. 4860. London: HMSO 1972.

Smith, K. and Keenan, D. J. *English law, 3rd Ed. London: Sir Isaac Pitman and Sons*, 1969.

U.K. Regulations. U.K. motor vehicles (construction and use) regulations. London: HMSO, 1969.

U.S. 88 Stat. 395, 1968.

# CHAPTER 25

# Externalities: An Assessment

In Chapter 22 we discussed the need to bear in mind the costs of abatement when determining the optimal output of noise; clearly it is important to choose that solution, or mixture of solutions, which attains the required result with maximum efficiency. Both a system of tax changes and a body of laws involve costs of information, administration, and enforcement. However, it is often maintained that the former, less "interventionist," governmental solution has substantial advantages in these, and other respects. A comparative appraisal of the solutions to noise pollution as described in the two previous chapters—legislation versus taxation, subsidies, or "bribes"—is now in order.

## THE CASE AGAINST LEGISLATION

It is generally accepted that in order to set a pollution tax, all that is needed is a knowledge of the output of pollution and the damage (marginal social cost) it causes. The tax is then levied on the polluting output, and each polluter adapts to it as best he can in the light of his own cost function. In this way, firms or individuals in different situations can choose their optimal level of noise output, as long as they pay the social costs—the tax—it engenders. Furthermore, the burden of such a tax encourages research into a technology which is less polluting.

On the other hand, it is claimed that in order to set standards a knowledge both of the damage function and of the marginal social costs of abatement* is required. This poses more information problems and makes an optimal solution less likely. In addition, inspection and enforcement of standards are often held to engender greater administrative problems than the devising and implementing of a tax system.

Thus, for the purist, the legal remedy has shortcomings. It can be shown that as far as resource allocation is concerned, fiat measures are more distorting than the other approaches: while a tax could theoretically be devised to equate marginal private with marginal social net product, there can be no fine balancing of marginal equivalances through a government ordinance. But the practical difficulties of devising such a tax make its use problematic for most noise situations.

When authority for noise control is delegated to regulatory bodies, the law is often framed in general terms, while specific standards are set by the administrators. In the process of setting the standards in public or private hearings, the better organized representative groups are usually those profiting from the noise producing activity. In the case of the FAA which deals with all aspects of civil aviation in the United States, the result was that standards set were not very high. Even where standards are detailed in the legislation, enforcement, at the hands of an agency whose aim is the furtherance of aviation, will be weak—as shown by the example of the U.K. Board of Trade in the previous chapter. In general more effective anti-noise measures will be taken if power is vested in independent agencies like the EPA.†

If a noise suit is filed in the courts, it is the judge who deliberates on the feasibility of preventive action. Here, too, the situation seems to favor the offending party. In the United Kingdom, for example, the Noise Abatement Act (1960) states, "In proceedings brought by virtue of subsection (1) of this section in respect of noise or vibration caused in the course of trade or business, it shall be a defense for the defendant to prove that the best practical means have been used for preventing and counteracting the

---

*That is, a complete knowledge of the curves in Fig. 22.3 in this Part.

†Caution is needed if the example of Britain's quaint anti-air pollution agency, the Alkali Inspectorate, is not to be followed. The much vaunted clean air over British cities is due more to the control over domestic fires brought by the Clean Air Act, than the activities of the Inspectorate which is concerned with Industrial emissions. The familiarity between the Inspectorate and the industry it polices is illustrated by the consideration that: ". . . on only three occasions in the last forty-seven years have court proceedings been brought," and methods were pursued ". . . to preserve what already exists and in particular to do nothing which might damage the goodwill and cooperation existing between industry and the Inspectorate" (Bugler, 1972).

effect of the noise or vibration" (NAA, 1960). Much turns on the judge's interpretation of "best practical means." While it is up to the defendant to prove that these means have been taken, it is very hard for the plaintiff to show that they have not. It is worth remembering that in common law such a defense is not available.

The importance of making such calculations explicit will be discussed again later, but it must be repeated that in the past the balance of advantage has seemed to lie with the noise producer, both in the noise limits set and by the laxity of enforcement. Furthermore, it is to be recognized that the charges of inefficiency and bureaucracy, leveled against government are often justified. It is therefore necessary to examine more closely the reasons for preferring the legislative solution.*

## THE CASE AGAINST TAXES

For a tax to be an efficient solution, the "peg" upon which it is hung must be specific and easy to monitor. Thus an impost on factories emitting a specific air pollutant like sulfur dioxide, or pouring chemical waste into a given river, may be feasible: the sources of pollution and the amount produced are easily definable and measurable. Even if the case is restricted to those industries which offend most, the same cannot be said of noise. Furthermore, there may be a high irreducible level of noise associated with any output. This means that in many cases the fundamental answer must be to encourage the design of quieter machines, putting the initial burden on the machine tools industry. Some of the reasons for doubting the efficacy of a tax to achieve this were given in Chapter 23.

What can be stated unequivocally is that a tax does not give the best solution from the workers' point of view. One of the most quoted advantages of a tax is that it gives a corporation the option of a flexible response, that is, it can pay the tax and keep polluting, or cut the pollution and pay less tax. If it decides not to reduce the noise at all, the conclusion is that the cost of the pollution as represented by the tax is less than the value of the marginal unit of the firms output.† But, of course, the costs of factory noise are not spread out over the whole city/nation/world, but are concentrated on the factory workers, and to a lesser extent, the surround-

---

*Charges for pollution are as much government action as laws, but the latter are usually taken to imply more official involvement than the former.

†Assuming here that noise varies with output, that is, the firm has the choice of less output and less noise.

ing community. Only if the tax reflects this social cost, in many cases a loss of hearing, is the result optimal. One could conceive of a tax based on a schedule of the marginal social cost of industrial deafness, but a law defining maximum permitted exposure based on physiological considerations would appear simpler. Moreover, in the case of a tax, equity demands that the revenue be shared among the sufferers, raising enormous administrative difficulties.

To the extent that a tax system would reduce noise from industry, aircraft and vehicles, the neighborhood noise would also decrease. However, the residue of generalized noise nuisance comes from the proximity of many diverse human activities, and varies according to human behavior. A tax on this is clearly absurd.

As we have seen in Chapter 23, vehicle and aircraft noise are the most likely candidates for the tax–subsidy remedy. However, a vehicle tax would face the same difficulty as legislation: while there is a relationship between engine size, fuel consumption, and air pollution, no clear conclusions can be drawn about noise characteristics and engine size, which limits the basis for taxation. Thus a certain amount of arbitrariness attaches to both solutions. Of greater importance perhaps, is the fact that the technical feasibility of a tax on the social costs generated by vehicles in cities has long been established*—but nowhere implemented. So, in addition to the practical problems, the greater political acceptability of legal standards seems to militate against a noise tax on vehicles.

Legislation is the most favored method of tackling aircraft noise through limits on the users of planes and by standards set for the producers, while taxes and subsidies are less in evidence. The problem is an international one, and it may be that international agreement is easier to reach on the more familiar setting of standards than on the relatively new concept of a noise tax. A serious drawback, again, would be a solution which allows the option of paying the full tax and maintaining an undiminished noise output. In this case such a solution is not acceptable because it is a large minority of people who bear such a disproportionate burden of the nuisance.

Finally, there are grounds for doubting the "scientific" basis for a tax on noise; in other words, granted that legislation is inevitably arbitrary

---

*This is true only in respect to the social cost of congestion. However, even the introduction of a tax on this basis alone, would bring benefits in terms of less air and noise pollution, fewer accidents, etc., which are no less real for being harder to measure.

(that is, there is no pretension of basing the standards on marginal costs and benefits of noise reduction), are there valid grounds for supposing that a tax is less arbitrary? The idea of a marginal cost of noise on which the tax would be based, though clear enough in diagrams, as in Chapter 22, raises two problems. One is the estimation of the total cost function (which we discuss in Chapter 26); the other relates to the peculiar additive nature of noise.

Restricting ourselves to vehicles as an example, if one vehicle is emitting 100 dB, doubling the noise energy by adding a second identical vehicle at the same distance from the measuring point, would produce 103 dB. The addition of *two* more would produce 106 dB, four more 109 dB, etc. But a doubling of the subjective *loudness* corresponds to an increase of 10 dB. So it takes seven extra vehicles to double the loudness produced by the original vehicle. As noise levels rise, the marginal social costs of noise increases. Yet the marginal increment in noise per vehicle is diminishing. Thus even the conceptual problems involved in using marginal costs to impute a tax on noise are daunting. While a tax based on average costs (e.g., total noise costs from a traffic flow, divided by the number of vehicles) is more feasible, it would violate our efficiency rule based on marginal equalities, which is the primary reason for choosing a tax in the first place.

### Two Problems of the Legal Solution

There are, however, two last stumbling blocks before we can accept wholeheartedly the exhibited preference of governments for legislation over taxes and subsidies, as the remedy for noise pollution. One has to do with the very nature of the political process. When legislators consider anti-noise statutes, they are making decisions on costs and benefits involved. There is a clear need for further research and empirical investigation into the costs of noise, in order that these decisions be made on a rational basis, and not as a compromise between opposing lobby groups. Unless this information is forthcoming there is the danger of too much deference to "economic factors," the balance of payments, and other statements of national interest. Where those economic interests which have most to lose by stricter noise control standards are well represented, improvements will be slow. Fortunately the new awareness of environmental issues, when channeled intelligently into political action and allied with other appropriate pressure groups, has achieved some victories—the most notable being the abandonment of the supersonic transport program in the United States.

Beyond this, there are those who fear that government interference in the market economy not only reduces economic freedom and thus efficiency, but also impinges on political liberty. This fear is usually directed more toward government ownership, rather than control, of resources.

## SUMMARY

However, although its adherents would obviously prefer the voluntary bargains approach wherever possible, agreement with individualism does not necessarily preclude the legislative solution. The role of the state in arranging the institutional framework to direct self-interest into channels beneficial to society as a whole, has long been accepted. In fact, as Tullock (1970) maintains, the government can be seen as a collective apparatus to remove externalities. Although at pains to point out that state action generates unwanted side effects of its own, he admits that the larger the externality in question, the higher the likelihood that government intervention will be of net benefit.

Noise constitutes a pervasive and extremely harmful externality, and the liberty to subject ourselves to such pollution is not very precious. It would seem, therefore, that the road to more noise-preventive legislation is clear.

## REFERENCES

Bugler, J. Polluting Britain. A report. Harmondsworth, Middlesex, England: Penguin Books, 1972.
NAA (*U.K. Noise Abatement Act 1960*). London: HMSO, 1960.
Tullock, G. *Private wants, public means: An economic analysis of the desirable scope of government.* New York: Basic Books, 1970.

# CHAPTER 26

# Cost–Benefit Analysis

## INTRODUCTION

We have seen that noise exists at its present high levels because people who create it are not necessarily those who suffer from it. The measures discussed in the previous chapter are designed to remedy this situation either directly or indirectly. Their aim is to reduce noise from current activities to the socially optimal level, which is the point at which the marginal social benefits and marginal social costs of noise reduction are equal: a criterion explicit in the voluntary bargains and tax subsidy approaches and implicit in the other approaches.

Cost–benefit analysis can be carried out in situations where the reduction of noise is a social benefit (such as measures to quieten jet engines, or to restrict takeoffs at night); or it can be used to examine a proposed investment project which will generate noise in the future, where the increase in noise is a social cost (as in the construction of a new airport). Here we shall concentrate on this second situation, but the discussion of how noise is valued is equally relevant to the first—the earlier chapters.

Cost–benefit analysis is a means of evaluating a project in terms of its impact on the community as a whole; it differs from normal investment appraisal mainly in the breadth of view taken. The aim in both cases is the maximization of the present value of benefits minus costs. However, while a business considers only monetary flows, a government is concerned, as far as possible, with the total impact of a given project on the community.*

The shift of emphasis means three things: first, more variables are included in the analysis; second, the variables have to be valued differently; third, since the capital is not raised in the private market, the rate of interest with which to discount the future flows of costs and benefits has to be decided upon.

In a major project it is probable that not only will social costs exceed private costs, but also social benefits will exceed private benefits. Thus a debit item must be entered for the noise created by a new airport, but a credit item must be included for the reduced congestion at other airports. Neither of these considerations would enter into a decision made in a private sector. Having decided on the type of social costs and benefits to be included, we must establish a cutoff point beyond which their magnitudes are no longer important. In the case of noise the costs to people living outside a certain "noise contour" are disregarded; but there is no economic basis for choosing the relevant contour. This problem will be raised again later.

As in a private appraisal, some variables enter into a public cost–benefit analysis, but with a changed price or value. If a firm constructing an airport takes on men who were previously unemployed, it includes their wages as part of costs. To society the cost of employing them on the same project is nil, since before it was begun they were contributing nothing to national output. For private investment, taxes are obviously an important consideration, but for the public sector they are a transfer payment, and are thus excluded.

While it is often easy to evaluate social benefits from a government investment—since in other contexts they are marketed—social costs pose a deeper problem. Attempts to value a social cost such as noise can only be made indirectly, and there is no ideal way of doing this. The pricing of noise is of such central importance to this discussion, that it is discussed separately in the next section.

---

*It might be argued that all government expenditure should be subject to cost–benefit analysis. But often the goals of policy are consensus goals, and the issue reduces to that of finding the most "cost-effective" way of reaching them. (Planning, Programming, and Budgeting systems are an indication of the contribution micro-economics can make in this regard.) Further, cost–benefit analysis is only applicable to projects which will "... not alter the constellation of relative outputs and prices over the whole economy" (Prest and Turvey, 1968).

For capital investment projects the cost and benefits will accrue in the future. When comparing two or more projects, there is an obvious need to reduce these future flows to a single figure. Even if only one project is under consideration the various costs and benefits will occur on different dates (e.g., capital and recurrent costs). To obtain this single figure, or present value, of future monetary values, it is necessary to discount them by a rate of interest.* A positive discount (interest) rate implies that future costs and benefits are valued less than present ones. People will not give up $100 today for $100 in one year's time, but will require $105 instead; the discount rate which equates $105 next year with $100 now is thus 5 percent.

While it is not our task here to inquire into the various proposals for determining the appropriate discount rate, it is certain that the rate at which society discounts the future (the social time preference rate) is not just some average of individual time preference rates; rather it is the result of a political decision, albeit one influenced by conceptual considerations.

Costs and benefits can both alter due to technological innovations, shifts in demand and political changes. Thus, often connected with the discussion of the choice of discount rate are methods of handling the uncertainty and risk attached to any future event. Some advocate that a premium be added to the discount rate, as was done in evaluating the Channel tunnel project (Mishan, 1971). This has the drawback that not all elements of the calculation carry the same risk; furthermore, a consideration as important as the uncertainty and risk of a future event should not be subsumed in an adjustment (determined by the analyst) to the discount factor, but should be made explicit in the deliberations of the decision makers themselves. More fruitful are attempts to arrive at the most likely single outcome, or alternatively the mean probability (expected value) of a range of outcomes, for those variables which exhibit uncertainty. Most promising perhaps is the idea of varying the probabilities attached to the critical variables and seeing how this affects the outcome of the analysis. If the conclusion of the analysis turns out to be sensitive to variations in the probability attached to noise costs, when a government makes its decision on the project it explicitly reveals how it views the future social costs of noise.

---

*There are other investment criteria, and difficult theoretical problems connected with the evaluation of projects. (See e.g., Prest and Turvey, 1968.)

## THE VALUATION OF NOISE

Seeking, as it does, to bring within the measuring rod of money all the pros and cons of a given enterprise, cost–benefit analysis faces three separate valuation questions.

In the first place, the direct benefits and costs are given by the market.* For example the direct benefits from an airport are measured by the revenue it earns; the direct costs are those of construction and operation, the provision of surface access (road and rail), etc. Secondly, other effects which do not enter directly into the account of the airport, but nevertheless are reflected in the G.N.P., must be valued. "Shadow prices" or "imputed values" can be used to assess the job creation effects of the investment, or the loss of future food production from agricultural land. Thirdly, there are effects which are not reflected in G.N.P. such as savings in leisure time and noise.† Here the valuation is perforce an indirect one; a price has to be elicited by examination of people's revealed preferences for speed of transport over extra cost, or for cheaper houses over higher noise levels, or through their answers to questionnaires. This section is devoted to a case study of these methods of evaluating the social costs of noise from an investment project, where noise is a joint product, *and* simultaneously with estimating the social benefits from noise abatement. We shall deal only with the effects on residential areas; a discussion of the direct costs of noise, for example, on industry and agriculture, is undertaken in the Appendix.

### The Roskill Commission

One of the largest and most recent cost–benefit studies was undertaken by the Research Team of the Commission on the now defunct plan for the Third London Airport (Roskill, 1970). Strictly speaking, it was a "cost–effectiveness" study rather than a full-blown cost–benefit one, because the Commission's terms of reference were limited to deciding where, and when, a third airport for the London area should be built. It was assumed that benefits would exceed costs whatever the site chosen, and that there were no differences in the benefits arising from an airport on either of the four sites on the short list. So, for the purpose of the Research Team's analysis, the problem was one of valuing noise costs and discovering the least cost site.

---

*With certain provisos on double counting (see Chapter 24).
†They may indeed be reflected perversely in the G.N.P., as discussed in Chapter 22.

The number of households affected by aircraft noise was estimated by the use of a noise contour map. The contour lines were drawn up on the basis of the Noise and Number Index (NNI), for values of 35–40 NNI (at the outer boundary considered by the Commission) increasing by steps of 5 NNI, to the highest contour of "over 55 NNI."

## Compensation for Different Categories of Households

The households within the areas considered were then divided into three groups (Table 26.1): those moving because of the airport; those moving anyway; and those who chose to remain. The noise cost to each of the groups was calculated as being equal to that amount of money which would have to be given to a resident to restore him to his pre-airport level of satisfaction, that is, to entirely compensate him for the imposition of the noise nuisance. No allowance was made for noise annoyance to new entrants, who were assumed to be fully compensated by the relative fall in house prices in the noisy zone. All costs were discounted to 1982, the target date of opening.

Persons moving because of the noise were deemed to suffer a loss due to depreciation on their houses ($D$), removal expenses ($R$), and a measure of the subjective value placed on the houses ($S$). The latter arises because people value the services of their house more than the market does: in a sense they enjoy a "householder's surplus," which is defined as the difference between the householder's subjective value of his house and the market value. The subjective value is the sum which the householder would consider just sufficient to compensate him for loss of the property, assuming he had to leave the noisy area altogether (Roskill, 1970); it is a recognition of the fact that market price is an incomplete measure of the

**Table 26.1** Different Categories of Hypothetical Compensation to Householders near an Airport.

| Householders | Hypothetical Compensation* |
|---|---|
| Moving due to the airport | $S + R + D$ |
| Moving anyway | $D$ |
| Staying | $N$ |
| New entrants | Zero |

*$S$: householders' surplus; $R$: removal costs; $D$: depreciation; $N$: noise annoyance disbenefit.

real value of a house. A home is obviously more than bricks and mortar, and whether because of friends, family, employment, love of the locality, or just plain inertia, people rightly value a house in their preferred area more highly than an identical one elsewhere.

Those people who would have moved irrespective of the airport will incur on moving a depreciation cost $(D)$, in addition to any costs which they would have incurred in the absence of the airport. Thus they suffer a capital loss of $D$.

The group which chooses to remain in spite of the construction of the airport was taken as suffering a noise annoyance disbenefit $(N)$, corresponding to the present value of the future noise nuisance.

## Computations of the Compensation

*Householders' surplus.* The figure for householders' surplus was arrived at by means of a social survey. The aim was to elicit directly from the householders the minimum sum they would accept to compensate them for moving to another area. After discovering what they thought was the market value of their house or apartment, the research team asked the respondents to suppose that a developer was willing to make an offer, and to say what price would just be sufficient to compensate them for leaving. The householders' surplus was measured by the percentage increase of the latter sum over the former.*

*Removal costs.* The second category of costs for those moving because of the airport—the removal costs $(R)$—were estimated at 16 percent of property value and were intended to cover both the removal expenditure and the disbenefits associated with the inconvenience of moving.

*Depreciation costs.* The third type of loss, the depreciation $(D)$, is clearly the same for those moving because of the airport, and those moving anyway. It was estimated from a survey of house prices around Gatwick (London's second airport) since the area was felt to be representative of the four sites under final consideration by the Commission. Real

---

*A different way of estimating the surplus would have been to ask how much the respondent would be willing to pay to stay in his present home, that is, to keep the airport away. This approach has the twin disadvantages of being an unreal question "how much will you pay to keep what you have," and of eliciting an answer which, if at all realistic, depends not so much on willingness, but on ability, to pay. The method adopted by the Roskill Commission avoids this source of bias, but has the drawback that a subjective valuation of the compensatory amount can be open ended.

estate agents in Gatwick were asked to assess the differential in price between houses within the various noise contours, and those outside the 35 NNI limit. This was done for low-, medium-, and high-priced properties, and revealed that depreciation increased with the price of the house as well as with noise levels. For example, in the 35–45 NNI area, the percentage depreciation of values for the three classes of property were 4.5, 9.4, and 16.4 respectively.

Within each noise zone and price category it was assumed that the average percentage depreciation figure reflected the median noise annoyance disbenefit. This simply means that for 50 percent of people, noise annoyance would be greater than that represented by the depreciation figure, and for the other 50 percent, it would be less.

Within each noise zone (between any two contour lines), the number of households in the three price ranges was known, but the frequency and intensity of annoyance at each NNI level* was not. To determine it, the McKennell social survey approach was used, which had devised a way of scoring aircraft noise annoyance on a five-point scale† (McKennell, 1963). A frequency distribution of annoyance scores was obtained for each NNI level; obviously the higher the NNI the more frequent were the high annoyance scores (i.e., the higher was the percentage of households recording). This is qualitatively illustrated by Fig. 26.1, which superimposes on one graph frequency distributions for each NNI.

For each distribution the median noise annoyance score could be calculated. It was then a simple matter to attribute the depreciation figure for each NNI to the median annoyance score‡ for that NNI, so as to arrive at a money value for all scores. Since for every NNI level the percentage of households with each annoyance score was known, it proved fairly easy to calculate the total number of households suffering monetary depreciation for every NNI level in the three different classes of property.§

*Noise annoyance costs.* The last type of cost (N) is the annoyance tolerated by those who do not move in spite of the airport. The suffering of this group symbolized was taken as an *annual* loss equal to the depreciation D in house prices due to noise.

---

*That is, how many people were annoyed and to what degree.

†See Appendix 1.

‡On the five-point scale.

§For example, if in the 55 NNI level the median annoyance score was four, and the depreciation on low house prices (average price = £3000) was 13 percent, then £390 is the cost of the noise for *each* household in the group. If there are 1000 low-priced houses at the 55 NNI level, the depreciation cost of noise is £390,000 for that group.

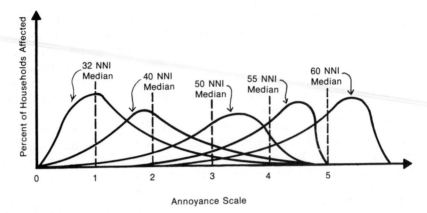

**Fig. 26.1**  Frequency distribution of annoyance scores for different NNI levels.

The final step in the Roskill Commission study was to calculate what fraction of the population in the vicinity of any site falls into the three groups.

The numbers moving irrespective of the proposed airport were estimated to run at 4.1 percent of the population of the noise-affected zones. After this, the fraction staying or moving was taken to be a function of the relative costs of either action: "Whether a particular household moves will therefore depend on the householder's own subjective values of $N$ and $S$ and on the values of $D$ and $R$ appropriate to the price of his house" (Roskill, 1971). The team estimated for each NNI level and house price, the percentage of people for whom $N$ exceeded $S + R + D$, who were then assumed to be the movers.

Finally, allowance was made for householders' surplus, $S$, and removal costs, $R$, to increase through time at the same rate as real income per head—3 percent a year, while depreciation $D$, was allowed to rise at 5 percent a year. These adjustments were made to incorporate the observed fact (from the house-price survey) that as incomes rise, quiet becomes more valuable.

## FURTHER CONSIDERATIONS

Despite the increasing sophistication of attempts, such as that of the Roskill Commission, to measure noise costs, the number of difficulties facing the analyst remains daunting. Let us mention—only briefly—some of the major problems.*

Of central importance to the Roskill model was the assumption that median noise annoyance disbenefits could be measured by the depreciation in house values. However useful an assumption this is, the Commission admitted in the Report that it was an unsubstantiated one (Roskill, 1971). Paul (1971) and others have pointed out that the differential for quiet in any house market depends partly on the ratio of quiet to noisy homes; the scarcer the quiet homes, the larger the price differential, and vice-versa. Also the ratio between noise sensitive and noise insensitive people in the area will affect by how much house prices fall. The Research Commission took cognizance of such criticisms and instructed its research team to perform the analysis on two alternative assumptions that would give an upper and lower limit to the noise costs: one, that $D$ measured the noise nuisance experienced by 75 percent of the population, and the other, that $D$ only measured the disbenefits of 25 percent of the population.

Perhaps a more potent criticism is that the fall in property value measures in fact how much the seller is willing to give up in order to get away from the noise. This measure is based, therefore, on "willingness to pay" and not on the "compensatory adjustment" required to bring the seller back to his pre-airport level of welfare, and to that extent it may underestimate the loss involved.†

Alternative models to estimate depreciation have been put forward by Wise (Roskill, 1970, 1971), Pearce (1972), and the British Airports Authority (BAA) (Plowden, 1970). The BAA model, perhaps agreeing with Pearce's conclusion that doubts as to the validity of any procedure based on property prices must remain (Pearce, 1972), decided to adopt a social survey technique in estimating the noise annoyance disbenefit, $N$.‡

In an ingenious manner the BAA team elicited from its respondents how much the price of an imaginary house, which fulfilled all their requirements, would have to be reduced if they were to accept certain defects.

---

*For detailed criticism of the Roskill noise-cost model see the work by Paul (1971), and the rejoinder by Walters (1972). A more general but no less critical discussion of cost–benefit analysis as applied to airports and air travel, is provided by Mishan (1970).

†In spite of the fact that the notion of "compensating" the noise sufferers was explicitly used only in evaluating household surplus, it was a conceptual underpinning of the entire analysis.

‡Although they did use a similar property model to the Roskill one to estimate $D$.

Among several "control defects" were three relating to different noise levels; the required reductions associated with these formed the basis of the costs. One of the more interesting results was that 54 percent of the respondents said they would not look at a house which had the defect of being close to a major airport (NNI 75). The same survey was used to arrive at householders' surplus, S.

Unfortunately there are problems facing this alternative method of pricing disbenefits, which are almost as intractable as those posed by the use of property price models. A critical question is what to do with "infinite responses." The Roskill research team's attempt to elicit S revealed that 8 percent would accept no price from a developer (the question was framed in these terms) as being sufficient compensation for moving; while out of the BAA respondents, in answer to the question of how much profit they would have to make on the sale of their present house (and repurchase of a comparable one, in a similar area, five or more miles away) to induce them to move, 38 percent said no amount of money would suffice.

The analysts in the former case valued the infinities at 200 percent of house value, and in the latter, at 20 percent. The dilemma is clear: purity in the calculations requires that an infinite sum be entered as being the household surplus, while practicality demands a finite figure. It is easy to concur with the opinion that "rather than play around with figures in this unmeaningful way, it would be better to exclude infinite costs from the numerical analysis, and treat what they represent in the way Norman churches and deaths ought to be treated—as items about which qualitative valuations cannot be escaped" (Paul, 1971).

In the use of surveys, the framing of questions (as well as the interviewer's technique) is all important. It is difficult to draw the line between posing unrealistic situations, or asking questions which give the respondent a false impression, and using a realistic survey which induces people to exaggerate or lie, in order to get rid of a proposed airport which threatens their homes.

A fundamental objection to noise-cost valuation, whether based on property prices or sample surveys, is that they will both underestimate the disbenefit since the ambient noise level is constantly rising. As the general level of noise increases, the individual will lack the context in which he can make a subjective valuation of the cost it imposes on him.*

---

*This "self-evident" notion has received substantiation in a survey of aircraft noise annoyance around London Airport (Second Survey, 1971).

In regard to property prices, Mishan has pointed out that absolute differences in noise, and therefore in price differentials, between two areas may stay constant as noise levels rise but disbenefit will have increased.

In the limiting case in which there is no escape whatever from aircraft noise in all inhabited areas of the country, noise being everywhere uniformly unbearable, noise-induced differences in property values will vanish; the measure of loss for all of us, on this indicator, being zero (Mishan, 1970).

## Equity

The final issue that we need to consider is the vexing one of equity. In Chapter 22 of this part we have seen that the Pareto optimum is the benchmark for policy in a static situation. Although exactly where society should be on the Pareto frontier is a value-judgment, there is general agreement that an attempt should be made to reach the frontier—that is, to make some better off without making anyone worse off.

The problem is that the Pareto optimum proves to be too rigorous a guide for policy, especially on a large investment project such as an airport, where undoubtedly some people will be worse off. An answer to this dilemma is to adopt a different criterion for such decisions, based on the idea of Kaldor and Hicks (Kaldor, 1939; Hicks, 1939). The essential idea is one of a "potential Pareto improvement;" that is, any change, as a result of which the gainers *could* compensate the losers and still remain better off themselves, is desirable. This can be expressed graphically by assuming a two-individual community, faced with a given utility possibility curve (Fig. 26.2).

The Pareto criterion only permits a move within the arc *EBD* as being an improvement. A move such as *E* to *A* is ruled out because Individual 1 gains at the expense of Individual 2. Under the Kaldor criterion, however, the move from *E* to *A* is an improvement since by a redistribution of wealth from Individual 1 to Individual 2, society can move along the utility frontier to a point such as *C*.

It is this theory which forms the basis of cost–benefit analysis. An investment project is justified if those who gain can potentially compensate those who lose, that is, if benefits exceed costs. Whether such compensation is actually paid is no concern of the analyst. He has proved that it *could* be paid, by getting us from point *E* to point *A* in Fig. 26.2; it is up to the government to take the necessary redistributive measures to bring society to point *C*. Thus justification of the pursual of allocative

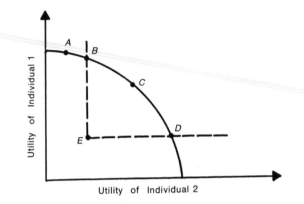

**Fig. 26.2**  Potential Pareto improvement for a community of two individuals.

improvements at the expense of distributional considerations, rests on the grounds that the progressive nature of the tax system will ensure that the economic growth generated by the project will be spread around to the losers too.

However, the machinery for dealing with equity issues is geared to the national rather than to the local levels to the extent that it depends on fiscal policy (Nwaneri, 1970). Thus issues will be more acute when a project such as an airport impinges very heavily on one area. While the beneficiaries from the airport are many and diffuse, the sufferers consist mainly of the communities living in the areas affected by the airport. In such cases even a tax system that would equalize all incomes would not completely remove the inequities of the situation. The concentration of ill-effects on relatively small numbers of people means that these effects are no longer marginal (Paul, 1971). In fact, as was seen in Chapter 4, individuals are precluded by law from seeking compensation through the courts.

More specific to noise–cost models based on property prices is the criticism that, the more expensive the houses in an area, the greater will appear the burden of noise. Yet it is not proven that low-income groups are any less perturbed by noise than their more affluent neighbors. The evidence seems to be confusing on this point. In the survey conducted around London Airport, only 29 percent of the "lowest" socio-economic group indicated that they found noise very disturbing and were worried about the problem, as opposed to 36 percent of the "highest" group, but 19 percent as against 8 percent said they thought their area was very noisy. Thus the authors of the survey state "This appears to be largely social attitude to noise related to the standard of amenity that they expect in their home environment since they are only marginally more sensitive to noise in general" (Second Survey, 1971).

Other problems concern the asymmetry in the evaluation of costs and benefits—for example in the Roskill Commission the social costs to people outside the 35 NNI level were not assessed, and the fact is that people may—and do—move into noisy areas, unaware of *how* bad the environment is, so that the relative cheapness of the houses is not adequate compensation. These are instances of the general question of how wide to cast the net in evaluating projects.

**Remedies**

Various proposals have been put forward for remedying the divorce of equity from efficiency in cost–benefit analysis (Nwaneri, 1970). Essentially the idea is to weight the costs and benefits according to the equity factors which are to be taken into account. For example Nwaneri recommends five weights (Nwaneri, 1970):

- income differences between beneficiaries and sufferers based on marginal tax rates;
- intrasite differences between sufferers;*
- the proportion of households affected;
- the extent of community disruption; and
- differences in the marginal utility of income.

Once the weights are calculated, they are applied either to scale down the costs and benefits to air travelers to a level comparable to the disbenefits incurred by the sufferers, or, to scale up the disbenefits of the sufferers while the costs and benefits to the beneficiaries are held constant.

Against this solution it can be said that some of the weights used, (e.g., marginal utility of income) and the method of their calculation, are debatable,† and that by tending to submerge so many considerations into a single figure, an appreciation of the breadth of the problem is lost. The

---

*For the same amount of noise nuisance, some lose more (in depreciation) than others. This may seem to conflict with our statement that property models were biased toward the rich, but income differences are ironed out by use of the first weight.

†This is basically the view of the Roskill Commission (Roskill, 1971).

more complete the analyst's work, the less the role of the decision maker—a point that will be stressed in the conclusions.

## APPENDIX:  ESTIMATES OF SOME COMPONENTS OF THE DOLLAR COST OF NOISE

Noise not only threatens health, disturbs or annoys, but also, if it has certain characteristics, can damage structures, impair the efficiency of work, and affect the output of farm animals. These are all effects that, if measurable, result in a direct dollar cost. However, the costs are very difficult to estimate accurately—thus explaining the claims of one recent report that "Data available on the entire subject of noise and its abatement are so rudimentary that they do not lend themselves to even the most primitive economic analysis" (EPA, 1971b). The problem, of course, is that noise is an external cost: there is no market in noise, and hence no price for it. Surrogate methods must be used to establish the social costs of noise pollution, or its corollary, the social benefits of noise abatement. In this chapter we have discussed in detail how the costs of aircraft noise can be evaluated by indirect means in cost–benefit models. Here we attempt to put a dollar figure on the costs of several sources of noise.

### The Effect of Noise on Efficiency

It has frequently been suggested that noise has an adverse effect on worker efficiency. The hypothesis is based primarily on the assumption that noise is a distraction, tending to reduce attention to work and/or increase the rate of fatigue. Numerous studies have been devised to test this hypothesis, with ambiguous results. Many have shown no significant deterioration of output under noisy conditions. Where an effect has been found, it has generally been adverse, although a few studies have shown an increase in efficiency when noise is present.

Severe difficulties arise in any attempt to summarize the data in a statistical manner, as there is little consistency in the experimental design. The majority have been laboratory experiments. However, they vary as to the type of task performed, the type and level of noise presented in both the "noisy" and the "quiet" situations, the duration of the experiment, and the measures used to define output. The first three sources of variance could (and probably did) affect experimental results, while the last makes comparison of results in a quantitative sense nearly impossible. Most experiments have attempted to determine the existence of a noise effect, but few have attempted to assess its magnitude in a particular situation.

One of the best known of the efficiency studies is the now classical one of Lancashire weavers, which actually took place in a work situation (Weston, 1935). The output of weavers wearing earplugs was compared with that of weavers with no ear defenders. The "personal efficiency" of the protected weavers increased 12 percent. However, the job was paced by equipment, and the overall gain in production was in the neighborhood of only 1 percent. Noise levels were 96 dB without earplugs and 81–86 dB with them. Some differences in weather conditions may have affected the results, as may the suggestive effect of wearing earplugs. However, this still represents one of the best field studies on the problem.

Another field study of note, conducted by Broadbent and Little, showed a definite noise effect upon film processors (Broadbent and Little, 1960). Unfortunately, the data were presented in the form of "errors made" and "incentive pay earned," which are not readily transferable to productivity.

Laboratory studies have attempted to study mechanical tasks, vigilance tasks, serial reaction tasks, and "intellectual" tasks (usually simple arithmetic or standardized tests). Perhaps the earliest major laboratory study was performed by D. A. Laird, using a mechanical task (Laird, 1933). The subjects were required to touch a metal stylus to a plate through holes in a moving tape. Noise levels were varied from 50 to 90 dB, with one run of the experiment lasting about 4 hours. Measures were in the form of errors made and holes missed; both were found to increase with noise. However, errors were a relatively small proportion of output and total output varied by less than 1 percent. Broadbent has run a number of laboratory tests on vigilance (Broadbent, 1953). His results show no immediate effect of noise on simple vigilance tasks. A decrease in efficiency does occur for more complex tasks and for serial reaction tasks. Again, the figures are not transferable into overall productivity measures.

Tests of mental tasks are difficult to find. One serious drawback to running a test is the difficulty of defining and measuring the output of an intellectual task. Tests of arithmetical ability show varying adverse effects indicating a fatigue effect and a possible after effect (Obata *et al.*, 1934). Clerical testing showed no effects, but its duration was only 30 minutes—hardly sufficient for a fatigue effect to appear (Smith, 1951).

To estimate the cost to the economy of whatever the overall decrease in efficiency might be is an extremely complex and uncertain undertaking. Yet, potentially these costs can be very high. For instance, in order to arrive at what at best can be only an extremely rough estimate for the United States, let us assume that the one-half of the working population exposed to noise greater than 80 dB (see Part V, Chapter 18) contributes to one-half of the G.N.P., and that a decrease in efficiency reduces this fraction of the G.N.P. by the same percentage. Thus, a loss in efficiency of only 1 percent would cause a reduction of approximately $5 billion in a G.N.P. of $1 trillion.

A recent World Health Organization Report estimated the total cost of accidents, absenteeism, inefficiency and compensation claims in the United States due to industrial noise at $4 billion annually (EPA, 1971a), a figure which is close to our rough estimate. Clearly these figures are sufficiently staggering to justify further enquiry.

The following sets of hypotheses are suggested by our current knowledge:

• Intermittent noise has a greater adverse effect than steady noise. (Although many researchers have suggested this, controlled studies on the subject are very limited.)

• Noise levels below 90 dB have no significant effect on work output, at least in well-structured tasks.

• The effect of noise decreases with duration as the subject adapts, increasing again as fatigue sets in.

• Noise may enhance the output of a very monotonous task through an "arousal" effect (e.g., Tiechner et al., 1963). Carpenter (1962) points out that noise seems to compensate for sleepiness. In some studies extra noise raised efficiency, and in others it reduced it (Broadbent, 1967). This may be explained by assuming that there is an optimum level of arousal for efficiency, and any departure from this level reduces efficiency.

• Personality differences may be very important. For example, a study indicates that extroverts may suffer more than introverts (Smith, 1951).

Thus far we have ignored the psychological and physiological effects on the worker which do not affect his performance. To be complete, an analysis of the costs of industrial noise would have to include an estimation of these "intangibles," which in reality may be more important than the noise cost of lower productivity.

## The Cost of Aircraft Noise

Although not an index of current aircraft noise costs in the United Kingdom, the figures generated by the Roskill Commission's research team using the methodology described in this chapter provide a rough guide to the size of the problem (Roskill, 1971).

The various sites were assessed on the basis of three main criteria: surface access, effects on defense, and noise. Some less important factors were also taken into account: air traffic control, site preparation, and land take. The noise costs for four sites are given in Table 26.2. The figures refer to the property affected within the 35 NNI contour, and exclude the costs of airport site and safety zone acquisition. The model was run for each year between 1971 and 2006, and the costs discounted to 1982, the projected year of opening. Since the original long list from which these four sites were chosen excluded any location which seemed likely to subject a population of 50,000 or more to over 50 NNI, it is likely that noise costs from existing major airports in the United Kingdom are considerably more than the highest figure shown of $180.5 million. In fact, since out of a total of 173 airports in the United Kingdom, there are some six major ones all located near conurbations, total aircraft noise costs are likely to be well in excess of $1 billion over the next 30 years.

Two indicative studies have been made by the EPA of aircraft noise costs in the United States (EPA, 1971b). The first was based on flyover easements, which are payments to property owners who suffer the unpleasant effects of aircraft operations (McClure, 1969). For the five airports studied the average cost of easement ranged from $1000 to $4625. On the basis of an estimated 15 million people exposed to undesirable

Table 26.2  Noise Costs of Four Alternative Sites for the Third London Airport (Source: Roskill, 1971).

| Site | Noise Costs ($ million)* |
|------|--------------------------|
| Nuthampstead | 180.5 |
| Cublington | 56.5 |
| Thurleigh | 39.0 |
| Foulness | 25.1 |

*All figures in 1969 prices discounted to 1982.

aircraft noise in 1968, and 24 million by 1978, the EPA estimated the costs to be between $4 billion and $18.5 billion for 1968, and $6 billion and $27.75 billion for 1978.*

In the second study the same estimate of 4 million households subjected to intolerable noise levels was used, together with figures based on the lowest average damages awarded per household in law suits brought against Los Angeles International Airport. The resulting estimate of the total cost of aircraft noise pollution was $75.2 billion. The EPA concluded that the plaintiffs must have inflated their damage claims, but pointed out that if 10 percent of the sums were paid in out-of-court settlements, the cost would be $7.5 billion, which is within the cost range given by the easements model.

In terms of structural damage the effects of subsonic jet aircraft are slight. On the other hand, the sonic boom caused by supersonic aircraft is made up of a transient increase of pressure above atmospheric pressure than can produce damage to plaster and windows. Data from the St. Louis Sonic Boom Study (see Part IV, Chapter 16) may be used to estimate the damage that could be caused by regularly scheduled SST overland flights. Let it be assumed, following Kryter (1967) that 50 million people are exposed to some 15 booms a day. Let us also assume, arbitrarily, that St. Louis is representative of all American cities, that the flight path over the eastern part of St. Louis is typical, and that Kryter's 50 million people are all living in cities. The total number, then, of valid incidents per flight per million population (that is, incidents for which damage claims were allowed), would be 2.72.

Taking $71 as the average claim (Nixon and Hubbard, 1965), the daily damage would be $150,000 ($2.72 \times 50 \times 15 \times \$71$) and the yearly damage $54 million, in 1965 prices. If we revise this figure in line with the rise in the cost of living index we arrive at the estimate of roughly $72 million per year by 1973 prices.

More recent figures for sonic boom damage can be gleaned from the damages awarded in the United Kingdom after some twenty trial runs of the Anglo-French Concorde were made over selected areas on the west coast. Total compensation paid amounted to roughly $72,000—3600 per flight (Adams and Haigh, 1972). It must be noted that these tests were carried out over sparsely populated areas, and over the Irish Sea.

---

*An average family size of four persons living on one parcel of land was assumed. In 1968, there were roughly 4 million plots whose easement compensation ranged from $1000 to $4625.

## The Cost of Noise from Surface Transportation

The EPA has made estimates of the cost of land acquisition and relocation of families in areas affected by noise from automobile transportation (EPA, 1971b). Assuming some 268,000 acres to be subject to undesirable noise levels by the nation's major urban freeway system, and an average land (plus structures) value of $10,000 per acre, the cost of noise easements would total about $2.68 billion.

On the basis of a population density of 5000 people per square mile, some 2.1 million people would be affected. The cost of relocation for 500,000 families would amount to an additional $1.25 billion ($2500 per family, based on expenditure figures allowed under the Federal Aid Highway Act of 1968).

Acquisition and relocation costs combined, therefore, total nearly $4 billion (1970 prices). This figure provides a rough approximation of the noise costs of only urban freeways in the United States, and does not include costs due to other types of road, nor other forms of ground transportation.

The conclusion that can be drawn from these extremely tentative cost estimates is that the external costs of noise pollution are extremely high. The recurrent costs accruing from industry and from aircraft noise alone amount to at least $12 billion—and this is probably a low estimate.

## REFERENCES

Adams, J. G. V. and Haigh, W. Booming discorde. *National Geographical Magazine*, London, July 1972.

Broadbent, D. E. Noise paced performances and vigilance tasks. *British Journal of Psychology*, 1953, **44**.

Broadbent, D. E. Private communication, 1967.

Broadbent, D. E. and Little, E. O. J. Effects of noise reduction in a work situation. *Occupational Psychology*, 1960, **34**.

Carpenter, A. Effects of noise on performance and productivity. NPC Symposium, The Control of Noise. London HMSO, 1962.

EPA (U.S. Environmental Protection Agency). Public hearings on noise abatement and control. Vol. III, 1971.(a)

EPA (U.S. Environmental Protection Agency). The economic impact of noise. December 31, 1971.(b)

Hicks, J. R. The foundations of welfare economics. *Economic Journal*, Vol. XLIX. London: MacMillan, December 1939.

Kaldor, N. Welfare propositions and interpersonal comparisons of utility. *Economic Journal*, Vol. XLIX. London: MacMillan, September 1939. Reprinted in: *Essays in value and distribution*, London, 1960.

Kryter, K. D. Acceptability of aircraft noise. *Journal of Sound and Vibration*, 1967, **5**.

Laird, D. A. The influence of noise on production and fatigue, as related to pitch, sensation level, and steadiness of the noise. *Journal of Applied Psychology*, 1933.

McClure, P. T. *Indicators of the effect of jet noise on the value of real estate.* Santa Monica Calif.: Rand Corporation, July 1969.

McKennell, A. C. *Aircraft noise annoyance around London (Heathrow) Airport.* London: Central Office of Information, 1963.

Mishan, E. J. What is wrong with Roskill? *Journal of Transport Economics and Policy*, Vol. IV, No. 3. London: LSE, September 1970.

Mishan, E. J. The ABC of cost–benefit. *Lloyd's bank review.* London: Lloyd's Bank, July 1971.

Nixon, C. W. and Hubbard, H. H. Results of USAF-NASA-FAA flight program to study community responses to sonic booms in the St. Louis area. NASA TN D-2705, May 1965.

Nwaneri, V. C. Equity in cost–benefit analysis. *Journal of Transport Economics and Policy*, Vol. IV, No. 3. London: LSE, September 1970.

Obata *et al.* The effects of noise on human efficiency. *Journal of the Acoustical Society of America*, 1934, **5**.

Paul, M. E. Can aircraft noise nuisance be measured in money? *Oxford Economic Papers*, Vol. 23, No. 3. London: OUP, November 1971.

Pearce, D. The economic evaluation of noise generating and noise abatement projects. *Problems of environmental economics.* Paris: OECD 1972.

Plowden, S. *The cost of noise*, London: Metra Consulting Group, 1970.

Prest, A. R. and Turvey, R. Cost–benefit analysis: A survey. *Surveys of Economic Theory*, Vol. III. New York: MacMillan, 1968.

Roskill. Commission on The Third London Airport. In: *Papers and proceedings.* London: HMSO, 1970.

Roskill. Commission on The Third London Airport. The Report of the Commission. London: HMSO, 1971.

*SECOND SURVEY of aircraft noise annoyance around London (Heathrow) Airport.* London: HMSO, 1971.

Smith, K. R. Intermittent loud noise and mental performance. *Science*, 1951.

Tiechner, W. H. *et al.* Noise and human performance, a psychophysiological approach. *Ergonomics*, January 1963, **6**.

Walters, A. A. Mrs. Paul on aircraft noise—a correction. *Oxford Economic Papers*, Vol. 24, No. 2. London: OUP, July 1972.

Weston, H. C. and Adams, S. The performance of weavers under varying conditions of noise. 15th Annual Report of the Industrial Health Research Board, Report No. 20. London, HMSO, 1935.

# Part VII  Conclusions

# CHAPTER 27

# *Toward the Future*

## INTRODUCTION

In this book we have discussed important aspects of a complex socio-technological problem, noise pollution. It now remains to elaborate upon some of the deeper issues that we have broached. There is no doubt that the problem of noise is serious. Large segments of the population in an industrialized society are exposed to high levels of noise, not only at their place of work, but also in their residences and in their leisure activities. In the United Kingdom, for example, more than 10 percent of the population is disturbed by the noise at a single airport, London Heathrow.

Even with the relatively ambitious steps currently being taken or envisioned to control noise in most countries, sound levels and exposure to noise will remain high, and possibly increase. At the same time rising living standards will bring about demands for better environmental quality and probably lead to more vigorous and more organized protests against noise. These protests may even be triggered by lower noise levels than in the past, for it is highly likely that as the public acquires more amenities it will want to be exposed to "comfortable" rather than merely tolerable levels of sound (Bauer, 1970).

In the 1950's the problem of noise was not generally perceived as urgent. In Europe there were few cars, and in the United States few airplanes. Everywhere little was known about the consequences of noise, and noise abatement. Many people accepted and were even proud of automobile noise. In Europe as well as in the United States there were very few airports and aircraft movements, and therefore very few people

379

affected. The jet engine had not yet arrived on the scene with the much higher noise level in comparison to the propeller planes. The prevailing attitude in Europe and in the United States was "Thank God for jobs." In Western Europe, recovering from World War II, and in the United States, where there were memories of the depression of the early 1930's, the unions pressed more for employment and high rates of pay than for solutions to environmental problems that did not appear to be as serious as silicosis or injuries.

What has dramatically altered noise levels since the 1950's is the enormous growth in population and per capita income and in industrialization; industry has also become more noisy because machines have become more powerful.

Furthermore, the lag time between the development of a given problem and a change in social attitudes and goals leading to action on the problem is long in our society; an engineer would say that the feedback circuits are slow (see Appendix 2). An example is the time needed to establish appropriate government agencies. Characteristically, major changes in policy in the United States occur with changes in administration. From 1952 to 1975 there have only been five presidents, Eisenhower, Kennedy, Johnson, Nixon and Ford. It is probably fair to say that the Eisenhower administration was not very concerned with the environment. The Kennedy and certainly the Johnson administration were more active in this area. Nixon's first term continued with less enthusiasm the environmental improvements that Johnson started; the second term, heavily affected as it was by the Watergate affair, was not very favourable to further environmental policy changes. Finally, in the Ford administration, the energy crisis has again overshadowed environmental concerns. In European countries, political changes are more rapid than in the U.S., and continuity in carrying out policies is more difficult to achieve.

## VALUE-JUDGMENTS AND DECISION MAKING

A recurring theme throughout this book has been that of values—personal, economic, technological, and social values. When these values conflict, they give rise to difficult questions: What noise levels should workers tolerate? What is the correct definition of hearing loss? (Is there indeed such a thing as a correct definition?) Who bears the cost of noise abatement? Can a dollar figure be put on good hearing, or on a tranquil environment?

It would seem to us self-evident that the ultimate response to these questions is a political one. Decisions, implicit or explicit, rational or irrational, democratic or autocratic, have to be, and are, made on these issues. Both the manner and the result of such decision making have implications which are fundamental to the type of society we are creating. While a full analysis of the political process is obviously beyond the scope of this book, it is useful to distinguish three different approaches to the solution of social questions involving noise.

## The Traditional Method

According to the traditional approach, decisions are made by elected politicians and appointed civil servants in deference to a host of varied considerations, some of which are never stated explicitly. In Part VI we discussed economic values at length and showed how misleading they are—in the sense that, uncorrected, they yield external costs such as noise. The role of the state in remedying this is widely accepted, although opinions still differ as to the best method. But what if the government itself is involved in the advancement of activities or projects which are polluting?

A prime example of this situation is the development of the supersonic aircraft (SST). This is a project that transcends mere economic values, and produces vast negative externalities. In statements made to the U.S. Senate Appropriations Committee on March 11, 1971, 10 of the United States' most eminent economists analyzed a government official's testimony on the United States SST.* Among them were three former members and one former chairman of the Council of Economic Advisors, as well as Milton Friedman and Wassily Leontief, men not normally in close agreement. Their conclusions were unanimous: the project was a gross blunder and should be abandoned immediately. The Nobel prize winner Paul Samuelson said: "In this day there is no excuse for pyramid building to make work, and add to a nation's spurious glory. Public expenditure must always take into account human as well as dollar factors. But in this case any realistic cost–benefit analysis will reach the same conclusion to which at every stage in the history of this project non-political commissions have arrived— namely that government subsidy of the SST or similar supersonic aircraft is at this stage of technology and economic development both on economic and a human disaster" (Samuelson, 1971).

---

*Mr. Magruder's testimony, made originally before the House Subcommittee on Transportation.

The arguments against the SST which led to its concellation in the United States apply with equal force to the Anglo-French plane. The project stands indicted on even the cost accountant's terms; it will never recover the estimated $2.5 billion that the French and British taxpayers (no commercial aircraft corporation would touch it) will have spent on research and development ($1.4 billion by April 1972), and only on the most generous estimates of sales can it recover the production costs of $75 million per plane.

The long catalog of environmental problems that the operation of a substantial fleet of this aircraft would create for mankind points up the ease with which ordinary prudence, social welfare, and even profitability, can be thrown to the winds by the traditional political process. The process worked well in the case of the U.S. decision concerning the SST but not in the case of the Anglo-French decision. Paul Foot, M.P., has summarized the position: "Governments and Oppositions on both sides of the Channel and of varying complexions were committed. Indeed they were tied up in what appeared to be an inextricable legal tangle, as the Labor Cabinet discovered when it made its attempt to escape in October 1964. Money, national prestige, international law, scientific pride, and what the Orientals are supposed to call face, all lined up on one side" (Wiggs, 1971).

One can conclude that the decision-making process which produced this decision, has at the very least some serious faults. Ross Stainton, Deputy Managing Director of BOAC has said, "Magnificent as Concorde is as a technical achievement, a rational assessment of cost and benefit has yet to be made" (Times, 1970).

### Cost–Benefit Analysis

An alternative method of decision making—cost–benefit analysis—holds the possibility of avoiding the pitfalls of the "old-style" politics so dramatically evinced by the example of the Concorde. Cost–benefit analysis is the most famous member of the whole new "intellectual technology" which has sprung up since World War II and which encompasses operational research, systems analysis, and cybernetics.

The possibility of making government decisions more rational is raised by those who feel that we have the information and techniques available to be able to solve social questions on a scientific basis. The notion of a group of experts routinely solving society's problems on the basis of elaborate cost–benefit and system analyses is accepted by some practitioners in the field. For instance, Stafford Beer has a lofty view of the role of cyberneticians. "It is that we are responsible. We are not responsible because we have been elected to govern affairs; we are responsible because cybernetics, that science of effective organization, is our profession. Such understanding of the subject as there is, we have. Therefore we must speak out .... We do not know as much as we would like to know before making such a stand as is here proposed .... We must use such tools as we have, and use them now .... Some who are here, and some great men and wonderful friends now dead, guessed that the tool-kit would not be finished in time. Today we know that the moment has come for us to start work, and we must do the best we can"* (Beer, 1971).

While Beer sees cybernetic control (via a meta-system) as the solution to society's problems, others take a more cautious, but essentially similar view: "the legislature could enact a bill setting up an engineering and economic computing center, which with respect to any particular externality, could apply the best methods available to determine what is the optimal amount of tax and subsidy to reduce the externality. It could then provide that whatever decision was produced by the technicians would automatically become law without further legislative action" (Tullock, 1970).

Aside from the fundamentally anti-democratic nature of the last step, the difficulty with this approach is that on a technical level we are still faced with the problem of putting a price on external costs, and since there can be no element of subjective decision making, *all* costs must be quantified. But this is merely postponing a value-judgment. As we have seen in Part VI, surrogate measures of value can be used to put a price on noise, etc., but considerable difficulties remain with even a sophisticated property-price model and there are many factors which elude even this process.

For example, in many cost–benefit analyses the question of putting a value on human life, or on human health, arises. This is done by adding the net present value of a man to some arbitrary figure for "subjective" loss (the former being his expected future lifetime production minus consumption discounted back to the date of death, the latter represents the anguish caused by the tragedy or loss).

But how can we put a value on anguish? We can no more do that than we can measure the cost of a medieval church or a historic building due to be demolished to make room for an airport, as the Roskill Commission at

---

*Reprinted by permission of *Futures*.

first attempted to do (Roskill, 1970).* Can a cash figure represent the loss due to destruction of wilderness areas and the wildlife in them? In the case of a national park where an entrance fee is paid, the cost–benefit analyst would value the loss at the fee, the travel costs incurred getting there, and some estimate of consumer surplus (what visitors would pay to see the park over and above the entrance fee). But if the amenity is free as in the case of quiet, and nobody counts how many people enjoy it, how then is the loss to be evaluated? The British Government decided (against the Roskill Commission's advice) to choose as the site for its third London Airport the coast at Foulness. This area is one of the most beautiful and desolate stretches of coast and marshland in England, and is also a nesting ground for the rare Brent geese. What price can we put on such things? (It is to be noted that in 1974 the U.K. Government abandoned completely the idea of creating a third airport for London).

Thus, there is no escape from subjective value-judgment by recourse to cost–benefit analysis. Doubt can even be cast on the meaning of some of the values which can be measured. For example, in the design of a transportation system, while noise is a cost, one of the benefits is travel time saved by the proposed system. This is usually valued as some fraction of the hourly wage for business travelers. For vacationers and children a lower figure is used. The time savings between a given route and a less noisy one may be very small, a matter of minutes. But as soon as these minutes are priced and accumulated for total passenger movements up to say the year 2000, the entry in the benefit ledger can be enormous. A saving of 6 minutes for 100 million passenger trips (for simplicity, equally divided among adult business and leisure) would, on the basis of the values used by the Roskill Commission research team yield a saving (benefit) of around $47 million per year (Roskill, 1971).† Yet how are we to relate this figure derived from saving 6 minutes per person with the noise annoyance caused to any substantial number of people?

### Participation

Cost–benefit analysis and other systems analysis techniques cannot therefore be a substitute for political decision making. But, as we have

---

*It later gave up this hope (Roskill, 1971).

†The 1968 value of business time was taken as 87.5¢ per hour, and that of leisure time as 68.75¢ per hour. A time saving of one-tenth of an hour gives us 87.5¢ × 50 million journeys + 6.875¢ × 50 million journeys = $47,187,500. The money values used are the low estimates of the Roskill research team.

seen, neither can the traditional political process be relied upon for rational and equitable decision making in areas involving values, because it tends to reflect the pervasive influence of pressure groups, for instance what has been called the urban-industrial complex (Goodman, 1972), rather than the interests of individuals. Corporate and labor influence is more concentrated spatially and financially than that of communities, and the need is to find a way of providing an equitable balance of power.

Although participation has been much abused as a catch phrase, we feel it can be a mechanism through which the people who are, or will be affected by noise can influence the decision-making process, both in the work place and in the community. A cardinal requirement for successful participation is that there be provision for more decentralized decision making and for maximum possible dissemination of information by politicians and bureaucrats.

As we have shown repeatedly in this book (in Part V for example), there is no such thing as the objective or non-ideological expert weighing up in a dispassionate manner what is to be done. The very selection of which facts to use implies some criterion as to what facts are important or relevant. Thus a price tag is put on the life of a victim in a traffic accident, the cost of noise outside a certain NNI contour is ignored, or hearing damage is defined as ability to comprehend sounds at given frequencies and at a given threshold. The argument for participation is simply that since unbiased judgment is intrinsically difficult or impossible, it is much better that the biases of those who are going to live with the results of policies actually determine such policies.

A society in which the community is the decision-making unit avoids the twin evils of central political control and value-assigning computations by the "rational managers" of society. It must be recognized that such a participatory system might well be inefficient in the traditional sense. For example, it would be a long and costly process for local neighborhoods to have a say in the location of a regional highway system.

But this inefficiency may well be the price of a more democratic decision-making process. In the developed countries, man is no longer engaged in a constant struggle for the necessities of life. As Alfred Marshall wrote in 1920 ". . . the nation has grown in wealth, in health, in education, and in mortality; and we are no longer compelled to subordinate almost every other consideration to the needs of increasing the total produce of industry" (Marshall, 1964). The rich nations of the world are now freed from exclusive concern with production and consumption to comtemplate some of the non-economic aspects of civilized social life. High on the list of such aspects we would put quiet. The present danger in that economic recession, inflation and the energy crisis will distract attention from environmental issues.

## Simulation

In Part V we raised the possibility of worker participation in setting standards for occupational noise exposure. Since the recent study by Burns and Robinson (see Chapter 3) we are in a position to give workers a fair idea of what risk they are undergoing in their employment.

Tapes are in existence which can simulate the distorted or muffled way in which a damaged cochlea perceives sound; tables can now be constructed which make it possible to suggest to someone contemplating work in a noisy environment what the odds are that after a given number of years he will hear sounds in the same distorted manner.

Simulation techniques can also be used when trying to assess community reaction to noise. This has been recommended as a means of avoiding the drawbacks of more formal ways of valuing intangibles like quiet (Plowden, 1970). The method used by the Roskill Commission, as we have seen in Part VI, was based on property prices; but variables other than noise affect prices. An alternative, a sample survey, was used by the British Airports Authority's Research Team in presenting their evidence to the Commission. The survey, perforce, relies upon people's stated intentions rather than what they actually do. Simulation of airport or freeway noise by tape recordings offers the possibility of gauging people's reactions more accurately. This can be viewed as a way of assessing the "endurance costs" for a particular noise. "People would (then) be asked to accept a machine in their house for a certain length of time which would play the tape continuously. To reward them for taking part in the experiment, respondents would be offered a certain sum of money" . . . (Plowden, 1970). Thus simulation could be used as a way of placing value on quiet as part of a cost–benefit analysis, or as a method of increasing people's awareness of risk. Not only must a community affected by a proposed airport or freeway be party to the planning and decision-making process, and be informed of the social and economic changes which will result, but it must also have some advance idea of the environmental effects. In the case of noise pollution, simulation methods would seem to provide for this.

## THE UNIQUE NATURE OF NOISE AS A POLLUTANT

The pervading issues of value-judgments and quantification of values can be seen more clearly in the case of noise than in the case of other pollutants which can cause death.* This consideration underscores the important fact that major differences exist between noise and other forms of pollution.

First, noise is everywhere. It is not as easy to control as those sources of water and air pollution which are more concentrated. Even with some concentrated sources of noise, such as airplanes near airports or ambulance sirens, reduction of noise through operational procedures can carry considerable risk. In the case of airplanes, for instance, steeper landings and reduced power climb-outs on takeoff cannot be made beyond a certain safety limit.

In the second place, although certain effects of noise, like those of many other pollutants, accumulate in the organism, if noise pollution were to cease there would be no noise residual in the environment, as there would be in the case of water pollution (for example, pesticide residuals) and air pollution.

Third, unlike air and water pollution, the effects of noise are felt only close to the source. While a river can carry pollution long distances downstream, noise problems are more local, making it difficult to mobilize support from distant groups to solve them.

Fourth, an essential awareness of noise and motivation to reduce the problem are not present. The ubiquitousness of noise and the importance of hearing, for example, to language acquisition and to thinking are generally underestimated. People are more prone to complain and demand political action about air pollution or water pollution than about noise. Noise is not effectively internalized because workers are not aware of the risk. Therefore, effective public measures against noise will be taken only when it is considered as pressing a problem as air pollution.

Fifth, noise is not likely to have genetic effects, while some effects of air and water pollution, such as radioactive pollution, can. Thus, even if the problem were to become much worse during our generation and the next, a solution would probably prevent harm to future generations. However, the annoyance, frustration, impedance of learning and the

---

*Indeed, noise pollution, which from the economic viewpoint is obviously not well internalized in the work place, opens up the thorny question of whether other forms of pollution, especially air pollution, are similarly not internalized in the work place.

general stress which noise pollution causes, all can have severe effects on our children's environment, and therefore on that of future generations.

Noise can be more important to the quality of life of an urban dweller, particularly a person who spends his entire life in the city, than the preservation of nature in some distant region. It also affects suburbanites who are moving away from the city, carrying to the new environment the power and the noise of the automobile and the lawnmower.

## THE ISSUE OF PUBLIC TRANSPORT

What must be done to reduce this source of noise? Obviously all programs aimed at quieting cars, trucks, airplanes, and machines at work should be supported. Possible approaches have been discussed throughout the book. But, all told, these approaches are only a stopgap; beyond them we must look to a reorganization of the way in which industrialized societies carry out their activities. Given the enormous significance of vehicles and airplanes as a source of noise, one of the major issues is that of public transport. Low population density areas, the suburbs, depend on automobiles. At this moment there is no economically viable public transport system that can effectively convey the traffic to and from these areas. In the United States the car is in effect, for many people, even poor people, the only form of transportation available. American cities and suburbs have been made possible by the automobile, and so have, to an increasing degree, European suburbs. Similarly, the airplane is at this moment the only rapid transportation link not only for large distances, but also for medium ones, particularly in the United States.

More effective public transportation systems, revitalized railroads, new urban systems, are essential ingredients (but clearly not the only ones) in a long-range solution to the noise problem. The issue of public transport also impinges on the problems of air pollution, of energy conservation, and of access to public services. Thus its solution becomes one of the most urgent and fruitful activities in which our society should become engaged.

Given the present technico-economic constraints of the problem, it is necessary to look at ways in which social practices could alleviate the problem. For instance, sharing of private transportation would have a beneficial effect not only on energy consumption, but also on air pollution and noise. A reversal in leisure patterns would help—sail boats, not motorboats; bicycles, not motorcycles, etc. One way of encouraging these practices would be more restrictive noise laws on leisure grounds, lakes, and harbors, and the establishment of *noise privacy as a major civilized covenant* (including, among other things, privacy from loud television advertisements or from the clatter of dishes in cafeterias).

## EPILOGUE

If it were possible to draw up a list of the various problems facing society, noise would rank among the most insidious. In the first place, the problem is enormous—vast numbers of people are exposed to noise at work, while traveling, and at rest. Secondly, the severity of the ill-effects has been underplayed and overlooked for too long. Thirdly, the nature of noise as an environmental stressor may well have a synergistic effect with other stressors and other forms of pollution. Finally, as we have seen, the very unique nature of noise as a pollutant presents us with very complex technical, social, political and legal issues.

For thousands of years man showed that he could adapt to the increasingly artificial world he was creating for himself, since changes took place so slowly as to mitigate undesirable effects and allow adaptation to take place gradually. The question now, however, is whether there are limits to adaptation of this kind; there is no aural equivalent to the eyelid, and no refuge for the factory worker or the tired city-dweller from the surrounding din. Not only is our physical environment itself deteriorating but our very means of perceiving it are becoming damaged. Society is built on the use and comprehension of words; any attack on that facility is an attack on civilization itself.

## REFERENCES

Bauer, R. A. Predicting the future. Transportation noise—a symposium on acceptability criteria, Washington, D.C., 1970.

Beer, S. The liberty machine. *Futures*, December, 1971, **3** (4), 338–348.

Goodman, R. *After the planners.* Harmondsworth: Pelican Books, 1972.

Marshall, A. *Principles of economics.* London: MacMillan, 1964.

Plowden S. *The cost of noise.* London: Metra Consulting Group, 1970.

Roskill. Commission on The Third London Airport. In *Papers and proceedings*, Volume VII, Stage III. Research and Investigation Parts 1 & 2. London: HMSO, 1970.

Roskill. Commission on The Third London Airport. The Report of the Commission. London: HMSO, 1971.

Samuelson, P. A. Testimony for Senate Appropriations Committee. March 11, 1971.

Times. (*The Times* London), *Business news*, October 13, 1970.

Tullock, G. *Private wants, public means.* New York: Basic Books Inc., 1970.

Wiggs, R. *Concorde—the case against supersonic transport.* London: Pan/Ballantine, 1971.

# Appendixes

# APPENDIX 1

# Measures and Indices of Noise and Annoyance

In this Appendix we briefly review basic definitions of acoustical parameters, and we describe some of the most commonly used measures and indices of noise and annoyance (summarized in Table A1.1). The descriptions given here are generally not mathematical and are far from encompassing the wide range of measures and indices that have been developed to characterize noise and annoyance. They are simply intended to provide the reader with a semi-technical appreciation of the nature of the measures and indices that have been used throughout the book. For more quantitative and comprehensive descriptions, the reader is referred to specialized references (Beranek, 1971; Power, 1971; EPA, 1971; Lyon, 1973; Harris, 1957).

In the context of the noise pollution problem, noise measurements are not an end unto themselves; their chief purpose is to provide an index of disturbance or annoyance, which is the primary psychophysiological factor governing reactions to noise, and the socio-technological actions necessary to control noise.

## NOISE: BASIC DEFINITIONS

### Sound Pressure

The increase or decrease in pressure with respect to the atmospheric pressure caused by the propagation of a disturbance (sound) through air, or for that matter through any other media, such as walls, plates or water is known as sound pressure. The sound pressures generated by human

393

**Table A1.1**   Summary of Some of the Most Frequent or Effective Noise-Rating Procedures.

|  | Units | Characteristics |
|---|---|---|
| A-weighted sound level | dB(A) | Simple measuring technique;<br>High correlation with NC and PNC;<br>Suitable for measure of fluctuating noise;<br>Adequate for predicting general public acceptance of most community noises |
| Equivalent sound level ($L_{EQ}$) |  | Most recent and simple single measure of noise which best correlates with cumulative noise effects;<br>Correlates also with many other noise effects |
| Loudness level | Phons | Subjective rating by listeners, by comparison with a narrow band reference noise |
| Loudness | Sones | Numerical designation of comparative loudness levels |
| Perceived Noise Level (PNL) | PNdB | Correlates with aircraft annoyance;<br>For steady sounds;<br>Takes into account both intensity and frequency of noise |
| Effective Perceived Noise Level (EPNL) | EPNdB | A refinement of PNL;<br>For fluctuating sounds;<br>Takes also into account maximum tone and duration of noise |
| Noise Exposure Forecast (NEF) |  | A major improvement over EPNL;<br>Takes into account mix of aircraft, time of day, etc.<br>Tends to be superceded by $L_{EQ}$ |
| Noise and Number Index (NNI) |  | Introduced and used in the U.K.; |
| Composite Noise Rating (CNR) |  | Used extensively in the past in the US;<br>Correlates with aircraft annoyance;<br>Tends to be superceded by $L_{EQ}$ |
| Noise index (R); Night noise index (R') |  | Introduced and used in France<br>Correlates with aircraft annoyance |
| Speech Interference Level (SIL) and Preferred Speech Interference Level (PSIL) | dB | For steady noise;<br>Rates ability to interfere with conversation |
| Noise Criteria (NC) curves |  | For rating of reasonably steady noises in buildings;<br>Combines speech interference and maximum permissible level of noise |
| Preferred Noise Criteria (PNC) curves |  | A refinement of NC, still experimental |

**Table A1.1** (continued)

| | Units | Characteristics |
|---|---|---|
| Noise Pollution Level ($L_{NP}$) | dB(NP) | For fluctuating noise, and for mixtures of different types of noises, both steady and intermittent; Considers both mean energy and range of variation of noise; Still experimental |
| Transport Noise Index (TNI) | dB(A) | Based on average noise level and noise increases over background; Fails to consider number and duration of noise occurrances |
| Single Event Noise Exposure Level (SENEL) | dB(A) | For sounds received from single-event noises; Integrates intensity over entire intensity of noise |
| Community Noise Equivalent Level (CNEL) | dB(A) | Essentially the same as $L_{DN}$ (a derivative of $L_{EQ}$) except for treatment of nighttime noises |

speech are very small, averaging 1 microbar, or 1 million times less than the normal atmospheric pressure of $1.013 \times 10^5$ newtons* per square meter at sea level. At the low end the ear responds to pressures as low as two ten-thousandths (0.0002) of a microbar, and at the high end to pressures as high as 2000 microbars.

## Sound Power and Intensity

Sound power, the acoustic power emitted by the sound, is measured in watts. Sound intensity is the power per unit area. It is usually measured indirectly, in terms of the square of the time-average of the instantaneous sound wave, and of the characteristic resistance of the medium.

## Decibels

As we have seen, there is an enormous difference between the sound pressures of the softest sounds people can hear, 0.0002 $\mu$bar and the loudest sounds they can tolerate, 2000 $\mu$bar. The ratio is 10,000,000 to one. This ratio is shrunk to manageable size by the use of a logarithmic scale.

---

*The newton is the unit of force in the MKS (meter, kilogram, second). It equals 0.2248 lb (force) or $10^5$ dynes (the unit of force in the CGS (centimeter, gram, second system).

Thus if one sound pressure $P_1$ is ten times another $P_2$, the sound pressure level is said to be 20 decibels (abbreviated to dB) higher. If $P_1 = 100\,P_2$ then the sound pressure level (SPL) is said to be 40 decibels higher, etc. In other words, an increase in sound pressure level by 10 times is measured as a doubling in decibels. The relevant formula is SPL (dB) $= 20\log_{10}(P_1/P_2)$. Thus a sound pressure level of 140 dB above the (usual) reference sound pressure of $0.0002\,\mu$bar represents a sound pressure $10^7$ times the reference sound pressure. The zero on the scale is an arbitrary level, corresponding to the threshold of hearing for the average person at 1000 Hz. The correspondence between sound-pressure levels in decibels and sound pressure in microbars is given in Fig. A1.1, together with the correspondence between sound-power levels in decibels and sound power in watts. The concept of decibel—of a logarithmic scale with a specified reference level—is a general one that can be used for sound pressures,

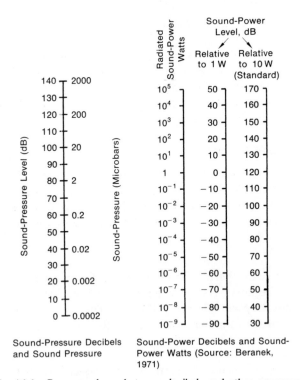

Sound-Pressure Decibels and Sound Pressure

Sound-Power Decibels and Sound-Power Watts (Source: Beranek, 1971)

**Fig. A1.1**  Correspondence between decibels and other measures.

sound power, sound intensity, etc. Whenever measurements are made in decibels, they are called measurements of sound levels.

### Frequency

Most sounds involve more than one cycle of overpressure and under-pressure with respect to the ambient pressure. The number of cycles per unit time defines the frequency of the sound. The most common unit of sound frequency is the cycle per second (cps), which is also called the Hertz (Hz). The ear of a normal adult human has the ability to hear a very broad spectrum of frequencies from 20 to 20,000 Hz. For other animals the range can be even broader—for instance, for the dog it extends to over 100,000 Hz.

Pure-tone sounds are those in which the sound waves (sound pressure) fluctuate sinusoidally at a constant frequency. In general, machinery that rotates comes close to emitting pure-tone sounds, or combinations of pure-tone sounds (combinations of harmonics). There are other sounds of an asperiodic nature, such as the sound of a rocket or a dishwasher, which cannot be decomposed into a set of harmonics (but can be described as the result of an infinite number of pure tones of different frequencies and amplitudes, spaced infinitesimally apart from each other). The *period* ($T$) of a sound is the reciprocal of the frequency. The *speed* of sound ($C$) is determined by the ambient conditions—the nature of the medium, its temperature, pressure, etc. For an ideal gas (a reasonable assumption for air at normal environmental temperatures and pressures), the speed of sound depends only on temperature.*

The range of frequencies of pure sounds can be subdivided in a number of ways, such as decade bands, octave bands, third octave bands. Figure A1.2 shows the center frequencies of such bands. Each decade band covers a 10–1 range of frequencies, and each octave band a 2–1 range. The utility of the third octave band stems in part from the fact that they encompass approximately one-tenth of a decade frequency band.

The practical use of frequency bands in describing a noise source is exemplified by Fig. A1.3, which shows the one-third octave-band level for an executive jet aircraft at an altitude of 500 ft during an approach operation. Sound-pressure levels from a series of contiguous bands can

---

*The speed $c$ is given by: $c = 20.05 \sqrt{T}$ m/s, where $T$ is the obsolute temperature in degrees Kelvin (temperature in degrees centigrades plus 273.2). For instance, at 20°C (68°F), $c = 20.05 \sqrt{293.2} = 300$ m/s.

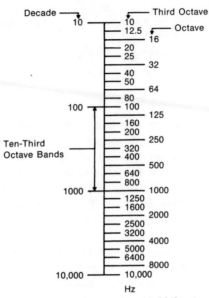

**Fig. A1.2** Center frequencies of decade, octave, and third octave bands (Source: Lyon, 1973).

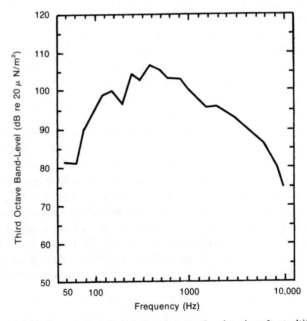

**Fig. A1.3** One-third octave-band level for an executive jet aircraft at altitude of 500 ft during approach operation (Source: EPA, 1971a).

be contained by procedures such as those in Fig. A1.4 to yield an overall sound-pressure level for the entire frequency range. The basic consideration in building up the overall level is the non-linearity of the superposition of sound when measured in decibels. Thus two sources of 70 dB yield 73 dB; this level combined with a 75 dB level yields 77.1 dB, etc.

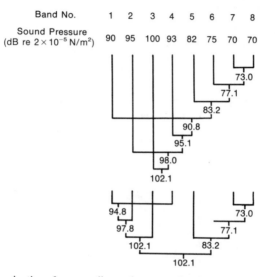

**Fig. A1.4**    Determination of an overall sound-pressure level from levels in frequency bands. Two methods (Source: Beranek, 1971).

## MEASUREMENTS AND RATING PROCEDURES (SEE TABLE A1.1)

### Sound Measurement and Weighted Sound Levels

Basically the sound pressure can be measured by a transducer, amplifier and a read-out device (Fig. A1.5).

The ear tends to attribute different loudness to sounds of different intensities. To account for this factor in the measurement of sound, most sound level meters include weighting networks with different response to sounds in octave-frequency ranges. Four weighting curves commonly used in the design of weighted networks are also shown in Fig. A1.5. The A-weighted level which discriminates against low-frequency sounds, is emerging as the most frequently used level. As shown by the figure, at a 50 Hz pure tone it yields a reading of 30 dB less than the C-scale.

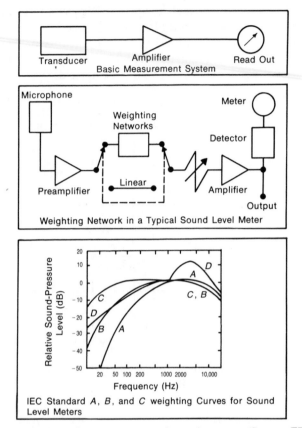

**Fig. A1.5**   Basic scheme for measurement of sound pressure (Source: EPA, 1971a).

If a spectrum analyzer is added to the basic measurement system, it becomes possible to determine the distribution of the sound pressure over the frequency range. A spectrum analyzer is simply a system of filters, each allowing the passage of a certain band of frequencies of the sound. Most commonly, analyzers are octave-band analyzers, but for more detailed work, third octave filters or even narrower band filters can be utilized.

### Peak Sound Level $L_{10}$ and Mean Sound Level $L_{50}$

Two sound levels are often useful in defining noise exposure: the $L_{10}$ level, the noise level, in dB(A) exceeded only 10 percent of the time, and the $L_{50}$ level, the mean level or the level exceeded 50 percent of the time.

## Equivalent Sound Level $L_{EQ}$ and Derived Measures $L_{EQ(24)}$, $L_{EQ(8)}$ and $L_{DN}$

One of the most recent descriptors of noise adopted by the U.S. Environmental Agency (EPA, 1974) for defining the tolerable limits of noise is the equivalent noise level $L_{EQ}$—the mean-square level of a sufficiently long sample of noise (in dB(A) relative to 20 Micro-Newtons per m$^2$ and per second). If the noise has an intermittent maximum level $L_{MAX}$ for a fraction X of the sample duration, and $L_{MAX}$ is 10 dB or more higher than the background noise, then $L_{EQ} = L_{MAX} + 10 \log X$. Otherwise, more complex calculations are necessary.

The equivalent sound level over a 24 hour period, $L_{EQ(24)}$, serves to characterize the cumulative noise exposure of an individual during such a period.

The equivalent sound level over an 18 hour period, $L_{EQ(8)}$ is a basis for identifying environmental noise which causes damage to hearing (with the 8 hours the continuous time period identified with the typical occupational exposure).

The day-night sound level, $L_{DN}$, is the equivalent sound level over a 24 hour period, with a greater weight given to night-time noises, since they are more intrusive than day-time noises (because of decreases in background noise).

$L_{EQ}$ and the measures derived from it are more recent than the indeces CNR, NEF and CNEL defined later. Both CNR and NEF consider day and night periods identical to those used for $L_{DN}$. CNEL is essentially similar to $L_{DN}$, except for the treatment of night-time noises (the 24 hours being divided into three periods). For most airports, the difference between a two-period and a three-period day is not significant.

### Loudness Level; the Phon

Looking at the way psychologists investigate loudness gives an insight into the problem of the measurement of something which cannot be exact because it is a subjective judgment by human beings.

The early work on loudness was concerned with establishing what sounds were equally loud. Accordingly, people were asked to compare pure tones of various frequencies with a reference pure tone of 1000 Hz and to judge when these test tones were equally loud. Their judgments were *averaged* and this resulted in equal loudness contour curves. The number used to characterize the loudness was the sound pressure level (SPL) of a 1000 Hz pure tone judged to be equally loud. The unit of measurement was (and still is) the phon. Thus a pure tone judged *on average* to be equally as loud as a pure tone of 1000 Hz having an SPL of, say, 80 dB, has by definition a loudness level of 80 phons. But the loudness level measured by different investigations is noticeably different even when the sound is presented the same way. In keeping with our view that decisions about noise levels are decisions about minorities we would suggest that if one must do loudness studies, one ought to give great attention to the statistics of loudness judgments—to the differences in individual judgments.

### Loudness; the Sone

The situation is even more subjective and dangerous when one moves from *loudness level* (i.e. the phon) to *loudness*, (the sone), a comparison of two loudness levels. The unit of loudness, the sone, is defined as the loudness of a sound whose loudness level is 40 phons. In an experimental judgement of loudness, subjects may be asked, for instance, whether a test tone is twice or half as loud as a reference tone, say of one sone. If, on the average, it is perceived to be so, then by definition the loudness of the test tone would be respectively two sones or one half sone. Individually there are wide variations in the response. For instance one subject thought a sound of 110 phons to be 100 times as loud as another subject did! Moreover, even the average numbers assigned to the different tones seem to have a significance beyond their size, a 27 dB test tone has been judged to be 1/20th as loud as a reference tone regardless of whether the reference tone was at 60, 70 or 80 dB! And this is on average!

We believe that neither saying a tone is so many times as loud as another nor saying that it is as much louder as the difference between two other tones is particularly useful. They are both artificial; perhaps what is relevant is to ask whether the tone of noise is acceptably or unacceptably loud *in a particular context* and then for the people affected to make decisions on the basis of whether the minority finding the tone unacceptably loud is too large or not.

### Perceived Noise Level (PNL) and Effective Perceived Noise Level (EPNL)

For many noises, the overall sound-pressure levels, as measured by a sound meter, tend to correlate poorly with the subjective perception of noise—annoyance. A scale developed by Kryter for the evaluation of aircraft noise based on such a perception, gives more weight to the high frequencies (EPA, 1971a). In the scale, the Perceived Noise Level (PNL) is expressed in Perceived Noise Decibels (PNdB). Thus, this measurement takes into account not only the intensity, but also the frequency of sound.

The contours of PNL's, as a function of noise intensity and frequency, show that annoyance approximately doubles with each increment of 10 PNdB. Thus the annoyance from an aircraft that generates 110 PNdB of noise is twice that of an aircraft generating 100 PNdB, and four times that of an aircraft that generates 90 PNdB.

Investigations of the effect of aircraft noise have shown that the duration as well as the tone (discrete frequency content) of the noise affect the perception of the noise. To the human ear, a doubling of duration is equivalent to adding approximately 3.5 dB to the noise source. This consideration led to the formulation by the U.S. Federal Aviation Administration of a new index, the Effective Perceived Noise Level (EPNL), measured in Effective Perceived Noise Decibels (EPNdB).

### Noise Exposure Forecast (NEF) Index

In order to provide a realistic single number rating of the cumulative noise produced in the vicinity of an airport by aircraft operation, it is necessary to take into account the noise level generated by each class of aircraft, the total mix of aircraft utilizing the airports, the flight paths, the number of operations during day and night periods, the operating procedures, etc. One index designed to accomplish this is the Noise Exposure Forecast (NEF) index, developed originally by the U.S. Air Force. A synoptic list of the factors that enter into its determination is given in Table A1.2, which also shows the relation of the index to the much simpler PNL and EPNL indices. Although computation of the NEF index cannot be accomplished in practice without a computer, it provides the most sophisticated measure available today for the assessment of noise generated by jet aircraft operation. A very rough and conservative estimate of NEF contours based on the total number of operations (takeoffs plus landings) estimated to occur in daytime at a typical American airport in 1975, is given in Fig. A1.6. It is interesting to note that the estimate attributes a much higher weight to night operations.

### Noise and Number Index (NNI)

The Noise and Number Index (NNI), used extensively by the Wilson Report in Great Britain (Wilson, 1963), is a measure both of the average

**Table A1.2**   Factors Included in Computing Perceived Noise Levels, Effective Perceived Noise Level, and Noise Exposure Forecast (Source: Power, 1971).

| | | |
|---|---|---|
| Absolute noise levels ⎤ PNL | | Perceived Noise Level (PNL) |
| Noise spectrum ⎦ | EPNL | Effective Perceived Noise Level (EPNL) |
| Maximum tone | | |
| Noise duration | | |
| Aircraft type | | |
| Mix of aircraft | NEF | Noise Exposure Forecast (NEF) |
| Number of operations | | |
| Runway utilization | | |
| Flight path | | |
| Operating procedures | | |
| Time of day | | |

value of the PNL and of the average number (N) of aircraft whose noise is perceived at the place where the measure is taken.*

**Noise Index (R) and Night Noise Index (R$^1$)**

The Noise Index (R) (also called the isopsophic index) has been used in France to obtain noise contours around many French airports, including

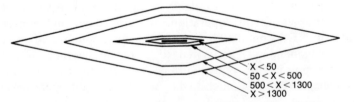

X < 50
50 < X < 500
500 < X < 1300
X > 1300

**Fig. A1.6**   Very rough estimate of extension of NEF contours (based on method in Beranek, 1971). [X = number of jet operations during daytime (7 a.m.–10 p.m.) + 17 times number of operations during nighttime (10 p.m.–7 a.m.).]

---

*NNI = PNL + 15 log N − 80.

the new Roissy Airport. It gives lesser weight than an NNI to the number of perceived aircraft movements;[†] thus, a forecast utilizing R is less strict concerning increases in traffic than one utilizing NNI. Also used in France is the Night Noise Index (R[1]), which gives different weights to noise during different periods of the night.

## Composite Noise Rating (CNR)

Before the introduction of the NEF, the Composite Noise Rating (CNR) index was used extensively in the United States. It differs from R but for a constant,[‡] thus facilitating comparisons between American and French measures and forecasts. The correspondent level of the three indices, NNI, R, and CNR for different noise levels and different numbers of noise occurrences is given in Table A1.3.

**Table A1.3**   Correspondence of NNI, R, and CNR Indices (Source: Alexandre, 1970).

| Number of Airplanes | 90 PNdB | | | 100 PNdB | | | 110 PNdB | | | 120 PNdB | | |
|---|---|---|---|---|---|---|---|---|---|---|---|---|
| | NNI | R | CNR | NNI | R | CNR | NNI | R | CNR | NNI | R | CNR |
| 1 | 10 | 60 | 78 | 20 | 70 | 88 | 30 | 80 | 98 | 40 | 90 | 108 |
| 10 | 25 | 70 | 88 | 35 | 80 | 98 | 45 | 90 | 108 | 55 | 100 | 118 |
| 50 | 36 | 77 | 95 | 46 | 87 | 105 | 56 | 97 | 115 | 66 | 107 | 125 |
| 100 | 40 | 80 | 98 | 50 | 90 | 108 | 60 | 100 | 118 | 70 | 110 | 128 |
| 200 | 45 | 83 | 101 | 55 | 93 | 111 | 65 | 103 | 121 | 75 | 113 | 131 |
| 500 | 51 | 87 | 105 | 61 | 97 | 115 | 71 | 107 | 125 | 81 | 117 | 135 |

## Speech Interference Level (SIL) and Preferred Speech Interference Level (PSIL)

The Speech Interference Level (SIL) correlates well with that of a steady, continuous noise interference with speech communication. (If the level of the noise fluctuates, speech communication is more effective, of course, during periods of lower noise level.) The level was first measured (by an octave-band set of filters) as the arithmetic average of sound-pressure levels in three octave bands: 600–1200 Hz, 1200–1400 Hz, and 2400–4800 Hz. Subsequently, a preferred way to measure the level was developed, which averaged the sound-pressure level in three octave

[†] $R = PNL + 10 \log N - 30$.
[‡] $CNR = R + 18$.

bands having the geometric-mean center frequencies at 500, 1000, and 2000 Hz.

Estimates can be obtained from A-weighted sound levels.* Lacking an instrument, very rough estimates are obtained from "walkaway" tests.† Table A1.4 shows a rough estimate of the correlation between the

**Table A1.4**   Walkaway Tests for Rough Estimation of PSIL or $L_A$ (Source: Beranek, 1971).

| Distance Apart, ft | (m) | PSIL, dB | $L_A$, dBA |
|---|---|---|---|
| 6–9 | (2–3) | 64–70 | 71–77 |
| 9–14 | (3–4.5) | 59–66 | 66–73 |
| 14–21 | (4.5–7) | 53–61 | 60–68 |
| 21–32 | (7–10) | 47–55 | 54–62 |
| 32–50 | (10–15) | 41–49 | 48–56 |
| 50–75 | (15–23) | 35–43 | 42–50 |

distance and the PSIL, as well as the sound level in dB(A). (The distances in the table are the average ones under normal atmospheric conditions at which a male talker conversing with average voice can just *not* be understood; the average in one column corresponds to the range in the others—for example, a distance of 11.5 ft corresponds to a PSIL ranging between 59 and 66.)

### Noise Criteria (NC) and Preferred Noise Criteria (PNC) Curves

These noise criteria curves (Fig. A1.7) represent an indication of the characteristics of noise that are most acceptable to persons within buildings. The Noise Criteria (NC) curves were first introduced in 1957 for the rating of reasonably steady noise levels in buildings. They specify both the maximum allowable speech interference and the maximum allowable sound loudness in a given space.

The Preferred Noise Criteria (PNC) curves were introduced in 1971, as an improvement of the NC curves. They describe more acceptable noise

---

*From the relationship PSIL = Sound Level (in dB(A)) − 7 dB (Beranek, 1971).

†On a calm day, the distance is determined at which a male walking away from another male can barely understand a word or two in a 10-second period of listening to an unfamiliar text. The test is repeated several times, alternating speakers.

| Preferred Noise Criteria Curves | 31.5 Hz | 63 Hz | 125 Hz | 250 Hz | 500 Hz | 1000 Hz | 2000 Hz | 4000 Hz |
|---|---|---|---|---|---|---|---|---|
| PNC-15 | 58 | 43 | 35 | 28 | 21 | 15 | 10 | 8 |
| PNC-20 | 59 | 46 | 39 | 32 | 26 | 20 | 15 | 13 |
| PNC-25 | 60 | 49 | 43 | 37 | 31 | 25 | 20 | 18 |
| PNC-30 | 61 | 52 | 46 | 41 | 35 | 30 | 25 | 23 |
| PNC-35 | 62 | 55 | 50 | 45 | 40 | 35 | 30 | 28 |
| PNC-40 | 64 | 59 | 54 | 50 | 45 | 40 | 36 | 33 |
| PNC-45 | 67 | 63 | 58 | 54 | 50 | 45 | 41 | 38 |
| PNC-50 | 70 | 66 | 62 | 58 | 54 | 50 | 46 | 43 |
| PNC-55 | 73 | 70 | 66 | 62 | 59 | 55 | 51 | 48 |
| PNC-60 | 76 | 73 | 69 | 66 | 63 | 59 | 56 | 53 |
| PNC-65 | 79 | 76 | 73 | 70 | 67 | 64 | 61 | 58 |

OCTAVE-BAND SOUND-PRESSURE-LEVEL VALUES
ASSOCIATED WITH THE 1971
PREFERRED NOISE CRITERIA (PNC) CURVES

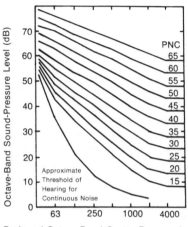

Preferred Octave-Band Center Frequencies (Hz)

| 1957 Noise Criteria Curves | 63 Hz | 125 Hz | 250 Hz | 500 Hz | 1000 Hz | 2000 Hz | 4000 Hz | 8000 Hz |
|---|---|---|---|---|---|---|---|---|
| NC-15 | 47 | 36 | 29 | 22 | 17 | 14 | 12 | 11 |
| NC-20 | 51 | 40 | 33 | 26 | 22 | 19 | 17 | 16 |
| NC-25 | 54 | 44 | 37 | 31 | 27 | 24 | 22 | 11 |
| NC-30 | 57 | 48 | 41 | 35 | 31 | 29 | 28 | 27 |
| NC-35 | 60 | 52 | 45 | 40 | 36 | 34 | 33 | 32 |
| NC-40 | 64 | 56 | 50 | 45 | 41 | 39 | 38 | 37 |
| NC-45 | 67 | 60 | 54 | 49 | 46 | 44 | 43 | 42 |
| NC-50 | 71 | 64 | 58 | 54 | 51 | 49 | 48 | 47 |
| NC-55 | 74 | 67 | 62 | 58 | 56 | 54 | 53 | 52 |
| NC-60 | 77 | 71 | 67 | 63 | 61 | 59 | 58 | 57 |
| NC-65 | 80 | 75 | 71 | 68 | 66 | 64 | 63 | 62 |

OCTAVE-BAND SOUND-PRESSURE LEVELS
ASSOCIATED WITH THE 1957
NOISE CRITERIA (NC) CURVES

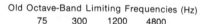
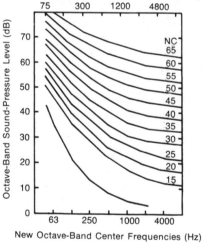

New Octave-Band Center Frequencies (Hz)

**Fig. A1.7**   Indoor Noise Criteria (NC) curves and Preferred Noise Criteria (PNC) curves (Source: Beranek, 1971).

qualities, particularly with regard to the noise of air-conditioning systems, and to the acceptability of background noise in open-plan architectural spaces, in which no major barriers are allowed between personnel, and the question of acoustic privacy becomes important.

### Noise Pollution Level ($L_{NP}$)

The Noise Pollution Level ($L_{NP}$), introduced in 1969, is one of the first methods for dealing with fluctuating noise (Robinson, 1971). It is based on the consideration that the annoyance due to noise is the sum of two terms: one term determined by the mean energy of the noise, and the other determined by the range of variation of the noise (because annoyance increases with the variability of the noise).* Data are insufficient at present to show how effective the $L_{NP}$ is as a rating quantity that correlates with annoyance in a wide variety of fluctuating noises.

### Transport Noise Index (TNI)

TNI of Langdon and Scholes (1968) is based on the appealing assumption that the louder the noise is on average *and* the more the noise rises above the level associated with quiet in the particular surroundings the more the noise will be thought annoying (a consideration similar to that on which $L_{NP}$ is based).† The index does not consider the number of occurrences of the noises nor how long each occurrence lasts. Thus it tends to underestimate the disturbance. $L_{10}$, on which TNI is based, correlates with dissatisfaction score and is used in planning in Britain.

### Single Event Noise Exposure Level (SENEL) and Community Noise Equivalent Level (CNEL)

In a community, the summation of annoyance from single event noise leads to a reaction to noise from those sources. Thus, it becomes important to find a way to rate single event noises, such as the noise from a car or from an airplane flyover, perceived at a given distance from the source. To do so, a Single Event Noise Exposure Level (SENEL) has been introduced, which integrates over the entire duration of the noise—

---

*$L_{NP} = L_{EQ} + 2.56\,\sigma$ dB(NP), where $L_{EQ}$ is the mean-square sound level of a sufficiently long sample of the noise, in dBA, and $\sigma$ is the standard deviation of the same sample.

†TNI $= 4(L_{10} - L_{90}) + L_{90} - 30$ dB(A) where $L_{10}$ and $L_{90}$ are the levels in dB(A) exceeded 10% and 90% of the time respectively, based on a twenty-four hour period.

as perceived at a given distance from the source—the $A$-weighted noise generated by the source.*

The total noise exposure for a day (24 hours) is the community noise equivalent level (CNEL). This index gives greater weight to noise between 7 and 10 P.M., and even greater weight to noise between 10 P.M. and 7 A.M.†

## ANNOYANCE

Annoyance is assessed through annoyance surveys, which endeavor to relate annoyance generated by exposure to noise, to physical measurements of the noise causing the annoyance. The most complex annoyance surveys are those that have been conducted in conjunction with aircraft noise, as discussed in Part IV.

### Annoyance Scales

Annoyance can be evaluated by an annoyance scale, which provides a hierarchical analysis of subjective reactions to noise. Each respondent is assigned an annoyance "score," which varies according to the disturbance felt (Guttman Scale). The annoyance scale must be designed so as to make it possible to test the coherence of the replies concerning noise, to assign a variable weight to each reply, and to rank these replies.

To achieve this objective, the questions used to establish the scale must be grouped in such a way that every individual who replies in the affirmative to a given question must necessarily have replied affirmatively to all the preceding ones (unidimensional and cumulative response). For example:

1. How much does aircraft noise annoy you?

---

*For noise from a single aircraft $SENEL = NL_{max} \pm 10 \log_{10} \tau/2$ dB(A), where $NL_{max}$ is the maximum observed noise level (on the A scale), and $\tau$ is the duration measured between 2 points 10 dB before and after the maximum noise.

For surface vehicles (automobiles, trucks, etc.) moving at velocity V an approximate formula for SNEL is (EPA, 1971b): $SNEL \simeq L_A(R) + 10 \log [(\pi/2)(R/V)]$ dB re 20 $\mu$N per m$^2$ and per second, where $L_A$ is the $A$-weighted noise level at distance R.

†The total *noise exposure* for a day can be expressed as $CNEL = SENEL + 10 \log N_C - 49.4$ dB(A), where SENEL is the energy mean value of SENEL for each single event, and $N_c = N_d + 3N_e + 10N_n$ with $N_d$, $N_e$ and $N_n$ respectively the total number of flights during daytime (7:00 a.m. to 7:00 p.m.), evening (7:00 p.m. to 10:00 p.m.) and night (10:00 p.m. to 7:00 a.m.).

2. Does aircraft noise disturb your listening to the radio or watching TV?
3. Does aircraft noise disturb your conversation?
4. Does aircraft noise wake you?
5. Does aircraft noise disturb or annoy you at other times or in another way?

The respondents are given scores. For the questions above, the score would vary from 0, for persons not annoyed at all, to 5 for the persons most annoyed. The results obtained by a survey of this kind are exemplified by data from the London (Heathrow) Airport study (Fig. A1.8) (McKennell, 1963).

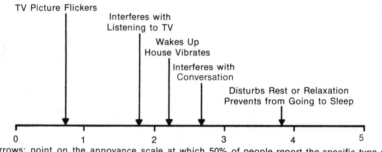

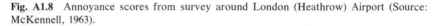

Arrows: point on the annoyance scale at which 50% of people report the specific type of disturbance.

**Fig. A1.8**  Annoyance scores from survey around London (Heathrow) Airport (Source: McKennell, 1963).

The annoyance caused by aircraft noise, or for that matter by other sources of noise, has also been described using scales of "noisiness," "acceptability", and "intrusiveness." A comparison of these scales with perceived noise level of aircraft flyovers is given in Fig. A1.9. It can be seen that the scales are very different; for example what is "moderately noisy" is "barely acceptable" and what is merely "noisy" is worse than "unacceptable".

A numerical index of annoyance, the noy, was introduced by Kryter in an investigation of aircraft annoyance which led to the definition of perceived noise levels, discussed in the previous section. The noy is defined as the noisiness of a sound 40 dB in pressure, at a frequency of 1000 Hz. The high correlations which obtain between average annoyance

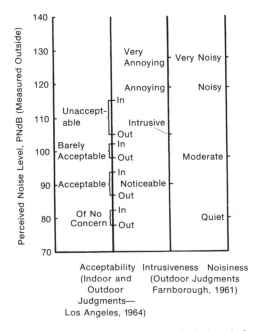

**Fig. A1.9** Comparison between perceived noise level of aircraft flyovers and category scales of acceptability, intrusiveness, and noisiness (Source: Sawyer, 1967).

and a well-chosen noise level index, indicate that the average annoyance due to noise can be precisely quantified and predicted. But this does not mean that the *individual* annoyance can.

It is very likely that other psychological, physiological, and even technical variables (such as standard deviations of the noise peaks, different acoustic insulation, way of life, etc.), not yet defined or still unknown, also exerted a direct influence on the feeling of annoyance. In the absence of more detailed information in this respect, one must accept the average annoyance scores for each noise level. While these averages do not reflect the feelings of each individual, they do reflect, nevertheless, what, on an average, is felt by the population in a given area. However if the study of noise teaches one nothing else, it should be that averages are not enough to describe a situation; the reactions of minorities are important. The less likely but more severe hearing damage or annoyance cannot be discounted.

## REFERENCES

Alexandre, A. Prevision de la gene due au bruit, autour des aeroports et perspectives sur les moyens d'y remedier. Doc. AA 28/70. Centre d'Etudes et de Recherches d'Anthropologie Appliqueé, Paris, 1970.

Beranek, L. L. (Ed.), *Noise vibration and control*. New York: McGraw-Hill, 1971.

EPA (U.S. Environmental Protection Agency). Fundamentals of noise: Measurements, rating schemes and standards. Washington, December 1971. (a)

EPA (U.S. Environmental Protection Agency). Transportation noise and noise: Equipment powered by internal combustion engines. Washington, December 1971. (b)

EPA (U.S. Environmental Protection Agency). Information on levels of environmental noise requisite to protect public health and welfare with adequate margin of safety. Washington, March 1974.

Harris, C. M. *Handbook of noise control*. New York: McGraw-Hill, 1957.

Langdon, F. J., and W. E. Scholes, The traffic noise index: a method of controlling noise nuisance, *Architects' Journal*, 1968, **147**.

Lyon, R. H. *Lectures in transportation noise*. Cambridge, Mass.: Grozier, 1973.

McKennell, A. C. *Aircraft noise annoyance around London (Heathrow) Airport*. London: Central Office of Information, SS 337, April 1963.

Power, J. K. Aircraft noise standards and regulations. Federal Aviation Administration, Report No. FAA-RD-71-24, Washington, 1971.

Robinson, D. W. Towards a unified system of noise assessment. *Journal of Sound and Vibration*, 1971, **14**.

Sawyer, F. L. Aircraft noise and the siting of a major airport. *Journal of Sound and Vibration*, 1967, **5**.

Wilson. Committee on The Problem of Noise. Noise, final report. Cmnd. 2056. London: HMSO, 1963.

# Technological Forecasting for Noise Control

## THE PROBLEM

Noise control can be viewed as a process of environmental health management.* Thus, the essential task is how to develop control mechanisms capable of acting before the perturbation of the health parameters of a community produced by noise goes beyond acceptable levels.

The difficulty of the task stems from the fact that neither the technological causes of noise nor many characteristics of the community are static. They undergo very rapid changes. Some of the most severe environmental problems that our society has encountered have arisen from the inability of existing feedback loops to react to such changes with sufficient rapidity. It becomes thus essential to develop predictive, rather than merely reactive feedback mechanisms. This requires the ability to forecast, as much in advance as possible:

- the changes in technology that are likely to generate noise capable of perturbing the physical and psychological health of the community,
- the characteristics of the community that can be affected by noise

---

*The reader should not lose sight of the fact that management implies managers or decision makers, and the crucial questions in decisions are the well known ones: Who benefits from the decision? Who suffers? Who decides, and *how* do they decide? To these questions should be added the concerns with the increasing centralization of government: if forecasting is to be carried out, this should certainly occur as a normal part of the democratic process, with full participation at the grass roots, rather than exclusively as a highly organized task at (central) government level.

in such a way as to result in perturbation of the health parameters of the community.

Although the forecasting of these two aspects requires quite different skills, there are multiple and essential interconnections. Thus, determination of the technological agents that can generate noise depends heavily on an understanding of the characteristics of the community, and involves taking into consideration a large number of interactions between technology and the community, between different components of the community, as well as between different specific technologies. Some technologies are relatively stable and may add no new noise, but the community characteristics may be changing, either because of other technologies, or, intrinsically, because of factors within the community that may be outside of the realm of technology. The decreasing willingness of a community, as its socio-economic status improves, to accept existing noise, or air pollution, is an example of how changes in social characteristics of a community can make existing technological inputs unacceptable.

The time span over which a forecast is required must be geared to the rate of growth of each technological process involved, the rapidity with which community characteristics may change and to the speed with which feedback mechanisms can be mobilized.

## FORECASTING TECHNOLOGICAL PROCESSES

Forecasting the noise produced by technological processes involves two distinct but complementary elements:

- forecasting of the technological processes that will come into being;
- forecasting the health effect of the noise produced by such processes.

The forecasting of technological processes presents in turn three distinct problems:

1. Forecasting over a specified time period, the level of operation (volume of production) of existing sources.

2. Forecasting the time scale of development and the outputs of technologies that are technologically feasible at present but not yet in operation. The process of prediction is not necessarily less urgent for this category, since the rate of growth of new processes may be quite rapid once these processes come into operation. This is exemplified by the rate

of growth of rock-and-roll bands with their physiologically damaging sound outputs, or of high rotational speed internal combustion engines of small displacement. In each of these cases, the speed of the technological development outstripped the ability of existing feedback loops to provide guidance and normative regulations for a health-preserving operation of the noise sources, thus highlighting the need for a predictive feedback loop.

3. Forecasting future technologies—both technologies which existing scientific knowledge would indicate to be feasible—and technologies based on yet unknown but probable or even possible future scientific developments. Although the technologies in this category are more chancy, their early forecasting, far from being an idle speculation, is at least as imperative as the forecasting of the technologies in the two previous categories. This is so on several accounts. In the first place, technologies that may appear to be still well below the horizon can frequently materialize very rapidly. Thus, the scientific feasibility of splitting the atom was generally not only questioned, but excluded during the first two decades of this century. The time between the first experimental operations of jet engines (1939–40) and their widespread commercial use, although substantial (15–20 years) has been much shorter than the ability of the community to react to the environmental effects of the jets through legislation and technological measures.

Secondly, future technologies, *qua* future, offer greater latitude in preparing for their interaction with the health parameters of the community.

In the third place, totally new technologies have exerted a more profound influence on the environment than the evolution of existing technologies. The advent of the propeller-driven airplane or, more generally, of the internal combustion engine—unforeseen less than a generation before their widespread use—added more noise and pollutants to the environment than the possible evolution of the steam engine, or of the horse-drawn carriage. Timely forecasting of these technologies, and of their consequences—in the form, for instance, of "scenarios" exploring their possible uses and influences in society would have made society better equipped to handle their consequences, and direct their evolution.

Thus, forecasts of new technologies should be performed even in the absence, at present, of sufficient knowledge supportive of their feasibility. Such forecasts are needed as inputs to scenarios portraying the possible uses and health consequences of the new technologies. Even if a technology fails to materialize (as can be expected to occur in a statistically large percentage of cases dealing with such chancy predictions) a collection of scenarios, continuously augmented, revised, and re-examined, becomes an extremely valuable tool for developing an ability to envision with imagination and foresight future environmental changes, and to plan for their containment within desirable limits.

## FORECASTING THE COMMUNITY CHARACTERISTICS

The concomitant step to prediction of technological development and of its health effects is the forecasting of the community characteristics—biometric, social, economic, political as well as geographic (such as changes in build environment). Such a forecasting provides an essential input to the forecasting of technological processes, since, clearly, the development of technology is determined by the characteristics of the community. Forecasts of community characteristics also provide "exposure profiles" which make it possible to predict what portion of a community of given biometric characteristics can be expected in the future to be exposed to noise, and how strongly. Forecasting of exposure profiles involves the prediction of the number of people in the community, and of their age, sex, relevant health condition, as well as the prediction of the noise dosage to which they each are likely to be exposed. It is also important not only to predict the dosage of noise, but also its time-distribution. We have seen that chronic exposure to a given level of noise in a subway can produce permanent threshold shifts of the hearing acuity if it occurs as a result of a daily routine of trips occurring within 2 or 3 hours from each other, rather than 6 or 7 hours apart.

## NOTES ON FORECASTING METHODOLOGY

In conclusion, the problem of forecasting the effect of technologically produced noise demands the answer to five distinct questions:

1. What are the noise sources (processes, industries, activities) that will be operating over the time span of the forecast?
2. What will be the noise produced by these sources?
3. What will be the actual physiopsychological effects of such noise?
4. What will be the exposure profile of a community to the noise?
5. What will be the aggregate effect on the community of all the ambient

noise, as well as of the combination of noise and other agents of annoyance and stress? Will the effects be linearly additive, reinforcing, etc.?

The answer to each of these questions requires different methodologies, skills and data bases. A variety of forecasting methods and mechanisms are already available for approaching certain elements of the problem (such as technological forecasting for industry, forecasting of population characteristics, market analyses and projections, general scenarios for economical and political forecasting of the type exemplified by the studies of the Hudson Institute) (Kahn and Wiener, 1967). Some imaginative and surprisingly accurate qualitative predictions have also been made from time to time by leaders in a particular field, as well as by inspired laymen—typified by Jules Verne or Karel Capek. It must be recognized, however, that:

1. Until recently, inventions and new products have been created with only secondary consideration of health factors. This had led to the development of methodologies for technological forecasting which are generally not sensitive to such factors.

2. Most of the current technological forecasting techniques (e.g., Bright, 1968) are geared primarily to the prediction of the development of existing technologies rather than to that of future technologies. Yet, even within the realm of existing technologies, the rate of error can be very large, as exemplified by the underestimate of the rate of growth of the transistor industry. The error can be reduced by using concurrently a multiplicity of techniques, attempting to analyze the reasons for discrepancies in estimates, formulating a prediction in terms of confidence limits, and continuously updating it.

3. The forecasting of technologies still below the horizon presents great difficulties, but, as suggested earlier, is essential. Such a forecasting can be approached from two different viewpoints:

- What can be called a need-driven forecast: a forecast in terms of projected societal needs for a given technology and of the historical experience of times elapsed between perceived needs—before any knowledge of scientific means for satisfying them existed—and inventions. Observation of the invention process indicates that invention often follows a strongly felt and clearly perceived need.
- What can be called a discovery-driven forecast: a forecast obtained from speculation as to probable scientific discoveries, coupled with an understanding of the possible technologies that could arise from them.

4. Prediction of the exposure profile of a population involves, among other factors, the ability to predict patterns of work and habits that lead to exposure to noise, as distinct from the relatively simpler task of predicting only numbers of a population.

5. The methodology and mechanisms for forecasting environmental factors of a physical nature such as noise, need not be essentially different from those for predicting factors of a biological or environmental nature. In particular, it appears desirable to pursue the study of biological similarity laws for exposure to noise, so as to make meaningful experimentation possible with organisms other than man. At present research on biological similarity in general has been focused primarily on biochemical rather than biophysical aspects—with the exception of studies of the response to vibration and physical shock.

## CONCLUSIONS

In brief, technological forecasting for noise is a task both essential and complex. Without comprehensive and up-to-date forecasts of technology and of the possible effects on community health of the noise it generates, we will be constantly protecting ourselves from the danger of yesterday, rather than from those of today or tomorrow.

The essential role that forecasting needs to play in noise control requires that this activity not be left to chance, or carried out in piece-meal fashion, as is the case today, but become a continuous and well-organized task carried out at the government level, with strong community participation.

## REFERENCES

Kahn, H. and Wiener, A. J. *The year 2000.* MacMillan: New York, 1967.
Bright, J. W. *Technological forecasting for industry and government.* Englewood Cliffs, N.J.: Prentice-Hall, 1968.

# Environmental Impact Statements for Noise

## THE NATIONAL ENVIRONMENTAL POLICY ACT AND THE COUNCIL ON ENVIRONMENTAL QUALITY

In the United States, the National Environmental Policy Act (NEPA) of 1969 requires environmental considerations to be given appropriate consideration in the Federal decision-making process (NEPA, 1970). The act also established the President's Council on Environmental Quality (CEQ) with authority to review Federal programs designed to comply with the NEPA. The Council published in August 1973 guidelines for the preparation of Environmental Impact Statements (CEQ, 1973). The guidelines apply to projects or actions:

- undertaken by the Federal government, or
- supported totally or in part through Federal contracts, grants or other funding assistance, or
- requiring a Federal permit, license or other entitlement for use.

and to any other "*major Federal actions significantly affecting the quality of the human environment.*" These major Federal actions are to be construed by agencies with a view toward the overall cumulative impact of the action or project proposed. Adverse significant effects that must be considered include those that:

- degrade the quality of the environment
- curtail the range of beneficial uses of the environment
- serve short-term environmental goals, to the detriment of long-term ones

- may have both beneficial and detrimental effects, *even if*, on balance, an agency believes that the effect will be beneficial
- are secondary effects (such as the impact of an airport or a highway on population growth).

To be a "Federal action," the action must be characterized by the presence of sufficient Federal control and responsibility. These are not present, for example, in the case of Federal funds distributed to State and local governments as general revenue showing.

Each Federal agency is required to review the typical class of actions likely to require environmental impact statements.

Resources of Federal agencies to these requirements are contained in specific rules and regulations issued by the agency (e.g., DOT, 1974, EPA, 1975 and HUD, 1975). Each of these agencies may make reference to its own existing criteria, standards, policies and regulations. For example, in the case of noise, the regulation of the U.S. Department of Housing and Urban Development (HUD, 1975) makes reference to the department's handbook on noise statement and control (HUD, 1971).

The guidelines of the Council for Environmental Quality (CEQ, 1973) identify Federal agencies and Federal State Agencies with jurisdiction by law—or with special expertize—to comment on various areas of environmental impact, from air quality to land use and management. In the case of noise, the agencies are:

- Department of Commerce—
  National Bureau of Standards
- Department of Health, Education and Welfare
- Department of Housing and Urban Development
  (land use and building materials aspects)
- Department of Labor—
  Occupational Safety and Health Administration
- Department of Transportation—
  Assistant Secretary for Systems Development and Technology
  Federal Aviation Administration, Office of Noise Abatement
- Environmental Protection Agency
- National Aeronautics and Space Administration

In addition, the guidelines identify offices with agencies which can provide information regarding the agencies' NEPA activities, and comments on other agencies' impact statements. These include, among others:

- Department of Defense: Office of the Assistant Secretary for Defense (Health and Environment)
- Federal Power Commission: Commission's Advisor on Environmental Quality
- Environmental Protection Agency: Director, Office of Federal Activities; also the ten Regional Administrators
- Department of Health, Education and Welfare: Office of Environmental Affairs in the Office of the Assistant Secretary for Administration and Management; also, the ten Regional Environmental Officers
- Department of Housing and Urban Development: Director, Office of Community and Environmental Standards; also, the ten Regional Administrators
- Department of Transportation: Director, Office of Environmental Quality in the Office of the Assistant Secretary for Environment, Safety and Consumer Affairs; also, the ten Regional Secretarial Representatives, the nine offices of the Regional Directors of the Federal Aviation Administration, the ten Regional Administrators Offices of the UMTA (Urban Mass Transportation Administration) Representatives.

Environmental impact statements are not limited to Federal agencies. A number of states and local governments now have, or are contemplating, laws similar to NEPA.


## THE ENVIRONMENTAL IMPACT STATEMENT

The process of preparing a Federal Environmental Impact Statement is described in Fig. A3.1. The major steps are as follows:

1. Determination, by project originator (a state, local or private agency) as to whether or not there will be Federal involvement in the project.
2. Federal contacts, to determine if an environmental assessment or statement are required, and the lead Federal agency (the "proposing" agency) with major responsibility concerning the "Federal action" discussed in the previous section.
3. Decision by the Federal agency, on the basis of the environmental assessment, as to whether or not the proposed project constitutes "a major Federal action" and thus requires an environmental impact statement.

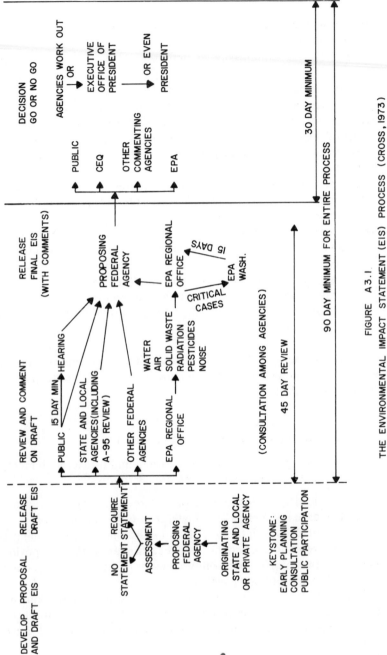

FIGURE A3.1

THE ENVIRONMENTAL IMPACT STATEMENT (EIS) PROCESS (CROSS, 1973)

4. Preparation, if the previous step has indicated this to be necessary, of a draft environmental impact statement, at least 90 days before the proposed action.
5. Review of the draft by the public, state and local agencies, other Federal agencies, the Regional Offices and if necessary headquarters of the Environmental Protection Agency. Public hearings should be held not earlier than 15 days after the draft has been completed, and the entire review of the draft of the impact statement should be expected to require no less than 45 days.
6. Final environmental impact statement, to be made available at least 30 days before the proposed action. The final statements must incorporate the comments received on the draft, the agency's response to the comments, and, if necessary, modifications of the original statement.

The final statement is then the basis for the decision, by the appropriate agencies, or if necessary the the Executive Office of the President or even the President, as to whether the project or action should be permitted or not.

An Environmental Impact Statement must contain eight parts (CEQ, 1973):

1. Description of proposed action, statement of its purposes and description of the environment affected, "adequate to permit an assessment of potential environmental impact by commenting agencies and the public."
2. Relation of the proposed action to land use plans, policies and controls for the affected area. In the case of conflicts or inconsistencies with approved or proposed Federal, State or local plans, policies and controls, the agency should state the extent to which it has reconciled it proposed plan, or why it has decided to proceed without a full reconciliation.
3. Probable impact of the proposed action on the environment (including secondary impacts).
4. Alternatives to the proposed action, including, where relevant, those not within the existing authority of the responsible agency (such as replacement of air transportation by surface transportation).
5. Any probable adverse environmental effects which cannot be avoided (such as annoyance).
6. Relationship between local short-term uses of man's environment and the maintenance and enhancement of long-term productivity (including trade-offs between short-term environmental gains and long-term

losses, and the extent to which the proposed action forecloses future options).

7. Any irreversable and irretrievable commitments of resources that would be involved in the proposed action.

8. Indication of what other interests and considerations of Federal policy are thought to offset the adverse environmental effects of the proposed action. Should cost-benefit analyses be included with the impact statement, a clear statement of environmental costs is required—or of the extent to which such costs have not been taken into account.

Experience with environmental impact statement for noise is currently limited. The statements must identify and quantify the source of unwanted sound, the effects on the receiver—both physiological and psychological (including the effects on structures and in the measure that these in turn may have an effect on humans)—as well as social impacts. The various chapters of this book should provide a base of information for many of these aspects, as well as an indication of the very considerable difficulties associated with the assessment of impacts.

## REFERENCES

CEQ (Council on Environmental Quality). Guidelines for the Preparation of Environmental Impact Statements, *Federal Register*, Vol. 38, No. 147, August 1, 1973.

Cross, F. Introduction to Preparation of Environmental Impact Statements, *Pollution Engineering*, March 1973.

DOT (U.S. Department of Transportation). Procedures for Considering Environmental Impacts. *Federal Register*, Vol. 39, No. 190, Sept. 30, 1974.

EPA (U.S. Environmental Protection Agency). Preparation of Environmental Impact Statements. Final Regulations. *Federal Register*, Vol. 40, No. 72, April 14, 1975.

HUD (U.S. Department of Housing and Urban Development). Departmental Circular 1390.2. Washington, 1971.

HUD (U.S. Department of Transportation). Procedures for Considering Environmental Impacts. *Federal Register*, Vol. 39, No. 190, Sept. 30, 1974.

NEPA (The National Environmental Policy Act of 1969). U.S. Public Law 91–190, January 1, 1970.

# Subject Index

# Name and Title Index